D1552659

Enforcing Equality

Enforcing Equality

Congress, the Constitution, and the Protection of Individual Rights

Rebecca E. Zietlow

NEW YORK UNIVERSITY PRESS
New York and London

NEW YORK UNIVERSITY PRESS
New York and London
www.nyupress.org

© 2006 by New York University
All rights reserved

Library of Congress Cataloging-in-Publication Data
Zietlow, Rebecca E.
Enforcing equality : Congress, the Constitution, and the protection
of individual rights / Rebecca E. Zietlow.
p.   cm.
Includes bibliographical references and index.
ISBN-13: 978-0-8147-9707-5 (cloth : alk. paper)
ISBN-10: 0-8147-9707-5 (cloth : alk. paper)
1. Equality before the law—United States. 2. Civil rights—United
States. 3. United States. Congress.   I. Title.
KF4764.Z54 2006
342.7308'5—dc22   2006012447

New York University Press books are printed on acid-free paper,
and their binding materials are chosen for strength and durability.

Manufactured in the United States of America
10 9 8 7 6 5 4 3 2 1

To David, Alice, and Zoe
and
To the memory of my dear friend, Denise C. Morgan

Contents

Acknowledgments   ix

1   Introduction   1

2   Congress and Rights before the Civil War   12

3   Belonging, Protection, and Equality:
    The Reconstruction Congress   38

4   Belonging and Social Citizenship: The New Deal
    and the Wagner Act   63

5   To Secure These Rights: The 1964 Civil Rights Act   97

6   The New Parity Debate   128

7   Rights of Belonging and Popular Constitutionalism   145

8   Considering Rights of Belonging, Moral Values,
    and Community   160

    Notes   169
    Bibliography   235
    Index   253
    About the Author   265

Acknowledgments

This book is the result of years of work and help from count-less friends and colleagues. It began as an analysis of the Supreme Court's interpretation of the Privileges or Immunities Clause of the Fourteenth Amendment after its ruling in *Saenz v. Roe*. As I researched the mean-ing of the privileges and immunities of citizenship and the Citizenship Clause, I delved into the history of the Fourteenth Amendment. I soon shifted my focus from court enforcement of those provisions to the po-tential of congressional enforcement of the rights of federal citizenship.

My focus on congressional enforcement power was due to recent Su-preme Court rulings striking down civil rights legislation as beyond the scope of congressional power. These rulings seemed particularly prob-lematic to me since I had always believed that the Court was the guard-ian of minority rights. Instead of guarding minority rights, in cases such as *City of Boerne v. Flores* and *United States v. Morrison,* the Court was preventing the majoritarian bodies from protecting those rights. I began to explore other sources of authority for Congress to use in en-acting civil rights legislation, including the spending power and enforce-ment of the Citizenship Clause.

In a related project, my friend Denise Morgan and I began to explore the role of state legislatures as protectors of rights and formulated the concept of rights of belonging. In research for our article, I learned more about the history of congressional efforts to protect individual rights. More importantly, I began to understand that my long-held be-lief that courts were the best guardians of minority rights was both his-torically and (in my view) conceptually flawed. It soon became apparent to me that this project was beyond the scope of a law review article or two, and it grew into this book.

One of the most satisfying aspects of writing this book was the oppor-tunity it gave me to connect with some of the finest scholars throughout the country. Akhil Amar, Richard Aynes, and Michael Kent Curtis were especially helpful and encouraging during the earliest phase, and Reva Siegel and Sandy Levinson have been crucial sources of guidance and support throughout this project. Denise Morgan was a friend and partner in this work and often helped in reading drafts and asking pointed questions. Her friendship was invaluable to me. Thanks to Theresa Beiner, Michael Kent Curtis, Nancy Levit, Richard Pious, Keith Whittington, and Bryan Wildenthal, who helped me to shape my idea into a book proposal. Special thanks to Martha Biondi, Courtney Cahill, Paul Finkelman, William Forbath, Risa Goluboff, David Koeninger, Denise Morgan, James Gray Pope, Joseph Slater, and David Stebenne for comments on drafts of parts of this book. Thanks are also due to the others who engaged in dialogues with me concerning aspects of this project, including Keith Aoki, Michael Les Benedict, James Brudney, Stephen Clark, Owen Fiss, James Fox, Robert Justin Lipkin, Wayne Moore, Todd Pettys, Mark Poirier, Robert Post, Robert Pushaw, and Tracy Thomas.

Thanks to the University of Toledo for summer research grants that funded this work, and to all of my colleagues there, especially Phil Closius, Beth Eisler, Llew Gibbons, Joseph Slater, and Daniel Steinbock, and Renee Heberle, Ben Pryor, Sam Nelson, and all of the members of the University of Toledo Law and Social Thought working group for their support and help. Thanks also to my excellent research assistants, Annelise Araujo, Michele Bracy, Cheri Budzynski, Melinda Campbell, Parri Hockenberry, Daniel Nathan, Victoria Shackelford, Kelly Tomlison, and Laurie Watson. I presented earlier versions of this work to several annual meetings of the Law and Society Association, as well as the Ohio Legal History Seminar, faculty scholarship workshops at Rutgers-Camden School of Law and the Salmon P. Chase School of Law, and symposia at the Temple University Law School and the University of Akron School of Law. Thanks to all who attended these presentations and provided helpful comments.

Thanks to my father, Paul Zietlow, for being my model of a teacher and a scholar and to my mother, Charlotte Zietlow, who taught me the value of political engagement.

Finally, thanks so much to my husband, David Koeninger, for his help, support, and love, and to my beautiful daughters, Alice and Zoe, for sharing their mother's attention and time with this project.

In the controversial chapter opposing judicial review in his book *Taking the Constitution Away from the Courts,* Mark Tushnet famously noted that his wife, an attorney for the American Civil Liberties Union, "disagrees with nearly everything that I have written in this chapter." My husband also works as a public interest lawyer, in the areas of government benefits, healthcare, and taxes. Over the years, he has become increasingly dissatisfied with the power of impact litigation to improve his clients' lives, and he has devoted an increasing amount of time to working within the political process to address the needs of his clients. David's experience has played an important part in shaping my thoughts on the issues explored here. Through the research for this book, I have learned that his experience is not an anomaly but, rather, is consistent with that of reformers throughout the history of this country.

1

Introduction

Every year, thousands of students in constitutional law classes throughout the country learn about the special role that the federal courts have in our constitutional system—the role of protecting discrete and insular minorities. With its roots in Justice Stone's famous footnote four in *United States v. Carolene Products,* the "representation reinforcement" theory of judicial review posits that federal courts are best suited for protecting individual rights in general, and the rights of minorities in particular, because they are insulated from political pressures experienced by the majoritarian political branches.[1] No less than one of the Founders of our Constitution, Alexander Hamilton, first made this argument, claiming that "the independence of the judges is equally requisite to guard the Constitution and the rights of the individual from the effects of those ill humors which [are] the arts of designing men."[2] To legal scholars educated in these classes and inspired by the Warren Court's ruling in *Brown v. Board of Education,* it is axiomatic that the primary protectors of individual rights within our constitutional system are the federal courts.[3] However, this theory does not accurately reflect the relationship among Congress, the federal courts, and individual rights throughout the history of our country. Repeatedly, and during key periods of our history, Congress, representing the majority of the people in our nation, has acted not to *infringe upon* but to *protect* equality norms. In this book I describe that history, question the primacy of federal courts as protectors of individual rights, and present an alternative picture—that of Congress, the majoritarian branch, protecting equality norms.

In this book I revisit one of the oldest and most important controversies in constitutional law: how to reconcile equality norms with democratic rule.[4] Most constitutional scholars believe that equality norms need protection from majority rule and that only the insulated federal courts can provide that protection.[5] To the contrary, I argue that democracy must be able to function without undue judicial interference to ensure the adequate enforcement of equality norms.[6] Throughout our history, groups of people have worked together to fight for constitutional change in order to expand the scope of individual rights. For example, abolitionists fought to end slavery and later to establish rights for newly freed slaves, labor leaders fought for the right to organize, and civil rights workers in the 1950s and 1960s fought for legislation to end race discrimination in society. These activists directed their arguments to the political branches, not to the courts, and they were successful in the political branches, often despite the opposition of courts. The voice of these political activists is mostly lost in the conventional "representation reinforcement" view of individual rights. Here I seek to restore their voice and to analyze the manner in which members of Congress translated the constitutional theories of these activists into statutes protecting individual rights.

At the outset of this analysis, it is useful to consider recent examples where the government has protected two separate individual rights: the First Amendment right to free exercise of religion and the Second Amendment right to bear arms. Defining the scope of the Free Exercise Clause has been the subject of a constitutional dispute between Congress and the Supreme Court throughout the past two decades. By contrast, the courts have shied away from enforcing the Second Amendment individual right to bear arms, leaving its enforcement to the political branches. While proponents of both rights enjoy strong public support, the second right is arguably more robust and less subject to restriction in our legal system.

On April 17, 1990, the Supreme Court decided the case of *Employment Division v. Smith,* holding that the Free Exercise Clause of the First Amendment requires that state policies that incidentally infringe on the free exercise of religion need only surpass rational basis scrutiny, the lowest level of constitutional review.[7] The *Smith* ruling marked a significant constitutional change because prior to *Smith,* the Court had applied strict scrutiny, the highest level of review, to such policies.[8] The ruling immediately generated a battle over constitutional meaning between the Court and Congress.

Public reaction to the Court's ruling in *Smith* was swift and negative. Members of the public, political interest groups, and politicians on both sides of the political spectrum condemned the ruling as insufficiently protective of religious freedom. Responding to this criticism, a broad-based coalition of religious organizations unsuccessfully took the unusual step of petitioning the Court to re-hear the case.[9] Members of Congress responded to the outcry by adopting the Religious Freedom Restoration Act (RFRA), which statutorily reinstated the strict scrutiny test for state actions incidentally infringing on the free exercise of religion. RFRA required state and local regulations that burden religious practices to be the least restrictive means of furthering a compelling governmental interest in order to pass statutory muster, effectively restoring the strict scrutiny test.[10] The statute passed both houses of Congress by an overwhelming margin and was signed into law on November 16, 1993. Members of Congress agreed almost unanimously that religious exercise deserved a higher level of protection than that provided by the U.S. Supreme Court.[11]

During the debate over RFRA, members of Congress on both sides of the aisle made it clear that they believed the Court had wrongly interpreted the Constitution. Oregon Republican Senator Mark Hatfield declared, "the Smith decision . . . has severely limited the first amendment's protection of the right to exercise religious beliefs," and his colleague, Dan Coates of Indiana complained, "The Court has effectively turned religious Americans into second class citizens."[12] On the other side of the aisle, Democratic Senator Bill Bradley agreed that "Smith has, in essence, removed any real or significant constitutional protection for the free exercise of religion. It has, in effect, gutted the Free Exercise Clause."[13] In the House, Republican Bob Goodlatte of Virginia opined, "The U.S. Supreme Court has allowed serious erosion of this right [to free exercise]," and his Democratic colleague, Charles Schumer agreed, "incomprehensibly, Justice Scalia's decision explained that requiring the Government to accommodate religious practice was a luxury. Tell to millions of Americans that religion is a luxury, and I think we get the reaction that we have had universally here on the floor from the most liberal to the most conservative member."[14]

Some members of Congress made it clear that they intended RFRA to overrule the Court's interpretation of the Free Exercise Clause.[15] Representative Henry Hyde of Illinois cautioned, "Of course the label restoration is inappropriate in this context since the Congress writes the laws —it does not and cannot overrule the Supreme Court's interpretation of the Constitution. We are unable to restore a prior interpretation of the first amendment."[16] Others were less circumspect. Representative Charles Schumer insisted, "The bill will restore the first amendment to its proper place as one of the cornerstones of democracy."[17] House Judiciary Chairman Jack Brooks, a Democrat from Texas, explained that overturning a Supreme Court decision "is not an action to be taken lightly," but, he added, "If the judicial branch is unwilling to afford adequate protection to our basic constitutional rights, Congress must step into the breach."[18] Signing the bill, President Bill Clinton agreed: "The power to reverse by legislation, a decision of the United States Supreme Court, is a power that is rightly hesitantly and infrequently exercised by the United States Congress. But this is an issue in which that extraordinary measure was clearly called for."[19] Hence, while they varied in the extent to which they were willing to directly challenge the Court, the president and the members of Congress who enacted RFRA asserted Congress's authority to independently interpret the meaning of the Free Exercise Clause.

The Court's response to RFRA was equally swift and correspondingly negative. In *City of Boerne v. Flores,* the Court struck down RFRA as applied to state governments on the ground that it exceeded Congress's Section Five authority to enforce the Fourteenth Amendment. The *Boerne* Court held that RFRA, and all future Section Five legislation, must satisfy a new "congruence and proportionality" test in order to ensure that Congress uses its Section Five powers only to enact "remedial," not "substantive," legislation.[20] In *Boerne,* the Court emphatically asserted its own preeminence in constitutional interpretation, maintaining that when Congress attempts to define the substance of unconstitutional conduct, it intrudes on the proper function of "the Judicial Branch . . . to say what the law is."[21] The Court cited to *Marbury v. Madison* for the proposition that congressional interpretation of the constitution would place the constitution "on a level with ordinary legislative acts."[22] Despite the fact that *Marbury* itself made clear that all branches of the government have an obligation to interpret the constitution,[23] the *Boerne* Court insisted that Congress lacks the institutional competence to interpret the Constitution, effectively ruling that Congress lacks the authority to interpret the Fourteenth Amendment more expansively than the Court's interpretation.[24]

After *Boerne,* some members of Congress continued the battle over the Free Exercise Clause. Senator Orrin Hatch complained, "the Court has once again acted to push religion to the fringes of society," and

Representative Charles Schumer opined that the Court's *Boerne* opinion forces citizens "to choose between their government and their God."[25] In 2000, Congress enacted the Religious Land Use and Institutionalized Persons Act (RLUIPA), a more modest, spending power–based statute that imposes the RFRA strict scrutiny test only on state regulations governing land use and institutionalized persons.[26] Recently, the Court held that RLUIPA does not violate the Establishment Clause, but it has yet to rule on whether or not Congress had the power to enact the statute.[27]

In contrast to the battle over the Free Exercise Clause, consider the Second Amendment right to bear arms, one of the few individual constitutional rights that have developed with little input from the courts. Scholars differ over whether the Second Amendment protects an individual's right to bear arms.[28] The Supreme Court has not decided a single case interpreting the scope of that right since its ambiguous ruling in the 1939 case of *United States v. Miller,* and lower courts consistently rule against Second Amendment claims.[29] However, the individual right to bear arms has flourished in the popular realm, and advocates of that right have achieved significant political success. Opponents of gun control have defeated numerous legislative proposals by asserting their Second Amendment right to bear arms, and Congress has recognized that right in at least three separate pieces of legislation.[30]

Supporters of the individual right to bear arms have often bemoaned the fact that courts shy away from enforcing the Second Amendment.[31] However, even if the courts were to enforce the Second Amendment, it is difficult to imagine that right being more robust than it is currently in the political realm. If the Court did recognize an individual right, it probably would qualify that right in the way that it has limited freedom of expression in its interpretation of the First Amendment. In point of fact, supporters of the individual right to bear arms have good reason to keep that issue away from the courts and in the political process.

In *Smith* and *Boerne,* the Court interpreted the Free Exercise Clause more narrowly than Congress had, and in RFRA, Congress was more protective of the rights of religious minorities than the Court had been. Hence, the story of RFRA and *Boerne* is inconsistent with the conventional theory that courts must protect individual rights from infringement by the majority. The story of the Second Amendment also is arguably inconsistent with that theory. Gun owners have been politically active precisely because they know they cannot count on the courts to protect their rights. The lack of court enforcement has added urgency to their concerns and enhanced their political appeal.[32] As a case study, the Second Amendment suggests that some rights actually might receive *more* protection *without* the institution of judicial review.

Of course, it is problematic to generalize based on two examples. Perhaps the First Amendment right to free exercise and the Second Amendment right to bear arms are different from other individual rights because they are supported by either a majority of Americans or at least a significant minority. Other rights are not as politically popular and likely would not achieve the same success in the political process. Thus, a more systematic analysis of the strengths and weaknesses of courts and legislatures as rights-protectors is warranted.

In this book I focus on a certain category of rights, what Denise Morgan and I have called "rights of belonging."[33] "Rights of belonging" are those rights that promote an inclusive vision of who belongs to the national community of the United States and that facilitate equal membership in that community. Legislation that defines and protects rights of belonging is the end product of a decision by the majority to embrace minorities and facilitate their inclusion in social and political institutions, as well as in the economic life of the country.

The term "belonging" is most closely associated with Kenneth Karst, who has written extensively about equal citizenship. Belonging, he explains, is essential to equal citizenship because "[a]mong full members of the community, the ideal of equality prevails; as to outsiders, the issue of equality seems irrelevant."[34] The term "rights of belonging" is intended to be more encompassing than the term "civil rights," including rights that historically were not considered to be civil rights such as economic and social rights. While it has its roots in the republican view of citizenship rights, the term "rights of belonging" also attempts to avoid the distinction between insiders and outsiders that the term "citizenship" implies.[35] National citizenship can be a force that brings people together, but the concept of national unity also can signal a sharp divide between those who belong and those who are excluded.[36] In sum, rights of belonging are best understood as the set of entitlements that are necessary to ensure inclusion, participation, and equal membership in our diverse national community.[37]

In general, rights of belonging are based in equality. In *Brown v. Board of Education*, the Supreme Court created a right of belonging for African American schoolchildren by holding that segregated elementary schools violated the Equal Protection Clause. Court decisions like

Brown, and statutes like the Reconstruction Era civil rights statutes and the 1964 Civil Rights Act, create rights of belonging because they facilitate the belonging of people of color as equal members in our society. In contrast, liberty interests, like the right to family autonomy and freedom of speech, in and of themselves are not rights of belonging. However, liberty-based rights can implicate equality-based rights. For example, the right to marry is a liberty interest, rooted in individual autonomy, but it becomes an equality interest when it is denied to one group of people based on immutable characteristics.[38] Similarly, the First Amendment protects liberty interests such as freedom of speech and association, but it can also facilitate belonging by enabling people to participate in the political process on an equal basis. Hence, the right to join a union, based in part in the First Amendment and protected by the Wagner Act (formally, the National Labor Relations Act),[39] is a right of belonging because it facilitates the equal participation of workers in the workplace and in the political process. Both rights are rights of belonging because they enable outsiders to become part of the larger community.

Because rights of belonging facilitate the inclusion of "outsiders" into the community in which they live, they appear at first glance to be precisely the type of individual rights best enforced by non-majoritarian courts. Indeed, there is a significant overlap between those who benefit from rights of belonging and "discrete and insular minorities," the term that invokes judicial solicitude. Yet here I show that precisely the opposite has happened during two of the periods of history marked by the greatest expansion of rights of belonging, post–Civil War Reconstruction and the New Deal Eras. The Court arguably preceded Congress during the third such period, the Second Reconstruction of the 1960s, with its ruling outlawing segregation in *Brown v. Board of Education.* However, even during that period, the ineffectiveness of judicial enforcement of the Court's mandate in *Brown* meant that congressional action was necessary to fulfill the promise of equality in that decision.

Like the recent dispute over RFRA, the periods in which Congress has acted to protect rights of belonging often have been marked by battles over constitutional meaning between Congress and the Supreme Court. The Fourteenth Amendment itself was enacted in the midst of such a battle. Moreover, as during the battle over the meaning of the Free Exercise Clause, Congress, and not the Court, often took on the role of the branch that is *more* protective of individual rights. Sometimes, as during Reconstruction and the New Deal Eras, members of Congress have taken a defiant attitude toward the Court and asserted their own authority to interpret the Constitution. In other times, including the New Deal and the Second Reconstruction Eras, members of Congress have acted in the shadow of the Supreme Court and shaped their strategy to conform to the Court's restrictive interpretation of their power. Only during the debate over the 1964 Civil Rights Act did members of Congress see themselves as acting in harmony with the Court's constitutional vision. Even then, though, their power to act was restricted by Supreme Court precedent, and members of Congress shaped their strategy to avoid a possible confrontation with the Court. The battles between the Court and Congress over constitutional meaning are more than just a power struggle between coordinate branches. What is at stake in those battles is the adequate protection of our rights of belonging.

The rights-protecting role of Congress was central to the constitutional vision of the principal architect of our constitution, James Madison, and is enshrined in the enforcement provisions of every constitutional amendment expanding individual rights since the Reconstruction Era. Nevertheless, until now constitutional scholars have largely overlooked Congress's important role as protector of individual rights.[40] This oversight is due in large part to the fact that many constitutional law scholars simply do not trust Congress to act as a constitutional interpreter. As Mark Tushnet describes this view: "Familiarity leads us to assume that constitutional review must occur in courts and that non-judicial actors—politicians, said in a disparaging tone of voice—would fail to do a decent job of constitutional review were they given a chance. Courts are said to be distinctly the forum of principle, the legislature and executive the forum of politics."[41] Many legal scholars simply ignore the role that Congress has in interpreting the Constitution. Others argues that as a political body, Congress cannot properly evaluate the kind of constitutional norms that underlie rights of belonging because it is not suited to determining matters of principle. In contrast to courts, which are institutionally designed to allow judges to determine matters of principle, members of Congress must pay attention to the desires of their constituents, hence, the "prevailing winds" of politics will affect their decision-making.[42]

In this book I take issue with those scholars and argue not only that Congress has the power and the competence to play an important part in creating constitutional norms but also that members of Congress have often used that power to protect rights of belonging. This book joins the growing body of work that Larry Kramer describes as "popular constitutionalism"—the study of constitutional interpretation outside of the courts. Some of this work, including Kramer's, focuses on the interpretation of the constitution by "the people themselves" apart from the influence of political bodies.[43] Other scholars, such as Mark Tushnet and Keith Whittington, focus on constitutional interpretation by the political branches, including Congress.

In this book I explore the relationship between the two phenomena.[44] Popular constitutionalism by "the people themselves" has always preceded congressional protection of rights of belonging. For example, the antislavery constitutional theories of abolitionists influenced the Framers of the Reconstruction Amendments and Reconstruction Era civil rights legislation. The labor movement's "constitution of freedom" influenced the New Deal Congress's protection of workers, and the demands for equality of civil rights activists in the 1950s and 1960s inspired Congress to enact the 1964 Civil Rights Act and numerous other pieces of civil rights legislation. Here I focus primarily on what members of Congress did with those constitutional theories.

Here I also explore in detail the congressional debates over legislation protecting rights of belonging during those three eras, and in doing so, I treat Congress as a constitutional actor with an important role in constitutional interpretation. Like federal judges, members of Congress also swear an oath to uphold and defend the Constitution and thus are expected to consider the constitutionality of their actions.[45] Keith Whittington calls the process of determining constitutional meaning in the political branches "constitutional construction—the method of elaborating constitutional meaning in the political realm."[46] Consistent with that view, in this book I take the words of the members of Congress at face value, just as a reader of a court decision would do. This methodology rejects the claim that the political nature of congressional decision-making necessarily results in unprincipled decisions. Many of the members of Congress debating the important statutes discussed in this book were acting on principle.

However, motive is not decisive to my analysis. Even those members who were not acting on principle, but instead acted according to political expediency, had to make convincing arguments in order to obtain their political objectives. Politicians make arguments in order to persuade, as do judges when they write decisions.[47] While it is undeniable that members of Congress make decisions based on political calculations, the political nature of congressional decision-making in and of itself does not make that decision-making either illegitimate or inferior to courts' interpretation of the Constitution. Extensive research by political scientists reveals that the rulings of federal courts tend to track public opinion at about the same rate as congressional policies, indicating that, like members of Congress, judges also may be influenced by politics.[48]

Still, constitutional construction is different from courts' interpretation of the constitution because, unlike judicial decisions, it is openly influenced by, and responsive to, political forces. In a majoritarian body, the most persuasive arguments resonate with popular sentiment and thus are useful to determining that sentiment. The vote on a piece of legislation is the final indicator of whether or not members of Congress succeeded in convincing their colleagues.

The study of congressional protection of rights of belonging is particularly salient given the Court's ruling in *Boerne* and other cases in the past decade, limiting congressional power to protect those rights. For example, in a series of recent cases, the Court has limited Congress's power to abrogate sovereign immunity, making it more difficult for individual plaintiffs to enforce their federal rights against state infringement.[49] In another group of cases, the Court limited Congress's use of the commerce power to establish individual rights.[50] Although the Court's ruling in *Boerne* placed the most stringent limitations on congressional power to define constitutional norms, all of these cases make it harder for Congress to create rights of belonging and to make them individually enforceable. These cases make it apparent that, to the current Supreme Court, other constitutional norms, including state sovereignty and protecting the Court's role as constitutional interpreter, take precedence over congressional protection of these important rights. More importantly, these decisions prevent Congress from adopting an alternative position—one that favors the protection of rights of belonging over these other constitutional norms.

The Rehnquist Court has been criticized widely for the restrictions that it has imposed on Congress's rights-enforcing power.[51] Much of this criticism contrasts the Rehnquist Court's lack of deference toward Congress with the deference of the Warren Court. While this criticism is justified, it is somewhat ahistorical because it treats the Warren Court as the norm. It is the Warren Court, and not the current Court, that is the historical anomaly. Throughout the history of this country, the Court has placed constitutional barriers in the way of congressional protection of rights of belonging, and it often has narrowly construed the statutes protecting those rights. Learning this history should cause constitutional scholars to reexamine their views on the role of legislatures and courts as protectors of rights of belonging. Advocates of rights of belonging should also should take note and reconsider their reliance on courts instead of political bodies as the principal enforcers of those rights.

Along with the history explored in this book, there are institutional reasons why Congress is better suited to protect rights of belonging than are the federal courts. The insulation of federal courts from the political process arguably make those courts better suited to protect minorities because courts need not answer to the will of the majority. However, political insulation also weakens courts and can lead to resistance when courts enforce equality norms. By contrast, legislatures benefit from the legitimacy of being politically accountable to the people they serve. The transparency of the decision-making process also contributes to its legitimacy. Moreover, legislatures speak with the power of the majority, and Congress speaks for the majority of the entire country. Thus, it is not surprising that even when courts act in concert with Congress, federal legislation protecting rights of belonging has been more successful than court enforcement of those norms. Finally, focusing on congressional protection of rights restores the agency of political activists that fought for constitutional change. Their arguments were not directed toward courts but toward political actors.

Moreover, there are also normative reasons why, whenever possible, debates over rights of belonging should be conducted in the political realm rather than within the courts. Rights of belonging represent the decision of the community to expand itself to include more members and to improve the treatment of those who live within that community. Legislatures are the more natural enforcers of these positive rights because legislatures represent the will of the community. Political debates over the meaning and scope of rights of belonging can strengthen the community because it fosters an open dialogue about those rights. Because rights of belonging express the values of our national community, they are integrally linked to the political process. Perhaps most importantly, relying primarily on judges to define and enforce rights of belonging diverts energy from political action and engagement in the community, which is the most effective means of bringing about social change.[52]

2

Congress and Rights before the Civil War

Prior to the Civil War, Congress played a very small part in protecting individual rights and had virtually no role in protecting rights of belonging. This was largely due to the fact that, although several provisions in the original Constitution and the Bill of Rights created individual rights, neither the original Constitution nor the Bill of Rights contained any provisions empowering Congress to enforce those rights. The lack of a congressional enforcement power was contrary to the intentions of the principal architect of the Constitution, James Madison. Madison strongly believed that Congress should have the power to act to protect individual rights, but he was unable to convince his colleagues at the constitutional convention. Even if Madison had prevailed, however, disagreements over the extent and meaning of individual rights during this era would have precluded federal legislation protecting rights of belonging. The issue of slavery loomed over Congress throughout this period, preventing members of Congress from reaching consensus over the role of the federal government in relationship to individual rights. The major constitutional crises of that era, including the crisis leading to the Missouri Compromise and the nullification crisis, revolved around the issue of slavery. Congress, not the federal courts, resolved these crises.[1] When the federal courts did get involved, they usually ruled in favor of slavery, especially in the decade preceding the Civil War.[2] Over time, the nation became increasingly divided over the issue of slavery, division that was reflected in tense congressional debates over individual rights in the years leading up to the Civil War.

The concept of "rights of belonging" was anachronistic prior to the Civil War because the Constitution contained no express provision requiring equality in the government's treatment of its citizens.[3] More important was the lack of consensus over who "belonged" to the national, or even the state, polity, and who *could* belong. This question was central to the congressional debates over the meaning of citizenship and the rights inherent in citizenship, in the years leading up to the Civil War. Members of Congress debated the question of who could be a state citizen or a U.S. citizen, whether the state or federal citizenship was primary, and the extent of rights to which those citizens were entitled. In *Dred Scott v. Sanford,* the Supreme Court held that people of African descent could not be citizens and thus were not subject to federal protections. Antislavery members of Congress rejected the Court's ruling, and opposition to *Dred Scott* became a rallying cry for opponents of slavery.[4] The division over slavery made any consensus over rights of belonging within Congress impossible prior to the Civil War.

Madison and the Federal Negative

James Madison believed that Congress should have the power to enforce individual rights. Indeed Congress's power to protect individual rights was crucial to Madison's constitutional vision, embodied in his theory of the extended republic and his proposed legislative veto, or federal negative, which would have authorized Congress to veto state legislation. Madison intended the legislative veto to serve as a mechanism for protecting individual rights by preventing factions in state governments from oppressing minorities.[5] However, while the Founders by and large adopted Madison's proposal for structuring the government, they rejected Madison's proposed federal negative, depriving Congress of the power to protect minority rights.

Protecting individual rights was one of Madison's chief concerns as he worked on the design of our government. Indeed, he believed that "justice" was the "object of government."[6] Madison was most concerned that factions would form in governments and prompt them to enact unjust laws that would intrude on individual rights. In Federalist No. 10, Madison described "factions" as "a number of citizens . . . united and actuated by some common impulse or passion, or of interest, adverse to the rights of other citizens or to the permanent and aggregate interests of the community."[7] He believed that factions were inevitable in all civilized societies because of the diversity of interests and the fallibility of human reasons and passions.[8] To remove the cause of factions would require destroying the liberty that Madison thought was essential to a republican government. Instead, he and the other Founders attempted to design a government with structural measures that would control the effects of factions.[9]

Structural measures for protecting individual liberty in our constitutional design include separation of powers, the system of checks and balances, and federalism. As Madison explained in Federalist No. 51, to preserve liberty each department in the federal government should have a will of its own and be protected from undue encroachment by the other departments. In addition, the federalist system, with its division of power between the national and state governments, would provide "a double security . . . to the rights of the people."[10] The horizontal and vertical distribution of power would prevent any one branch or level of government from becoming too powerful, thereby protecting individual rights from government oppression. All of these mechanisms were designed to ensure that the government would enact just legislation and help protect individuals from government interference. However, Madison believed that the most important structural mechanisms for protecting individual rights were the extended republic and the federal negative.

At the time of the framing of the Constitution, Madison believed that states, and not the federal government, posed the greatest danger to individual rights and liberties.[11] He was worried about "the unrestricted power of majorities in state legislatures to pass laws that violated the rights of individuals and minorities."[12] Prior to the constitutional convention, Madison explained that the vices of the political system of the United States included the "want of guaranty to the states of their Constitutions and laws against internal violence" and the "injustice of the laws of the states."[13] Therefore, Madison strongly believed that the national government should have the power to act decisively in the presence of a wrong perpetrated by state legislatures.[14] He maintained that "[t]he evils which prevail within the states individually . . . affect the whole."[15]

Madison believed that the extended republic would do a better job at protecting individual rights than would state legislatures. In his Vices Memo, Madison explained: "As a limited Monarchy tempers the evils of an absolute one; so an extensive Republic ameliorates the administration of a small republic."[16] In Federalist No. 10, he elaborated that an extended republic would be more likely to enact just laws because it enjoyed three advantages over smaller republics. First, there would be a lower probability that any one faction will amount to a majority. Second, there would be fewer opportunities for factions to coalesce, given the larger distances. Third, elected officials' wider constituencies would make it more likely that they would take a broader view of the public interest. Madison explained: "The influence of factious leaders may kindle a flame within their particular states but will be unable to spread a general conflagration through the other states. . . . In the extent and proper structure of the Union, therefore, we behold a republican remedy for the diseases most incident to a republican government."[17]

Madison's theory of the extended republic explains why he thought that Congress would probably enact better laws than state legislatures would, and why he believed that Congress would be less likely than state legislatures to violate individual rights. However, the extended republic alone could not prevent states from intruding on individual rights. The second element of Madison's plan was to create a mechanism for Congress to police state legislatures, which he called the federal negative, or legislative veto. Madison's federal negative would have empowered Congress to veto state legislative measures "in all cases whatsoever," in order to prevent them from intruding on individual rights.[18] Under Madison's proposal, congressional review of state laws would be a routine aspect of state lawmaking. Madison hoped that the negative would serve as a preventive measure because it would cause state legislators to stop and think about how Congress would react before adopting unjust legislation, and it would allow members of Congress to screen out state measures that were a product of a factious majority.[19] Madison linked the federal negative to his theory of the extended republic, explaining that because Congress served the people of an extended republic, it would serve as a "disinterested and dispassionate umpire in disputes between different passions and interests in the State."[20] Madison believed that the federal negative was the most important constitutional protection for individual rights, and he fought for it at the constitutional convention, proposing it three times without success.[21]

Scholars have debated the meaning of Madison's proposed federal negative. Charles Hobson argues that its chief purpose was to maintain federal power over state governments.[22] More recently, scholars have emphasized the role that the negative would have had in protecting individual rights against infringement by the majority.[23] This theory is supported by a letter that Madison wrote to George Washington explaining that the negative would curb "the aggressions of interested majorities on the rights of minorities and of individuals."[24] Madison believed that the governmental structure should prevent majorities from carrying into effect "schemes of oppression."[25] Because Madison believed that Congress, serving a larger republic, would be more enlightened than state legislatures, he thought Congress would be well suited to protect individual rights from infringement by oppressive combinations in the states.[26] He explained that the negative was intended to "control bad or unjust majorities in one arena (the states) with better and more just majorities (Congress) in another."[27]

Notwithstanding the importance of the federal negative to Madison, there is little evidence that the other delegates to the constitutional convention shared his view.[28] Though Madison proposed the negative three times at the constitutional convention, he lost every time.[29] Many delegates who favored a more state-centered government opposed giving the federal government too much power over the states in this manner.[30] Members of the convention such as Thomas Jefferson feared that an unlimited federal veto would unduly threaten state sovereignty.[31] As a compromise, the convention adopted the Supremacy Clause and strengthened the powers of the federal judiciary. These measures, as well as the limited protections for individual rights against state infringement contained in Article I, Section 10, "were expected to serve the purpose of Madison's negative."[32] The defeat of the federal negative and its replacement with the Supremacy Clause shifted the burden of protecting individual rights from Congress to the federal courts.

The option of judicial review as a mechanism for protecting individual rights undoubtedly contributed to the defeat of Madison's federal negative.[33] Others of the Founders thought courts, and not Congress, should play the primary part in protecting individual rights. For example, Alexander Hamilton argued that the judiciary's life tenure, stability, and independence tend to insulate them from popular pressures, making them more neutral than frequently elected officials, and thus more likely to protect minority rights.[34] In a letter that he wrote to Madison, Thomas Jefferson also claimed that the independence and integrity of judges would make them well-suited to enforce individual rights.[35] During the later debate over the Bill of Rights, Madison indicated that he was willing to rely on judicial review as a backstop, explaining that he expected that courts would enforce the Bill of Rights and thus provide an "impenetrable bulwark against every assumption of power in the legislative or executive."[36] However, Madison strongly disagreed with Hamilton's view that judicial review would provide the best protection of individual rights.

Although Madison was well aware of the potential for legislatures to intrude on individual rights,[37] he also believed that Congress, and not the courts, would be most effective at protecting those rights. Madison believed that "interior" or structural controls like the federal negative would be far more effective than "exterior" or admonitory controls, like the Bill of Rights, that would be enforced by the courts.[38] At the constitutional convention, Madison explained the negative in terms of separation of powers, as a systemic check on the lawmaking process that would prevent unjust laws from being made. Madison thought the automatic, preventative legislative veto was far superior to the ad hoc system of judicial review of laws after they were made.[39] In a letter to Jefferson he explained, "it is more convenient to prevent the passage of a law, than it is to declare it void after it was passed."[40]

Moreover, Madison was not convinced that judicial review would be an effective protection for individual rights. He pointed out that the fact that judges were not elected was a double-edged sword. While on the one hand it enhanced their independence, on the other hand it reduced their power because, unlike legislatures, their power did not come from the people. Knowing that any agency of government that attempts to act against the will of the people is going to have difficulties, Madison predicted that after-the-fact orders would be met by resistance and doubted whether states would follow adverse judicial decrees. Presciently, Madison feared that the use of force would be necessary to ensure the orders of federal courts would be followed.[41] Moreover, Madison was not convinced that judges would rule in favor of minority interests. He argued that it was equally likely that the judge's independent powers would align him with the unjust majority as with the rightful interests of the minor party.[42]

Madison believed that any attempt to check state legislatures must come from an institution of similar strength that also derived its power directly from the people. Because Congress represents all of the people, and thus has the most power, it could use that power most effectively to protect individual rights.[43] As we have seen, Madison believed that Congress would have the wisdom and the will to use the federal negative to protect individual rights. After the Alien and Sedition Acts of 1798, Madison become more suspicious of the power of the federal legislature and began to believe that Congress also posed a danger to liberty.[44] In his later years Madison's opinion of judicial review changed, and he came to believe that the judicial department was the surest expositor of the Constitution.[45] Indeed, later in his life, Madison supported judicially imposed limitations on congressional power and criticized John Marshall's opinion in *McCulloch v. Maryland* as too deferential to Congress. He thought that it was essential for Congress to consider the constitutionality of its actions, but by then he distrusted the ability and willingness of congressional representatives to do so.[46] However, at the constitutional convention, Madison stated that Congress, and not judges, should be the primary guardian of individual rights.

Although they rejected Madison's most far-reaching proposals, the Framers of the Constitution did adopt some protections for individual rights, based on the protective structure of the federal government. They recognized that, without a strong federal government, balkanization would threaten individual rights. Therefore, they incorporated certain basic protections into the original Constitution to ensure some centralized protection.[47] These protections included the Full Faith and Credit Clause,[48] which requires states to give full faith and credit to judgments entered into in other states; the Privileges and Immunities Clause of Article IV,[49] which states that the citizens of each state shall be entitled to all privileges and immunities of the citizens of the several states; and the Article III Diversity Clause,[50] which provides federal jurisdiction when citizens of different states sue each other.[51] These provisions indicate that the Framers intended the federal government to further uniformity of rights, even if it was not intended to serve as a proactive protector of those rights.[52]

After the Constitution was ratified, Madison stopped advocating congressional enforcement of rights, but he persisted in his concern about state legislatures. He voiced this concern again during the debate over the primary constitutional protections for individual rights prior to the Civil War, the Bill of Rights. Although Madison originally opposed the Bill of Rights, calling them "parchment guarantees" that would have little effect, he later became the lead advocate for its adoption because he believed the Bill of Rights would do little harm and that it was politically necessary.[53] When he first proposed the Bill of Rights to Congress, Madison's version included a provision that would have strengthened the power of the federal government to protect individual rights from state interference. The proposed amendment would have added to the limitations on state power in Article I, § 10, the following clause: "No state shall violate the equal rights of conscience, or the freedom of the press, or the trial by jury in criminal cases."[54] Madison regarded this proposal as "the most valuable [one] on the whole list."[55] In a speech to the House of Representatives, he explained: "I think there is more danger of those powers being abused by the state governments than by the government of the United States. . . . It must be admitted, on all hands, that the state governments are as liable to attack these invaluable privileges as the general government is, and therefore ought to be as cautiously guarded against."[56]

Once again, however, Madison appears to have been virtually alone in his views. The Bill of Rights grew primarily out of the antifederalists' fear of the national government, and, as states rights supporters, the antifederalists were not interested in reducing state sovereignty in the manner that Madison suggested.[57] Madison's proposed amendment passed the House but was defeated in the Senate without much discussion.[58] His vision of federal enforcement of rights against state governments, and Congress's role in enforcing those rights, was not resurrected until the ratification of the Fourteenth Amendment after the Civil War.[59]

In retrospect, Madison was probably overly idealistic in his belief in the extended republic's ameliorative effect on factions. As Hamilton warned, oppressive local factions can also find common cause at the national level.[60] Moreover, it is difficult to imagine how the federal negative would have functioned in the modern day United States. Impractical and unwieldy even in its own day, it is likely that it "would surely have collapsed under the weight of the modern administrative state."[61] To a certain extent, history has borne Madison out. As he predicted, over the years the federal courts have not been sufficiently protective of rights of belonging, and congressional action has been necessary to achieve their adequate protection. However, due in large part to the lack of congressional enforcement provisions like Madison's proposed federal negative, Congress lacked the power to protect rights of belonging during the first eight decades of our country's history.

Rights in Congress: Slavery, Nullification, and Citizenship

Congress's failure to protect individual rights prior to the Civil War was not only due to lack of power but also, and more importantly, due to the lack of political will. The shadow of slavery prevented a national consensus over the meaning and extent of individual rights during that era. Congress did act to protect the rights of slaveholders, at the expense of the rights of slaves and free blacks, with the Fugitive Slaves Acts of 1793 and 1850.[62] Those members of Congress who wanted to act to protect other individual rights did so by requiring states to adopt rights-protecting measures in their constitutions as a condition of their admission to the Union. Further efforts were stymied by a lack of consensus among members of Congress and the growing division between representatives of free and slave states that developed during the first half of the nineteenth century. As the century wore on, slavery loomed increasingly large over all congressional debates, especially those regarding individual rights. In the two decades leading up to the Civil War, members of Congress became consumed with debate over the meaning of citizenship rights and the extent of their power, if any, to protect those rights.

The original constitution represented a compromise between proslavery and antislavery forces. Important provisions of the constitution, including the Three-Fifths Clause and the Fugitive Slave Clause, were intended to protect slavery.[63] Even those provisions intended to protect individual rights and strengthen the Union, such as the Full Faith and Credit and the Privileges and Immunities Clauses of Article IV, could be interpreted to protect the rights of slaveholders.[64] Thus, historian Paul Finkelman argues: "On every issue at the Convention, slave owners had won major concessions from the rest of the nation, and with the exception of the commerce clause they had given up very little in return."[65] Northerners were willing to sacrifice the issue of slavery in order to obtain concessions to create a strong national union. Of course, the issue of slavery ultimately caused the union to fall apart. The constitutional compromise depended on the states' treating each other with comity. Fugitive slaves, traveling slave masters, and traveling free blacks created tension, which challenged the compromise and led to the collapse of comity between the states.[66] The rising tension over slavery was reflected in debates over the principal controversy of the era—the extent of the federal government to make improvements—and the two principal constitutional crises of the era: that leading to the Missouri Compromise and the nullification crisis.

The only major legislation that Congress enacted prior to the Civil War to protect individual rights were the Fugitive Slave Acts, which were intended to "protect" the property rights of individual slave owners.[67] In 1793, Congress enacted the first Fugitive Slave Act, relying on its implicit power to enforce the Fugitive Slave Clause. The statute made it a federal crime to interfere with either process or harbor a known slave.[68] Congress enacted the statute in response to a dispute between the governors of Pennsylvania and Virginia over a slave who had been freed under Pennsylvania law but kidnapped and taken back to Virginia.[69] During the debate over the act, Congress considered, but ultimately rejected, a provision that would have created a presumption of freedom for blacks living in northern states and required that their slave status be proven in trials in their home states.[70] The final version removed the protective provision and allowed the hearing to be held without evidentiary protections.[71] Like the Fugitive Slave Clause, the 1793 act was a major victory for slave owners and their supporters in Congress. Since the Fugitive Slave Clause did not have an enforcement provision, the act also represented an extension of congressional power.[72]

During the first half of the nineteenth century, an increasing number of northern states resisted the Fugitive Slave Act, with some state legislatures enacting measures protecting escaping slaves and other state officials refusing to enforce the act.[73] As a result, in 1850, Congress enacted a more stringent statute, which provided for the appointment of a federal commissioner in every county of the nation to enforce it, and authorized federal marshals and, if necessary, federal troops to aid the capture of fugitive slaves.[74] The 1850 act not only deprived the northern states of the power to shelter fugitive slaves but also, in a blow to the sovereignty of the northern states, superceded the authority of reluctant northern officials and enlisted federal "help" to ensure that the task would be carried out. As a result of this federal law, northern blacks were in danger not only when they traveled to southern states, and, because of the weak evidentiary standards of the federal act, in danger of being kidnapped in the very northern state in which they lived.[75]

Hence, prior to the Civil War, Congress acted repeatedly to support the interests of slave owners. While representatives of the slave states were happy to use federal power to enforce the institution of slavery, however, they fiercely resisted federal power in other areas, fearing that opponents of slavery would use it to limit that institution. Throughout this period, members of Congress hotly debated the extent of congressional power to make "improvements" by levying tariffs and appropriating federal money for development projects and establishing institutions such as the federal bank, creating what prominent congressman Henry Clay called the "American system."[76] These debates primarily focused on the proper contours of federalism and Congress's threat to state autonomy. The positions of members of Congress on internal improvements became intertwined with their positions on the issue of slavery. Southerners such as John Calhoun, who initially supported the American system, became some of its harshest opponents as they realized that the system created precedent for Congress to legislate against slavery.[77]

Of course, other members of Congress opposed slavery. From the very beginning, members of Congress unsuccessfully proposed measures to end the institution of slavery and protect free blacks.[78] The most important victory for antislavery forces in Congress occurred prior to the Constitution's adoption, when the Confederate Congress enacted the Northwest Ordinance, which governed the territory that contained many of the early new states, including Indiana, Ohio, and Illinois. Article VI of the ordinance provided that "there shall be neither slavery nor involuntary servitude in the said territory."[79] The ban on slavery in the Northwest Ordinance became almost sacred to northerners, especially abolitionists.[80] However, the overall effect of the ordinance was ambiguous. Like the Constitution, it contained a fugitive slave clause, and other provisions of the ordinance appeared to condone slavery.[81] Some slavery persisted in the territory after it was outlawed, in part due to the lack of an enforcement provision in Article VI.[82]

Nonetheless, in the early nineteenth century, northern members of Congress relied on the Northwest Ordinance as a means of protecting individual rights. Along with prohibiting slavery, the Northwest Ordinance also required the territories to treat their inhabitants with equal representation and privileges. When the states within the territory were admitted to the Union, Congress required that they institutionalize that requirement in their state constitutions as a condition of admission.[83] Congress also extended the same requirement to other new states, including Louisiana and Mississippi.[84] Hence, conditions on admission were a means of assuring that some states at least formally pledged to protect basic individual rights, even if those rights were not enforced. When members of Congress attempted to use this same mechanism to address the issue of slavery, however, a crisis ensued. While the issue of slavery was implicit in debates over internal improvements, some of the fiercest congressional debates over slavery occurred in the context of admitting new states. These conflicts escalated over time as tension mounted over slavery in the territories.

In February 1819, Representative James Tallmadge of New York proposed conditioning the admission of Missouri as a state on the gradual abolition of slavery within the state.[85] The House voted to accept the amendment, but the Senate rejected it, and the Fifteenth Congress ended before the issue was resolved. When the new Congress met, Representative John Taylor of New York renewed the proposal, but his renewed proposal was more extreme—that Missouri would have to forbid slavery altogether, except for persons already "held to service or labor" there.[86] As a compromise, Illinois Senator Jesse Thomas proposed to ban slavery in the northern territories, rather than in Missouri, and both Houses agreed.[87] The compromise bill provided that slavery could be legal in Missouri but not in the new state of Maine, and that slavery would be prohibited in the remaining territory acquired from France in 1803 and lying north of 36°30'.[88]

The congressional debate over the admission of Missouri focused on whether Congress had the power to ban slavery within a state. The basic power that Congress relied on to limit slavery in Missouri was its Article IV power to admit states into the Union. Representative Taylor relied on the precedent of conditions imposed on other states that had been admitted.[89] Supporters also argued that the ban fell within Congress's commerce power, as well as the principle that Congress could require a republican form of government.[90] Opponents of the slavery ban strongly resisted the last argument because it is implied that all slave states were not "republican."[91] Opponents principally argued that such a ban would impose an unconstitutional condition on the admitted state. They maintained that the right to permit slavery was reserved to the states by the Tenth Amendment.[92] Finally, southerners strongly resisted the argument that Congress could use the commerce power to regulate slavery within the states.[93]

The constitutional arguments over congressional power to regulate slavery in the territories and the states were not resolved in 1820. Instead, the Missouri Compromise temporarily eased the concerns of both sides of the debate, but its aftermath was increased tension.[94] The events surrounding the Missouri Compromise caused southerners such as John Calhoun to harden their opposition to federal power to make improvements such as roads and canals, as a means of fostering national unity. After the 1820 crisis, Calhoun dedicated himself to opposing congressional power in all realms, including improvements. Calhoun realized that "[i]f Congress can build roads and canals, it can emancipate slaves."[95] The Missouri debate had shown Calhoun how easily some northern members of Congress could distort grants of federal power into threats to the institution of slavery.[96]

Calhoun was the primary instigator of the other major crisis to arise in Congress during this era, the nullification crisis of 1832. The nullification crisis involved the protective tariffs that Congress imposed on imported goods.[97] South Carolina officials, including then Vice President Calhoun, viewed the tariffs as an unconstitutional and intolerable burden on the states. In November 1832, encouraged by Calhoun, the South Carolina state legislature declared the tariffs unconstitutional and resolved not to enforce them. The South Carolina legislature asserted its own power to nullify the tariff and threatened secession in response to the use of federal force to enforce the tariffs.[98] This doctrine of nullification threatened the constitutional order because of its implicit connection to the incendiary issue of slavery and resistance to federal restrictions on slavery. President Andrew Jackson recognized this fact, and responded to the resolution by asking Congress to authorize the use of force to enforce the tariffs. He proclaimed that if the United States could not defend itself against nullification, "the supremacy of the (federal) laws is at an end."[99]

Within Congress, the strongest response to Calhoun's construction was Daniel Webster's. He was the premier representative of the traditional center of nationalist sentiment and an attorney responsible for some of the Court's nationalist decisions. Webster argued that the nullifiers were trying to undermine the Constitution and maintained that nullification threatened the Union.[100] With President Jackson's support, the nationalist Representative Henry Clay engineered a compromise measure that included the passage of a bill authorizing federal officials to use force to enforce the tariff and a gradual reduction of the tariffs to a level suitable to South Carolina.[101]

Although the nullification crisis was ostensibly about economic policy, to Calhoun and his southern supporters, the controversy was really about slavery. In September 1830, Calhoun drafted a message to the South Carolina state legislature, explaining that if the federal government could levy this tariff, it could do anything, thereby reducing the states to mere corporations. He explained:

Such a power in the hands of the General Government is itself sufficient to control the whole industry and institutions of the country. . . . On all questions connected with the monied action of the government, we have been and must continue to be a minority. Our peculiar productions, and our peculiar domestick institutions, mark us, as its certain victim, unless we can be protected by the interposed sovereignty of the States.[102]

Since "our peculiar domestick institution" was a favorite contemporary euphemism for slavery, this speech makes clear that the tariff was only "the occasion, rather than the real cause of the present unhappy state of things."[103] And although the compromise resolution resolved the issue of tariffs, doing away with them until the Civil War era, it only exposed the depth of feeling about the underlying issue of slavery and the danger that the mounting tension over slavery posed to the Union.

As tension mounted in Congress over the issue of slavery, popular opposition to slavery was growing in the north. Opponents of slavery had been active since the founding of our nation, but the organized abolitionist movement gained momentum in the early 1830s. William Lloyd Garrison's newspaper, the *Liberationist,* was founded in 1831, and the American Anti-Slavery Society was founded in 1833. "For the next thirty years, the movement's main arguments depended on the principles of the Declaration of Independence" and its promise of equality for all.[104] However, abolitionists were divided over their opinion of the Constitution. One group, led by Garrison, held that the Constitution was "a covenant with Death and an agreement from Hell" because it was fundamentally a proslavery document. They argued for the dissolution of the Constitution. A second group acknowledged the proslavery provisions but argued that it essentially was an antislavery document.[105] A third group argued that the Constitution already forbade slavery.[106] From the start, the third group of antislavery constitutionalists asserted a strong form of popular constitutionalism and challenged the authority of the Court. This group of abolitionists is the most important for understanding the Fourteenth Amendment because of its influence on members of Congress during the antebellum era, including the men who would become the Framers of that Amendment.

Antislavery constitutionalists maintained that the Bill of Rights was enforceable against the states and that the Due Process Clause, the Privileges and Immunities Clause of Article IV, and principles of natural law forbade the institution of slavery.[107] Notwithstanding the Court's ruling in *Barron v. Mayor and City Council of Baltimore* that the Bill of Rights was not enforceable against the states, these abolitionists "continued to insist that the Bill of Rights, with which slavery is obviously incompatible, imposed positive duties on the states."[108] Abolitionist lawyer Joel Tiffany expressed this view in his influential 1849 book, *Treatise on the Unconstitutionality of American Slavery,* in which he argued that "the *object* of the national government was to protect the natural and inalienable rights of each citizen."[109] Other abolitionist lawyers argued that the Due Process Clause of the Fifth Amendment forbid slavery.[110] They maintained that free blacks were citizens and developed a legal theory by which the states, as well as the federal government, could not deny the fundamental rights of American citizens.[111] Influenced by these abolitionists, northern members of Congress began to assert the authority of their states to allow free blacks to be citizens.

Members of Congress had debated the extent and nature of the rights of citizenship from the very beginning of our nation. While members of the First Congress appeared to believe that they had broad authority to enact "naturalization" laws that included a general power to define or confer citizenship, even then, it was apparent that it would be problematic for southern states if Congress decided to make slaves citizens.[112] Based in part on these concerns, Congress asserted a more limited authority over citizenship in subsequent naturalization acts.[113] The uncertain relationship between slaves, free blacks, and citizenship rights continued to haunt Congress and sparked numerous contentious debates. In Congress, antislavery constitutionalists took a strong position on the meaning of citizenship, arguing the fact that a person was a citizen of one state meant that his basic rights could not be taken away from him by another state. Those views were not shared by a majority of Congress until the Reconstruction Era. During Reconstruction, the antislavery constitutionalists were highly influential. Ten of the fifteen members of the Joint Committee on Reconstruction were associated with them. The most important of these was Ohio Representative John Bingham, who later became the principal author of Section One of the Fourteenth Amendment.[114] As early as 1820, however, some members of Congress expressed a broad view of citizenship rights in their debates.

For example, the Missouri Compromise was jeopardized when Missouri presented a proposed draft constitution that would have prohibited free blacks from entering the state.[115] Rhode Island Senator James

Burrill argued that the provision violated the Privileges and Immunities Clause of Article IV and that Congress could not admit a state whose law was repugnant to the U.S. Constitution.[116] South Carolina's William Smith replied that the clause only protected citizens, and blacks were not citizens anywhere. He pointed out that every northern state discriminated against blacks in some way or another.[117] Representative James Strong replied that official discrimination did not mean that people were not citizens, pointing out that women and children could be citizens even though they were not able to vote.[118] Representative Charles Pinckney, who had been at the constitutional convention, claimed to have drafted the Privileges and Immunities Clause and insisted that it had never been intended to apply to blacks.[119]

Defenders of Missouri also adopted a more extreme argument: that Congress had no right to pass on the constitutionality of the provision because Missouri was now a state. Of course, Missouri's enabling act expressly required the state to submit its constitution to Congress, but the far-reaching implications of this argument's rejection of federal power to protect individual rights was apparent to all of the participants in the debate.[120] Henry Clay brokered a compromise on this issue as well. Appealing to the good faith of Missouri's leaders, he declared: "There cannot be a doubt but that Missouri, solicitous as she must be, to participate in all the high advantages of our excellent Union, will eagerly seize the opportunity of testifying her attachment to the Federal Constitution, by giving the solemn pledge which she is asked to make, to respect the privileges and immunities which it secures to citizens of other States."[121] Missouri was admitted on the condition that the state legislature could not enact any law to implement that provision that would violate the Privileges and Immunities Clause.[122] That compromise was made possible by Congress's failure to define the privileges and immunities of citizenship. However, the underlying debate lingered and arose repeatedly in the antebellum years.

In 1849, the issue of citizenship resurfaced in debates over the "Seaman's Acts," laws enacted by the states of South Carolina and Louisiana, which authorized state police officers to arrest and imprison free black men that entered their states.[123] At that time, conflicts over traveling blacks and freed slaves had become commonplace between free states and those, like South Carolina, that allowed slavery.[124] The Seaman's Acts were enacted in response to the arrest of Denmark Vesey in Charleston. Vesey was a free black man from the north who allegedly came to Charleston in order to foment a rebellion there.[125] Members of Congress from Massachusetts were particularly concerned about the Seaman's laws because their state had a large shipping industry that employed many sailors who were people of color.[126] Representatives George Ashmun and Charles Hudson decried these laws, arguing that the South Carolina law violated the Privileges and Immunities Clause of Article IV because it authorized the imprisonment of free citizens from their state.[127]

"In the state of Massachusetts the black man was as much a citizen as a white man," said Hudson, complaining that if one of those citizens of color were to go to South Carolina, "his person, and perhaps his life, may be in danger" solely because of the color of his skin.[128] Similarly, Ashmun explained that his problem with the South Carolina law was that it was enforced against "our citizens."[129] Thus, even though they thought that the rights of the freed citizens of color adhered to state, not federal, citizenship, they articulated a national view of citizenship that would protect the rights of state citizens, once those rights were bestowed upon them, against interference by other states. Hudson and Ashmun believed that the Article IV Privileges and Immunities Clause required comity between the states, comity that included respecting the rights that each state bestowed on its own citizens.[130] Their concern was undoubtedly due to the fact that by 1849, southern courts had become extremely reluctant to recognize the manumission of slaves under the laws of northern states.[131]

Representative Hudson argued that the South Carolina law was unconstitutional and accused the state of avoiding Supreme Court review of its law through the doctrine of interposition.[132] Other members of Congress shared this view and articulated their concern by telling the story of Samuel Hoar, a minister from Massachusetts who traveled to South Carolina for the purpose of challenging the constitutionality of the South Carolina law.[133] Rather than arrest Mr. Hoar and his companions, which would have set up the possibility of a legal challenge, South Carolina officials ordered Mr. Hoar to leave town.[134] Members of Congress who advocated a broad view of federal citizenship rights often mentioned the story of Mr. Hoar to illustrate their concerns about southern laws that, they believed, violated the constitutional principles of citizenship.[135] It served as a powerful example of what they did not like about the treatment of their citizens by southern states—that northern citizens could have their most basic human rights taken away from them by southern states, solely due to the color of their skin.[136] Further, it reflected disrespect for the northern states' conveyance of citizenship rights and their power to manumit slaves through their laws.[137] From that time, reference to the Hoar affair implicated not only the substantive rights of Rev. Hoar and the black seaman who accompanied him "but also the underlying issue of national government authority to protect those rights."[138]

In response to the citizenship-based argument of their northern colleagues, southern members of Congress argued that the constitution did not protect people of color from other states because those people were not, and could not be, citizens of the United States. For example, Senator Andrew Butler of South Carolina stated that "colored persons . . . are a species of persons having such rights only as may be conferred upon them by state jurisdiction; they have no federal eligibility, or federal recognition, as citizens of the United States."[139] Butler explained that his understanding was that a state can give a colored person a "status" of being free, but that "status" did not govern in other states and would depend on the local law of each state. "Their condition must be assimilated under the law that operates on them."[140]

More importantly, shortly after Hudson's and Ashmun's dissertation on the rights of citizenship, Congress refuted them by enacting the 1850 Fugitive Slave Act, assisting southern slave owners in capturing slaves that had escaped to northern states. That the southern view of citizenship predominated in Congress during the antebellum era is illustrated by the passage of this act, which protected the rights of slave owners to their "property" but implicitly refuted any claim of individual rights that the fleeing slaves, or for that matter, free blacks, themselves might have enjoyed.[141]

Like the majority of the members of Congress at the time, the Supreme Court adopted the southern view of the Privileges and Immunities Clause in its *Dred Scott* decision.[142] Prior to *Dred Scott*, the federal courts adjudicated many political controversies associated with slavery, and they almost always ruled in favor of the interests of slave owners.[143] In the 1841 case of *Groves v. Slaughter,* the Court held that Congress could not use the commerce power to regulate the slave trade.[144] However, the Court sided with congressional power in its 1842 decision, *Prigg v. Pennsylvania.* In *Prigg,* the Court upheld the 1793 Fugitive Slave Act and found that it preempted the Pennsylvania Personal Liberty Act. The Court upheld the act, even though the Fugitive Slave

Clause contained no congressional enforcement provision, based on an extremely broad reading of implied congressional powers and Justice Story's view that "the clause manifestly contemplates the existence of a positive, unqualified right on the part of the owner of a slave, which no state law or regulation can in any way qualify, regulate, control or restrain."[145] Although the Court's subsequent ruling in *Dred Scott* is considerably better known, Judith Baer has argued that *Prigg* "in historical importance far outweighed the *Dred Scott* decision of 1857, because it invalidated all efforts of the Northern states to protect the civil rights and the liberties of an important class of persons under their jurisdiction."[146]

The *Prigg* decision arguably set the precedent for members of Congress to legislate to protect other individual rights, including the privileges and immunities of citizenship protected by the same Article IV that contained the Fugitive Slave Clause.[147] Until *Prigg,* members of Congress were hampered in their efforts to protect individual rights by another Supreme Court decision of that era, *Barron v. Baltimore.* In *Barron,* the Court held that the Bill of Rights did not impose limitations on the states, but only on the national government.[148] This obviously limited Congress's power to legislate to protect individual rights against state infringement. However, the Privileges and Immunities Clause of Article IV expressly limited the power of the states and might have provided an avenue for Congress to circumvent the impact of *Barron.*

In the influential circuit court case of *Corfield v. Coryell,* Justice Bulrod Washington defined the privileges and immunities of citizenship extremely broadly:

> What these fundamental principles are, it would perhaps be more tedious than difficult to enumerate. They may, however, be comprehended under the following general heads: Protection by the government; the enjoyment of life and liberty, with the right to acquire and possess property of every kind, and to pursue and obtain happiness and safety . . . the right of a citizen of one state to pass through, or to reside in any other state . . . to claim the benefit of writ of habeas corpus . . . (and) to institute and maintain actions of any kind in the courts of the state.[149]

Although a lower court case, *Corfield* was influential during its time because Justice Washington was a supporter of the Constitution at the Virginia ratifying convention and had studied law with one of the Framers, James Wilson.[150] Washington's opinion in *Corfield* was the most extensive, and the highest court's exposition of the fundamental rights of "citizens of all free governments."[151] The *Corfield* court's broad reading of citizenship rights was an inspiration for antislavery constitutionalists, who championed its promise of federal citizenship. However, as we have seen, members of Congress strongly disagreed about the question of who could become a citizen of the United States, subject to congressional protection. As tension over this issue mounted, the Supreme Court attempted to resolve the issue in *Dred Scott v. Sanford*, a last-ditch effort by the Court to end the controversy over slavery and stave off the impending Civil War.

Dred Scott originally petitioned for freedom in Missouri state court, alleging that he became free when he and his master traveled with him to the free territory of Illinois and the portion of the Louisiana Territory that is now known as the state of Minnesota.[152] The question of whether a slave who traveled into a free state had become free was often litigated during the antebellum era. Under Illinois law, and Missouri precedent, Scott would have been considered free. Indeed, Scott prevailed in his state court trial, but his master's widow appealed. First the Missouri Supreme Court, and later the U.S. Supreme Court, held that Scott was still a slave.[153] By 1852, the year that the Missouri Supreme Court heard the case, tension over slavery in the territories had caused comity between free and slaves states to deteriorate almost to the point of collapsing. The Missouri Court was simply not willing to follow precedent granting comity to Illinois law, nor was it willing to recognize congressional authority to regulate slavery in the territories.[154] In an opinion resounding in state's rights, Missouri Supreme Court Justice Scott, an ardent proslavery Democrat, referred to Illinois law as "foreign" law and warned that the abolitionist sentiments reflected in that law would cause "the overthrow and destruction of our government."[155]

Notwithstanding his loss in state court, the intrepid Mr. Scott filed a second case in federal court. By 1850, the federal courts were mostly ruling in support of slavery.[156] Scott lost in a jury verdict and appealed to the Supreme Court. Justice Taney released his opinion by reading it aloud from the bench in March 1857, two days after the inauguration of Democratic president James Buchanan.[157] The first issue considered by the Court was whether Mr. Scott was a citizen who could invoke diversity jurisdiction. Chief Justice Taney described the question presented as whether "a Negro, whose ancestors were imported into this country, and sold as slaves, [could] become a member of the political community formed and brought into existence by the Constitution of the United States and as such become entitled to all the rights, and privileges, and immunities, guaranteed by that instrument toward the citizen," including the privilege of suing in United States Court.[158] Taney answered the question with a resounding "no." He explained that slaves are not "constitutional members of this sovereignty" and thus were not intended to be included in the word "citizens." On the contrary, stated Taney, neither slaves nor their descendants were part of the "people" protected by the Constitution and the Declaration of Independence, because they were "considered as a subordinate and inferior class of beings who had been subjugated by the dominant race."[159]

Even though he found that the circuit court lacked jurisdiction, Taney went on to invalidate the Missouri Compromise on the grounds that Congress unconstitutionally deprived slave owners of their property rights when it outlawed slavery in the free territories. This portion of the opinion was particularly threatening to northern states because "it made slavery national, in the sense that slavery would be legal in any part of the United States where a state government had not abolished it."[160] Moreover, as the only case to strike down a federal statute since *Marbury v. Madison*, *Dred Scott* eviscerated Congress's power to resolve the issue of slavery on its own.

Contrary to the hopes of the members of the Supreme Court, the *Dred Scott* decision did not resolve the national conflict over slavery. Instead, the decision added fuel to the fire, inflaming northern fears about the expansion of slavery and emboldening southern leaders to demand nationalization of the institution.[161] Slaveholders heartily approved of the decision because the Court's ruling gave them a stamp of approval to take and hold slaves in any territory.[162] In the north, the prevailing attitude was outrage at the majority opinion, and the Court was widely attacked by northerners and Republicans.[163] The *Dred Scott* decision was one of the most important political issues in the 1858 congressional election and the 1860 presidential election, and it contributed significantly to the victory of Republicans in both elections.[164] Indeed, the chief effect of *Dred Scott* was to raise political consciousness in the north, "rousing a considerable segment of the public to adopt views that were openly anti-Court and anti-judicial supremacy as well as anti-slave power."[165]

Antislavery Republicans simply refused to accept the authority of the Court's ruling in *Dred Scott*. Instead, they challenged the Court's authority to interpret the Constitution. Abraham Lincoln often articulated a similar view of the *Dred Scott* decision. Opposing *Dred Scott* became one of Lincoln's principal campaign issues. He argued that *Dred Scott* proved that, unless Republicans were elected, the Supreme Court would extend the institution of slavery into the northern states, warning, "We shall lie down pleasantly dreaming that the people of Missouri are on the verge of making their state free; and we shall awake to the reality, instead, that the Supreme Court has made Illinois a slave state."[166] Between March 1859 and April 1860, Lincoln made at least sixteen speeches in which he raised the specter of a "nationalization of slavery." Lincoln warned that "a new Dred Scott decision" would eventually "carry slavery into the free states" and "bring slavery up into the very heart of the North."[167] Lincoln also attacked *Dred Scott* in debates with Douglas and in his First Inaugural Address, conceding that it bound the parties before the Court, but challenging its authority as a rule of law.[168] After he was elected, "Lincoln's Administration acted consistently with these views, too, by ignoring the Court's opinion and recognizing black citizenship in a range of contexts, such as the regulation of coastal shipping and the issuance of passports and patents, not to mention by abolishing slavery in the territories and the District of Columbia."[169]

In Congress, Lincoln's allies agreed. Criticizing *Dred Scott* in a speech before Congress in April 1860, Representative John Bingham of Ohio defiantly exclaimed:

> With Jefferson, I deny that the Supreme Court is the final arbiter on all questions of political power, and assert that the final arbiter on all such questions is the people. . . . While I could condemn armed resistance to any decision of the Supreme Court . . . I would claim for myself, in common with my fellow citizens, the right to question their propriety, to denounce their injustice, and to insist that whatever is wrong therein shall be corrected.[170]

Similarly, Maine Senator William Fessenden stated that he did not believe *Dred Scott* "accurately states the law."[171] Later, many Republican members of Congress simply disregarded both *Dred Scott* and *Barron*, arguing that, notwithstanding those opinions, the Fourteenth Amendment merely clarified existing law when it expressly stated that all persons born in the United States are citizens and identified rights that were enforceable against states.[172]

Hence, the Court rejected the broad view of citizenship rights held by

the antislavery constitutionalists in *Dred Scott*. However, to the abolitionists and their supporters, the Court's decision in *Dred Scott* did not
resolve the principal legal question addressed by the Court—whether
blacks could be citizens within the United States. The antislavery constitutionalists' lack of deference to courts is not surprising given that
"[b]oth in its origins and for most of history, American constitutionalism assigned ordinary citizens a central and pivotal role in implementing their Constitution."[173] During the early nineteenth century, departmentalism, the view that each branch had its own autonomous role in
constitutional interpretation, continued to dominate political thought,
and Presidents Jefferson, Jackson, and Lincoln explicitly asserted their
authority to interpret the Constitution in a manner inconsistent with the
courts' interpretation.[174] In the antebellum era, popular constitutionalism remained ascendant and was a central tenet of the abolitionists.[175]
In the streets, the Court's decisions in *Prigg* and *Dred Scott,* and the federal court's imprisonment of abolitionist Passmore Williamson for his
efforts to assist fugitive slaves in Pennsylvania, fueled the abolitionist
movement, and opposition to federal courts became a central component of the abolitionists' constitutional vision.[176] Antislavery constitutionalists on the streets and in Congress rejected the Court's ruling and
continued to maintain that slavery was unconstitutional and that the
federal government had broad power to protect citizenship rights.

John Bingham was chief among congressional advocates of national
citizenship regardless of the Court's ruling in *Dred Scott.* Prior to the ruling, in a speech given during the debate over the admission of Kansas to
statehood in January 1857, Bingham expressed a broad view of the individual rights protected by the Constitution, steeped in the language of
equality:

> It must be apparent that absolute equality of all, and the equal protec-
> tion of each, are principles of our Constitution, which ought to be
> observed and enforced in the organization and admission of new states.
> The Constitution provides, as we have seen that *no person* shall be de-
> prived of life, liberty or property, without due process of law. It makes
> no distinction either on account of complexion or birth—it secures
> these rights to all persons within its exclusive jurisdiction.[177]

Bingham also emphasized the importance of freedom of expression and
condemned the laws of the Kansas territory that criminalized antislav-

ery speech.[178] According to Bingham, the individual rights to equality of treatment and freedom of expression were part of the rights of federal citizenship.[179] After *Dred Scott,* Bingham maintained his beliefs. In 1858, he explained, "It has always been understood that the citizens of each state of the Union are *ipso facto* citizens of the United States."[180] Moreover, like those before him, Bingham believed that the fact that one state had recognized a person as its citizen triggered the Privileges and Immunities Clause of Article IV, preventing any other state from taking the rights of citizenship, conveyed to him by his home state, away from him.[181]

However, Bingham differed from his predecessors in his belief that the federal government, and not merely the states, had a rights-generating function.[182] Bingham believed that the Privileges and Immunities Clause of Article IV protected the rights of national, rather than state, citizenship. In a speech during the debate over the admission of Oregon to statehood, Bingham explained that the privileges and immunities protected by Article IV belonged to citizens "in" the several states, not "of" the several states.[183] This interpretation of Article IV "implies the existence of substantive national rights which states may not deny."[184] This view was inconsistent with the Court's decision in *Barron,* but Bingham simply believed that *Barron* had been decided wrongly.[185] Bingham stressed the importance of federal supremacy in the debates over the admission of Oregon to statehood and in other debates. For example, during a debate over the funding of the Union Army, Bingham argued, "The Republic can no more live without its supreme law duly obeyed or duly enforced than can its citizens who compose it live without air."[186] Simply put, what mattered most to Bingham and his allies was federal power to enforce the rights of federal citizenship.

During the Oregon debates, Bingham explained that, in his view, once a person was recognized as a citizen, he acquired certain rights that could not be taken away from him by any state, including "the equality of all to the right to live; to the right to know; to argue and to utter, according to conscience; to work and enjoy the product of their toil . . . the rock on which that Constitution rests."[187] Bingham and others were especially concerned about Oregon's provision that would have denied people of color access to her courts. Bingham explained that he could not consent to "mutilate and destroy . . . the Constitution of my country" by supporting a bill that allows a state to deny "the right to a fair trial in the courts of justice."[188] Regarding the Privileges and Immunities

Clause, he opined that "this guaranty of the Constitution of the United States is senseless and a mockery, if it does not limit state sovereignty and restrain each and every State from closing its territory and courts of justice against citizens of the United States."[189] Again, Bingham emphasized equality, but this time the vision of citizenship rights that he expressed was even more expansive and eloquent.

Similarly, Senator William Fessenden of Maine, who later became the chair of the Joint Committee on Reconstruction, explained during the Senate debate over the admission of Oregon that because Maine had free colored citizens, he could not agree to admit Oregon as a state. Oregon would not allow citizens of his own state to visit.[190] Said Fessenden: "By the laws of Maine, and under the constitution of the state of Maine, free Negroes are citizens . . . just as much citizens of the state of Maine as white men. . . . I cannot vote for the admission of any State with a constitution which prohibits any portion of my fellow citizens of my own state from the enjoyment of the privileges which other citizens of the state have."[191] Senator Henry Wilson of Massachusetts agreed, pointing out that the prohibition on access to the courts would have prevented a free citizen of color from Massachusetts from filing suit if he was injured in Oregon.[192] Others agreed that the bar on access to the courts violated the Privileges and Immunities Clause.[193]

Of course, these views did not go unopposed in Congress. Some members of Congress simply cited the *Dred Scott* decision as a decisive refutation of Bingham's and Fessenden's arguments.[194] Several members of Congress also maintained that states had the power to exclude whomever they chose and that the Privileges and Immunities Clause did not prevent them from doing so.[195] For example, Representative Linus Comins of Massachusetts, while stating his "regret" about the exclusion provision, argued that the provision was not a reason to prohibit Oregon from becoming a state, because it was consistent with the West's treatment of free blacks.[196] Senator Steven Douglas of Illinois, who later ran against Abraham Lincoln in the presidential campaign of 1860, pointed out that Illinois had a similar provision excluding free people of color, and he argued that Illinois, like Oregon, had a sovereign right to do so: "Whether she does so or not is a question for herself, and not for any other state to interfere with."[197] Democrats continued to articulate such a cramped reading of the rights of citizenship during the debate over the ratification of the Fourteenth Amendment.[198]

Thus, prior to the Civil War, members of Congress hotly debated issues of constitutional meaning, including the extent of their role and the role of the federal government as a protector of individual rights. On the eve of the Civil War, as the conflict over slavery intensified, it was unclear whether Congress had the power to end slavery or to do anything to protect individual rights. Perhaps members of Congress could have relied on the precedent of *Prigg* to enforce the privileges and immunities of citizenship, but there was no consensus as to what those rights were and whether the federal government or the states had the role of enforcing those rights. Moreover, the Court had held in *Dred Scott* that the Privileges and Immunities Clause did not apply to slaves, precluding federal action on the principal civil rights issue of the day, and the Court's ruling in *Barron* precluded Congress from enforcing the Bill of Rights against the states. By 1866, most Republicans shared Bingham's and Fessenden's view that free blacks were citizens[199] and "believed in a body of national rights that states were required to respect."[200] However, due in part to the Court's proslavery rulings in the antebellum era, Congress needed the enforcement powers granted by the Reconstruction Amendments in order to implement this vision.

The events leading up to the Civil War proved correct Madison's theory that congressional protection of individual rights was necessary to hold the union together and prevent states from violating those rights. In the antebellum era, abuses of individual rights by southern states grew increasingly egregious. In slaveholding states, free blacks were subject to legal disabilities that impaired their right to travel, establish residence, and enjoy the economic privileges of citizenship.[201] Because of the 1850 Fugitive Slave Act, free blacks in nonslavery states were in danger of being kidnapped and subject to the same disabilities.[202] Southern states also enacted numerous laws that threatened the rights of white abolitionists, outlawing antislavery speech and even banning the importation of abolitionist literature.[203] The 1856 campaign slogan of the newly formed Republican Party—"Free Speech, Free Press, Free Men, Free Labor, Free Territory, and Fremont"—reflected the Republicans' concern about the restrictions on freedom of expression imposed by those laws.[204] A growing number of members of Congress chafed at their lack of authority to address those abuses. As we shall see, empowering themselves to protect individual rights became the central goal of the members of the Reconstruction Congress.

3

Belonging, Protection, and Equality
The Reconstruction Congress

The themes of the antebellum congressional debates over the meaning of individual rights played themselves out during the Civil War. Central to that war was the question of "whether a citizen owed his primary allegiance to the national or state government."[1] When the Confederate states seceded from the Union, they asserted, in the most dramatic fashion possible, their sovereign right to treat individuals as they chose, regardless of any protections in the United States constitution that might otherwise have existed. The conflict between state autonomy and federal power was resolved in favor of federal power, particularly the power to bestow national citizenship rights, when the Union won the Civil War.[2] Following the war, the antislavery constitutionalists' vision of national citizenship and the rights that adhered thereto became an animating force behind the Reconstruction Amendments and the Civil Rights statutes of the Reconstruction era.[3]

Concerned about the plight of the freed slaves who had been loyal to the Union, Republican members of Congress enacted measures to enable their belonging, protection, and equality. The Reconstruction Era was marked by the genesis of congressional protection of rights of belonging because Republican members of Congress wished to establish freed slaves as members of the national community and to create statutory rights that would ensure their equal membership. As Judith Baer explains, the Republicans who led Congress during Reconstruction were committed to the ideal of "equality in terms of entitlement or endowment, a notion that all human beings have a right to equal respect and concern." They enacted open-ended, generous guarantees of rights to try to ensure that this ideal became a reality.[4]

Republicans in the Reconstruction Congress also intended both the

1866 act and the Fourteenth Amendment to implement structural changes related to the enforcement of rights of belonging. They were mindful of the impact that this power would have on our system of federalism, and they intended to alter that system, establishing the federal government, and not the states, as the principal branch of government responsible for protecting rights of belonging. Finally, in part because they still viewed the Supreme Court as representing the interests of slave owners, Republican members of the Reconstruction Congress saw themselves, and not the Court, as the primary enforcers of rights of belonging.[5] Empowering Congress to protect rights of belonging was central to the mission of the Thirty-Ninth Congress and the raison d'être of the Fourteenth Amendment.[6]

During this era, Congress, not courts, took the leading role in creating the first federal rights of belonging. Indeed, members of the Reconstruction Congress were acting against the backdrop of proslavery Supreme Court decisions, and consistently and repeatedly they expressed their distrust of the Court.[7] Congress also acted against the opposition of President Andrew Johnson, who vetoed virtually every Reconstruction measure, including the Freedmen's Bureau Act, the Reconstruction Act, and the 1866 Civil Rights Act.[8] However, Republicans dominated both the House and Senate throughout Reconstruction, and although the Republicans were divided among themselves as to how far they were willing to go with Reconstruction measures, they exhibited remarkable unity in approving Reconstruction legislation and overcoming Johnson's many vetoes.[9]

Even before the Civil War was over, members of Congress began to debate the question of how to maintain the Union victory and protect freed slaves from their former masters. In 1865, Congress enacted the Thirteenth Amendment, abolishing slavery and giving Congress the power to enact "appropriate" measures to enforce abolition. Members of Congress used that enforcement power to enact the 1866 Civil Rights Act, which proclaimed that freed slaves were citizens and protected their basic civil rights from discrimination on the basis of race. Concerns that the Civil Rights Act would be overturned by subsequent Congresses and doubts about the constitutionality of the 1866 act led Congress to enact the Fourteenth Amendment that same year. Throughout these two momentous years, members of Congress were immersed in debates over the rights of freed slaves and the extent of congressional power to protect those rights.

According to historian Eric Foner, when Congress enacted the Thirteenth Amendment, "already, many Republicans envisioned a nation where North and South, Black and White, were ruled by 'one law impartial over all.'" They believed that once ratified, the Thirteenth Amendment would establish free blacks as citizens whose fundamental rights could be protected by Congress.[10] Freed blacks held the same hopes. Foner explains: "Many former slaves saw freedom as an end to the separation of families, the abolition of punishment by the lash, and the opportunity to educate their children." Others stressed that freedom meant the enjoyment of "our rights in common with other men." As emancipated slave Henry Adams told his former master in 1865: "If I cannot do like the white man I am not free."[11] Former slaves expected Congress to legislate to protect their rights. Thus, in January 1866, blacks in the South Carolina Sea Islands rejected generous offers from former Governor William Aiken and Major General James P. Roy to work as hired hands on land they thought they should own. "Several remarked," Major Roy reported, "that they knew Congress was in session and would provide for them."[12]

The pleas for help from freed slaves and northern sympathizers in the south grew stronger as the initial, weak "presidential Reconstruction" faltered. Southern states enacted measures to subordinate freed slaves, known as "Black Codes," which prohibited blacks from enjoying such fundamental rights as purchasing property, entering into contracts, and traveling without passes.[13] Republican members of Congress were sympathetic and responsive to those pleas. Radical Republicans, led by Thaddeus Stevens in the House and Charles Sumner in the Senate, believed in a "utopian vision of a nation whose citizens enjoyed equality of civil and political rights, secured by a powerful and benificient national state" and insisted on the incorporation of black suffrage into any plan of Reconstruction.[14] Although the majority of the members of the Thirty-Ninth Congress were not willing to go so far as to grant political rights to blacks, conservative Republicans leaders such as John Bingham in the House and Lyman Trumbull in the Senate shared in the "emerging consensus within the Republican party that the freedman was entitled to civil equality short of suffrage."[15] As historian Michael Les Benedict observes: "By 1865 congressional Republicans were united primarily by shared convictions about racial justice, slavery and the restoration of the Union."[16] This vision is reflected in the broad measures enacted by Congress in 1866, including the 1866 Civil Rights Act and the Fourteenth Amendment.

The debates over the 1866 Civil Rights Act and the Fourteenth Amendment reveal several consistent themes. First, both measures were enacted in reaction to reports of widespread violations of fundamental rights of freed slaves and Union sympathizers in the former slave states. Members of Congress frequently recited testimony before the Joint Committee on Reconstruction, letters from freed slaves and employees of Freedmen's Bureaus complaining about new racist laws backed up by rampant violence that denied fundamental rights to freed blacks.[17] Second, virtually all members of Congress who spoke in support of these measures believed that the freed slaves were citizens of the United States and thus entitled to the fundamental rights of citizenship. They intended both measures to establish and protect these rights. Third, supporters of both measures shared a broad view of congressional power to legislate to define and protect rights of belonging.

Illinois Senator Lyman Trumbull, the chair of the Senate Judiciary Committee and one of the most influential men in Congress, introduced the 1866 Civil Rights Act on January 27, 1866.[18] Trumbull's bill defined as citizens "all persons of African Descent born in the United States" and proclaimed that "[a]ll citizens of the United States shall have the same right, in every State or Territory, as is enjoyed by white citizens thereof to inherit, purchase, lease, sell, hold and convey real and personal property." The act also guaranteed "all persons" in the United States "the same right . . . to make and enforce contracts . . . and to the full and equal benefit of the laws . . . as is enjoyed by white citizens."[19] It contained enforcement provisions enabling individuals to sue state officials in federal court when their rights were violated "under color of state law" and establishing a federal enforcement structure.[20]

Trumbull explained that the bill would protect all persons of the United States in their civil rights by "giv[ing] effect to [the] declaration [of freedom in the Thirteenth Amendment] and secur[ing] to all persons within the United States practical freedom."[21] Trumbull argued that the bill was necessary because of the Black Codes' discrimination against former slaves. According to Trumbull, the codes "still impose upon them the very restrictions which were imposed upon them in consequence of the existence of slavery, and before it was abolished."[22] He explained: "A law that does not allow a colored person to go from one county to another [or allow him] to hold property, does not allow him to teach, does not allow him to preach, is certainly in violation of the rights of a free man."[23]

Many other members of Congress agreed. For example, Senator Jacob Howard of Michigan argued that the Black Codes effectively reduced former slaves to the status of slavery: "Such was not the intention of the advocates of this amendment. Its intention was to make him the opposite of the slave, to make him a free man."[24] In the House, Representative Burton Cook of Illinois agreed: "It is idle to say these men will be protected by the States . . . those states have already passed laws which would virtually re-enslave them."[25] And Representative Martin Thayer of Pennsylvania asked, if the states are allowed to enact the Black Codes, "of what practical value is the amendment abolishing slavery in the United States?"[26] Thus, Republicans in the Thirty-Ninth Congress believed that the 1866 act was necessary to enforce the abolition of slavery.

Trumbull and his allies believed that the most effective way of ensuring the rights of freed slaves was to affirm the fact that they were U.S. citizens, thus entitled to the fundamental rights of citizenship. The Republicans explained that free blacks were entitled to citizenship because of their loyalty to the Union and the sacrifices that they had made in support of the Union. For example, Senator Clark explained that the free black man became a citizen "when he helped to achieve the independence of the country equally with white men."[27] Representative Hubbard of Connecticut pointed out that freed slaves "are loyal and faithful, every one." They helped on the battlefield and "prayed to God for the success of the nation's banner. . . . We owe them protection in return for their faithful allegiance."[28] Representative William Windom of Minnesota dramatically proclaimed that this bill "declares that the colored soldier, who has worn the uniform of the Republic and periled his life for its defense, shall have an equal right, nothing more, with the white rebel yet reeking with the blood of our murdered defenders."[29]

As loyal citizens, the Republicans continued, the freed slaves were entitled to the protection of the federal government. Representative William Lawrence of Ohio responded to the presidential veto of the act: "It is barbarous, inhuman, infamous, to turn over four million liberated slaves, always loyal to the Government, to the fury of their rebel masters, who deny them the benefit of all laws for the protection of their civil rights."[30] Representative John Hubbard of Connecticut explained that the bill "is intended to cast the shield of protection over four million American citizens," and the chair of the House Judiciary Committee, James Wilson of Iowa, stated that "[b]y our laws and our courts we may intervene to maintain the proud character of American citizenship."[31] Representative John Broomall of Pennsylvania summed it up: "The rights and duties of allegiance and protection are corresponding rights and duties. Upon whatever square foot of the earth's surface I owe allegiance to my country, there it owes me protection."[32] Hence, the Republican members of Congress intended the 1866 act to establish freed slaves as members of the national community and facilitate their membership by defining and protecting their rights.

This view of "allegiance and protection [as] reciprocal rights"[33] reflected the "social compact" theory of John Locke, who argued that people submit to the authority of the government in return for its protection.[34] However, the protections of the 1866 act were not limited to freed slaves. Supporters of the act also hoped that it would remedy southern persecution of northern sympathizers.[35] They explained that the rights outlined in the statute belonged to "every free person," and that it was intended to "provide that all people have equal rights."[36] The statute originally protected all "inhabitants" from discrimination. That term was replaced by the more restrictive term, "citizens," as a result of uncertainty about congressional jurisdiction over states' treatment of aliens.[37] Of those sympathetic to the act, only Representative Bingham protested the fact that the statute would only apply to citizens.[38] When he drafted Section One of the Fourteenth Amendment, John Bingham of Ohio used the more inclusive term "person" in its equal rights provisions. Nevertheless, the statute's link between rights and citizenship was consistent with the theories of Bingham and other antislavery constitutionalists, who had argued for a broad reading of federal citizenship rights prior to the war.

Along with aliens, the act also expressly excluded "Indians, not taxed" from its protection. This exclusion is due to the fact that Republicans were divided about whether or not Native Americans were subject to the protections of the federal government. Many members of Congress believed that Native Americans owed their allegiance to tribal governments, not the federal government, and thus were not eligible for the protections of federal citizenship.[39] While Native Americans who lived on reservations presented members of Congress with a conceptual dilemma because they arguably had forsaken their tribal allegiance, members of Congress were also divided about the extent to which they wanted to extend rights to any Native Americans.[40] The phrase "Indians, not taxed" was a compromise phrase, allowing the inclusion of some Native Americans in the protections of the act.[41] The exclusion of most Native Americans from the protections of the 1866 Civil Rights Act is a glaring exception to its message of belonging. The exception was partially remedied by the fact that Native Americans were not excluded from the subsequent Citizenship Clause of the Fourteenth Amendment.[42] However, it is undeniable that aliens and Native Americans simply did not fit easily within the vision of belonging held by the Framers of the Fourteenth Amendment.

The substantive rights protected by the 1866 Civil Rights Act were those that the antislavery constitutionalists had earlier linked to federal citizenship. The act enabled all citizens to participate in basic legal processes, such as purchasing property, entering into contracts, and using the court system, and gave them the right to personal security; all these would facilitate their belonging to their community. Introducing the bill to the House, James Wilson said that it would "protect and enforce those [rights] which already belong to every citizen."[43] Representative Thayer agreed: "The sole purpose of this bill is to secure to that class of persons the fundamental rights of citizenship . . . those rights which secure life, liberty and property, and which make all men equal before the law."[44] That some states had denied free persons of color access to their legal systems had prevented them from belonging to the legal polity. The 1866 act was intended to remedy this situation and provide a uniform federal baseline of fundamental human rights that could not be denied by states. It extended the rights of belonging, protection, and equality to all those who fell within its scope.

There was considerable debate over the source of congressional power to enact the 1866 statute. Supporters of the act asserted broad congressional authority to define rights of belonging and make them enforceable. Senator Trumbull stated, "There is very little importance in the general declaration of abstract truths and principles unless they can be carried into effect, unless the persons who are to be affected by them have some means of availing themselves of those benefits."[45] He and his allies believed that congressional enforcement was the best means for enforcing the promises of equality in the Thirteenth Amendment, as well as protections for citizens in the original Constitution and Bill of Rights.[46] Trumbull believed that Congress's power to enforce the

Thirteenth Amendment was sufficient to justify the bill. He argued that "[a]ny statute which is not equal to all, and which deprives any citizen of civil rights which are secured to other citizens, is an unjust encroachment upon his liberty; and is, in fact, a badge of servitude which by the Constitution is prohibited."[47] Representative James Wilson also thought that the Bill of Rights, and especially the Due Process Clause, gave Congress the power to pass the Civil Rights Bill. He said that citizens of the United States were entitled to "certain rights," and being entitled to those rights "it is the duty of the government to protect citizens in the perfect enjoyment of them."[48] Many other members of Congress agreed, maintaining that the rights outlined in the bill were simply the "ordinary rights of a freeman," necessary to secure the freedom of former slaves.[49]

Trumbull did not rely solely on the Thirteenth Amendment as a source of power to enact the statute. Trumbull argued that other provisions of the constitution also authorized Congress to protect the rights of citizenship.[50] First, he and his allies maintained that congressional power over naturalization included the right to define citizenship and establish rights pertaining to citizenship. Trumbull declared, "The authority to declare who shall be citizens of the United States is, as I understand, vested in Congress and nowhere else."[51] The extent of congressional power over citizenship had been highly contested in the decades leading up to the Civil War, with southerners consistently arguing that only states, and not the federal government, had the right to define the citizenship of persons who were born within the country. By 1866, however, a majority of those in Congress agreed with Trumbull that congressional power over citizenship was plenary, providing an ample source of authority to enact the 1866 measure.[52]

The other citizenship-based source of power relied on by Senator Trumbull was the Privileges and Immunities Clause of Article IV, which, Trumbull explained, secured to citizens "such fundamental rights as belong to every free person."[53] Trumbull maintained that the clause was self-executing and provided a source of congressional authority to define and protect the privileges and immunities of citizenship. In *Prigg v. Pennsylvania,* the Supreme Court had upheld the Fugitive Slave Act of 1793 as a proper exercise of Congress's power to enforce the Fugitive Slave Clause of Article IV. Trumbull and others argued that under *Prigg,* Congress enjoyed similarly broad authority to enforce the Privileges and Immunities Clause.[54] This theory helped to justify what troubled opponents (and some supporters) most about the 1866 act—the fact that the bill supplanted state law and created remedies against state government officials.

The 1866 act's remedies against state officials and the federal enforcement scheme were modeled on the remedial portions of the Fugitive Slave Acts of 1793 and 1850.[55] Supporters of the 1866 Civil Rights Act pointed out that it was less intrusive on states than were the Fugitive Slave Acts, since the 1866 act would only apply when states failed to protect the civil rights of their residents.[56] As Trumbull explained: "Now, sir, we propose to give the provisions of the fugitive slave law for the purpose of punishing those who deny freedom, not those who seek to aid persons to escape to freedom."[57] These members of Congress intended to turn *Prigg* on its head, protecting the rights of those freed from slavery with the very powers once used to enslave.[58]

Opponents of the Civil Rights Act made two basic arguments against it. First, they argued that the bill unconstitutionality interfered with state sovereignty and violated principles of federalism. For example, Senator Reverdy Johnson, a Democrat from Maryland, maintained that the bill violated the Tenth Amendment: "What doubt can there be but that if a State possessed the power to declare who should be her citizens before the Constitution was adopted that power remains now as absolute and conclusive as it was when the constitution was adopted? The bill, therefore, changes the whole theory of the government. . . . This bill, in my opinion, strikes at the reserved rights of the states[;] . . . it abolishes the states."[59] Senator Willard Saulsbury, a Democrat from Delaware, agreed that the bill intruded on the police powers of the state: "Such an assumption of power on the part of Congress ought to arouse the people of the whole country to the sense of impending danger."[60] In his veto message, President Andrew Johnson echoed this sentiment, characterizing the bill as "another step, or rather, stride, toward centralization and the concentration of all legislative power in the national Government." He warned, "The tendency of this bill must be to resuscitate the spirit of rebellion."[61] In the same ominous tone, Senator Johnson predicted that, just as the Fugitive Slave Acts proved to be unenforceable in the northern states, the 1866 act would prove unenforceable in the south.[62]

Opponents of the act also maintained that Congress lacked the power to enact the statute. They maintained that the Thirteenth Amendment was intended merely "to liberate the Negro slave from his master" and that Congress's power over citizenship was limited to naturalizing those who were born in foreign countries.[63] Democrats denied that Congress had the power to define freed slaves as citizens or bestow citizenship-based rights upon them. For example, Senator Saulsbury remarked archly, "If you intended to bestow upon the freed slave all the rights of a free citizen, you ought to have gone further in your constitutional amendment."[64] Several cited the Supreme Court's ruling in *Dred Scott,* that blacks could not be U.S. citizens, to support their view.[65] Indeed, *Dred Scott* was the "elephant in the room" throughout these debates. If the Court's opinion was still good law, it would appear to preclude Congress from declaring freed slaves to be citizens and bestowing citizenship based rights upon them.

In response, supporters of the 1866 act strongly asserted their authority to interpret and enforce the Constitution, notwithstanding Supreme Court precedent to the contrary. Senator Trumbull simply ignored the decision, explaining, "In my judgment, persons of African descent, born in the United States, are as much citizens as white persons who are born in the country. . . . If there were any question about it, it would be settled by the passage of a law declaring all persons born in the United States to be citizens thereof. That this bill proposes to do."[66] Virtually every member of Congress who spoke in support of the bill agreed with Trumbull that freed blacks were citizens and that the provision of the bill defining citizenship was "but declaratory of existing law."[67]

When reminded of *Dred Scott* by their opponents, the Republicans' criticism of that decision was virulent. Representative James Wilson described the Court's opinion as "a mere partisan subterfuge" designed to support Democratic President James Buchanan's position on the issue of slavery in the territories. Wilson accused the Court of delaying the decision until after the 1856 presidential election because "it was not safe to cast the monstrosities of that decision into the presidential campaign of 1856." However, he pontificated, "instead of becoming a triumphant platform for the Democratic Party, [*Dred Scott*] proved to be the scaffold on which the party was executed."[68] In the same vein, Representative John Broomall of Pennsylvania described the Court's *Dred Scott* opinion as "the political speeches of the judges of the Supreme Court of the United States on the occasion of their assembling to celebrate the election of James Buchanan, called in mockery their decision in the

Dred Scott case."[69] Thus, while the Republicans in the Thirty-Ninth Congress were willing to cite *Prigg* to support their own power, they rejected the limitations on their power imposed by *Dred Scott.*

Not all of the Republicans were as sanguine about the Court's negative precedents. Crucially, some supporters of the 1866 Civil Rights Act, including John Bingham and conservative *New York Times* publisher Henry J. Raymond, shared the Democrats' view that Congress lacked the power to enact the statute. Bingham had long been a proponent of a broad view of the rights of federal citizenship, and he agreed with his Republican colleagues that the introductory clause was simply "declaratory of what is written in the constitution." In the debate over the 1866 act, Bingham reiterated that he shared "an earnest desire to have the bill of rights in your Constitution enforced everywhere" and maintained that "if [the bill of rights] had been enforced in good faith in every state of the union the calamities and conflicts and crimes and sacrifices of the past five years would have been impossible."[70] However, he believed that Congress lacked the power to impose the limitations and remedies upon the states that made up the heart of the bill. Bingham explained that Congress could remedy this problem by amending the constitution, "expressly prohibiting the states from any such abuse of power in the future."[71] Raymond shared the belief that Congress lacked the power to impose penalties on those who violated civil rights "under color of state law." He agreed that "Bingham's proposed amendment" would remedy his concern.[72]

Opponents of the act seized on Bingham's comments, claiming that they proved the bill's unconstitutionality.[73] They failed to carry the day. The 1866 Civil Rights Act passed by overwhelming margins, and Congress wasted little time in overriding President Johnson's veto.[74] According to the *Congressional Globe* reporter, the announcement of the vote to override was greeted with an outburst of applause, in which "the throng of spectators heartily joined, and which did not subside for some moments."[75] This reflected public opinion in general, which was strongly in support of the bill.[76] However, Bingham and the other members of the Joint Committee on Reconstruction were well respected, and they had recommended passage of the Fourteenth Amendment to ensure that Congress had the power to enact measures like the 1866 act.[77] With doubts about the act's constitutionality hanging over their heads, members of Congress turned almost immediately to debate the proposed Fourteenth Amendment, approving it only two months after the passage of the 1866 act.[78]

The original draft of the Fourteenth Amendment was written by John Bingham and presented to Congress on behalf of the Joint Committee on Reconstruction as the central measure of their Reconstruction plan.[79] Well prior to the Fourteenth Amendment, Bingham believed that the rights of federal citizenship had a substantive component, including the Bill of Rights, and that those rights were enforceable against the states. To Bingham, the problem was that those rights lacked a remedy because Congress lacked the power to enforce them.[80] Two years before the Fourteenth Amendment was ratified, Bingham had made his theory of enforcement clear, speaking in general terms about what was to become the Fourteenth Amendment. Bingham explained that this "general" amendment would give Congress the express power to enforce "the rights which were guarantied [*sic*] . . . from the beginning, but which guarantee has been unhappily disregarded by more than one state of this Union . . . simply because of want of power in Congress to enforce that guarantee."[81] Presenting his original draft to Congress, Bingham stated that "every word of the proposed amendment is today in the Constitution of our country," located in the Privileges and Immunities Clause of Article IV and the Due Process Clause of the Fifth Amendment, "save the words conferring the express power upon the Congress of the United States." He explained, "Sir, it has been the want of the Republic that there was not an express grant of power in the Constitution to enable the whole people of every state, by congressional enactment, to enforce obedience to these requirements of the Constitution."[82] His Fourteenth Amendment would provide the enforcement power.

Many members of Congress agreed with Bingham that congressional power was necessary to ensure that the guarantees described in the Fourteenth Amendment would be implemented. Congressman Ignatius Donnelly, speaking in favor of the proposed amendment, argued, "Why should this not pass? Are the promises of the constitution mere verbiage? Are its sacred pledges of life, liberty and property to fall to the ground through lack of power to enforce them? Or shall that great Constitution be what its founders meant it to be, a shield and a protection over the head of the lowliest and poorest citizen in the remotest region of the nation?"[83] In addition, William Lawrence of Ohio, a widely respected lawyer and former judge, argued that Congress had the incidental power to enforce and protect civil rights. Lawrence said, "The Constitution declares these rights to be inherent in every citizen, and Congress has the power to enforce the declaration. If it does not, then the declaration of rights is in vain, and we have a government powerless to secure or protect rights which the Constitution solemnly declares every citizen shall have."[84]

These members of Congress focused on congressional power because they believed that courts were unable, or unwilling to adequately protect rights of belonging. For example, William Higby, Republican of California, implicitly criticized the courts when he opined that lack of enforcement of the Privileges and Immunities and Due Process Clauses had led those provisions to be "nugatory." Higby predicted that the congressional enforcement provision of the Fourteenth Amendment would "give vitality and life to the portions of the Constitution that probably were intended from the beginning to have life and vitality."[85] They saw themselves, not the courts, as the primary enforcers of those rights.

The version of the Fourteenth Amendment that was eventually approved by Congress was revised from Bingham's original draft. The final version separated the declaratory portion of individual rights, now found in Section One, from that describing the congressional enforcement power, now found in Section Five.[86] In *City of Boerne v. Flores,* the current Supreme Court claimed that the change was due to the Framer's concerns that Bingham's version would bestow too much power on Congress.[87] It is true that some opponents of the Fourteenth Amendment argued against increasing congressional power. For example, Senator Rogers argued that the amendment would "be found to be the embodiment of centralization and the disenfranchisement of the States of those sacred and immutable State rights which were reserved to them," and Representative Robert Hale, Republican of New York, declared that he would vote against the amendment because it introduced a power never before conferred on Congress.[88] However, these men were greatly outnumbered by the amendment's proponents, and there is strong evidence that the Framers did not intend their alterations to weaken congressional enforcement power.[89]

The supporters of the Fourteenth Amendment continued to emphasize the importance of congressional enforcement power after the amendment was changed.[90] Introducing the revised version to the Senate, Senator Howard explained, "The great object of the first section of this amendment is, therefore, to restrain the power of the States and compel them at all times to respect these fundamental guarantees. How will it be done under the present amendment? . . . [I]f they are to be effectuated and enforced, as they assuredly ought to be, that additional power should be given to Congress to that end. This is done by the fifth section of this amendment." He emphasized, "Here is a direct affirmative delegation of power to Congress to carry out all the principles of all these guarantees, a power not found in the Constitution."[91] Senator Luke Poland, a Republican from Vermont, agreed. A week before the final Senate vote on the amendment, Poland explained that he supported it because "[i]t certainly seems desirable that no doubt should be left existing as to the power of Congress to enforce principles lying at the very foundation of all republican government if they be denied or violated by the States." Thus, even after the amendment was altered, its supporters, who prevailed overwhelmingly in the congressional vote, continued to emphasize the enforcement power of Congress, not the courts, as the principal reason for the amendment.[92]

The final colloquy in the congressional debate over the Fourteenth Amendment further illustrates the fact that the Framers did not change their views that Congress would take the primary role in enforcing the Fourteenth Amendment. After Senator Howard introduced the amendment to the Senate, Senator Wade expressed concern that Section One included the term "citizen" but did not define it. He explained that if the government were to fall into the "wrong hands," the term might be misconstrued "unless we fortify and make it very strong and clear."[93] A few days later, Senator Howard responded to this concern by proposing the Citizenship Clause of the Fourteenth Amendment.[94] Howard did not believe that it was necessary to debate the meaning of that clause. Referring to the debates over the 1866 Civil Rights Act, he stated, "The question of citizenship has been so fully discussed in this body as not to need any further elucidation."[95] These remarks tied the substantive meaning of the Fourteenth Amendment to that of the 1866 Civil Rights Act, which had been debated so extensively directly prior to the amendment.[96]

In support of his motion, Howard's colleagues argued that Congress should define citizenship in order to keep the courts from limiting the protections promised in the amendment. For example, Senator Henderson opined, "The state courts are already deciding the civil rights bill to be unconstitutional. . . . Should the Supreme Court of the United States affirm the judgment of these inferior tribunals, the present period would be no better for the rights of the Negro than that when the Supreme Court once before supposed he had no rights which the white man was bound to respect."[97] Senator Yates agreed, noting that "[w]e have here, in the Constitution of the United States, a guarantee which protects us from future judicial tyranny such as we have experienced under the decisions of the Supreme Court. We have a declaration as to who are citizens of the United States."[98] Hence, the Framers of the Fourteenth Amendment made it clear that they did not believe the Supreme Court would be trusted to protect the freed slaves who were the objects of their legislation. They emphatically declared their power to determine the substance of the rights of their citizens directly prior to enacting an amendment that gave them the power to enforce those rights.

A better explanation for the change in the language of the Fourteenth Amendment than that of the Supreme Court in *Boerne* is that the Framers knew that the Radical Republicans would fall out of power and that subsequent Congresses might lose their enthusiasm for protecting rights of belonging. The Republicans were acutely aware that their majority in Congress was likely to be short-lived once the southern states were re-admitted to the Union. For that reason, most of the debates over the Fourteenth Amendment focused on Sections Two through Four, which laid out the rules for apportioning representation and restricting the voting rights of rebels, and most of the battles in the Thirty-Ninth Congress centered on whether or not to enfranchise freed slaves.[99] This context helps to explain why, speaking in favor of the motion to postpone the vote on Bingham's version of the amendment, Representative Hotchkiss asked, "We may pass laws today, and the next Congress may wipe them out. Where is your guarantee then?"[100] In the same vein, Thaddeus Stevens, the Radical leader in the House, warned that the 1866 Civil Rights Act was not sufficient to guarantee racial equality because "a law is repealable by a majority."[101] Hence, while the Framers of the Fourteenth Amendment believed that congressional power was essential to protecting individual rights, they feared that congressional enforcement alone would not be sufficient. They wanted the self-enforcing Section One to serve as a backstop to congressional enforcement.[102]

The Framers' primary emphasis on congressional power was natural given that they viewed the Court as proslavery and anti-Reconstruction. During this era, Congress and the Court engaged in a power struggle over constitutional meaning. Key provisions of the Fourteenth Amendment were directed at overturning rulings of what they viewed as the proslavery Supreme Court. The Citizenship Clause of the Fourteenth Amendment was expressly intended to overrule the Court's decision in *Dred Scott*,[103] and the language "no state shall" in Section One was intended to overrule the Court's decision in *Barron*.[104] In 1866, the Court issued two decisions with negative implications for Reconstruction measures, leading members of Congress to believe that the Court was hostile to the Reconstruction effort.[105] Congressional suspicion of the Supreme Court also had an important role in one of the major constitutional controversies of the day, the case of William McCardle.

William McCardle was a reporter for the *Vicksburg Times* who was being held in military custody for disturbing the peace, inciting to insurrection and disorder, libel, and impeding reconstruction, on the basis of several editorials that he had written which were critical of Reconstruction.[106] McCardle brought a habeas petition to challenge his imprisonment, relying on a jurisdictional provision that was enacted by Congress in 1867.[107] The district court denied his petition, and he appealed it to the Supreme Court. McCardle challenged not only his own incarceration, but the constitutionality of Reconstruction in general. Leaders in the Reconstruction Era Congress assumed that the Court would hold Reconstruction itself to be unconstitutional if given the opportunity. Hence, in 1868, they repealed the 1867 jurisdictional provision upon which William McCardle had relied. As James Wilson explained, the Repealer Act was intended to "prevent the threatened calamity falling upon the country . . . that the McCardle case was to be made use of to enable a majority of the Court to determine the invalidity and unconstitutionality of the reconstruction laws of Congress."[108]

President Johnson vetoed the Repealer Act, proclaiming, "Thus far during the existence of the Government the Supreme Court of the United States has been viewed by the people as the true expounder of their Constitution," and warning that "any act which may be construed into or mistaken for an attempt to prevent or evade its decisions . . . cannot fail to attend with propitious consequences."[109] Congress emphatically rejected Johnson's position that the Court had a supreme role in interpreting the constitution when it overrode Johnson's veto. The Court then famously held that Congress had the power to take away its jurisdiction, thus avoiding further confrontation with Congress over the most controversial political issue of the day.[110]

Congress's swift and decisive action restricting the Court's power to review their enforcement of equality norms in the Repealer Act indicates that not only did they not view the Court as the principal protector of "discrete and insular minorities" but also they fiercely distrusted the Court and feared that the Court would impede congressional protection of those minorities. Further evidence of this view is the fact that a bill that would have required an extraordinary majority vote of the Justices to invalidate an act of Congress cleared the House of Representatives in 1868. Given that in 1868, Congress's primary legislative agenda was effectuating the Reconstruction Amendments, the success of this bill in the House of Representatives is striking evidence that those members of Congress viewed the Court not as a protector of rights of belonging but as a barrier to their enforcement. Given Congress's view of the Court at the time, it is not surprising that members of the Reconstruction Era Congress placed such importance on congressional power to enforce those norms. What is surprising is that this history has gotten lost, not only in the contemporary Court's juriscentric approach to enforcing equality norms but also in the constitutional scholarship analyzing the relationship between the courts and Congress in effectuating those norms.

Moreover, the Framers had a very broad view of congressional power in mind when they enacted the enforcement provisions of the Reconstruction Amendments. The Supreme Court's broad interpretation of congressional power in *McCulloch v. Maryland*[111]—that the "Necessary and Proper" Clause of Article I authorized Congress to enact any legislation that was "appropriate" to furthering a "legitimate end"—remained the standard on congressional enforcement power throughout the antebellum era.[112] The Framers of the Fourteenth Amendment invoked *McCulloch* in Section Five, when they authorized Congress to enact "appropriate" legislation to enforce the rights established by the amendment.[113] Some Framers even believed that *Prigg* meant that the Fourteenth Amendment was unnecessary because the existence of rights necessarily meant that Congress had the power to enforce them.[114]

Republicans in the Thirty-Ninth Congress were also mindful of the impact that this expansion of congressional power would have on our system of federalism. Prior to the Civil War, the basic rights of citizens of one state did not extend beyond the borders of that state. The Framers of the Fourteenth Amendment were extremely dissatisfied with this situation. Above all, they sought the uniformity of rights that only federal enforcement could bring. They intended to alter the system of federalism, transferring the role of protecting individual rights from the states to the federal government.[115] Thaddeus Stevens explained that the problem with the original constitution was that "the constitution limits only the actions of Congress, and is not a limitation on the States."[116] Many members of the Reconstruction Congress agreed with Stevens and argued that adequate protection of rights of belonging would require a change in the federalist system. The Fourteenth Amendment represented a commitment to nationhood that changed the relationship between state and federal citizenship. Federal citizenship was now clearly supreme.[117]

During the debates over the 1866 Civil Rights Act, John Bingham cautioned that the bill might go beyond congressional power because under the then existing system the states, and not the federal government, had the responsibility of enforcing the Bill of Rights.[118] Responding to Bingham, James Wilson explained that he believed that, given the history of state deprivations of rights, the remedy "must be provided by the Government of the United States, whose duty it is to protect the citizen in return for the allegiance he owes to the government. . . . Without it the Republic becomes an oppressor, exacting a discharge of duty by the citizen, in the absence of a power to return a protective compensation."[119] Representative Samuel Shellaburger, Republican of Ohio, noted that even John Calhoun recognized that states were prohibited from denying the rights of federal citizenship.[120] Similarly, responding to President Johnson's criticism of the enforcement provisions of the 1866 act in his veto message, Senator Trumbull quoted President Andrew Jackson's condemnation of the nullification doctrine. Trumbull asserted the authority of federal power, pointing out, "The right to punish persons who violate the laws of the United States cannot be questioned."[121] Bingham also relied on the supremacy clause in his speech introducing the Fourteenth Amendment.[122]

These members of Congress believed that federal power to establish uniform rights was necessary to preserve the Union. Introducing the amendment, Bingham explained, "Nothing could be plainer to thoughtful men than that if the grant of power had been originally conferred upon the Congress of the nation, and legislation had been upon your statute books to enforce these requirements of the Constitution in every state, that rebellion, which has scarred and blasted the land, would have been an impossibility."[123] In a later debate, Bingham elaborated, "Is the bill of rights to stand in our Constitution hereafter, as in the past five years within eleven States, a mere dead letter? It is absolutely essential to the safety of the people that it should be enforced." Bingham insisted that federal enforcement power was essential to the "unity of the government."[124] These remarks illustrate the extent to which "national supremacy became intertwined with black freedom, civil rights guarantees, and the protection of white unionists" during the Reconstruction Era.[125]

The record is less clear with regard to which substantive rights encompassed in the broadly worded provisions of the Fourteenth Amendment.[126] Scholars have long debated the scope of the rights protected by the Fourteenth Amendment.[127] While this chapter does not pretend to present an exhaustive analysis, it is possible to discern a general paradigm from the congressional debates. Due in large part to the Court's ruling in the *Slaughter-House Cases,* the Privileges or Immunities Clause became something of a dead letter shortly after it was enacted. In the twentieth century, courts and Congress focused attention primarily on its companion, the Equal Protection Clause. However, the debates over the 1866 act and the Fourteenth Amendment reveal that its Framers focused primarily on the Privileges or Immunities Clause.[128] To the extent that the Framers discussed the substance of rights protected by the Fourteenth Amendment, they focused primarily on defining the privileges and immunities of citizenship.

There is ample evidence that the Framers believed that the privileges and immunities of citizenship include at least the trio of rights referred to in the Declaration of Independence—that is, the right to life, liberty and property. This is clear from the language of the 1866 Civil Rights Act and from the debates over the meaning of the act. During those debates, Representative William Lawrence expressed this widespread view: "There are certain absolute rights which pertain to every citizen, which are inherent, and of which a state cannot constitutionally deprive him . . . the absolute right to live, the right of personal security, personal liberty, and the right to acquire and enjoy property."[129] Included in the meaning of "liberty" was the freedom of speech and religion that southern states had denied to many citizens prior to the Civil War.[130] Others, including John Bingham and other antislavery constitutionalists, believed that the privileges and immunities of citizenship, protected by the Fourteenth Amendment, at least included the Bill of Rights.[131] Thus, in March 1871, Bingham noted that the Bill of Rights "chiefly defined" the privileges and immunities of citizenship.[132]

As expressed in the remedial provisions of the 1866 Civil Rights Act, the members of the Thirty-Ninth Congress also believed that access to government facilities, such as courts, and the right to enter into legal contracts, as well as the right to travel, were privileges and immunities of citizenship.[133] The right to travel was particularly important for freed slaves, who had hitherto been forbidden from doing so. Newly freed slaves traveled often, and "[t]he ability to come and go as they pleased would long remain a source of pride and excitement for former slaves."[134] However, a majority of the Republicans did not see the right to vote as a right of citizenship.[135] The majority differentiated "civil rights," centering on the right to participate in the legal system in such basic means as entering into contracts and owning real property, from "political" rights, like the right to vote. Radical Republicans vehemently disagreed, insisting that voting was a right of federal citizenship.[136] However, in this matter, the Radicals in the Thirty-Ninth Congress were outnumbered and defeated, and the Republicans officially adopted the position that only the former "civil" rights were considered to adhere to federal citizenship.[137]

There is also considerable evidence that some Framers of the Fourteenth Amendment intended the rights encompassed in the Fourteenth Amendment to be considerably broader, encompassing all fundamental human rights based on a "natural law" view of rights.[138] For example, when Senator Howard introduced Section One of the Fourteenth Amendment to the Senate, he indicated that in order to find the privileges and immunities of federal citizenship, one should look to the Bill of Rights and to the Circuit Court's opinion in a well-known case, *Corfield v. Coryell*,[139] a lower court case that was well known for embodying a broad, natural rights theory of citizenship.[140] Similarly, in the debate over the 1866 act, Representative Senator Lyman Trumbull declared, "To be a citizen of the United States carries with it some rights, and what are they? They are those inherent, fundamental rights which belong to free citizens as free men in all countries," and Representative James Wilson said simply "civil rights are the natural rights of man."[141]

Though they disagreed on the substance of the rights of citizenship, the Republicans all agreed that those rights should be applied equally throughout the country. The theme of equality of rights directly reflects the concerns expressed by northern members of Congress in debates over the rights of citizenship prior to the Civil War.[142] Prior to the Civil War, Republicans in Congress were outraged that citizens of one state could be denied their most basic rights by another state, and they intended the Fourteenth Amendment to rectify this situation by creating a baseline of rights that would be uniform throughout the country.

During the debate over the 1866 act, members of Congress repeatedly spoke of the importance of equality of rights. For example, Representative William Windom explained that the act's "object is to secure a poor, weak class of laborers the right to make contracts for their labor, the power to enforce the payment of their wages, and the means of holding and enjoying the proceeds of their toil."[143] In the same vein, introducing the Fourteenth Amendment to the Senate, Senator Howard proclaimed that it "establishes equality before the law, and it gives to the humblest, the poorest, the most despised of the race the same protection before the law as it gives to the most powerful, the most wealthy, or the most haughty."[144] Thus, that the rights of citizenship should be equal regardless of the state of one's residence was expressed not just in the Equal Protection Clause but throughout the Fourteenth Amendment.[145]

Legislation enacted pursuant to the Fourteenth Amendment enforcement power reflects the same themes of belonging, protection, and equality that permeated the 1866 debates. To eliminate all doubts about the constitutionality of the 1866 act, Congress reenacted its provisions as part of the 1870 Enforcement Act.[146] Congress enacted the Enforcement Acts of 1870 and 1871 in response to reports of overwhelming violence against freed slaves and the formation of the Ku Klux Klan.[147] The 1871 Enforcement Act prohibited conspiracies by state or private actors to prevent a person from "exercising any right or privilege of a citizen of the United States," including the right to vote, serve on juries, and "obtain equal protection of the law."[148] Members of Congress were concerned that states were not actively prosecuting the instigators of this violence, so they created federal causes of action, hoping to use the jurisdiction of the federal courts to protect their citizens from that violence when the states would not.[149]

Protection was the theme of this legislation, which made it a crime to interfere with a citizen's exercise of his rights of citizenship. The 1871 act was enforceable against private individuals as well as state officials because members of Congress were concerned about the denial of equal protection by local officials. Thus, Michael Kent Curtis has argued, "In 1871 most Republicans thought that when states failed to provide adequate protection, Congress could supply it by laws operating directly on private individuals."[150]

The Civil Rights Act of 1875 went further in its substantive provisions, prohibiting race discrimination in privately owned places of public accommodation. The act, entitled "An act to protect all citizens in their civil and legal rights," took the theme of belonging one step further, attempting to equalize the rights of citizens in their private transactions.[151] The 1875 act reflects a very broad view of rights of belonging, prohibiting race discrimination even in the "social" realm. Moreover, the 1875 act provided that the freedom from race discrimination was such a fundamental right that its denial, even by private parties, would be a federal offense.[152] The 1875 act was the result of years of advocacy by Radical Senator Charles Sumner, who died before his bill was adopted. The seven blacks in the Forty-Third Congress also spoke out eloquently in favor of the bill, and the 1875 act was finally approved by a lame duck Republican Congress in large part as a tribute to Sumner's memory.[153] Sadly, the bill was never really enforced, and according to Eric Foner, "well before the Supreme Court declared it unconstitutional in 1883, the law had become a dead letter."[154] Social equality did not become a legal reality for most African Americans until almost one hundred years later.

Congress's active use of their newfound rights-generating power during the later period of Reconstruction was due in large part to their sense of urgency caused by rampant violations of rights throughout the south.[155] It was also due at least in part to distrust of court enforcement of constitutional rights. For example, supporters of the 1871 Enforcement Act, responding to unchecked Ku Klux Klan terrorism in the south, argued that federal legislation was needed to enforce the Fifteenth Amendment because they were concerned that southern judges would not enforce the Amendment.[156] This is not to say that the Reconstruction Era Congress mistrusted all courts. Indeed, an important provision of the 1871 Enforcement Act gives federal courts jurisdiction for causes of action arising under the act. Moreover, the same Congress that enacted the most far-reaching measure, the Civil Rights Act of 1875, also bestowed general federal question jurisdiction on the federal courts.[157] Wary of the incoming Democratic majority, the Republicans took their chances on judicial enforcement, hoping that in the short run the judges would be more solicitous to rights of belonging.

Unfortunately, however, the members of the Reconstruction Era Congress were right to be distrustful of the Supreme Court. Even while their Reconstruction efforts were still active, the Court began dismantling the political successes of the freed slaves and their protectors. In two major cases, the *Slaughter-House Cases* and the *Civil Rights Cases,* the Court significantly limited the scope of the Fourteenth Amendment and of Congress's power to enforce that amendment. In the *Slaughter-House Cases,* the Court rejected the broadest, natural rights theory of the privileges and immunities of citizenship held by some Framers of the Fourteenth Amendment, when it held that those rights did not include the right to pursue an occupation.[158] The Court held that states, not the federal government, have the responsibility of defining and protecting the fundamental rights of citizens.[159]

James Fox has argued that the *Slaughter-House Cases* had a significant impact on Congressional debates about civil rights legislation immediately following the Court's ruling.[160] Fox points out that the first version of the 1875 Civil Rights Act, which prohibited race discrimination in privately owned places of public accommodation, was introduced in 1870, and was heavily debated in Congress throughout the period. After the Court's opinion in *Slaughter-House,* opponents of the Bill argued that it now fell outside Congress's power to protect the privileges and immunities of citizenship because of Justice Miller's narrow interpretation of those rights in the *Slaughter-House Cases.*[161] In response, supporters argued that freedom from discrimination remained a right of federal citizenship, emphasizing the equality-based nature of citizenship rights.[162] However, Fox is doubtless correct when he points out that *Slaughter-House* played an important part in "effect[ing] the subtle elimination of fundamental privileges of national citizenship from the congressional and national political discourse over the Fourteenth Amendment and Reconstruction."[163]

In the *Civil Rights Cases,* the Court directly limited congressional enforcement power when it struck down the Civil Rights Act of 1875, which prohibited "any person" from denying to "any citizen" access to privately owned places of public accommodation on the basis of race.[164] In that case, the Court held that Congress's power to enforce the Fourteenth Amendment is limited to remedying state action.[165] The Court articulated a cramped view of congressional power, stating in dicta that the legislation which Congress is authorized to adopt under the Fourteenth Amendment "is not general legislation upon the rights of the citizen, but corrective legislation such as may be necessary and proper for counteracting such laws as the States may adopt or enforce."[166]

By the turn of the century, Congress had abdicated its responsibility to protect rights of belonging and the Supreme Court had sanctioned state-sponsored segregation in the case of *Plessy v. Ferguson*.[167] The responsibility to protect rights of belonging thus fell back to the states, and state protection was spotty at best.[168] The segregated Jim Crow system took hold in the south, as did rampant racial violence against African Americans. The states' failure to protect rights of belonging eventually led to renewed federal intervention in the twentieth century.

Finally, the legacy of Reconstruction is almost as important as what actually happened during that time. Though the Northern Democrats lost in the Reconstruction Congress, for years they prevailed in the battle of history.[169] For many years, the Reconstruction Era was reviled as a period in which vindictive northern carpetbaggers exploited the conquered south.[170] More recently, historians have celebrated the Reconstruction Era and have argued, to the contrary, that the problem with Reconstruction is that the Republican reformers did not go far enough.[171] However, as Pamela Brandwein has recently argued, the Northern Democrats' version of history had left its mark on our country. For almost a century after Reconstruction ended, segregationists relied on that version to justify Jim Crow laws that disenfranchised blacks and made them into second-class citizens, contrary to the intent of the Republicans who supported the Fourteenth Amendment, until the latter half of the twentieth century.[172]

The Reconstruction Era has enjoyed a similarly controversial position in the annals of legal scholarship, primarily in the context of the debate over whether or not the Fourteenth Amendment was intended to incorporate the Bill of Rights against the states.[173] Volumes of literature have been written about this debate, which is well beyond the scope of this work. What merits attention, though, is the role of the views of courts held by participants in this debate. One of the leading opponents of incorporation, Charles Fairman, argued that the Supreme Court's ruling in *Barron v. Mayor and City Council of Baltimore* precluded incorporation of the Bill of Rights. In his work, Fairman discounted the Reconstruction Era Republicans' critique of *Barron* because he maintained that only courts, and not members of Congress, had the power to interpret constitutional meaning.[174] Responding to Fairman, William Crosskey argued that the Framers of the Fourteenth

Amendment intended to overrule *Barron* and incorporate the Bill of Rights against the states.[175]

Crosskey pointed to the Republicans' numerous critiques of the Court and argued that Bingham and others were reformers who were trying to fix the law that the Supreme Court had broken. According to Crosskey, the Republican members of Congress were attempting to define constitutional meaning and bypass hierarchical court rulings. As Brandwein explains, "What is clear is Crosskey's view that the key to understanding the debates was the Republican's rejection of the Supreme Court as the ultimate authority on the Constitution."[176] Fairman ridiculed Crosskey and argued that his conclusions were illogical and unbelievable.[177]

While Fairman prevailed in that round, since then, numerous scholars have argued convincingly that Crosskey's views more accurately reflected the views of the Framers of the Fourteenth Amendment.[178] Thus, almost one hundred years after Reconstruction, the battle over constitutional meaning continued. Once again, the supporters of a broad view of rights rely primarily on congressional authority, while those with a more narrow view of rights rely on a juriscentric view of the courts.

Perhaps most importantly, the new congressional enforcement power in the Reconstruction Amendments marked a significant change in Congress's role in our constitutional structure.[179] While prior to Reconstruction, the Constitution did not contain a single provision authorizing Congress to protect rights of belonging, all of the Reconstruction Amendments contain congressional enforcement provisions, as does every amendment enacted since Reconstruction that expands individual rights.[180] The Reconstruction Amendments thus represent a major departure from the constitutional protections for individual rights prior to the Civil War by naming Congress, not the courts, as the principal enforcer of those rights.

4

Belonging and Social Citizenship
The New Deal and the Wagner Act

While the New Deal Era is widely recognized as a significant time of constitutional change, most constitutional scholars view the change in terms of federalism and separation of powers because of the expansion of the federal government and the administrative state. However, the New Deal legislative program had another, broader meaning as well—the expansion of rights of belonging.[1] During the New Deal Era, Congress created rights of belonging with statutes protecting the rights of workers and establishing a federal safety net for those who could not work.[2] The centerpiece of the New Deal, and the focus of this chapter, is the Wagner Act (also known as the National Labor Relations Act), which established the right of workers to form unions and bargain collectively with their employers. While the Wagner Act and other New Deal statutes protecting the rights of workers are conventionally viewed in economic terms, proponents of this legislation saw their primary goal as enforcing human rights.[3] The New Deal Era thus represents another period in which Congress acted to protect rights of belonging, continuing in the tradition of their Reconstruction Era predecessors.

According to legal historian William Forbath, the New Deal embodied a constitutional vision that centered on individual freedom and the ideology of social citizenship that continued the tradition from Reconstruction.[4] As Forbath points out, that vision developed, not within the courts but on the streets and within the political branches, in opposition to the courts.[5] The debate over the Wagner Act well illustrates his point because members of the New Deal Congress saw themselves, not the courts, as the primary protectors of citizenship rights. Rather than turning to the courts to enforce their rights, during this era, as during Reconstruction, reformers viewed courts as an obstacle to achieving social reforms. While labor was often successful at advocating a collective vision of freedom within the political realm, courts championed the individual liberty of contracts and struck down the protective legislation that had been supported by workers. Hence, like the Reconstruction Era, the early twentieth century was marked by conflict over constitutional meaning between the political branches and the courts.

During the New Deal, supporters of the Wagner Act in Congress adopted labor's constitutional vision, but they had to contend with the conservative vision of the Court. As a result, they framed the act in two different registers: as a means of protecting human freedom and of regulating interstate commerce. Supporters of the act eventually prevailed before the Supreme Court, which upheld the Wagner Act as an exercise of Congress's commerce power, despite earlier rulings construing that power narrowly.[6] However, in the debate over the Wagner Act, members of Congress were concerned, not just about the extent of their power to regulate commerce but, more importantly, about the meaning and significance of belonging to the national community, and whether the individual liberty of contract, or the collective freedom to belong to a union, should prevail.

Members of the New Deal Congress linked the workers' right to organize into unions with social citizenship and belonging. Labor leaders had long advocated this view, arguing that the right to organize was necessary for the equal citizenship of workers. They argued that the right to join a union was a fundamental human right that would empower workers economically, but also politically. As an editorial in the *Iron Molder's Journal* argued in 1904, "Political equality is not sufficient and unless the wage-earner possesses an industrial equality that places him on par with his employer there can never exist that freedom and liberty of action which is necessary to the maintenance of a republican form of government."[7] During debates over the Wagner Act, members of Congress agreed, framing the right to organize in terms of the freedom, equality, and human dignity that had characterized their predecessors' discussion of belonging during the Reconstruction Era.

The right to organize into a union and bargain collectively is arguably the quintessential right of belonging because it facilitates the formation of communities of workers who benefit both economically and socially. To join a union is to join a community, and in the first half of the twentieth century union membership facilitated the social integration that was especially important for the many industrial workers who had recently immigrated.[8] Equally importantly, the right to organize enabled workers to use collective action to achieve economic and political gains. Union membership not only empowered workers within the workplace, it also enabled workers to participate more fully in the political arena because unions became a strong political force. Workers who joined unions were also more likely to feel invested in their communities and engage in political action, from voting to direct engagement in politics.[9] Finally, labor leaders believed that the right to join a union was essential to the human dignity of workers. Under the authoritarian tradition of master/servant, workers were cowed, both psychologically and socially, and intimidated by their employers into working under difficult conditions. Belonging to a union empowered these workers psychologically, giving them a mechanism to demand respect from their employers and enforce that demand.[10] Thus, many workers saw the right to organize as a fundamental human right, essential not only to their economic well-being but also to their personal autonomy. For all of these reasons, the right to organize facilitates the belonging of workers in our society.

To many of labor's leaders in the early twentieth century, the right to join a union was not just a political goal but a constitutional right. They claimed a constitutional tradition of their own, what James Gray Pope describes as "labor's constitution of freedom."[11] Labor's philosophy was rooted in the Reconstruction civil rights tradition, based on the right to equality embodied in the Fourteenth Amendment, the freedom from involuntary servitude guaranteed by the Thirteenth Amendment, and the freedom of expression guaranteed by the First Amendment and democratic ideals.[12] They relied on Reconstruction Era rhetoric to fight their campaign against "wage slavery" and for protective labor legislation.[13]

Many union leaders viewed the Thirteenth Amendment as a pro-labor amendment with impact significantly broader than the ending of chattel slavery. This view has roots in the Reconstruction Era and the philosophy of "free soil, free labor" advocates such as Henry Wilson and John Bingham. Prior to the Civil War, they saw the abolition of slavery as necessary to improve conditions of white workers but felt that banning slavery alone was not enough—addressing extreme conditions of labor exploitation was also necessary.[14] Those members of the Reconstruction Congress who held these views anticipated the profound effect that abolishing slavery would have on the entire structure of labor relations, raising the floor because slaves occupied the bottom rung in the progression of labor status.[15] During the Thirteenth Amendment ratification debates, Senator Henry Wilson was the strongest advocate for equality for all laborers, proclaiming that "we have advocated the rights of the black man because the black man was the most oppressed type of the toiling men of this country."[16] In the House, John Bingham also advocated equality for workers, declaring that citizenship rights included "the equality of all to the right to live . . . [and] to work and enjoy the product of their toil."[17] Of course, the Reconstruction Congress did not speak with one voice, and Congress did not officially adopt their vision of the amendment.[18] However, the vision of Wilson and Bingham lived on within the labor movement, where it was nurtured and passed on from generation to generation. Invoking the Reconstruction Era, labor leaders such as Samuel Gompers, founder of the American Federation of Labor and AFL president until 1924, recalled days of civil disobedience by abolitionist ministers prior to the Civil War. Gompers characterized the Thirteenth Amendment as the "glorious labor amendment" and argued that the right to strike meant "the difference between voluntary and involuntary servitude, between freedom and slavery."[19]

Other labor leaders shared Gompers's view of the Thirteenth Amendment, and to at least some of the rank and file, the link between the right to organize and that Amendment's prohibition on slavery became a deeply held belief and important motivating force.[20] Pope details how coal miners in the early 1900s from Kansas to West Virginia long cited the Civil War and the abolition of slavery as precedents for their own struggles for freedom.[21] This was a particularly strong tradition in West Virginia, where many of the miners were African Americans and some were former slaves.[22] Advocates of this view argued that *individual* freedom to take or leave a job was not enough. To these workers, the rights to organize into unions, bargain *collectively,* and strike were fundamental to human freedom.[23] Hence, they saw the right to organize as essential to the true freedom that would enable workers to belong as full, productive members of society. Decades later, this language of freedom would prove important in congressional debates as members of Congress created a statutory right to join a union in the Wagner Act.

Of course, the free labor ideology of the Reconstruction Era had been transformed from its original sources. Most of the Reconstruction Era free labor advocates had the ideal of an artisan or other independent worker in mind.[24] They had no idea of the changes that would come about in American society as a result of industrialization, mass unemployment, and mass urban poverty. As a result, they believed that the government had an important role in ensuring the freedom of workers, but they did not envision the need for the state to provide the social insurance and other workers' protections advocated by labor during the New Deal Era.[25] Indeed, prior to the Depression, most workers did not expect the government to do much to meet their needs. However, the severe economic needs occasioned by the economic crisis of the Great Depression caused workers to rely increasingly upon the protection of the government.[26] As workers became more invested in government, they also became more involved in politics. These workers advocated "the strengthening of two institutions to rebalance power within capitalist society"—the federal government and unions.[27]

Another basis for labor's belief in a constitutional right to join a union was the link between unionization and democracy. Many labor leaders linked political and economic empowerment in their concept of industrial democracy. Native-born American working-class radicals like Eugene Debs championed this egalitarian strain in the nineteenth-century tradition of working-class republicanism, calling for extending basic civil and political rights into the realm of production and the market sphere.[28] These labor leaders and their progressive allies maintained that in order for a political democracy to flourish, the workplace needed democratization as well. Building on this view, teachers in Seattle attempting to unionize in the 1920s maintained that the right to unionize was a fundamental right of citizenship that the state could not deny. Those teachers challenged the school board's "yellow dog contract" policy, maintaining that the policy required them to "surrender the rights of citizenship to secure public employment."[29] They strongly asserted their constitutional right to join a union. While the language of industrial democracy was most popular during the World War I era,[30] the link between unions and democracy continued to be a potent vision because it invoked the importance of participation for full citizenship in our society. The language of industrial democracy most effectively evokes the right to belong, and it strongly influenced members of Congress during debates over the Wagner Act.

Prior to the New Deal, however, labor's constitutional vision achieved mixed success, often prevailing in the political process only to lose in the courts. During the first third of the twentieth century, the early labor movement convinced state legislatures to enact statutes adopting safety regulations, restricting the number of hours an employer could require his employees to work, and prohibiting antiunion practices such as "yellow dog" contracts.[31] However, labor's political success was stifled by both federal and state courts, which struck down much of this protective legislation as undue interference with the "right to contract."[32] During this era, common law governed the substantive rights of workers.[33] Though the courts did not strike down all of the legislation that they reviewed, overall the rulings of courts, both state and federal, had a distinctly antilabor bent.[34] William Forbath argues persuasively that the hostility of courts toward workers' rights played a significant part in shaping labor's political agenda during the first third of the twentieth century, shifting that agenda from "broad, class-based legislative initiatives" to the legislative protection of workers' organizations, so that they could bargain for protections in the private sector.[35]

However, achieving this "voluntarist," form of workplace reforms required using the political process to limit the involvement of courts in labor relations. This was also the era of "rule by injunction," with courts issuing numerous orders preventing labor from organizing and engaging in political action.[36] As a justification for enjoining union activities, courts defined property rights broadly, justifying their intervention as necessary to protect an employer's interest in his employees' labor and in his employees' nonunion status.[37] As a result, by the early 1920s labor leaders made anti-injunction legislation their top legislative priority, and attacks on the courts were central to their political program.[38] Labor leaders were also successful at their campaign for anti-injunction statutes, but state courts routinely invalidated anti-injunction statutes on the grounds that they were "class legislation" that unduly intruded in the judiciary.[39]

The prevailing view of the *Lochner* era is that of the Progressives, who believed that the constitutional vision held by the vast majority of courts during this era was based on an extreme view of liberty based in laissez-faire economics, protecting business from pro-worker regulations that interfered with the property rights of business. Recently, however, some scholars have noted the link between the *Lochner* ideology of freedom of contract and the Free Soil, antislavery ideology of the Reconstruction Era.[40] If correct, this observation arguably puts the *Lochner* rulings in a more favorable light than the Progressive view of courts as pro-business and antiworker. However, even if the sources of the two competing ideologies were the same, the conclusions drawn by courts and labor were diametrically opposed. While the labor movement's "constitution of freedom" is premised on the view that workers were coerced by their employers and the state, the *Lochner* doctrine of contractual liberty is premised on the lack of coercion in labor contracts.[41]

More importantly, the *Lochner* courts focused on *individual* liberty, emphasizing the right of each individual employee to form his or her own contract. By contrast, labor held a *collective* vision of freedom, maintaining that the constitution protected the freedom of workers to associate in *groups* and bargain as a group. Labor economist Robert F. Hoxie observed in 1923, "As the [common] law in spirit is individualistic, it makes the freedom and sacredness of the individual contract the touchstone of absolute justice, and as the unions are formed to escape the evils of individualism and individual competition and contract . . . the [common] law cannot help being in spirit inimical to unionism."[42] Of course, there was a strong practical reason why labor focused on group rights rather than individual rights. Labor leaders and their supporters in Congress believed that freedom to bargain collectively was essential because the worker's individual bargaining power was simply not sufficient to counter the vastly superior resources of individual employers.[43]

Moreover, whether or not the revisionist scholars are correct, it is undeniable that reformers during this era, including progressives, populists, and labor activists, saw courts not as champions, but as a major *impediment* to obtaining rights for workers.[44] During the first third of the twentieth century, labor leaders and their progressive supporters actively engaged in efforts to limit the power of courts in order to protect their successes in the political realm.[45] While President Franklin Roosevelt's attacks on the Courts in early 1937 are well known, his confrontation with the Court was "merely the culmination of a struggle that had raged with varying degrees of intensity for a half century."[46]

The first third of the twentieth century was marked by an on-going battle between, on the one hand, labor and their legislative allies and, on the other hand, courts with their conservative constitutional doctrines based on the liberty of contract. Although labor's constitutional vision often prevailed in the political process, it rarely prevailed in the courts. As a result, principled disobedience to injunctions became the official policy of the American Federation of Labor. Samuel Gompers proclaimed, "contempt of court was obedience to law."[47] Gompers's statement reflects his view that the rule by injunction was antithetical to the principles of freedom protected by the Thirteenth Amendment. His was an assertion of popular constitutionalism in direct opposition to the laissez-faire constitutional view of the courts. Gompers and other labor leaders argued that injunctions not only violated their freedom but also undermined their First Amendment rights and their rights to trial by jury.[48] Labor leaders were not alone in attacking the courts during this era. Progressives and populist leaders also alleged that a "judicial oligarchy" had usurped the powers of Congress and joined labor in calling for anti-injunction legislation and for other reforms that would decrease the power of courts.[49]

Congress also became involved in the constitutional dispute between labor and the courts. As with state legislatures, labor achieved some success in Congress, only to have those successes struck down or limited by courts. The dispute between Congress and the Supreme Court over the constitutionality of federal statutes proscribing child labor is perhaps the most dramatic example of these disputes. In 1916, Congress enacted a statute prohibiting the shipment of goods manufactured by child labor in interstate commerce, but the Court struck the statute down as beyond the scope of the commerce power.[50] Congress tried again to limit the use of child labor by imposing a tax on products manufactured by children, but the Court again struck the statute down, as beyond the taxing power.[51] These federal measures had enjoyed widespread popular support, and the Court's decisions striking them down provoked despair and anger within progressive and union circles. The Court's position on child labor became a rallying cry for the Courts' opponents and prompted Congress to consider a constitutional amendment that would have expressly authorized Congress to regulate child labor. The amendment prevailed in Congress but foundered in the states during the ratification process.[52]

Another dispute involved the 1914 Clayton Act, in which Congress prohibited antilabor injunctions in federal courts. When it was enacted, Samuel Gompers hailed it as "labor's magna carta" since it curtailed the power of courts over unions.[53] However, the Clayton Act was equivocal because it allowed an exception for "lawful" injunctions to protect property rights. This exception invoked the common law, and courts accepted the invitation, broadly construing the exception and continuing to issue numerous injunctions.[54] The Supreme Court upheld this practice, effectively gutting the Clayton Act and robbing labor of its principal legislative victory.[55]

The anticourt movement fostered labor's principal legislative success in Congress prior to the Wagner Act, the 1932 passage of the Federal Anti-Injunction Act, also called the Norris-LaGuardia Act.[56] The Norris-LaGuardia Act has the same general goal as the Clayton Act, depriving federal courts of jurisdiction to issue injunctions in cases "involving or growing out of a labor dispute."[57] However, the Norris-LaGuardia Act was considerably more effective at preventing federal courts from issuing injunctions against unions. The roots of the act ran deeper and its purpose was wider, echoing labor's constitution of freedom. As its preamble reflects, the act linked unionization with the freedom of association and self-representation, and it was intended to protect those rights.[58] The Supreme Court eventually upheld the constitutionality of the Norris-LaGuardia Act.[59] However, that decision only took place after a showdown between the courts and the political branches in which the Wagner Act had a major role.

The intervening event and catalyst was the Great Depression, which began in 1929 when a major stock market crash wiped out savings and hurt consumer confidence. At first, economists thought the downturn would be brief, but unemployment rose steadily in 1930, the stock market continued to decline, and farm prices collapsed. That year also saw the beginning of the drought that caused the "dust bowl" and a large number of bank failures.[60] By 1931, the Depression had become a catastrophe. Banks failed, farm prices collapsed, and manufacturing output plummeted. Large industrial cities, like Detroit, Toledo, and Cleveland, saw 50 percent unemployment among blue-collar workers. In the southwest, hundreds of thousands of farm families lost their farms and became migrant workers.[61] The Great Depression brought hardship and suffering for millions of Americans, but it also was a fertile time for economic, political, and social change.[62] The economic impact of the Depression brought about the ascendancy of labor's constitution of freedom, including its ideology of social citizenship and belonging, at the expense of the conservative constitutional vision held by the courts.

The initial impact of the Depression on labor relations was inconclusive because Roosevelt was still dependent on the support of business leaders.[63] However, workers' interest in unions increased during this time because they had learned to distrust welfare capitalism and because the work force was increasingly American, educated in the United States, and employed under conditions of mass production. Over time, labor enjoyed enhanced political clout.[64] Hence, the Great Depression created a favorable climate for the Wagner Act to succeed because "it diminished the influence of businessmen, caused union leaders to turn their backs on voluntarism, and created an experimental political climate."[65] Supporters of the Wagner Act believed that economic planning and increasing the purchasing power of workers were essential to the recovery of the U.S. economy.[66] However, throughout the congressional debates, supporters of the act also framed the right to organize as a fundamental human right based on freedom of expression, freedom of association, and freedom from wage slavery.

The statutory right to organize had its genesis in the centerpiece of the Roosevelt's First New Deal, the National Industrial Recovery Act (NIRA).[67] Pursuant to the NIRA, the federal government would allow business and industry to fix prices and required them to pay higher wages, through "codes of fair competition."[68] For labor, the key provision of the NIRA was its Section 7(a), which guaranteed the right to organize in a union.[69] Many unions saw Section 7(a) as a green light to organize. They engaged in extensive campaigns, especially in the coal, clothing, textile, and iron and steel industries, with a large degree of success.[70] Employers responded by forming "company unions" as a sole means of employee representation. Labor strongly opposed those "unions."[71] The ambiguous language of Section 7(a) on issues such as company unions, and the lack of enforceability of the entire NIRA, led to numerous conflicts between management and labor. A pattern developed whereby workers joined unions at the invitation of Section 7(a), but their employers refused to recognize the unions.[72] The result was a wave of strikes in 1933, more than in any year since 1921.[73]

In an attempt to resolve the burgeoning disputes between labor and management, in the fall of 1933 Roosevelt established a National Labor Board (NLB) to resolve disputes by mediation or arbitration and asked Senator Robert Wagner to act as chair.[74] Wagner had a long history of support for labor. Prior to entering politics, he had been a union side labor lawyer, winning one of the few appellate victories overturning an antilabor injunction.[75] Wagner was also a close ally of Roosevelt, and he sponsored a majority of the president's New Deal measures in the Senate.[76] Under Wagner, the NLB had created a new, pro-worker "common law" that would protect the right to organize, require reinstatement of employees fired for union organizing, create an employers' duty to bargain fairly, and mandate that employers should keep "hands off" union elections.[77] Wagner and the other members of the NLB soon learned that they had little power to enforce their rulings because the only form of sanction available to them was to remove the "Blue Eagle" that signaled that the employer was cooperative with the government.[78] By March, 1934, Wagner became convinced that Section 7(a) needed better enforcement provisions in order for it to be effective, so he introduced a new bill "to effectuate further the policy of the NIRA."[79]

Wagner intended his bill to legislatively reinforce the right of employees to unionize, to prohibit employer discrimination against these employees, and to counterbalance the relaxation of antitrust laws for business, enabling business to work together more closely, with "the equal organization and equal bargaining power of employees."[80] In a speech given shortly after he introduced his bill, Wagner explained that the nascent economic recovery of the United States had exposed the "paradox of poverty and progress," in which the falling wages of workers made it impossible for them to purchase the goods that they were producing. To combat this, Wagner argued, workers had to have equal bargaining power, and the best means for securing equal bargaining power was "by securing for employees the full right to act collectively through representatives of their own choosing."[81] Hence, Wagner framed his first bill in terms of economic equality. Other supporters maintained that the bill was necessary to prevent labor unrest that resulted from the lack of the workers' rights to organize.[82]

Although the AFL and the NLB strongly supported Wagner's statute, in early hearings the Roosevelt administration had adopted an ambivalent attitude toward Wagner's bill.[83] Labor Secretary Frances Perkins testified that the Department of Labor had investigated over 3,200 complaints charging 264 employers with discriminating against employees who wanted to join a union. Echoing the language of industrial democracy, she argued, "Workers should be reassured and reconfirmed in the rights of free speech, free assembly, free association in any organization of their choice, and in the right to elect representatives."[84] However, Perkins was lukewarm toward the bill, calling it "very interesting."[85] The Roosevelt administration's ambivalence was due to the fact that corporate America solidly opposed the bill. The press was also overwhelmingly hostile to the bill, with twelve out of fifteen major newspapers writing editorials opposing it.[86]

In 1934, corporate opposition to Wagner's bill prevailed.[87] Instead of Wagner's bill, Congress enacted a stop-gap measure, Public Resolution 44, which authorized the president to form a board or boards to investigate labor disputes arising under Section 7(a), but did nothing to remedy the lack of enforcement power that had plagued the NLB.[88] The summer and fall of 1934 were marked by a series of massive and violent strikes.[89] In 1934 alone, there were 1,856 strikes, involving over 1.47 million workers, 51.5 percent of the country's total workforce.[90] Many of these strikes involved clashes between pickets, strikebreakers, police, and the National Guard, causing numerous injuries and deaths. For example, during the May 1934 Auto-Lite strike in Toledo, two strikers were killed and twenty were wounded from gunfire, and ten National Guardsmen were wounded when strikers hit them with bricks.[91] Over twenty striking workers were killed and hundreds were wounded in San Francisco, Minneapolis, and in the textile workers strikes that spanned the south through New England.[92] By January, members of the NLRB and organized labor were now convinced that Section 7(a) "could not and would not be enforced."[93] They demanded legislation that would create rights that were truly enforceable. In Congress, the debate resumed, allowing labor's supporters in Congress to amplify their constitutional vision. In the meantime, the 1934 congressional elections were crucial to the eventual success of the Wagner Act. They represented a landslide victory for the president's allies and his New Deal, with Democrats winning a majority of 45 seats in the Senate and 219 in the House. "The election for all practical purposes eliminated the right wing of the Republican party," and, "hence, the legislature was prepared to entertain more progressive measures."[94] By February 1935, Senator Wagner was determined to win permanent legislation in this favorable climate.

To defeat Wagner's bill, representatives of business engaged in one of the largest lobbying efforts in history to prevent Congress from enacting its provisions.[95] Business leaders were frightened by the bill's collective view of labor relations and its apparent assumption that the interests of capital and labor would always be in conflict, but especially by their fear that "the federal government was now totally behind the effort of the union movement to organize workers."[96] The National Association of Manufacturers, a business association that formed in order to oppose pro-labor legislation, prepared industry witnesses to testify, issued press releases, and sent out brochures to employees and customers, urging them to lobby their federal representatives against the bill.[97] Business groups ran numerous radio and newspaper ads and organized speeches, broadsides, and correspondence to lobby against legislation protecting the worker's rights to organize.[98] They also worked directly with conservative members of Congress, suggesting amendments to cripple the bill.[99]

From the beginning, the debate over the Wagner Act reflected the ongoing constitutional debate over the rights of workers. Business evoked the constitutional vision of the courts as the primary basis for their opposition to the bill. Testifying at the Senate hearings, business leaders and their lawyers objected to the majority rule provision, the outlawing of company-supported unions, and the failure to include control over unions.[100] Opponents also argued that the bill would create a monopoly for the AFL, and that the bill was biased against employers because it imposed no limits on unions.[101] However, their primary tactic was to argue that the bill was unconstitutional. Tracking the major relevant Supreme Court decisions, they claimed that the bill violated principles of federalism and due process, depriving employers of their right to contract with individual employees.[102] For example, during a Senate hearing, James Emery, council for the National Association of Manufacturers, testified that the bill would affect "among the most fundamental rights that man possesses, whether labor or employer," the right to contract and the right "to decline to associate with others" along with the right to select one's agent.[103] Hence, the Court's conservative constitutional vision was the mainstay of business opposition to the Wagner Act.

Proponents of the Wagner Act responded with a constitutional vision of their own, one rooted in labor's constitution of freedom. Introducing his bill, Wagner echoed the constitutional philosophy of the labor movement and spoke out against the constitutional philosophy of the courts. Wagner called Section 7(a) of the NIRA a "veritable charter of freedom of contract" and argued that without the right to bargain collectively, "there would be slavery by contract."[104] Wagner juxtaposed his view of freedom of contract with the view, predominantly held by courts, that the principle of collective bargaining violated freedom of contract. "Nothing could be more fallacious," he declared. "The fathers of our Nation did not regard freedom of contract as an abstract end. They valued it as a means of insuring equal opportunities, which cannot be attained where contracts are dictated by the stronger party."[105] Thus, from the outset of the congressional debate over his bill, Wagner asserted a version of popular constitutionalism that favored "labor's constitution of freedom" over what he saw as the oppressive constitutional views held by the Supreme Court and many lower courts.

However, because of the institution of judicial review, Wagner and his allies were also compelled to frame their measure in the more conservative terms that were more likely to persuade the Supreme Court when it ruled on the constitutionality of the act. Although many members of Congress asserted their own authority to interpret the Constitution, all of them were clearly aware that the Court had its own power to review the constitutionality of the measure, and that the Court would rely on its own constitutional vision when doing so. The Court's conservative constitutional vision overshadowed the congressional debate over the Wagner Act. Throughout the debate, both supporters and opponents of the Bill believed that the Court would probably hold it unconstitutional. This required congressional supporters of the Wagner Act to argue at two different levels because they were arguing to two very different audiences: the public and their elected representatives on the one hand, and the courts on the other.

Hence, the constitutional debate over the Wagner Act occurred at two parallel levels, one court-centered and the other centered on the political process. In the political process, members of Congress framed the act in terms of freedom and human rights. Wagner's language of freedom was addressed to an audience (the public and Congress) that was receptive to such arguments and most likely to be persuaded by them. The Court, however, would have been highly unlikely to accept the argument that there was a constitutional right to join a union. Thus, supporters of the act also conducted a parallel debate over how best to frame the act so that the Supreme Court would uphold its constitutionality, framing the bill in the conservative narrative of removing burdens to interstate commerce.[106] Thus, the congressional debate over the 1935 Wagner Act focused on economic policy, as well as rights of belonging.

Throughout the debates over the Wagner Act, many members of Congress made it clear that they believed the right to organize was a fundamental human right that would facilitate workers' belonging to society as equal citizens. The act's congressional supporters often evoked the language of freedom and slavery, maintaining that without the right to join a union workers were virtually enslaved in their jobs. Senator Wagner repeatedly compared working without a right to join a union to slavery. For example, in a speech given on the day he introduced his first bill, he called the right to bargain collectively "a veritable charter of freedom of contract; without it there would be slavery by contract."[107] During Senate debate, Wagner insisted, "I would not buy peace at the price of slavery."[108] Years later, Wagner's legislative aide, Ken Keyserling, recalled that Wagner always said that the purpose of the act was "to make the worker a free man."[109] Wagner's Senate colleague, Senator Walsh, agreed that "any injunction or any law that prevents a man from striking, is a law of servitude, and that is the principle we have to keep in mind. It is the difference between freedom and servitude."[110]

In the House, Representative Carpenter of Nebraska echoed the sentiments of his Senate allies. He declared, "Some remedy must quickly be found for the misery and wretchedness which presses so heavily on the large majority of the laboring class. . . . A small number of rich men have been able to lay upon the masses of the poor a yoke little better than slavery itself." Carpenter called the workers' right to form labor unions and bargain collectively "inherent rights."[111] Representative William Connery of Massachusetts agreed that the statute raised "human rights above property rights" and represented a "continuation of the fight which has raged ever since man was freed from serfdom." Connery maintained that nominally free people were still toiling in "virtual economic slavery."[112] Similarly, Representative Vito Marcantonio of New York asked rhetorically, "Unless Congress protects the workers what liberty have they? Liberty to be enslaved, liberty to be crucified under the spread-out system, liberty to be worked to death under the speed-up system, the liberty to work at charity wages, the liberty to work long hours."[113] Representative Wood agreed that "[This bill] involves an age-old principle—the desire for freedom . . . all this bill is designed to do is to make men free."[114] In the same vein, Representative Truax of Ohio explicitly invoked the Reconstruction Era, calling the bill an "emancipation for labor" and claiming "as Lincoln freed the blacks in the South, so the Wagner-Connery bill frees the industrial slaves of this country from the further tyranny and oppression of their overlords of wealth."[115] Thus these members of Congress evoked labor's constitution of freedom during the congressional debate and made it clear that they believed the right to join a union was essential for the freedom of workers: an essential predicate to their belonging in society.

Supporters of the Wagner Act also linked the right to organize to other constitutional values such as freedom of speech and democracy.[116] Testifying before Congress, labor leaders argued that the right was necessary for workers' participation in the political realm.[117] The Senate report on the first Wagner bill echoed labor's claims and called it an attempt to prevent employers from impairing "the exercise by employees of rights which are admitted everywhere to be the basis of industrial no less than political democracy. A worker in the field of industry, like a citizens in the field of government, ought to be free to form or join organizations."[118] In Senate debates, Wagner maintained that collective bargaining brought "an element of democracy into the government of industry" and explained that the principle of majority rule was intended to conform to the democratic procedures that are followed in business and government life.[119] In a newspaper interview, Wagner said, "Let men know the dignity of freedom and self-expression in their daily lives, and they will never bow to tyranny in any quarter of their national life."[120] Thus, Wagner evoked the language of industrial democracy that had proven so effective for labor decades earlier, and he indicated that the right to join a union was essential, not only to the empowerment of workers in the workplace but also to workers' belonging to the political community.

Other New Dealers in Congress evoked industrial democracy, arguing that an employee at a nonunion plant was like a nonvoting member of society.[121] For example, Representative Withrow explained, "The right of self-government through fairly chosen representatives is a right which is inherent to the American people and to our American form of government. The bill does no more than guarantee that right to American labor."[122] Similarly, Representative Carpenter of Nebraska proclaimed, "The worker's right to form labor unions and to bargain collectively is as much his right as his right to participate through delegated representatives in the making of laws which regulate his civic conduct. Both are inherent rights."[123] Representative Truax of Ohio called the bill "a new bill of rights, a new declaration of independence, if you please."[124] Like union organizers before them, these members of Congress framed the Wagner Act as a measure that would enhance democracy by strengthening the ability of workers to participate in the national polity and belong to that community as equal citizens.

Congressional supporters of the act also championed the concept of economic empowerment for workers. For Wagner, his staff, and other supporters of the act, it "signified recognition that a national economy required national regulation and that a stable one needed a more equitable distribution of income and wealth."[125] Wagner viewed the right to bargain collectively as not only a sensible way to conduct business affairs but also essential to social justice for workers.[126] At the 1935 hearing before the Senate Labor Committee, Wagner explained that the bill was one of several efforts to establish balance in the economy, as well as an example of congressional action in face of wealth and power.[127] Wagner and his allies advanced a theory of mass purchasing power, arguing that long-term prosperity depends on higher wages and a more even distribution of income. They explained that collective bargaining would promote these ends.[128] This argument responded to the pleas of workers throughout the country who believed that workers were entitled to their fair share of the wealth they created. These workers wanted both economic equality and social equality.[129]

Finally, supporters of the bill also presented a more conservative narrative in support of the bill—that it would promote industrial peace by reducing the number of strikes. They pointed out that many of the strikes that were plaguing the U.S. economy were caused by the situation in which employers denied their employees the right to organize. In turn, these strikes interfered with interstate commerce.[130] The Wagner Act's statement of findings and policy took this approach, pointing out that inequality of bargaining power between unorganized workers and employers tended to depress wages and aggravate recurrent business depressions.[131] Hence, Wagner's committee report described the first objective of the bill as removing the basic cause of strikes—the failure to bargain—and the second objective as the equalization of bargaining power.[132] Supporters argued that without this legislation, labor was likely to become more radical and disrupt the economy even more. For example, at the 1935 hearing in the Senate Labor Committee, Lloyd Garrison, then head of the NLRB, testified that the act was "our chief bulwark against communism and other revolutionary movements."[133] These arguments were intended to shore up support from moderates and lay out the argument for the constitutionality of the act that was bound to occur before the Supreme Court.[134]

At the hearings on the act, some union officials had urged Wagner to rely on the Thirteenth Amendment as a source of congressional power to enact the statute.[135] Not only would this approach have provided an avenue for Congress to avoid the Court's restrictive commerce clause precedent, but also it was more consistent with the arguments of the supporters of the bill, who, we have seen, "framed their claims in the language of human rights, not commerce."[136] The preamble of the bill mentioned the freedoms advocated by labor.[137] "To eliminate the causes of certain substantial obstructions of the free flow of commerce," the act stated that it intended to "encourag[e] the practice and procedure of collective bargaining" and protect "the exercise by workers of full free-dom of association, self-organization, and designation of representatives of their own choosing."[138] However, though Wagner spoke in the lan-guage of freedom, for a source of power he relied on Congress's power to regulate commerce instead of the rights-generating provisions of the Reconstruction Amendments.[139] The preamble dryly concluded that "de-terrents to mass purchasing power have a detrimental effect upon, and that strikes obstruct, interstate commerce."[140] This language evoked the more conservative narrative that the bill was necessary to reduce labor strife.

Legal historians James Gray Pope and William Forbath have debated the meaning of Wagner's seemingly inconsistent approach to this legisla-tion. This debate is best understood within the context of the ongoing battle between the Court and Congress over constitutional meaning. Pope traces Wagner's ultimately conservative emphasis on removing barriers to interstate commerce to the influence of legalistic technocrats on Wagner's staff, who believed that labor's reliance on the Thirteenth Amendment was foolish and preferred to argue in the more conven-tional language of interstate commerce.[141] Pope argues persuasively that the right to organize would have fared better politically and before the courts in subsequent years had it been understood as a fundamental hu-man right.[142]

In response, Forbath points out that Wagner and his allies wanted to avoid the pitfalls of the kind of open-ended language that would have invited the courts' common law approach that had been so problematic for labor.[143] They wanted legislators, and not courts, to define the rights of workers. This viewpoint is reflected in the labor-supported Worker's Rights Amendment, proposed in 1935. That amendment would have authorized Congress to regulate the hours and conditions of labor, es-tablish a minimum wage in any employment, and regulate production and industry.[144] Proponents of the amendment argued that it would "unmistakeably establish the right of the people to have an industrial democracy."[145] The Amendment's focus on congressional enforcement power indicates that reformers had confidence in Congress's ability to define the *substance* of the individual rights of workers and were most concerned about whether Congress had the *power* to do so. The juris-dictional choice to place rights enforcement in democratic politics, and not the courts, was consistent with labor's experience with the two bodies. To them, workers' rights were best enforced by democratic politics, not by the courts.[146]

The evidence supports Forbath's argument. Congressional supporters of the Wagner Act wanted to prevent the courts from robbing labor of its legislative rights. The New Dealers' distrust of courts was evident during the Senate's consideration of the act prior to the Court's ruling in *A. L. A. Schechter Poultry Corporation v. United States.* Part of the strategy of the act's opponents was to propose some amendments to derail the bill.[147] The most significant such amendment, originally drafted by the National Association of Manufacturers and proposed by Senator Millard Tydings of Maryland, would have prohibited "coercion from any source," including union organizers. The NLRB opposed the amendment as "a joker" that would "defeat the very objectives of the bill."[148] Proponents of the Wagner Act uniformly agreed, and all fiercely opposed the amendment. The reason for their opposition is telling. They were opposed not to the term "coercion" but to the courts' interpretation of that term.[149] As Senator Walsh explained, they were concerned that courts might construe as "coercive" the efforts of one employee to organize a union.[150] In support of this argument, Senator Norris, the coauthor of the Norris-LaGuardia Act, pointed to courts' construction of the Clayton Act which "took away all of its practical effect," and recited the history of antilabor injunctions, to explain his opposition to the Tydings amendment.[151] Hence, proponents of the Wagner Act worried that the Court would construe it narrowly or against labor, as it had the Clayton Act. The Senate's distrust of courts revealed itself in the lopsided defeat of the Tydings Amendment, which lost with a margin of 50 to 21.[152]

The debate over the Tydings Amendment reflects the extent to which New Dealers were sensitive to the power of courts to undo the rights that they were trying to create in the Wagner Act. Time after time, they had seen workers lose their rights before conservative courts, and they took pains to prevent this loss from occurring again. Thus, it may be unfair to fault Wagner for his technocratic focus on regulating interstate commerce, even if that focus caused a conservative bent to his framing of the act. Wagner was using any means necessary to enforce what he saw as essential human rights and protect those rights from conservative courts.

For years, labor activists had directed their rights-based arguments to political bodies, not courts, and the New Dealers embraced their rights-protecting role. However, Pope is correct that, in retrospect, it might have been better if supporters of the Wagner Act had confronted the courts head on and more strongly asserted their congressional authority to define rights of belonging by basing those rights in the constitutional principles that they evoked during the debates over the act. In that view, the problem with Wagner's strategy was that he and his allies were not firm enough in their challenge to the courts.[153] They knew that the courts could not be trusted with workers' rights, but they also knew that if they did not speak the language of the Court, the Court was certain to invalidate their measure. If Wagner and his allies had been more firm about their role as constitutional interpreters, and asserted the link more strongly that they saw between the right to organize and belonging, perhaps that right would have fared better before subsequent Courts to whom the language of rights strongly resonated.

Of course, that strategy would have only worked if government lawyers arguing in favor of the act before the Court had accepted the view that the right to organize was a fundamental right. To the contrary, Forbath points out that the progressives who worked for the Roosevelt administration made the choice to stick with the language of commerce for another reason. Although they were often labor's allies, they also distrusted labor and didn't want to give them the latitude that might have resulted from framing the right to organize in the broad language of fundamental rights.[154]

While the strategies of both labor and the progressives were effective before Congress, the progressives' pragmatic approach prevailed before the Court. The Court upheld the Wagner Act solely as a regulation of commerce based on Wagner's more conservative rhetoric. The language of freedom and belonging that permeated congressional debates is simply absent from the Court's opinion, and from the Court's interpretation of the act in subsequent years. Hence, the progressives got what they wanted—a more pragmatic, less rights-bound version of the Wagner Act.

The shadow of the Supreme Court hung heavy over the congressional debates on the Wagner Act. Members of Congress assumed that the Court would strike down the statute, and this awareness permeated the debate. Opponents of the Wagner Act, who made the unconstitutionality of the act central to their opposition, often asserted the Court's authority as the sole interpreter of the constitution. For example, Senator Frederick Steiwer of Oregon exclaimed, "there is no conceivable justification for the effort of Congress to take final action in connection with the National Recovery Act until the Supreme Court shall have defined the jurisdiction of the Congress to such an extent that we can say with certainty that we know our power and know that which is denied to us under the organic law of the country."[155] By contrast, proponents of the act varied in their attitudes toward the Supreme Court. Some members of Congress asserted their right to regulate the workplace within the existing framework established by the Court, but others challenged the Court's authority to define those constitutional norms. All of them distrusted the Court and saw it as a natural enemy in the fight to protect the rights of workers.

Hence, the debate over the Wagner Act reflected the ongoing dispute between members of Congress and the Court. This dispute intensified after May 27, 1935, a day known as "Black Monday" because it was thought to signal the end of the New Deal. On that day, the Supreme Court held that the National Industrial Relations Act was unconstitutional in the case of *A.L.A. Schechter Poultry Corporation v. United States*.[156] The Court's ruling in *Schechter* placed the constitutionality of the entire New Deal, including the Wagner Act, in doubt. However, the Court's ruling in *Schechter* turned out to be one of the most important factors in the success of the Wagner Act for three reasons. First, *Schechter* was the catalyst that caused President Roosevelt to back the statute.[157] Second, the decision bolstered the resolve of the act's proponents to defy the Court and enact the measure. Finally, *Schechter* ironically weakened congressional opposition to the statute because opponents assumed that the Court would do their job and strike down the statute.

Prior to the Court's ruling in *Schechter,* the Roosevelt administration had remained ambivalent about the Wagner Act. However, the Court's ruling gutted Roosevelt's labor policy, leaving him with nothing but the Wagner Act, and thus arguably forced him to support the bill.[158] On the day that the *Schechter* decision was released, the president held a press conference attacking the Court.[159] A week later, on June 4, Roosevelt announced that he had determined that "the New Deal program including [the Wagner Act] would proceed, if necessary, in defiance of the court," and added the act to his list of "must enact" legislation.[160] Because the president was enormously popular, his support for the Wagner Act was important to its success.

The Court's ruling in *Schechter* also had a strong impact on the congressional debate over the Wagner Act.[161] Initially, the decision "had a shock effect on the proponents of the Wagner legislation." Congress responded immediately to *Schechter,* going into recess for a week. After the president came out in support of the bill, it was brought back to the House Labor Committee for reexamination.[162] Most concerned about the success of his statute, Wagner responded to *Schechter* by reverting to his conservative constitutional narrative. Aides changed the language of the bill, striking out references to "the general welfare" and altering the definitions of "commerce" and "affecting commerce" to make that showing as well. The amended bill contained "findings and policy" explaining in detail "how industrial strife affects interstate commerce."[163] Hence, the *Schechter* ruling caused Wagner to revert to his more conservative narrative. After *Schechter,* rather than emphasizing the Wagner Act's promise of freedom for labor, Wagner presented it from the more business-friendly viewpoint, as a measure designed to foster industrial peace.[164]

Notwithstanding Wagner's protestations, most lawmakers assumed that *Schechter* meant the Court would probably hold the Wagner Act unconstitutional. This assumption had a varied effect on the congressional debate. Congressional opponents of the Wagner Act argued that *Schechter* had sounded the act's death knell. For example, Representative Hollister of Ohio proclaimed that the bill was "manifestly unconstitutional." Citing *Schechter,* Hollister accused the bill's proponents of disregarding repeated warnings given by the Court. He exclaimed, "It is inconceivable that the sponsors of this bill have had proper legal advice, for I am sure that they would not knowingly mislead their followers."[165] Many opponents simply cited the Court's decision in *Schechter* as proof the bill's unconstitutionality.[166] For example, Representative Thomas Blanton of Texas asked rhetorically, after *Schechter,* "Is there a good lawyer in this House who for one moment believes that such a law would be upheld by the Supreme Court?"[167] Others accused the proponents of the act of seeking to either avoid or circumvent the unfavorable Court ruling.[168]

Other members of the House used language from *Schechter* to support their position that the bill would unconstitutionally intrude on states' rights. For example, Representative Howard Smith denounced the bill: "We cannot change the Constitution by undertaking to define interstate commerce. We are merely fooling ourselves and holding out false hopes to others. . . . I appeal to you not to further strip the states of their police powers."[169] Echoing the Court's approach in *Schechter,* therefore, Smith maintained that the bill would intrude on the state's prerogatives by destroying the distinction between production and commerce. These arguments were consistent with the position that opponents had taken throughout the congressional debates over the statute, that the Court had the ultimate authority to interpret the constitution.

However, even some opponents of the Wagner Act asserted the authority of members of Congress to determine the act's constitutionality for themselves. For example, Representative Charles Halleck of Indiana proclaimed, "I say to you that the first line of defense against attack on the Constitution is the Congress of the United States." He argued that members of Congress could not justify the passage of such an unconstitutional act because that would contravene their constitutional duty.[170] Representative Robert Rich of Pennsylvania also argued that members of the House of Representatives should vote against it because it was unconstitutional. He cautioned against passing the issue on to the courts. "We are agents with limited powers, and the Court gives every reasonable presumption to the constitutionality of what we do, because it believes that we have settled our own doubts."[171] These arguments by opponents of the Act illustrate the extent to which the language of popular constitutionalism had become acceptable within the New Deal congressional debates.

Not surprisingly, however, the strongest assertions of popular constitutionalism came from the Wagner Act's supporters. The Court's ruling in *Schechter* fueled the anti-Court sentiment already manifest among labor's allies in Congress. After *Schechter,* many supporters of the act asserted their own authority to interpret the Constitution in opposition to the Court. For example, in a radio speech on May 31, 1935, Representative William Connery defined the "question of the moment" as whether Congress will be able to legislate "constructively for the best and humane interests of the people of the United States" or whether the Supreme Court could be allowed to "set aside continually the mandate of the people and the action of the Congress of the United States." Connery pointed out that the Supreme Court is not elected and therefore not accountable to the people.[172] Representative Reuben Wood of Missouri was probably the most explicit in his defiance of the Court. When asked whether he believed that the Wagner Act was constitutional, he replied that although the constitutional lawyers in Congress had opined that the act was constitutional, "I don't know what is going to be constitutional so long as we have the present set-up of the Supreme Court."

When asked further whether he accepted the decision of the Court as the right interpretation of the law, Wood declared, "No, I do not. I differ with the Supreme Court and I have the right to differ with them." Wood explained that though he was not a lawyer, "I have been affected by a number of previous decisions of the Supreme Court. . . . I think we as a free people have a right to express our own opinion when the Supreme Court hands down a decision."[173]

Following up on Wood's remark, Representative Walter Pierce of Oregon opined, "The gentleman might also cite Abraham Lincoln in speaking of the Supreme Court with reference to the celebrated *Dred Scott* decision."[174] Representative Adolph Sabath of Illinois added, "As to the constitutionality of this measure, during the twenty-nine years I have been here, every time we have had a bill in the interest of the deserving labor, I have heard the learned lawyers of the nation raise the question of constitutionality."[175] The most strident language was that of Representative Charles Truax of Ohio, who described the Supreme Court disparagingly as "that American dictatorship appointed and sitting for life, the nine men in black."[176] He continued, "We see the same old faces that oppose all progressive humanitarian legislation. . . . What are you going to do with this sacred old constitution? You cannot eat it, you cannot wear it, and you cannot sleep in it."[177] Truax also argued that rather than precluding the statute, the *Schechter* decision made the bill more important because with no Recovery Act there would be a greater threat of strikes.[178] This more conservative argument was persuasive given the tense atmosphere that prevailed in many workplaces during this time.

Other proponents argued that the country was in a time of constitutional transition due to changes in the complex industrial economy. In this vein, Representative Moritz argued that given the economic situation, "it is up to us to find an easier way to amend our Constitution that the people may be given a fair deal."[179] Representative Norton agreed: "We live in a changing period. Conditions are not what they were when the Constitution was written."[180] Hence, months before president Roosevelt's Court-packing plan, members of Congress presaged Roosevelt's arguments for judicial reform. The popular constitutionalism of congressional proponents of the Wagner Act came naturally to them. As supporters of workers' rights, they had lived the history of courts overturning the legislative successes of labor, including some that they themselves had enacted. Now, during this crucial time of crises, they again saw the courts as their principal opponents. No wonder they claimed the constitution for themselves, as labor activists had for years before them.

More subtly, it is also likely that the *Schechter* decision weakened opposition in Congress because members of Congress essentially believed that they could have their cake and eat it too. By voting for the bill, they could avoid antagonizing labor, but business would also be satisfied because the Court would surely strike it down.[181] As Philip Levy, a member of the NLB opined, "The *Schechter* decision persuaded most lawyers and most members of Congress that the Wagner bill was unconstitutional so that 'the opposition just folded up.'"[182] This phenomenon helps to explain why many southern conservatives, hardly champions of labor, nevertheless voted for the bill.[183]

Once the bill had cleared the House Labor Committee, it encountered little opposition. After only one day's debate on the House floor, the bill passed on a voice vote.[184] The conference report was adopted by the House on a vote of 132 to 45 and by a voice vote in the Senate on July 5, 1935.[185] The president signed the bill on the same day.[186] Labor leaders compared *Schechter* to the Court's nineteenth-century *Dred Scott* opinion, and they rejoiced that Congress had not been daunted by the *Schechter* opinion.[187] Though Congress enacted the measure as a regulation of commerce, members of the labor movement nevertheless viewed these statutes as essential to human freedom.[188]

Given the bill's rocky history, why was the final vote so lopsided? While the *Schechter* decision is one reason for the vote, historian Irving Bernstein also explains, "The bill was presented at the most favorable possible moment since 1935 was the apogee of the New Deal as a progressive domestic reform movement. The influence of labor was at its height and Senators with little enthusiasm for [the Wagner Act] feared to face the AFL at the polls with a negative vote on their records."[189] The gravity of the economic situation and the uncertainty generated by the end of the NIRA also were important factors because they were the main reason for the widespread public support for the bill.[190] The bill had been discussed for more than a year in Congress, in the press, and over the radio. Even though the mainstream press was against the bill, the American public flooded Congress with mail, most of it in favor of the bill.[191] Finally, Senator Wagner's tireless fight was crucial to the success of the act that bore his name: "He mobilized the draftsmen, devised the political strategy, and carried the brunt of the fight with the public, Congress and the White House."[192]

After its passage the future of the Wagner Act remained in doubt. The act still had to pass the hurdle of the Supreme Court, which had been so hostile to protective labor legislation and had struck so many federal measures down as beyond congressional power to regulate pursuant to the commerce clause.[193] Hence, the battle between Congress and the Court continued. In 1936, as the Wagner Act made its way up through the lower federal courts, the Supreme Court struck down the 1935 Bituminous Coal Act, which gave coal miners the right to organize and bargain collectively, sending an ominous signal for the future of the Wagner Act.[194] In 1936 and early 1937, the general shared assumption was that the Court would invalidate the act when it had a chance to do so. Every single federal appellate court to consider the issue ruled against the constitutionality of the act, and district courts uniformly issued injunctions restraining its enforcement.[195] The constitutional uncertainty surrounding the Wagner Act took its toll on the act's enforcement. Initially, no one wanted to serve on the NLRB because they were certain that the Court would strike the Wagner Act down.[196] Because its future was in doubt, in 1936, the NLRB also had little or no public or political support.[197] Following the advice of their lawyers, many business owners decided not to comply with the Act.[198] As a result, union members began to feel that it was useless to rely on the protections of the Act.[199]

In response to the atmosphere of constitutional uncertainty, supporters of the act used the political realm not only to argue for the act's validity but also to challenge the authority of the Court to determine that validity. It was a skirmish of popular constitutionalism, in which labor leaders, members of Congress, and the president of the United States engaged the Court, calling on the people to assert their authority to legitimate the measure that had been enacted by Congress.

In Congress, Senator Robert La Follette of Wisconsin convened a special committee to investigate civil liberties violations by businesses fighting unionization on their premises.[200] At these hearings, witnesses testified about extensive employer espionage and antilabor practices. The hearings were highly publicized and resulted in increased public support for the efforts of the NLRB. As Malcolm Ross, the director of information for the NLRB in 1936, later explained, "The newspaper coverage of finks and criminals on company payrolls shamed the opposition into silence. It worked on the public conscience when appeals to reason had failed."[201] Hence, La Follette's hearings put the pressure on business and the Court to support the act.

Other members of Congress proposed measures to curtail the power of the courts. Long-time labor supporter Senator George Norris of Nebraska introduced a bill that would have required a unanimous Supreme Court opinion to strike down an act of Congress. Another bill was sponsored by one of Roosevelt's main opponents, Senator Burton Wheeler of Montana. Wheeler called for a constitutional amendment that would have enabled Congress to reenact a statute with a three-fourths (later two-thirds) majority vote after the Court had struck it down as unconstitutional.[202] These members of Congress chafed at the Court's power to overturn their hard-fought measures.

In the streets, labor leaders engaged in a wave of sit-down strikes in early 1937 to test the provisions of the Wagner Act, and, as James Gray Pope has observed, "the sit down strikes became a form of constitutional politics."[203] As a result, late 1936 and early 1937 marked the most tumultuous phase of New Deal transformation of labor relations in the United States.[204] In December 1936 alone, over 39,000 workers staged eighteen sit-down strikes.[205] The most dramatic of the sit-down strikes occurred in Flint, Michigan, in February 1937 as United Automotive Workers members protested General Motors' refusal to bargain with them. The Flint strike idled nearly all of General Motors' 200,000 workers, as the strikers compared their fight to the 1861 fight against slavery. Although the strike was considered illegal, Roosevelt and the governor of Michigan, Frank Murphy, urged General Motors to negotiate with the union. General Motors did so and entered into a contract with the United Auto Workers. As a result, UAW membership swelled.[206] The Flint strike dominated the national headlines as Roosevelt announced his court-packing plan.[207] By collective action, workers forced compliance with the act and summoned the support of the president, prevailing in this round of constitutional politics.

Finally, President Roosevelt also had a prominent role in this skirmish with the Court. By 1936, he had adopted the language of belonging, freedom, and citizenship that had been used by labor and their allies in Congress. In speeches during his 1936 reelection campaign, Roosevelt emphasized the workers' need for economic freedom, as well as the role of the national government in obtaining that freedom, as he described the role of government in language of slavery and freedom, tyranny and democracy.[208] Roosevelt won overwhelmingly that year, and during the subsequent Flint strike, CIO founder John Lewis announced that Roosevelt's victory meant that "[l]abor will . . . expect the protection of the federal government in pursuit of its lawful objectives."[209] Roosevelt agreed with this assessment.

In the fall of 1937, Roosevelt proclaimed the authority of the people to interpret the constitution and claimed that the 1936 election had affirmed the constitutionality of the Wagner Act even before the Court ruled on the issue. In that speech, Roosevelt described the constitution as "a layman's document, not a lawyer's contract. *That* cannot be stressed too often. Madison, most responsible for it, was not a lawyer."[210] Roosevelt continued, "You will find no justification in any of the language of the Constitution for delay in the reforms which the mass of American people now demand. . . . [T]he Bill of Rights was put into the constitution not only to protect minorities against intolerance of majorities, but to protect majorities against the enthronement of minorities."[211] Hence, the president asserted the authority of the political branches to enforce constitutional norms in order to protect the rights of the people.

In a well-known confrontation, Roosevelt challenged the Court more directly when he announced his plan requesting congressional authorization to add Justices to the Court in February 1937.[212] Although he originally presented the plan as an issue of competence, by early March it became clear that Roosevelt was attacking the Court because of its disregard for the national will in striking down New Deal measures.[213] Roosevelt's plan was extremely controversial, and despite his huge popularity, he was roundly condemned for suggesting it on the grounds that it violated principles of separation of powers.[214] The Senate Judiciary Committee emphatically rejected Roosevelt's proposal on June 14, 1937. By then, however, the Court had already upheld the Wagner Act, arguably capitulating to the constitutional vision held by labor and the political branches.

Despite the failure of his court-packing proposal in Congress, Roosevelt's proposal may have ultimately obtained his desired effect. Soon after he presented it, the Court reversed a fourteen-year-old precedent and upheld a state minimum wage law for women in the case of *West Coast Hotel v. Parrish*.[215] Two months later, the Court upheld the Wagner Act in *NLRB v. Jones & Laughlin Steel Corp.*, embracing a broad reading of Congress's commerce power.[216] The Court's decision was a huge victory for supporters of the act. In Alquippa, Pennsylvania, workers paraded through the streets carrying a banner reading "The Workers in Alquippa are now free men."[217] Senator Wagner gave a speech on the radio and said that Court's decision had "changed a controverted measure into a 'bulwark of industrial peace and justice.'"[218] Many historians have argued that the Court was bowing to political pressure in its *Jones & Laughlin* ruling.[219] Of course, it is not possible to identify now what factors motivated the Justices who upheld the Wagner Act. However, it is clear that popular constitutionalism prevailed in this instance, enabling Congress to expand the rights of belonging of workers throughout the country.

The Wagner Act was a momentous piece of legislation that had the potential to radically alter the American social and economic order.[220] Like the Reconstruction Era legislation, the Wagner Act represented a congressional redefinition of citizenship, by supplanting the common law of employment and labor market.[221] It was the cornerstone of the "Second New Deal," a comprehensive and reformist legislative program, which also included the Agricultural Adjustment Act, the Fair Labor Standards Act, the Social Security Act, and the Work Progress Administration, which employed over one million people in public works projects.[222] These and other New Deal Era statutes created a new federal regulatory state that greatly expanded the role of the federal government's relationship to the daily lives of people within its jurisdiction, creating a shift in federal-state relations so significant that Bruce Ackerman has termed it tantamount to a constitutional amendment.[223] It also represented a historic congressional commitment to expand rights of belonging in the face of the conservative opposition of the courts.

Unfortunately, the Wagner Act's success at achieving its goals of worker empowerment and economic justice was limited. In 2005, unionization was down, the real wages of workers were falling, and job displacement had become an economic crisis. Many scholars have analyzed the reason behind the act's failures. For example, Karl Klare blames the statute for contributing to the privatization of the marketplace and the depoliticization of workers.[224] On the other end of the spectrum, Christopher Tomlins maintains that the Wagner Act involved the state too deeply in labor relations, subordinating unions to the state. While Tomlins acknowledges that the Wagner Act "held out the opportunity of participation in determining the direction of the American political economy which organized labor had been seeking since the

turn of the century," he maintains that the act offered unions "ultimately no more than the opportunity to participate in the construction
of their own subordination."[225] While a detailed analysis of this question is well beyond the scope of this chapter, both of these scholars ac-
knowledge that courts have taken major steps in limiting the scope of
the act.[226] The courts served as the mechanism of the state that deprived
workers of the potential for social change inherent in the right to organize and engage in collective bargaining. Congress also limited the act's
reach with the 1947 Taft Hartley Act, and never returned to the prola-
bor stance that it held in 1935.[227] In the seventy years since the passage
of the Wagner Act, however, the Court has done considerably more
than Congress to reduce its effectiveness.[228]

After the Court upheld the Wagner Act, it also initially issued some
important decisions in favor of unions, establishing picketing as a protected aspect of free speech and "emancipat[ing] unions from the
clutches of antitrust laws." However, the Court later overruled its picketing decision.[229] More importantly, the Court construed the Wagner
Act narrowly from its very inception. Most notably, as early as 1938 the
Court held that employers had the right to hire replacements for striking workers, effectively undermining the right to strike that was expressly written into the Wagner Act.[230] Wagner aide Ken Keyserling
later explained that he believed the express provision was necessary because "some courts would have construed the opposite: that they had to
exercise this right [mutual aid and protection] as a condition precedent
to the right to strike."[231] Sadly, even the express statutory language was
insufficient to withstand the Court's undermining of this right, turning
the right to strike from a powerful weapon of workers into a weapon
for employers.[232] Shortly thereafter, the Court limited the NLRB's remedial power and held that the act did not protect workers engaged in sit-
down strikes.[233] James Gray Pope argues that in these cases, the Court
continued its common law tradition of construing the rights of employers broadly to gut some of the act's most important protections. As
Pope points out, though the Court long ago rejected *Lochner*, its antilabor conservative constitutionalism lives on in these rulings and others
that have effectively taken the teeth out of the Wagner Act.[234] Hence,
labor's supporters in Congress were correct in distrusting the courts and
in their unsuccessful attempts to limit the court's influence.[235]

Nonetheless, the Wagner Act had a powerful impact on the lives of
millions of American workers. With the Wagner Act, Congress legis-

lated the rights that labor had long demanded—the right to organize and to strike. The Wagner Act institutionalized unions, and union membership increased dramatically after its passage. Whereas in 1930, only 2.3 percent of the nation's workforce belonged to a union, by 1940 that number had risen to 27.6 percent, and from 1930 to 1945, the number of workers who belonged to unions jumped from around 3 million to over 12 million.[236] Wagner aide Ken Keyserling later called this rise in union membership the greatest contribution of the Wagner Act.[237]

Because joining a union empowers workers economically, politically, and socially, the ability to join a union enhanced the belonging of workers in the United States as equal citizens. Of course, the right to join a union only enables the belonging of workers who are able to join unions. Race discrimination permeated American society in the first half of the twentieth century, and a number of unions, especially trade unions, discriminated on the basis of race. While the relationship between labor and race during this era is complex, it is true that during the first half of the twentieth century many labor leaders were willing to sacrifice racial equality when necessary to achieve political victories for white workers. Notwithstanding their invocation of slavery, most labor leaders in the first half of the twentieth century were no champions of racial equality, and some condoned, or even encouraged, race discrimination.[238] Law professor David Bernstein has seized on this history to argue that the labor-backed reforms struck down by courts during the *Lochner* era were intended to exclude blacks from decent employment.[239] If this is correct, it was arguably the courts, and not the legislators who enacted those statutes, that were champions of rights of belonging. While Bernstein has been widely criticized for historical inaccuracies in his work,[240] he is correct that racial justice was compromised by New Deal measures, including the Wagner Act.

The tradition of activists linking race and class issues goes back to the pre–Civil War era. Though abolitionists were divided over the question of whether there was a link between "chattel" slavery and "wage" slavery, a significant number identified a direct link between the exploitation of slaves and wage laborers.[241] For example, when campaigning on behalf of Lincoln in 1860, Representative Henry Wilson argued that slavery hurt white workers in two ways: direct competition with slave labor in the south and associating the efforts of industrious white workers with those of the degraded slaves.[242] During Reconstruction, Wilson reiterated these themes in support of the Thirteenth Amendment and during a dramatic showdown with Representative Edgar Cowen in January 1866 over whether to extend the Freedman's Bureau statute. Responding to Cowan's speech against the extension, Wilson responded, "I tell you, sir, that the man who is the enemy of the black laboring man is the enemy of the white laboring man the world over."[243]

During the New Deal, however, labor was split at the time on issues of racial relations. This division is illustrated by the conflicting positions of labor organizations on Roosevelt's proposed Fair Employment Practices Commission (FEPC). On the one hand, the Congress of Industrial Organizations championed racial equality and supported the FEPC as part of their commitment to civil rights. The AFL, on the other hand, resisted federal attempts to eliminate racial discrimination in the labor market, and joined with business groups, southern Democrats, and conservative Republicans in resisting a permanent establishment of the FEPC after the war.[244] In Congress, supporters of the Wagner Act and other New Deal legislation failed to address issues of racial justice and made significant compromises that largely excluded African Americans from legislative protections.

Explicit discussion of race is absent from the congressional debates over the Wagner Act. Representative Vito Marcantonio, a leftist Italian-American representative from East Harlem, implicitly raised the issue of race when he proposed an amendment to extend the bill's coverage to farm workers, many of whom were southern blacks. He argued, "It is a matter of plain fact that the worst conditions in the United States are the conditions among the agricultural workers."[245] Representative Connery, the bill's sponsor in the House, claimed to be sympathetic to the amendment but explained that he wanted to take things one step at a time, since representatives from rural districts who would otherwise vote for the bill would oppose that amendment. The House defeated the amendment, and NLRA protections never were extended to agricultural workers.[246] Similarly, while the NAACP supported an amendment to the Wagner Act that would have prohibited race discrimination by unions, Wagner failed to get behind the amendment and the amendment failed. Wagner agreed to take out the nondiscrimination language, bowing to pressure not from southerners but from the AFL.[247]

The exclusion of the majority of African American workers from Wagner Act protections was consistent with the general failure of the New Dealers in Congress to address issues of race.[248] During the 1930s, Jim Crow was in full swing in the south and race discrimination preva-

lent in the north as well. Yet the Wagner Act and other New Deal legislation did little or nothing to address this extreme racial injustice. This
was so because Roosevelt, Wagner, and the other New Deal Democrats
depended on the votes of the southern Democrats for the success of
their legislation.[249]

Hence, it is clear that the Wagner Act never was intended to facilitate
the belonging of all workers by fighting race discrimination. However,
to a larger extent than Bernstein acknowledges, unions played an important part in the early civil rights movement. While many trade unions remained racially exclusionary during the New Deal Era, industrial
unions in the Congress of Industrial Organizations (CIO) had a particularly important part in crusading for racial justice during the 1930s and
1940s. In the 1930s and 1940s, the right to organize was significant for
the fledgling civil rights movement. CIO organizers understood the extent to which business used racial prejudice as a tool to divide workers.
Hence, "[r]acial unity became a watchword of the CIO's campaign in
the 1930s."[250] CIO organizers combated racism on political, economic,
and social fronts. For example, in the south, the CIO founded the
Southern Conference on Human Welfare, a biracial coalition of southern trade unionists and civil rights activists that organized a huge southern voter registration drive in 1944.[251] In Chicago, CIO organizers combated racial segregation to organize the multiracial meat-packing and
steel-working industries. CIO supporters organized boycotts and pres-
sured the taverns to integrate so they could serve as a location for union
meetings. Union organizers also fostered racial and ethnic unity by
sponsoring social events that were attended by members of all races.[252]
Their goal was to create a new workers' community where members
would focus on their class commonality and put aside their racial and
ethnic differences. Of course, some of these successes were short-lived,
and racial tension increased among unionized workers as competition
for jobs from blacks increased in the 1950s.[253] However, for a brief
period of time these union members foreshadowed the civil rights movement and created a community, however small, that facilitated the
belonging of all workers regardless of their race.

Perhaps more importantly, the right to belong to a union empowered
many black workers psychologically, inspiring them to work for social
change. In the 1940s, the labor movement had a crucial role in the
nascent civil rights movement. As historian Martha Biondi has pointed
out, the "struggle for Negro rights" in postwar New York began as a

fight to keep jobs.[254] During the war, African American workers swelled the ranks of wartime defense employers, many left the south to work in war industries of the north and west, and many of those workers became involved in the union effort.[255] Black industrial workers were enfranchised in the workplace by the "one man, one vote" system imple mented by the NLRB elections. This helped to generate a militant civil rights consciousness because those workers began to demand similar enfranchisement in the political process.[256] In the CIO in the 1930s, and with the alliance between the UAW and the NAACP in Detroit, "the labor movement and the civil rights movement [became] closely linked."[257] As black union members experienced the ability to partici- pate in the workplace as equal citizens with their union brothers, they came to desire, and then demand, the same kind of treatment in society at large. Hence, while Bernstein is correct that unions sometimes acted as agents of racial exclusion, his implication that unionism by nature is racially exclusionary is incorrect. To an important degree, the right to organize facilitated the belonging of blacks in America because union membership empowered many black activists to demand racial justice as well as economic justice.

Hence, the end of the New Deal Era marked the beginning of the Second Reconstruction. Issues of racial justice began to come to the fore after World War II, and the northern civil rights movement became ac- tive. At the same time, the Supreme Court started to actively engage in enforcing constitutional provisions against race discrimination.[258] Nev- ertheless, the expansion of rights during this tumultuous period resulted primarily from political activism and popular constitutionalism on the part of labor activists and progressives in Congress. Politicians, not judges, brought about the greatest expansion of rights of belonging since the Reconstruction Era.

5

To Secure These Rights
The 1964 Civil Rights Act

During the New Deal, most members of Congress avoided addressing issues of racial justice. However, shortly after the New Deal political actors, including some northern state legislatures and members of the federal Executive branches, became actively engaged in fighting racial discrimination.[1] For institutional reasons, Congress took considerably longer to act. However, as a civil rights movement grew and flourished following World War II, political momentum turned in favor of civil rights. In 1957 and 1960 Congress enacted relatively ineffective voting rights measures, but when members of Congress acted decisively in 1964, that legislation had a significant impact. The passage of the 1964 Civil Rights Act was one of the most momentous events in the expansion of rights of belonging in American history.[2] The public debate surging in the streets made its way into Congress. The battle in Congress over the act was fierce, and it paralyzed Congress for almost a year. However, it was ultimately successful. Unlike other eras in which Congress acted to expand rights of belonging, this time Congress had help from the Supreme Court. The Court and the majority of members of Congress agreed that it was necessary to outlaw race discrimination. The Supreme Court preceded Congress with its 1954 ruling outlawing state-mandated segregation in *Brown v. Board of Education.*[3] The Court's ruling in *Brown* is often cited as the prime example of the Court acting to protect minority rights.[4] However, in 1964, members of Congress responded to the will of the *majority* when they enacted the strongest legislative protections for rights of belonging since the Reconstruction Era.

Like the Civil Rights Act of 1875, its Reconstruction Era predecessor from almost one hundred years before, Title II of the 1964 act prohibits race discrimination in places of public accommodation. Title VII of the

1964 act also prohibits discrimination on the basis of race, color, sex, or religion in employment,[5] and Title VI prohibits race discrimination by recipients of federal funds.[6] The act also included important provisions authorizing the U.S. Department of Justice to enforce its antidiscrimination mandates.[7] These provisions established the right to participate in society free from discrimination based on race, a quintessential right of belonging. In the south, African Americans were treated as second-class citizens, subjected to both state and private discrimination. They were relegated to the back of the bus and to the cheapest accommodations, and they were barred from many commercial establishments. African Americans were also subjected to private race-based segregation in the northern states. Throughout the country, both public and private race discrimination excluded blacks from belonging as equal members of society. Congress intended the 1964 Civil Rights Act to restore their citizenship rights and enable them to participate as equal members of society in their everyday lives.

Of course, the 1964 Civil Rights Act was not limited to protecting southern blacks. The statute bars all race discrimination, and Title VII also prohibits discrimination in employment based on ethnicity, religion, and gender. Hence, the statute extended the promise of equality to millions of Americans and enhanced their right to belong as equal citizens. The symbolic impact of the 1964 Civil Rights Act may have been its most important contribution. The statute established a national policy against race discrimination in all contexts, and against discrimination in employment based on other immutable characteristics. On behalf of a majority of people in our country, the act emphatically affirmed the rights of belonging of people of color, women, and members of religious minorities in our society.

Congressional supporters of the 1964 Civil Rights Act were well aware of the historical significance of their effort. They saw themselves as completing the work of Reconstruction and enforcing the equality norms of the Reconstruction Amendments. During this debate, leaders in the presidential administrations and in Congress often invoked the spirit of Reconstruction.[8] As President John F. Kennedy explained when he introduced the bill, "One hundred years of delay have passed since President Lincoln freed the slaves, yet their heirs, their grandsons, are not free. . . . Now the time has come for the Nation to fulfill its promise."[9] Later, President Lyndon Johnson repeatedly linked the bill to Abraham Lincoln and the fact that the nation had recently celebrated the anniversary of the Emancipation Proclamation.[10] A group of House supporters of the bill, including Representatives Bill McCulloch and John Lindsay, echoed this theme in their statement in support of the bill, arguing in a memorandum that "the badge of citizenship—extended to Negro as well as white by the 14th Amendment—demands that establishments that do public business for private profit not discriminate on the grounds of race, color, national origin or religion."[11] Like their Reconstruction Era colleagues, members of the 1964 Congress hoped to extend the rights of belonging, protection, and equality to all Americans, regardless of their race.

The 1964 Civil Rights Act resulted from the efforts of civil rights activists dating back to the New Deal Era. World War II caused both an increased migration north of African Americans, and an increased awareness of racism among blacks and whites alike.[12] After the war ended and many of their jobs were taken away by returning white soldiers, many northern blacks became politicized and joined the nascent civil rights movement.[13] The northern civil rights movement achieved some important political successes at the state level, including the 1945 passage of a New York statute that was the first law prohibiting race discrimination in employment in the country.[14] Northern black voters also had an impact at the federal level. Their vote was important in presidential elections in the 1940s because they were concentrated in key swing states.[15]

Both Presidents Franklin Roosevelt and Harry Truman responded to the concerns of northern blacks and used executive orders to address race discrimination.[16] In 1939, Roosevelt installed the first Civil Rights Section in the Justice Department since the Reconstruction Era.[17] In 1941, he created the first federal Fair Employment Practices Commission.[18] Of course, the most important executive action on behalf of civil rights in the pre-*Brown* era was President Harry Truman's executive order banning segregation in the armed forces.[19] Truman also created a presidential committee on Civil Rights and commissioned it to study the condition of race relations in America.[20] In 1947, the committee issued its report, entitled *To Secure These Rights,* a reference to the guarantees of the Declaration of Independence.[21] The report detailed widespread racial injustice throughout the United States and called on Congress to enact civil rights legislation.[22] *To Secure These Rights* influenced civil rights advocacy for the next twenty years, and a number of its recommendations were incorporated into the 1964 Civil Rights Act.[23]

In the 1950s, the civil rights movement expanded into the Jim Crow South. Like the northern civil rights movement, the southern movement had its roots in the postwar unrest of returning GIs. The southern movement's strength increased significantly after the success of the Montgomery bus boycott in 1956.[24] Early civil rights activists engaged in boycotts of segregated businesses such as lunch counters. Perhaps the most dramatic early demonstration was that of the Freedom Riders, who sought to desegregate interstate travel by riding buses through Alabama and encountered brutal racial violence.[25] They invoked the federal arena of interstate travel and sought federal protection from mob violence.[26] These civil rights demonstrations were directed at political actors, and participants demanded political change. Eventually, southern activists succeeded in convincing mainstream America that major new legislative measures were needed to protect racial minorities in this country.[27] Civil rights activists heightened both the demand and the need for federal civil rights legislation.[28]

Unlike Reconstruction and the New Deal, other eras in which Congress acted to protect rights of belonging, this time, the Court was an important ally for those members of Congress who wished to expand those rights. During the New Deal, the Court indicated that it would take part in protecting the interests of minorities against majority abuse. In footnote four of *United States v. Carolene Products*,[29] Justice Stone stated that while the Court should apply a deferential level of review to economic legislation, it should apply heightened scrutiny to legislation that adversely affects "discrete and insular minorities"—those who have been historically excluded from the political process.[30] While the Court failed to uphold minority rights in the first case in which it invoked the concept of heightened scrutiny for race based classifications, *Korematsu v. United States*,[31] in the ensuing years, the Court repeatedly acted to protect the constitutional rights of minorities against majority infringement. Some of the most important decisions during that era include *Smith v. Allwright*,[32] in which the Court held that white primaries violated the Fifteenth Amendment; *Morgan v. Commonwealth of Virginia*,[33] in which the Court held that race discrimination in interstate commerce violated the Fourteenth Amendment; and *Shelley v. Kraemer*,[34] in which the Court held that state court enforcement of racially restrictive covenants violated the Fourteenth Amendment.

In 1954, the Supreme Court weighed in against segregation in what is widely regarded as the most important decision of the twentieth century, *Brown v. Board of Education.* The Court held that segregated elementary schools violated the Equal Protection Clause of the Fourteenth Amendment.[35] In a series of decisions following *Brown,* the Court struck down state-sponsored segregation in other state-run facilities, contributing to the eventual dismantling of the Jim Crow system in the south.[36] In *Brown,* the Court protected minority interests against the will of majorities in the southern states, where people heavily favored racially segregated schools.[37] Although both the Truman and Eisenhower administrations submitted briefs in favor of the plaintiffs in *Brown,* there was no clear national political consensus against segregation in 1954, when the Court decided the case, and the overwhelming majority of people in the southern states supported segregation at that time.[38] Due to strong southern opposition, however, the Court's rulings alone were not sufficient to end racial discrimination in this country. Political developments after *Brown* made it increasingly clear that congressional action was necessary to fulfill the promise of the Court's ruling in that case.

Although the Court had declared segregation to be illegal, during the 1950s the country remained powerfully divided over the issue of segregation. In the south, state governors strongly opposed segregation, and their opposition deepened, rather than decreased, after the Court's ruling in *Brown.*[39] Numerous southern state legislatures enacted pro-segregation statutes after *Brown,*[40] defying the Court's rulings and raising once again the antebellum doctrines of interposition and nullification. Many state judges in the south also voiced their opposition to the Court's mandates.[41]

When *Brown* was decided, lead attorney Thurgood Marshall said that he thought it might take about five years to implement the decision. He predicted that by the one hundredth anniversary of the Emancipation Proclamation in 1963, segregation in all forms would be eliminated from the nation.[42] Unfortunately, Marshall was overly optimistic. Instead of being met with compliance, the Court's ruling in *Brown* met with strong criticism and resistance by politicians and the general public in the south. While the Court's rulings following *Brown* did succeed in ending segregation in some state-run facilities, the Jim Crow south did not come to an end until after the enactment of the 1964 Civil Rights Act.

After *Brown,* instead of ordering compliance with the Court's mandate, state legislators throughout the south enacted a variety of pro-segregation laws in direct defiance of the Court. Between the 1954 *Brown*

decision and 1957, those legislatures enacted at least 136 new pro-segregation laws and amendments to their state constitutions.[43] Many
southern state political leaders strongly opposed desegregation efforts.[44]
James J. Kilpatrick, the influential editor of the *Richmond News Leader,*
revived the antebellum doctrine of interposition and argued that the
states had the power to ignore the federal mandate.[45] Following the
cues of their leaders, many southern school boards closed the public
schools in order to avoid the mandate of *Brown,* and others simply
refused to comply. The southern lower court judges charged with implementing the Court's ruling dragged their feet, either because they opposed desegregation or because they feared reprisals from the communities in which they lived.[46] In the deep southern states, notwithstanding
Brown, only 1.2 percent of black children attended school with white
children from 1954 to 1964.[47]

Even as southern resistance grew, however, the cause of civil rights
gained support throughout the northern states. From 1945 to 1964,
numerous state legislatures enacted measures prohibiting race discrimination in places of public accommodation. By 1964, twenty-eight states
and forty-eight cities had enacted measures that prohibited private race
discrimination.[48] Hence, after *Brown,* the country was increasingly divided over the issue of race, creating an atmosphere of constitutional
uncertainty, notwithstanding the ruling of the Court. Over time, it became increasingly apparent that Congress needed to step in and attempt
to unify the nation over this crucial issue.

The years leading up to the 1964 Civil Rights Act were also marked
by constitutional uncertainty over the details of the desegregation mandate. As a result of the Court's ruling in *Brown* and its extension of
Brown to other public facilities, state-mandated segregation was illegal
in almost all contexts by the late 1950s. However, there remained no
legal mechanism that clearly addressed private discrimination. In addition, it was unclear whether state assistance to discriminatory private
companies, such as bus companies and restaurants, also was illegal. Private discrimination was a significant barrier to the dismantling of the
Jim Crow system, yet the Court was constrained from addressing private action by its self-imposed state action doctrine.

In the *Civil Rights Cases,* the Supreme Court had struck down a provision in the 1875 Civil Rights Act that outlawed race discrimination in
privately owned places of public accommodation. The Court held that
Congress could not use its Section Five Fourteenth Amendment enforce-

ment power to address private discrimination.[49] Eighty years later, the state action doctrine was subjected to considerable strain. By the early 1960s, numerous civil rights activists staged "sit-in" protests of race discrimination in privately owned places of public accommodation, including buses, lunch counters, and restaurants.[50] Many of them were arrested and prosecuted for trespassing, and the Court was required to decide whether such prosecutions violated the Fourteenth Amendment. While several members of the Supreme Court indicated that they might be willing to overturn the *Civil Rights Cases* and reject the state action requirement, there was a lack of consensus on the Court about this important constitutional issue.[51] Resolving the state action dilemma nearly paralyzed the Court and also gave rise to the need for federal legislation.[52]

Hence, by the early 1960s, it was clear that federal legislation was needed to address the growing crisis over civil rights. Until then, Congress had been reluctant to act. From 1937 to 1950, a flood of civil rights legislation was introduced in Congress. During this time, 252 bills against discrimination were introduced, with 72 presented in the 1949–1950 session alone.[53] However, all of that legislation failed. Blacks were disenfranchised throughout the south, so members of Congress from that region were accountable only to white constituents who favored segregation.[54] Although those southern representatives composed a minority in Congress, it was a powerful minority. Because of the seniority system, staunch segregationists chaired some of the most important committees, including the House Rules Committee and the Senate Judiciary Committee, and those committee chairs did everything in their power to block civil rights legislation.[55] Legislation that bypassed those committees encountered an even more insurmountable obstacle in the Senate—the filibuster, which allowed southern senators to block or weaken legislation.[56] Most importantly, until the late 1950s most northern members of Congress simply lacked the will or the popular support to attack the Jim Crow system of the south.

As the civil rights movement strengthened and expanded to the south in the late 1950s, members of Congress became more responsive to the movement's demands.[57] The number of civil rights bills introduced in Congress increased steadily from 1948 until the early 1960s, but no legislation was successful until dramatic developments in the civil rights movement spurred congressional action.[58] The Montgomery bus boycott of 1956 spurred Congress to enact the first civil rights measure of the twentieth century, the Civil Rights Act of 1957. However, proponents of that bill encountered an insurmountable filibuster in the Senate and were forced to agree to weakening amendments. As a result, the 1957 act's measures were widely regarded as weak and ineffectual.[59] Early sit-in demonstrations throughout the south prompted Congress to enact another civil rights bill in 1960 that also focused primarily on voting rights. That bill met a similar fate because proponents of the bill were once again forced by a filibuster to remove effective enforcement measures.[60] In 1962, the Senate failed to even consider a civil rights bill that had passed the House when it became clear that supporters of the bill did not have the votes for cloture.[61] However, as the civil rights movement gained national prominence, the time was becoming ripe for meaningful federal legislation.

In the spring of 1963, Martin Luther King led protestors in sit-in demonstrations in Birmingham, Alabama, which resulted in massive confrontations with the police, led by Police Chief Bull Connor.[62] Chief Connor's forces responded brutally to the demonstrators, many of whom were children, allowing police dogs to attack and turning fire hoses on the nonviolent activists.[63] Pictures of these events were broadcast on the national news, and public opinion surged in favor of the activists, prompting President John F. Kennedy to act.[64] Kennedy had spoken out in favor of civil rights during his 1960 presidential campaign.[65] Once in office, however, Kennedy was faced with the same problems as his Democratic predecessors—he relied on southern Democrats and did not want to split the party over racial issues.[66] However, as civil rights advocates demanded protection from the federal government, the Kennedy administration became more actively involved in the cause of civil rights. Members of the Department of Justice realized that piecemeal enforcement of Reconstruction Era legislation was insufficient to effect meaningful change and advocated for new legislation.[67]

On June 19, 1963, Kennedy sent a newly strengthened, wide-ranging civil rights bill to Congress, aimed primarily at addressing private discrimination in places of public accommodation.[68] President Kennedy's administration fully committed itself to the success of his bill. Attorney General Robert Kennedy's staff wrote the original bill, and he, Assistant Attorney General Burke Marshall and his deputy Nicholas Katzenbach, were intimately involved throughout the congressional consideration of the bill.[69]

The congressional battle over the 1964 Civil Rights Act was epic, including the longest filibuster in the history of the Senate. The intensity of the congressional debate reflected the fact that the battle over segregation touched a raw nerve with the American public, generating both intense opposition and enthusiastic support. In the south, public opinion was solidly against the legislation because southerners saw it as a threat to their way of life. However, a significant majority of the American public supported the bill throughout the debate, and support grew as the debate wore on. The magnitude of public support for the bill, and the bill's eventual success, was due in large part to the effective advocacy of civil rights leaders who actively participated in the legislative process and in grass roots efforts to foster public support for the bill.

Public opinion in favor of the 1964 Civil Rights Act was informed not only by activists but also by the constant presence of the press at the Senate proceedings. On the first day of the Senate floor consideration of the bill, CBS president Fred Friendly stationed a reporter, Roger Mudd, in front of the capitol to give frequent television and radio updates. As the filibuster wore on, CBS news broadcasts began to show a superimposed clock, ticking off the hours, minutes, and seconds that had passed since the filibuster began.[70] On the day of the cloture vote, as the senators voted on the motion for cloture, Mudd announced each vote live on national television as it was cast.[71] In this way, the national media dramatized the importance of the 1964 Civil Rights Act, undoubtedly intensifying the emotion of the members of Congress involved in the debate and probably contributing to the public support for the act.

The Kennedy administration introduced the Civil Rights Act, then known as H.R. 7152, in the House of Representatives. This choice was due to the fact that the Senate Judiciary chair, James Eastland, was a staunch segregationist, but the chair of the House Judiciary Committee, Emmanuel Celler of New York, was a strong supporter of civil rights.[72] However, the bill had strong adversaries in the House as well. The foremost opponent of H.R. 7152 in the House was Representative Howard Smith, the eighty-year-old segregationist Democratic chairman of the House Rules Committee. Getting past Smith's committee was the most difficult hurdle in the House.[73] Because the congressional Democrats were divided by regional differences, the bill required a bipartisan effort. The bill's sponsors knew that they would need help, and they enlisted a moderate Republican from Ohio, William McCulloch. Over the Fourth of July recess following the introduction of the bill, Deputy Attorney General Burke Marshall traveled to Piqua, Ohio, McCulloch's hometown, to enlist his support. McCulloch made a commitment to back H.R. 7152, but on the condition that the administration not back down in the Senate and agree to weakening amendments. Marshall gave his word, and a key alliance between liberal Democrats and moderate Republicans was formed in the House.[74]

That Fourth of July break was important to the bill's success for another reason. Members of Congress who visited their districts throughout the country learned that their constituents had heard of the bill and that they liked it.[75] Their experience was reflected in polls taken during the summer of 1963, which revealed that a majority of whites supported the president, although they thought he was moving too fast. Perhaps even more significant, a July 1963 *Newsweek* article revealed that 40 percent of blacks had taken part in some civil rights demonstration.[76] Whites favored civil rights, and blacks demanded them. In August 1963, civil rights leaders including Martin Luther King and Bayard Rustin staged a March on Washington in which the participants called for federal civil rights legislation.[77] In September, many members of the House of Representatives returned to work ready to act on civil rights.

Tragic events in the fall of 1963 also contributed to the success of H.R 7152. On September 15, 1963, a bomb ripped through the Sixteenth Street Baptist Church in Birmingham, Alabama, killing four young girls who were attending Sunday school.[78] That event shocked the American public and strengthened the commitment to civil rights of the members of the House Judiciary subcommittee who were then considering the bill. In the weeks following the bombing, the subcommittee adopted several strengthening amendments, including the addition of Title VII's protections against employment discrimination and a provision empowering the attorney general to enforce the act.[79]

The second tragic event, of course, was the assassination of President John Kennedy on November 22, 1963. Grieving members of Congress worried that Kennedy's assassination could signal the end of H.R. 7152. Johnson had not been a strong supporter of civil rights when he was in the Senate, and he had shown himself willing to compromise on weakened legislation in 1957.[80] In retrospect, however, Kennedy's assassination may have been the single largest contributor to the ultimate success of the bill. The bill was widely viewed as Kennedy's legacy because he had supported it so strongly shortly before his death. Sympathy for Kennedy generated increased popular support for its provisions. Moreover, immediately upon becoming president, Johnson embraced the legislation and the cause of civil rights. In a nationwide television address on Thanksgiving Day, less than a week after Kennedy's assassination, Johnson said that civil rights legislation was necessary,[81] and Johnson's first State of the Union address echoed this commitment.[82] In retrospect, both supporters and opponents of H.R. 7152 agreed that Johnson's involvement was the most important factor to achieving the success of the bill.[83]

During their Christmas break following President Kennedy's assassination, members of Congress found that their constituents supported the bill and that they blamed Congress for not enacting it. Polls taken during this time showed that 62 percent of the general public supported H.R. 7152.[84] The popular support for the bill put pressure on the segregationist chair of the House Rules Committee, the bill's archenemy, Howard Smith, to relinquish control over the bill and allow his committee to consider, and eventually approve, the bill.[85] At the beginning of February 1964, the House considered the bill, with its opponents offering many amendments to weaken it, most of which were rejected.

The most significant amendment to H.R. 7152, the addition of "sex" as a protected category in Title VII, was proposed by the bill's archenemy, Howard Smith. Smith intended the amendment not to strengthen but to sink the bill.[86] However, to Smith's surprise, his proposed amendment was immediately greeted by an outpouring of support for the Bill from the female members of the House. For example, Martha Griffiths, a Democrat from Michigan, rose in support, arguing that if Title VII did not prohibit sex discrimination:

> White women will be last at the hiring gate. . . . You are going . . . to have white men in one bracket, you are going to take colored men and colored women and give them equal employment rights, and down at the bottom of the list is going to be a white woman with no rights at all. . . . A vote against this amendment today by a white man is a vote against his wife, or his widow, or his daughter, or his sister.[87]

A number of other female members of Congress agreed.[88] The only woman who opposed the amendment, Representative Edith Green, a Democrat from Oregon, was a supporter of the bill who explained that she did not want to take any action that would jeopardize the bill.[89]

Other supporters of the bill, including Representatives Manny Celler, Bill McCulloch, and John Lindsay, protested that the amendment was inopportune, but it passed, 168 to 133.

The addition of "sex" as a class protected by Title VII was highly significant. Thanks to that amendment, H.R. 7152 covered over 100 million people, rather than the 20 million it would have covered had it only applied to race, and it was an important influence on the feminist movement in the late 1960s and early 1970s.[90] Although the adoption of the amendment appeared haphazard, it was more carefully planned than was apparent from the public debate. Several years after the enactment of the bill, Representative Martha Griffiths told an interviewer that she originally had intended to sponsor the amendment but held off when she heard of Smith's intent to introduce it. She knew it would get many more votes, including the votes of one hundred southern Democrats, if Smith introduced the amendment instead of her, and that she needed those votes to get it passed since civil rights supporters such as Representatives Cellers and McCulloch opposed the amendment.[91] Notwithstanding the fears of the proponents of H.R. 7152, adopting the amendment turned out to be a gamble that paid off. On February 10, 1964, the House adopted the bill by a vote of 290 to 130, without any significant weakening amendments.[92] H.R. 7152 proceeded to the Senate, where it would face one of the longest and toughest legislative battles in congressional history.[93]

When H.R. 7152 arrived in the Senate, Senate Leader Mike Mansfield declared, "The time is now. The crossroads is here in the Senate."[94] As Mansfield well knew, any civil rights bill would face formidable obstacles in the Senate. The Senate Judiciary Committee, chaired by James Eastland, was known as the "graveyard" of civil rights legislation.[95] Any legislation that made it out of that committee would face a certain filibuster, with opponents of the bill led by Senate Minority Leader Dick Russell, a Georgia Democrat who strongly believed in segregation and white supremacy.[96] All civil rights legislation faced these barriers, but H.R. 7152 was not just "any" legislation; it was the most sweeping civil rights legislation considered in Congress since Reconstruction. Southern senators viewed the bill as an attack on their entire way of life, and they vowed to use every effort to fight off that attack.[97]

Supporters of the bill in the Senate knew that defeating the filibuster would take a major effort that required organization and cooperation.

Mansfield appointed Senator Hubert Humphrey, a Democrat from Minnesota and long-time supporter of civil rights, as the floor manager for H.R. 7152.[98] Humphrey was joined by Minority Whip Thomas Kuchel, a Republican from California and former protégé of Earl Warren.[99] Humphrey and Kuchel set up a bipartisan team of senators to shepherd the bill.[100] They adopted a new strategy to overcome the filibuster that was certain to come. Simply wearing out their opponents had failed in 1957, 1960, and 1962, so they decided to try to work for cloture, a procedure to end debate that requires a two-third majority vote.[101] Cloture was a risky option. Twenty-eight cloture votes had been taken since 1917, and only five had succeeded. Cloture had been tried, and failed, eleven times for civil rights bills.[102] Given the magnitude of their task, the Senate leaders also knew that rallying public opinion would be crucial to their effort. In March 1964, Humphrey and Kuchel met with church representatives and the Leadership Conference on Civil Rights to plan a rally in support of the bill, and they planned civil rights meetings all over the country. They also made sure that supporters of the bill had frequent access to the media.[103]

From the outset, it was clear that attaining cloture would be extremely difficult. Senate leaders planned to bypass the Judiciary Committee and bring the bill directly to the Senate floor.[104] Yet even the motion to bypass was filibustered for three weeks before the Senate as a whole was able to consider the bill, and the filibuster over the consideration of the bill lasted eighty-two days.[105] The filibuster was a grueling experience for the supporters of the bill. Throughout the filibuster, no other business was conducted in Congress. Members of the Senate were required to stay around, however, because their filibustering colleagues could, and did, call for a quorum vote at any time.[106]

As in the House, Senate leaders knew that a bipartisan effort would be needed to overcome the filibuster. In this regard, the most important member of the Senate was Illinois Senator Everett Dirksen, a conservative Republican from Illinois. Dirksen was widely respected and could bring enough votes to achieve cloture. Johnson and his advisers knew that convincing Dirksen to support the bill was crucial,[107] but they were also aware that Dirksen opposed Title II and Title VII and that getting his support would be difficult without making major concessions that would offend their allies in the House of Representatives.[108] Humphrey developed a strategy for winning Dirksen's support. Humphrey understood that Dirksen was getting near the end of his career and thinking about his place in history and correctly anticipated that Dirksen would like the idea of being a hero for the bill.[109]

Throughout the spring of 1964, as the filibuster wore on, Humphrey gave most of his attention to winning Dirksen's support for the bill. On April 20, that effort paid off.[110] Dirksen offered several amendments to the bill and made it clear that he would support the bill if his amendments were adopted.[111] Dirksen's principal amendments limited the authority of the Department of Justice to file suit when addressing "patterns or practice" of discrimination and permitted an initial period of state jurisdiction over cases arising under Title II and Title VII. Humphrey made it clear that they would only make those changes if Dirksen agreed to cloture on the entire bill. On May 19, Dirksen agreed and made a public appearance in support of the bill, setting the stage for the cloture vote.[112] Once he had changed his mind, Dirksen threw himself behind the bill and devoted himself wholeheartedly to its passage. Dirksen's involvement was crucial to the success of the bill because of his leadership qualities and because his amendments made the bill palatable to the moderates and conservatives who until then had been undecided.[113]

The cloture vote was held on June 10, 1964. It was a dramatic day in congressional history. Senator Robert Byrd, a former member of the Ku Klux Klan, ended the filibuster with a speech that lasted all night long.[114] Before the cloture vote, Senator Richard Russell stated one more time, "We have opposed [the bill] because the broad abdication of power and authority by the legislative branch that it provides would destroy forever the doctrine of separation of powers." Senator Humphrey responded that members of the Senate would "make that dream of full freedom, and full justice, and full citizenship for every American a reality."[115] As the savior of the bill in the Senate, Dirksen was allowed to give the final speech before the vote. He said, "The time has come for equality of opportunity in sharing the government, in education, and in employment. It must not be stayed or denied." Dirksen compared the bill to other landmark legislation, including the Pure Food and Drugs Act, creation of the civil service system, the eight-hour workday, the direct election of senators, the women's right to vote—all of which ultimately had become law because "their time has come."[116] The final tally was 71 to 29. Thus ended the longest filibuster in the history of the U.S. Senate.[117] It was the first successful cloture vote of a civil rights measure in the history of the Senate.

After the cloture vote, the vote on the bill, held June 19, 1964, was almost anticlimactic. The vote on the bill in the Senate was 73 to 27, and the bill returned to the House, where the vote in favor of the bill, 289 to 126, took place on July 2, 1964. President Johnson signed the bill that night, saying of the bill, "Its purpose is not to divide, but to end divisions—divisions which have lasted too long. Its purpose is national, not regional. Its purpose is to promote a more abiding commitment to freedom, a more constant pursuit of justice, and a deeper respect for human dignity."[118]

Hence, the congressional debate over the 1964 Civil Rights Act was long and dramatic. This was due to the fact that during that debate, members of Congress addressed both fundamental constitutional issues and the fundamental values that underlie American society. Both sides understood the historic nature of their debate. Proponents of the bill saw themselves as completing the work of the Reconstruction Era Congress. Opponents of the bill saw themselves as protecting the southern way of life based on racial segregation. These dynamics prompted a spirited constitutional debate.

Republican supporters of civil rights were especially eager to point out the link between themselves and their early Republican predecessors who had drafted the Fourteenth Amendment and the Reconstruction Era civil rights legislation.[119] Former President Dwight Eisenhower evoked his vision when he expressed his public support for the bill in a May 1964 letter to the *New York Herald Tribune*. In the letter, Eisenhower argued that because the Republican Party was the party of Lincoln, Republican members of Congress had a special obligation "to be vigorous in the furtherance of civil rights."[120] This connection showed itself most strongly during the debate over the proper constitutional source for the 1964 bill. Many Republican supporters of civil rights initially wanted to base the bill in the Fourteenth Amendment, which they saw as their historical legacy.[121]

Congressional supporters of the 1964 Civil Rights Act evoked not only the spirit of their Reconstruction Era predecessors but also their constitutional vision of ensuring the belonging, protection, and equality of federal citizens.[122] During Reconstruction, this vision was often expressed by Representative John Bingham, and by Senator Fessenden of Maine, speaking for the Joint Committee on Reconstruction, who stated that the goal of the Fourteenth Amendment was the equal participation of all in the rights of citizenship.[123] Other members of the

Reconstruction Congress wanted the Amendment to protect "the rights and privileges of citizens,"[124] "the personal and natural rights of citizens,"[125] the "fundamental rights of citizens,"[126] and the "civil rights of citizens."[127]

In 1963 and 1964, members of Congress evoked the language of their Reconstruction Era predecessors when explaining the need for the civil rights bill. For example, in a speech introducing the bill to the House, Ohio Congressman William McCulloch explained, "an obligation rests with the national government to see that the citizens of every state are treated equally without regard to their race or color or religion or national origin."[128] Similarly, Representative Archie Moore argued, "The right to be free from all forms of racial intolerance is so fundamentally the privilege of each and every citizen of the United States that it cannot be made the plaything of politics."[129] In stump speeches promoting the bill to the public, Senator Hubert Humphrey often evoked what he called "the citizenship gap," contrasting the gap between the rights of white and black citizens in the United States.[130] Senator Everett Dirksen probably summed it up best in his final speech before the Senate vote on the bill: "There is involved here the citizenship of the people under the Constitution who, by the 14th Amendment, are . . . citizens of the United States of America. That is what we deal with here. We are confronted with the challenge, and we must reckon with it."[131]

Opponents also evoked the Reconstruction Era, relying on negative images of that period to illustrate their arguments against the bill. Throughout debate on the bill, southern members of Congress compared it to Reconstruction legislation, calling the bill a "reinvasion" of the south that was comparable to Reconstruction.[132] For example, the foremost opponent of the bill in the Senate, Richard Russell of Georgia, was a Civil War buff who brought up images of that war in response to any civil rights proposal. In debates over civil rights measures, Russell would evoke images of the brave southern soldiers who fought in the Civil War, Sherman's march, the tyranny of northern Reconstruction, the removal of northern troops, and the restoration of white supremacy.[133] According to Russell, the 1964 act was "much more drastic than any bill ever presented during the days of Reconstruction. . . . [N]o member of the Reconstruction Congress, no matter how radical, would have dared to present a proposal that would have given such vast governmental control over free enterprise in this country."[134] Hence, even as proponents of the bill embraced the history of the Reconstruction

Era, southern opponents rejected that history with equally strong emotion and refused to compromise on its provisions.[135]

Proponents of the bill harked back not only to Reconstruction but also to a more recent era in which Congress legislated to protect rights of belonging, the New Deal. During the New Deal, the president and Congress had used their federal power to solve a national crisis, creating a precedent for Congress to act to address the crisis in race relations that it faced in the early 1960s. However, the New Deal Congress had excluded many blacks from the protections of its labor and social legislation.[136] The New Deal Congress expanded the use of the commerce power to create economic rights, and in 1964, in Title VII, Congress relied on that power to protect not only the right to racial equality but also the economic right to work free of discrimination. Proponents of H.R. 7152 argued that race discrimination had deep economic roots and a strongly negative effect on the United States economy. They also pointed out that the commerce clause had often been used to legislate on moral grounds, citing legislation prohibiting, among other things, kidnapping, child labor, and adulterated food.[137] Hence, the 1964 act addressed the intersection of economic and racial equality that Congress had avoided during the New Deal Era.

Clearly, then, members of the 1964 Congress knew that the 1964 Civil Rights Act had a special constitutional meaning, and that their actions were reminiscent of those of the Reconstruction and New Deal Congresses before them. In both of those periods, members of Congress took a leading role in protecting rights of belonging and effecting constitutional change. In 1964, members of Congress realized that the protections of the earlier eras were insufficient to protect the rights of minorities. Continuing in the tradition of their predecessors, they claimed the constitution for themselves as they legislated to enforce its protections of individual rights and equality norms.

Members of Congress engaged in extensive debates over the constitutionality of H.R. 7152, a debate in which participants disputed fundamental constitutional values. Proponents of the act believed that it was an appropriate measure to enforce the equality norms of the Fourteenth Amendment and to use the commerce power to address deep-seated economic issues that resulted from racial discrimination. However, they recognized the need to get around important constitutional roadblocks that had been created by Supreme Court rulings. Opponents raised numerous constitutional objections to the bill, invoking the state action requirement, individual rights, and structural provisions during congressional debates.

The principal constitutional obstacle to H.R. 7152 was the state action doctrine. Title II, the public accommodations provision of the bill, was similar to the 1875 Civil Rights Bill that the Court had struck down in the *Civil Rights Cases*.[138] In that case, the Court held that congressional power to enforce the Fourteenth Amendment could not be used to criminalize private discrimination because it was restricted to addressing state action. Members of Congress were reluctant to challenge the Court's ruling in the *Civil Rights Cases,* and many thus felt constrained from using their Section Five enforcement power to remedy private discrimination. Instead, they relied primarily on their power to regulate interstate commerce pursuant to the commerce clause, which contains no state action limitation. After the New Deal, the Court had adopted a highly deferential stance to the commerce power, and Kennedy administration officials advocated the use of the commerce power for that reason.[139] In addition, many members of Congress pointed out the economic impact of discrimination, including its toll on the ability of African Americans to travel and obtain employment.[140] It is clear from the congressional debates that the act was about both equality and economic rights.

Other supporters of the bill initially resisted the use of the commerce power, because they believed that the bill was intended primarily to enforce equality norms. For example, Senator John Sherman Cooper argued, "If there is a right to the equal use of accommodations held out to the public, it is a right of citizenship and a Constitutional right under the Fourteenth Amendment. It has nothing to do with whether a business is in interstate commerce. . . . Rights under the Constitution go to the equality of all citizens, the integrity and dignity of the individual, and should not be placed on any lesser ground."[141] They argued that the state action requirement could be met by state licensing, or through a *"Shelley v. Kraemer"* type enforcement theory.[142] Some Republicans opposed resort to the commerce clause because they linked it to Democratic New Deal economic legislation, such as the Wagner Act and the Fair Labor Standards Act, legislation based on the commerce clause that they had opposed. Therefore, they instinctively resisted further expansion of the clause.[143]

Many of the congressional opponents of the use of the commerce power were persuaded by the brief of Harvard Law professor Paul

Freund, which Robert Kennedy relied on when he testified before the Senate Commerce and Judiciary Committees during the summer and fall of 1963. Freund and Kennedy pointed out that the state action theory that Republicans had supported would have far-reaching effects if it was adopted by the Supreme Court. The result would be that any private discrimination would violate the Fourteenth Amendment, which would have an extremely broad impact on free enterprise. Relying on the commerce clause would allow Congress to more carefully calibrate the scope of the bill.[144] In the end, members of Congress adopted a compromise, proposed by New York Representative Kenneth Keating, to base the bill on both Section Five and the commerce power.[145]

Opponents often cited the *Civil Rights Cases* to argue that the bill was unconstitutional, contending that H.R. 7152 was essentially the same legislation that the Court had rejected in the *Civil Rights Cases*.[146] The southern critique of the bill also raised numerous other constitutional issues. First and foremost, they argued that the bill violated basic principles of federalism and separation of powers, and they claimed that the bill would establish a centralized government. For example, Senator Ed Willis called the bill "the most drastic and far-reaching proposal and grab for power ever to be reported out of a committee of Congress in the history of our Republic."[147] Senator William Tuck predicted that it "would confer upon the attorney general autocratic powers such as may benefit a commissar of justice in a totalitarian country," and Richard Russell explained, "We have opposed (this bill) because the broad abdication of power and authority by the legislative branch that it provides would destroy forever the doctrine of separation of powers."[148] Similarly, one of the only nonsouthern senators to vote against it, presidential candidate Barry Goldwater of Arizona argued that the bill "will require the creation of a federal police force of mammoth proportions."[149]

Opponents of the bill also claimed that it violated several individual rights. First, they claimed that it represented an invasion of private property rights, which included a "natural right to discriminate."[150] This critique echoed the most popular theme of opponents outside of Congress, who focused primarily on property rights. For example, Lester Maddox, the owner of the Pickrick Restaurant in Atlanta, was more combative but his argument was the same: "I knew then just as I know now, that I was trying to protect not only the rights of Lester Maddox, but of every citizen, including the three men I chased off my property, for if they could violate my right of private property, then there would

Loevy has argued, "It can be said of the Civil Rights Act of 1964 that, short of a declaration of war, no other Act of Congress had a more violent background—a background of confrontation, official violence, injury, murder that has few parallels in American history."[159] Second, the activists of the civil rights movement had a crucial role in creating a political atmosphere that was conducive to congressional action on their behalf. Passage of the bill became a national issue, with public support at a level that mirrored the super-majority vote that was necessary for the bill's success in Congress.[160] Third, the bill owed its success to the strategy of civil rights activists to convince lawmakers that the issue of civil rights was a moral issue.

Many of the bill's supporters themselves held a strong commitment to civil rights and believed that the bill's passage was a moral imperative. As Senator Humphrey explained while speaking in opposition to the filibuster, they saw passage of the bill as a "national issue. . . . [I]t is above all a moral issue, and not merely a political issue."[161] Some congressional leaders, including Hubert Humphrey, Manny Celler, Jacob Javitz, and John Lindsay, had long publicly supported the cause of civil rights. Charles Halleck reported that he came to believe in the cause of civil rights because of contact with African Americans who had suffered in the Jim Crow system. Others, such as Bill McCulloch and Clarence Brown, both of Ohio, cited the abolitionist tradition in their home states as reasons for supporting H.R. 7152.[162] The deeply held convictions of members of Congress on both sides of the bill contributed significantly to the tenor of the constitutional debate over the 1964 Civil Rights Act.

Civil rights activists also played an important part in the process of enacting the legislation. Civil rights and labor lobbyists had worked incessantly on getting the bill enacted and were intimately involved in the success of the effort. As early as July 1963, United Auto Workers president Walter Reuther had organized a meeting of labor and civil rights leaders to set up a "super lobby" to get the bill passed.[163] In the summer and fall of 1963, members of the Leadership Conference on Civil Rights met with Presidents Johnson and Kennedy a number of times and engaged in a national effort to drum up popular support for the bill.[164] Civil rights lobbyists Clarence Mitchell and Joseph Rauh, Jr.,[165] met often with House leaders while the bill was pending in the House, and while the bill was pending in the Senate, they were invited to weekly strategy sessions held by the Senate leaders.[166]

be nothing to prevent me from violating theirs."[151] Second, they argued that the bill violated individual freedom of association. Said Senator Strom Thurmond of South Carolina: "Freedom of the individual to choose his associates or his neighbors; to use and dispose of his property as he sees fit; to be irrational arbitrary and capricious, even unjust in his personal relations are things all entitled to a large measure of protection from government interference."[152] Hence, opponents of the bill championed individual property and liberty rights to oppose the equality rights that the statute represented.

Congressional proponents of the act largely ignored the property rights critique. Instead, they spoke more directly to the federalism-based critique, pointing out that many states already had provisions similar to those of the act, but arguing that federal enforcement was needed to ensure uniformity of rights. For example, Senator Clark pointed out that twenty-eight states and forty-eight cities already had enacted legislation toward fair employment practices, but added, "[N]ot a single state of the Old Confederacy has such a law. This is perhaps the most cogent argument in support of Title VII. Roughly 60 percent of the non-white population lives in 22 states where there are no FEPC laws." In Clark's view, these statistics illustrated the need for nationally uniform regulation.[153]

Thus, in 1963 and 1964, members of Congress were consumed by a debate over the meaning of equality, citizenship, individual rights, and the structure of our government. This congressional debate was also a debate over the meaning of what it is to be American. Northern members of Congress saw segregation as antithetical to the American way of life, yet southern members of Congress saw it as central to their American way of life. While neither side convinced the other of the correctness of their position, these debates eventually were resolved by the mechanism of the democratic process. The success of the act gave a congressional stamp of approval to the constitutional vision of the act's proponents, one of broad congressional power to protect rights of belonging, in which the principle of racial equality trumped property and states' rights. A majority in the 1964 Congress rejected, for once and for all, the idea that common law property rights included the right to discriminate on the basis of race.[154]

The 1964 Civil Rights Act not only established a federal commitment to racial justice and created an effective enforcement mechanism to carry out that goal, but it also marked a reconfiguration of federalism norms. Like the key provisions of the Reconstruction Era and New Deal legislation, the 1964 act greatly enhanced federal power to protect rights of belonging. In negotiating the bill, members of Congress carefully worked out a compromise balancing state and federal power to protect rights of belonging. For example, the key breakthrough in the Senate debate was the adoption of Dirksen's amendment that gave first priority to the rights enforcement of state administrative agencies, reducing the extent of the federal bureaucracy necessary to enforce the act, and ensuring a state role in the protection of civil rights. Thus, the 1964 Civil Rights Act became a constitutional milestone, reinforcing the enduring role of Congress as a protector of rights of belonging and altering the structure of federalism by empowering the federal government to protect those rights, while maintaining a sphere of state autonomy to do the same.

By enacting the 1964 Civil Rights Act, Congress resolved two areas of constitutional uncertainty, whether race discrimination could be legal anywhere in the country, and whether Congress had the power to address private discrimination. The act resolved that uncertainty by establishing a nationally uniform policy against racial discrimination and a congressional commitment to enforcing equality rights against private discrimination.[155] While members of Congress did not directly challenge the Court's decision in the *Civil Rights Cases,* it is arguable that the act constituted a de facto overruling of the state action requirement established by that case.[156] By relying on the commerce power, however, Congress avoided confronting the Court or testing the Court's precedent-limiting Section Five. Nonetheless, the bill marked a commitment to congressional enforcement of equality norms and to federal protection of minority rights against public and private infringement.[157] Ultimately, the success of the 1964 Civil Rights Act signaled that "the struggle against discrimination by private actors had become a legitimate end of the federal government."[158]

The story of the 1964 Civil Rights Act is therefore one of political actors responding to strong political pressure for legislation to create equal rights for minorities in this country. Three factors contributed to the passage of the bill, despite the many obstacles that it confronted. First, the inconvenience felt by the members of Congress during the filibuster were nothing compared to the sacrifices of the civil rights leaders and rank and file who were engaged in a public, brutal struggle with southern segregationists throughout the debate over the bill. As Robert

Civil rights lobbyists also helped out with the mundane details of the battle to enact H.R. 7152. For example, during the House debate, the Leadership Conference on Civil Rights helped maintain discipline by posting people in the audience to report when a member was absent from the floor at a significant moment. When they spotted someone, they reported him or her to the Democratic Study Group, a group of House Democrats who followed up by hunting that member down and getting him or her to the floor.[167] Civil rights activists also had an important role in the defeat of weakening amendments in the House of Representatives. Throughout the amendment process, they packed the gallery, and members of Congress took note. "All I could see was a sea of Black faces," said one representative; "I couldn't tell, therefore, whether my constituent was there or not, so I didn't take any chances. I voted on all of the Amendments."[168] In this way, even the rank and file activists played an important part in shaping the 1964 act. Rauh, Mitchell, and the other lobbyists from the Leadership Conference also had an impact on the content of H.R. 7152. The civil rights leaders demanded federal enforcement, and the labor leaders demanded equal employment opportunity provisions. They were successful at convincing their Senate allies not to budge on those issues.[169]

While these lobbyists were working behind the scenes, civil rights and religious leaders organized grass roots support throughout the country. Martin Luther King and his supporters stepped up public demonstrations demanding change, and both supporters and opponents of the bill referred to those demonstrations throughout the debate over the bill.[170] In a less high-profile effort, the National Council of Churches organized a grass roots campaign, urging church members to contact their senators and contacting influential people in senators' communities to aid in lobbying. The religious leaders placed their opponents on the defensive, and they were quite persuasive, convincing some of the most conservative members of Congress to support the bill on religious and moral grounds.[171] Adding drama to this effort, starting on April 19, 1964, theology students from all denominations engaged in a round-the-clock prayer vigil at the Lincoln Memorial that would continue until the bill cleared the Senate.[172] Rauh and Humphrey both cited the support of the National Council of Churches as extremely helpful in building national support.[173] These activists worked tirelessly to expand rights of belonging, and they were successful at the political level.

Immediately after President Johnson signed H.R. 7152 into law, it was challenged on constitutional grounds.[174] The federal courts heard the cases on an expedited basis, and in October 1964, the Supreme Court heard oral arguments on the constitutionality of the act.[175] The oral arguments before the Court echoed the constitutional debate that already had taken place in Congress, but the arguments before the Court were much more constrained than the congressional debate. Arguing on behalf of the act's constitutionality, Assistant Attorney General Burke Marshall focused almost exclusively on the question of whether the act was a justifiable use of Congress's commerce power. In oral argument, Marshall compared the 1964 act to the Wagner Act, arguing that the Civil Rights Act was similar "in the sense that it was intended to deal with a national problem that had been marked by a good deal of emotion and controversy and even violence in the streets."[176] Thus, Marshall evoked a connection between two of the most important statutes expanding rights of belonging in this country, urging the Court to take as deferential an approach to this statute as it eventually had toward the Wagner Act.

Attorneys for the act's challengers, like the congressional opponents of the act before them, primarily stressed property rights arguments, claiming that the act took away the property rights of business owners without due process of law. In his brief, Roger Smith, counsel for Ollie's Barbecue, argued, "It has long been assumed that a businessman, as an incident of the right to use and control property as he wishes, may deal with or refuse to deal with whomever he pleases."[177] Challengers also raised federalism-based arguments, claiming that the bill amounted to congressional overreaching. For example, at the oral argument before the trial court on the plaintiffs' motion for an injunction, plaintiff Moreton Rolleston, the owner of the Heart of Atlanta Motel, maintained that he was essentially bringing an ideological protest against the expansion of power of the federal government. "We could get along with Negro guests. . . . But the next step after this act, there may be just one more step, that's taking over all legislation by Congress, so setting up the stage for a dictatorship by Congress."[178] Before the Supreme Court, Rolleston also emphasized property rights and federalism, avoiding a discussion of the commerce clause.[179]

The Supreme Court upheld the 1964 Civil Rights Act in *Heart of Atlanta Motel v. United States*[180] and *Katzenbach v. McClung*[181] as falling within Congress's commerce power.[182] Although the vote within the Court in *Heart of Atlanta Motel* to uphold the act was unanimous, members of the Court were not unanimous in their reasoning as to why the act was constitutional. The Court's decision echoed the congressional debate over the proper source of the act. All of the justices agreed that the act was a proper exercise of Congress's power to regulate interstate commerce, but two members of the Court, Justices Goldberg and Douglas, also felt that it was a proper exercise of congressional power under Section Five. Justice Douglas's concurrence noted that he was "somewhat reluctant to rest solely on the Commerce Clause" and explained that he would have preferred to uphold the act as an appropriate use of Section Five power to protect the rights of federal citizenship.[183] Justice Goldberg agreed with Douglas, emphasizing that the primary purpose of the act was "the vindication of human dignity and not mere economics."[184] However, the other seven members of the Court were content to rest their decision on the commerce clause, and Justice Clark, author of the majority opinion, confined himself to a discussion of Congress's commerce power.[185]

Thus, the Court's consideration of the constitutional issues raised by the 1964 Civil Rights Act was considerably more narrowly focused than the constitutional debate that occurred in Congress. The Court appropriately focused solely on the issue of whether Congress had the power to enact the statute, rather than rehashing the issues of constitutional policy considered by members of Congress. Most notable is the Court's deferential approach to congressional power to make those determinations and act to protect minority rights. As Robert Post and Reva Siegel have argued, this deferential approach illustrates the fact that the Warren Court saw Congress as a partner in making its vision of the Fourteenth Amendment "more firmly law."[186]

Even before the Court upheld the 1964 Civil Rights Act, the public response to the act was markedly different than the response to *Brown*. Administration officials and civil rights advocates had all expected the act to be met with massive resistance, as had the Supreme Court's ruling in *Brown*. As the 1964 Civil Rights Act neared passage, President Johnson voiced his concern that government enforcement of the act would meet massive resistance in the south. On June 19, when the bill passed the Senate, Johnson said to Roy Wilkins, the NAACP chair, "Our troubles are just beginning. I guess you know that."[187] This time, the leaders were overly pessimistic. Initially, southern political leaders such as George Wallace condemned the act, and some opponents vowed not to comply but to resist the act.[188] For example, Louis W. Hollis, a Jackson

Mississippi official of the segregationist Citizens' Councils of America, warned that noncompliance would be like the Prohibition era: "Most businessmen feel that the law is unconstitutional and are going to treat it like they did the Supreme Court decision of May 17, 1954. . . . [I]t will be like the speakeasies of Prohibition when people went on drinking as if there was no prohibition."[189] However, these predictions proved to be unfounded.

Although court challenges were filed the day after the 1964 Civil Rights Act was signed, by and large from the start, business owners complied with Title II of the act, which prohibited race discrimination in public accommodations. The anticipated resistance to Title II simply did not materialize. Once they had lost, a few southern senators, including Herman Talmadge of Georgia and Allen Ellender of Louisiana, urged their supporters to comply with the law,[190] and even in cities in the deep south such as Birmingham, most places of public accommodation quietly complied. The NAACP's Constance Baker Motley reported that voluntary compliance had been "unexpectedly good. I would have lost every penny I've got if I had made a bet."[191]

After the Supreme Court upheld the bill in December 1964, business compliance with Title II was virtually universal.[192] An editorial in the *Atlanta Constitution* stated that the "cause of orderly government can only be served now by acceptance of the law." Presidents of the Atlanta Motel and Restaurants Associations said that their members would obey the law. Prominent restaurant owner Lester Maddox initially refused to follow the Court's order, and he eventually closed down his restaurant and ran for governor. His success in that campaign reflects residual opposition to the federal nondiscrimination mandate.[193] Employers quietly resisted the desegregation mandate of Title VII, which has been the subject of numerous and continued disputes over its mandates, especially in the area of affirmative action.[194] However, in the area of public accommodations and education, the rapid pace of the acceptance of the validity of the 1964 act by the majority of people in the south was truly amazing compared with the decade of strife and noncompliance that followed the Court's ruling in *Brown*.[195]

Like the Court's ruling in *Brown*, the 1964 Civil Rights Act functioned as a constitutional milestone because, like court decisions, statutes have precedential value. Statutory precedent does not have the same binding impact on legislatures as court precedents have on courts, but a statute can certainly influence the future actions of lawmakers.

The 1964 Civil Rights Act set the precedent for Congress to legislate broadly to protect rights of belonging, and this precedent influenced congressional action for the following quarter century. The success in overcoming the filibuster of a major civil rights bill empowered congressional supporters of civil rights legislation. Congressional leaders realized that it was possible to overcome filibusters of civil rights measures, and the American people continued to demand change. After the success of the 1964 Civil Rights Act, "a political logic took hold in which the elected branches of government perceived distinct rewards for approving civil rights legislation."[196] Since then, a national consensus has emerged that recognizes protecting minority rights as a central conviction of the federal government.[197]

The 1964 Civil Rights Act thus represents a paradigm for congressional action to protect the rights of the American people. Beginning in 1964, statutes became central to the nation's civil rights agenda.[198] Having embraced the cause of protecting civil rights in the 1964 act, members of Congress then expanded their definition of civil rights in subsequent legislation. Most significantly, one year later, Congress enacted the Voting Rights Act of 1965, which gave teeth to the Fifteenth Amendment's prohibition of race-based denials of the franchise. Like the 1964 act, the voting rights bill also responded to the demands of civil rights activists, for whom registration of black southern voters was a top priority.[199] The Voting Rights Act was arguably even more significant than the 1964 Civil Rights Act because federal enforcement enabled blacks to vote throughout the south, finally allowing them to engage in the mainstream political process.[200] As southern blacks started to vote, they encouraged Congress to continue to act to enforce equality norms throughout the following decade.

By the mid 1970s, Congress had adopted the most far-reaching measures to protect rights of belonging in our history. Other legislation prohibiting discrimination on the basis of race includes the Fair Housing Act, which prohibits race discrimination in real estate transactions,[201] and the Equal Credit Opportunity Act of 1974.[202] In the late 1960s, the women's rights movement gained momentum, and Congress responded by enacting multiple pieces of legislation prohibiting discrimination on the basis of gender, including Title IX of the Education Amendments of 1972 and the Pregnancy Discrimination Act of 1998.[203] During this period, Congress expanded the classifications of people whose rights were entitled to protection, prohibiting discrimination against the disabled[204] and the elderly,[205] and requiring that public education be accessible to disabled children.[206] Congress was not solely concerned with anti-discrimination law during this era. In the mid 1960s, Congress also enacted President Johnson's Great Society program, a body of legislation to help the poor.[207] Congress also enacted more antipoverty legislation in 1968, responding to the rash of urban riots following the assassination of Martin Luther King.[208] Like Title VII of the 1964 Civil Rights Act, this legislation combined racial and economic rights.

The cooperation between the Court and Congress also initially extended beyond the Court's ruling upholding the 1964 act. Throughout the 1960s and early 1970s, both the Court and Congress acted to expand rights of belonging.[209] Like Congress, the Court expanded its notion of classes protected by the equal protection clause, finding gender, sometimes alienage, and "illegitimacy" to be protected classes warranting heightened scrutiny in equal protection challenges.[210] The Court also played a part in creating the historical and political circumstances that fostered civil rights legislation.[211] Aside from the obvious example of *Brown*, the Court also issued numerous rulings that enabled the civil rights movement to function effectively. Notable cases supporting the civil rights movement include the Court's holding that membership in the NAACP was protected by the First Amendment in *NAACP v. Button*,[212] its decision that civil rights leaders could not be sued for libel absent a showing of "actual malice" in *New York Times Co. v. Sullivan*,[213] and the Court's holding preventing states from raising "procedural subterfuges" to deny civil rights advocates review of their First Amendment claims in *NAACP v. Alabama ex rel Patterson*.[214]

Finally, The Warren Court also read congressional power to protect civil rights broadly during this era, enabling Congress's proactive approach toward those rights. In *Heart of Atlanta Motel*, the Court defined the limits of the commerce power broadly, allowing Congress wide latitude to shape antidiscrimination law.[215] The Court applied the deferential "rational basis" test to Congress's Section Five power and Congress's power to enforce the Fifteenth Amendment when it upheld the 1965 Voting Rights Act.[216] The Court also applied a deferential approach to Congress's power to enforce the Thirteenth Amendment, holding that Congress could use that power to address what *Congress* considered to be the badges and incidents of slavery.[217] The Court's deference to Congress undoubtedly also influenced members of Congress in considering the 1964 act, who were deferential to the Court during their deliberations.

Proponents of the bill struggled with the Court-imposed state action requirement, which they saw as the chief constitutional obstacle to the act. They chafed at the restrictions on congressional power imposed by the Court in the *Civil Rights Cases,* but they were unwilling to test the Court on the Section Five state action issue. During the debate over the act, only one member of Congress even suggested that the Court's interpretation of Section Five in the *Civil Rights Cases* was incorrect. Senator Edmund Muskie came closest to challenging the Court in a debate with Senator Ellender over whether or not the bill violated the Tenth Amendment. Discussing the Fourteenth and Fifteenth Amendments, Muskie commented, "I realize that for many years the Supreme Court narrowed the interpretation of those amendments, but I urge that my colleagues reread them, and reconsider them in the light of the original Bill of Rights and the determination of the Founding Fathers to insure the blessings of liberty to themselves and their posterity."[218] Here, Muskie not only questioned the Court's interpretation of the Constitution but also challenged his congressional colleagues to engage in their own interpretation. However, Muskie's challenge was exceptional in this congressional debate. Most members of Congress were unwilling to test the Court on the Section Five state action issue and, instead, adopted the more cautious approach of relying on the commerce clause to address private discrimination. The compromise approach adopted by Congress enabled the Court to avoid the difficult state action issue and uphold the statute based on Congress's commerce power alone.

Robert Post and Reva Siegel have argued that members of Congress missed an important opportunity to end the state action requirement when they chose not to rely solely on Section Five and test the Court's resolve on the issue.[219] There is ample evidence that the Framers of the Fourteenth Amendment intended that amendment to address the failure of the state to act to protect minorities, and hence would have encompassed the 1964 act.[220] Moreover, as Post and Siegel point out, the Court was showing signs that it might have been willing to overturn the *Civil Rights Cases* and abandon the state action requirement by upholding a civil rights statute based on Section Five.[221] Congress's failure to challenge the Court on state action would come back to haunt members of Congress wishing to legislate to protect rights of belonging. Recently, in *United States v. Morrison,* the Supreme Court struck down the civil rights provision of the Violence against Women Act as beyond Congress's Section Five Power because it regulated private action.[222] The Court revived the Civil Rights Cases, etching the state action requirement into stone and thus greatly restricting Congress's Section Five power.[223]

The deference toward the Court by the members of the 1964 Congress contrasts significantly with that of Congress during Reconstruction and the New Deal, the two other eras in which Congress acted to greatly expand rights of belonging. This deference is not surprising, given that members of Congress strongly supported the Court's ruling in *Brown* and other cases upholding racial justice.[224] Indeed, an important provision of the act, Title VI, was intended to enforce the mandate of *Brown* and provide an effective remedy to supplement judicial action.[225] Title VI prohibits recipients of federal funds from discriminating on the basis of race. Speaking in favor of Title VI, Senator Humphrey pointed out that some lower courts had held that federal statutes contemplating "separate but equal" were unconstitutional, but he did not want to wait for courts to make the decision. He explained, "It is clearly desirable for Congress to wipe them off the books without waiting for further judicial action."[226] Humphrey believed that statutes would be more effective than piecemeal court enforcement, but he clearly saw both efforts as working toward a common goal.

Later, the harmony between the Court and Congress subsided. In early cases, the Court interpreted Title VII expansively, most notably finding that Title VII of the Civil Rights Act authorized disparate impact litigation and affirmative action.[227] From 1970 to the early 1990s, however, the conservative Supreme Court often interpreted civil rights statutes narrowly, and Congress often responded with amendments that reasserted a broader view of equality rights than that held by the Court.[228] For example, the Pregnancy Discrimination Act of 1978[229] and the Civil Rights Restoration Act of 1991[230] were direct responses to narrow Court readings of equality rights.[231] Most recently the Court has greatly restricted congressional power to protect rights of belonging. Hence, even during an era in which the Court was relatively receptive to rights of belonging, it was Congress, and not the Court, that took a leadership role in protecting minority rights.[232] These subsequent developments show once again the need for congressional assertiveness in defining and protecting rights of belonging.

In retrospect, the cooperation of the Court and Congress during the Second Reconstruction had a mixed impact. Because the Court was deferential to Congress, members of Congress were reluctant to challenge the Court. When the Court reverted to the restrictive approach toward rights of belonging that was more consistent with its historical attitude in cases like *Boerne* and *Morrison,* Congress was left in a bind. In this book I have illustrated the fact that the Warren Court's favorable attitude toward rights of belonging, and not that of the restrictive Rehnquist Court, is the historical anomaly. In retrospect, the need for congressional assertiveness in defining rights of belonging was equally acute during the Warren Court era. Had members of the 1964 Congress followed Muskie's lead and challenged the state action requirement, they could have eliminated one of the greatest obstacles to congressional protection of rights of belonging. As they had during the New Deal Era, members of Congress could have asserted their power to define constitutional meaning; if they had done so, they likely would have expanded the meaning of the constitution to be more protective of rights of belonging.

6

The New Parity Debate

Congress and the federal courts are not the only governmental bodies that can act to define and protect rights of belonging. Both states and the federal government protect rights of belonging, just as both states and the federal government have denied rights of belonging.[1] There has been a long and heated debate among scholars concerning whether federal and state courts are equally competent fora for the enforcement of federal constitutional rights.[2] In this chapter I consider another alternative—state legislatures.[3] Unlike Congress, state legislatures have unlimited power to define rights of belonging, and some states and localities have enacted laws that are *more* expansive in protecting rights of belonging than is federal law. Thus, a new parity debate is emerging over whether state and local lawmakers, on one hand, and Congress, on the other, are equally competent in this arena. Here I consider the possibility that state legislatures can substitute for Congress as protectors of rights of belonging, making congressional enforcement unnecessary or even justifying court-imposed restrictions on congressional power. I conclude that while state autonomy to experiment with measures protecting rights of belonging is valuable, congressional power is necessary to create a strong baseline of rights of belonging.

Several different theories of the proper role of states in our federal system support the proposition that state legislatures may supplant Congress as a protector of rights of belonging. The first theory, traditional states' rights federalism, asserts that the autonomy of states to determine their own policies has a value in and of itself, which is protected by federalism. Although states' rights federalism has fallen out of favor because of its historical attachment to racial supremacy, there are other valid reasons why preserving states' autonomy enhances their rights-generating function. One reason is that our federalist system divides the functions of state and federal governments in order to preserve individual liberty. Another reason is that several structural features of state governments, including their accountability to their constituents and their ability to serve as laboratories for experimentation, weigh in favor of state autonomy to define and protect rights of belonging.

The second theory is that there are powerful institutional reasons for state legislatures to be an inadequate substitute for Congress. For example, as James Madison explicated in his theory of the extended republic, Congress represents a large number of diverse people, and thus it is less likely than state legislatures to be controlled by factions and oppress minorities. Moreover, the centralized nature of Congress enables that body to act more efficiently, and more effectively, than the piecemeal nature of state legislation. In addition, only Congress can create rights of belonging that are uniform throughout the country. Finally, the distance between Congress and its constituents enables effective enforcement of rights of belonging against local prejudice. All of these institutional factors justify broad congressional power to generate a strong baseline of rights of belonging.

Throughout history, states' rights federalists have argued that a state's autonomy to establish its own rules has a value in and of itself. They point out that states existed prior to the federal government, and they argue that the states retained a significant measure of sovereignty, even after they ceded some of that sovereignty to the federal government when they ratified the Constitution.[4] States' rights federalists cite the Framers' fear of an all-powerful, overarching federal government, in support of limits on the power of Congress to encroach on state sovereignty.[5] They argue that states have a level of sovereignty that is equal to that of the federal government, and that federal interference in that autonomy is offensive to state sovereignty. According to these advocates, the process of self-government is a central virtue of federalism, and one of the primary goals of federalism is protecting the states' right to self-government.[6] However, state officials have rarely raised states' rights federalism as an argument in favor of their power to generate rights of belonging. To the contrary, with one significant exception, states' rights federalism has been used as a tool of oppression, in opposition to federal protection of rights of belonging.

The notable instance in which states have asserted their autonomy on behalf of protecting rights of belonging occurred prior to the Civil War. Officials in northern states opposed federal fugitive slave laws that required them to cooperate in returning fugitive slaves to their southern masters.[7] Northern states strongly resisted enforcing the federal laws.

Some states enacted laws making it illegal under state law to comply with the federal act, others enacted laws imposing procedural barriers to enforcement of the act,[8] many northern state judges refused to hear cases brought under the Fugitive Slave Act, and some northern governors refused to cooperate with southern efforts to retrieve fugitive slaves.[9] During the antebellum era, politicians in both nonslave and slave states raised states' rights arguments against federal intervention in their treatment of slaves. However, leaders of southern states were considerably more vehement in their states' rights rhetoric. Most notably, John Calhoun of South Carolina argued that states had the power to nullify federal law.[10] Other southern leaders repeatedly threatened to secede from the United States.[11] When Abraham Lincoln was elected president, the southern states carried through on their threat to secede, leading the United States into the Civil War.

After the Civil War, southern opponents of federal power continued to articulate states' rights arguments. Among other things, they fashioned a revisionist history of the Civil War, calling it the "war between the states" and insisting that the war was only about states' rights and not about slavery.[12] When Reconstruction ended, the south entered the Jim Crow era of state-mandated segregation and rampant racially motivated violence, and states' rights federalism became firmly identified with the segregationist cause.[13] In 1954 the Supreme Court's ruling in *Brown v. Board of Education,* striking down state-mandated segregation of public schools, inspired a revival of John Calhoun's doctrine of nullification, as southern politicians sought justification for ignoring the desegregation mandates of *Brown* and federal civil rights statutes.[14] States' rights federalism thus was a significant impediment to federal enforcement of rights of belonging for much of the twentieth century.[15]

Even putting aside the sinister political ends with which states' rights federalism has been most closely associated historically, the argument that congressional power to protect individual rights must always yield to preserve the sovereignty of states to govern themselves is inconsistent with some fundamental constitutional principles. The Fourteenth Amendment mandates a federal role in the protection of individual rights and authorizes Congress and the federal courts to invalidate state laws that violate those rights. The Fourteenth Amendment soundly rejects states' rights federalism by creating federal constitutional rights that individuals can enforce against state governments and giving Congress the power to legislate to enforce those rights.[16]

Because of the negative historical connotations associated with states' rights federalism, asserting states' rights in favor of protecting rights of belonging seems an anomaly in the twenty-first century. Nonetheless, there are two significant reasons why states should enjoy autonomy to protect rights of belonging. First, our federalist system limits the power of either level of government to oppress people and is thus an important protection for individual liberty. Preserving this liberty-enhancing feature of federalism is often raised as a justification for limiting federal power. Second, structural aspects of state governments arguably make them better suited than the federal government to protect rights of belonging. These structural features favor state legislatures as protectors of rights of belonging.

The federalist system of dual sovereignties was designed to protect liberty because each level of government will serve as a check on the power of the other, preventing the other from becoming overly oppressive.[17] The idea that our federalist structure of government helps to protect individual liberty dates back to the writings of James Madison. In Federalist No. 51, Madison explained:

> In the compound republic of America, the power surrendered by the people is first divided between two distinct governments and then the portion allotted to each subdivided among distinct and separate departments. Hence a double security arises to the rights of the people. The different governments will control each other, at the same time that each will be controlled by itself.[18]

Contemporary antifederalists argue that since the New Deal, the federal government has become too large and the danger of federal oppression has increased significantly.[19] They believe that states are more protective of individual liberty than is the federal government, and they point out that oppressive federal measures are considerably more dangerous than oppressive state measures since they are harder to escape through personal mobility.[20] Contemporary antifederalists argue that protecting state autonomy is necessary to enable states to counteract this concentration of power in the federal government. Thus, according to contemporary antifederalists, judicial limits on congressional power imposed in the name of federalism are at least as important to individual liberty as are those imposed in the name of individual rights alone.[21]

While preserving state autonomy may theoretically help to protect individual liberty, the problem with this approach to federalism is that it is difficult, if not impossible, to draw clear lines demarcating the limits of federal and state power. Recently, the Court has adopted the position that categorical limitations on congressional power are essential to preserving state sovereignty.[22] In the past, however, when the Court tried to impose categorical limitations on federal power, those attempts have failed.[23] Moreover, even if protecting individual liberty does justify some limits on federal power, it does not necessarily require judicially imposed limits on Congress's rights-generating function. Federalism requires a balance between state and federal power, but to the extent that the Court becomes involved in imposing the balance it must realistically assess the relationship between the state and the federal government in regulating any particular issue. The states and the federal government both have important roles to play in defining and protecting rights of belonging, roles that should not be restricted by categorical limits.[24]

While the debate over federalism's protection of individual liberty focuses on the question of whether or not to restrict federal power, another debate has emerged over the rights-generating functions of states themselves. Arguably, several aspects of state legislatures make them, and not Congress, best situated to protect rights of belonging.[25] Structural aspects of state governments make them uniquely responsive to smaller progressive groups advocating broad views of rights of belonging. Perhaps court-imposed limitations on federal power are justified because they protect state autonomy to enact more progressive measures.[26] This argument is different from the traditional claim that broad federal power to enforce individual rights threatens state autonomy. Rather, this debate questions the extent to which states may do a *better* job than the federal government at protecting rights of belonging, and should be able to do so free from federal interference.[27]

There are a number of historical examples of states and municipalities generating rights of belonging that were more protective than existing federal measures. The most striking example is the measures protecting fugitive slaves enacted by northern states prior to the Civil War, discussed previously. Other examples include the state of Wyoming allowing women to vote in 1890, thirty years prior to women obtaining the federal right to vote with the Nineteenth Amendment. The state of Wisconsin pioneered unemployment compensation, and the state of Massachusetts was the first jurisdiction to establish minimum wage laws for women and children.[28] At the turn of the twentieth century, state legislatures enacted labor legislation that was significantly more protective than that enacted by Congress.[29] Finally, numerous state legislatures enacted laws prohibiting race discrimination in employment and public accommodations prior to the 1964 Civil Rights Act.[30]

States and cities also were on the forefront of protecting rights of belonging at the end of the twentieth century. For example, while the proposed Employee Non-Discrimination Act,[31] which would prohibit discrimination in employment on the basis of sexual orientation, has failed repeatedly before Congress, numerous states and municipalities have enacted laws providing similar protections.[32] Moreover, states and cities played leading roles in implementing international human rights norms during that era. While Congress was reluctant to incorporate human rights norms into federal law, some states and cities were willing to do so. For example, whereas federal implementation of the international Convention on Elimination of All Forms of Discrimination against Women (CEDAW) has been lax since its creation at the United Nations Fourth World Conference on Women in 1995, the city of San Francisco adopted CEDAW as part of its local law in 1998.[33] Both in the past and in the present, states and municipalities have served as progressive laboratories of experimentation, often acting on the forefront in generating laws protecting rights of belonging.

States have also recently taken the initiative in making rights of belonging enforceable. When the Supreme Court held that Congress lacked the power to authorize private individuals to enforce many of their rights of belonging,[34] several state legislatures stepped in to fill the gap. Some state legislatures considered measures that would waive sovereign immunity.[35] For example the legislature of the state of Illinois enacted a provision waiving sovereign immunity to individual suits enforcing federal rights of belonging, including the Age Discrimination in Employment Act, the Americans with Disabilities Act, Title VII of the Civil Rights Act of 1964, the Fair Labor Standards Act, and the Family Medical Leave Act.[36] In the same vein, the state of Maine enacted a law to include state employees under state wage and overtime law.[37] That bill was designed to fill the rights-remedy gap created by the Supreme Court's holding in *Alden v. Maine* that private individuals could not sue to enforce federal overtime measures in state courts.[38] By enacting these measures, state legislatures affirmed their support for individual rights of belonging.

Several widely recognized values of federalism favor states and municipalities serving to help define and enforce rights of belonging. First, federalism is often praised for decentralizing the decision-making process, creating more forums for diverse views in that process and enhancing the sense of political community in cities and states.[39] This makes states and localities well-suited to protect rights of belonging. In smaller communities, smaller interest groups have a larger say, allowing some minorities to successfully lobby for legislation that is favorable to their interests at the state and local level, even though they may not be able to do so at the national level.[40] To put it another way, Madison's factions are not always oppressive—sometimes factions will protect rights of belonging.[41] One example of the formation of those factions toward the end of the twenty-first century is the migration of gays and lesbians in the United States to urban centers in the northeast, the west coast, and the upper midwest. As a consequence, those areas have enacted legislation that is more protective of the rights of belonging of sexual minorities than current federal law.[42] This pattern illustrates the fact that states and localities may serve as protective loci where rights of belonging can flourish.

A second widely recognized value of federalism is that it furthers government innovation because states can serve as laboratories for experimentation.[43] Because of the diversity of their populations and the strong tradition of democratic activism at the state and local level, states and city governments are likely to experiment with legislation that is more progressive than federal legislation.[44] This insight is contrary to the conventional view of "localism," which views it as a *barrier* to enforcement of rights of belonging.[45] As we have seen, there is also a countervailing tradition of states and cities experimenting with laws that are more protective of rights of belonging than are comparable federal statutes.[46]

A third value of federalism is that enhances a sense of political community and accountability. Federalism allows opportunities for people to participate meaningfully in state and local governments and makes it more likely that those governments will be accountable to the people they serve.[47] These opportunities create a favorable climate for rights of belonging at the state and local levels because the strength of states and localities is their diversity, and diverse groups of people are more likely to interact directly with each other in the democratic process at the state and local levels.[48] The participation of diverse groups in the local democratic process enhances the accountability of state and local officials to those whose rights need protection.[49] Moreover, decision-makers are likely to respond more compassionately to the injuries of their neigh-bors than they are to injuries of strangers who live far away.[50] Thus, the accountability of state and local officials often weighs in favor of states as primary protectors of rights of belonging.

Fourth, there is a credible argument that bottom-up, grass roots re-forms may be more effective than top-down, federal reforms. With states and cities at the forefront enacting protective laws, reform movements gain a momentum of their own and achieve the acceptance of their goals by the majority nationwide.[51] Change effected in this way may become more enmeshed in societal norms than top-down change imposed by Congress or the federal courts; or at least, such change might meet with less resistance.[52] Finally, unlike the federal government, states have a general police power. State legislatures therefore enjoy unlimited power to define rights and make them enforceable by waiving sovereign im-munity.

Finally, Steve Clark makes the normative argument that the best poli-cies may result from a decentralized conception of individual rights.[53] He opposes a universalist conception of human rights in favor of cul-tural relativism because relativism allows for progressive policies to be enacted someplace, even if they affect a limited number of people.[54] Be-cause obtaining a national consensus requires compromise, Clark points out that national policies will never be as protective as those enacted by the states that are progressive enclaves.[55] Of course, the policies of progressive states only apply to the people who live there. However, progressive antifederalists argue that people who live in less progressive jurisdictions and are dissatisfied with their state or local government's failure to protect their rights can simply move to more protective lo-cales.[56]

Given the institutional strengths of state legislatures as generators of rights of belonging, and the history of states and municipalities in gen-erating those rights, why does congressional power matter? It matters because states alone have not done and cannot do an adequate job of protecting rights of belonging. This country's history is replete with ex-amples of states denying rights of belonging. From slavery to the Jim Crow era and beyond, congressional enforcement of rights of belonging against state infringement has often been necessary to protect the most fundamental human rights. Moreover, when states have protected rights of belonging, federal power and federal rights have been instrumental in supporting the rights-generating function of states. For example, state and local officials would not be accountable to many of their constituents if those constituents did not benefit from federal voting rights. Prior to the 1965 federal Voting Rights Act, states routinely denied voting rights on the basis of race. A vast majority of African Americans were disenfranchised by states throughout the south, ensuring that local elected officials did not need to be accountable to them.[57] Federal legislation was needed to force many states and municipalities to function as centers of democracy.

Similarly, states could not serve as laboratories for experimentation without the federal right to travel. One of the principal rights of federal citizenship, the right to travel is needed to enable people who are dissatisfied with their state or local government's protection of their rights to move to a more protective locale.[58] Indeed, the fact that proponents of state autonomy rely so heavily on the right to travel highlights the disadvantage of relying on individual states to define rights of belonging: physical mobility is an inadequate safety net for ensuring individual rights. Todd Pettys explains that "[c]itizens who might one day want or need to move across state lines have an interest in securing federal legislation aimed at maximizing the number of jurisdictions in which they would be happy to live."[59] The level of protection afforded to individual rights in other jurisdictions is directly related to one's ability to comfortably exercise one's right to travel. Similarly, "citizens in a mobile society have an interest in favorably shaping the norms and regulatory preferences of their future neighbors, no matter where in the country those future neighbors currently reside."[60]

Moreover, people should not have to move in order to protect their most fundamental individual rights. The Jim Crow era, a time of great flux in our country because blacks fled oppression and violence in the south, is now nearly universally condemned as a shameful time in our history.[61] History aside, any system that relies on high mobility to ensure fairness is unlikely to adequately serve the needs of the poor or others who do not have the wherewithal to relocate.[62] There is a very real danger of a "race to the bottom" with regard to states and cities providing economic rights.[63] Rights that vary from locality to locality encourage migration to those jurisdictions that provide extensive, and often expensive, legal protections. Local governments may tend to cut back on individual rights out of fear of an influx of needy people.[64]

Finally, though states and municipalities have an important role in defining and protecting rights of belonging, that role simply does not justify restricting federal power. States and municipalities need flexibility to protect rights of belonging without federal interference, but it does not necessarily follow that Congress must be restrained in order to provide that flexibility. State autonomy to protect rights of belonging is best ensured not by restricting congressional power to protect those rights but by congressional measures limiting the preemptive effect of federal legislation on state attempts to protect rights of belonging. Congress has repeatedly included such measures in legislation to protect rights of belonging, making that legislation a floor, not a ceiling, of rights of belonging.[65] Consistent with Congress's intent, the Supreme Court and the lower federal courts have also adopted a presumption against federal preemption of state-generated rights of belonging.[66] Hence, preemption does not pose a significant barrier to states' protection of rights of belonging. Because there is little danger that federal law will preempt a more progressive state measure, there is no need to curtail congressional rights-generating power to protect the rights-generating function of states.[67]

While there is at least a theoretical danger of the national government becoming a totalitarian government, American history indicates that localism, not national government, poses more of an oppressive threat. As Kenneth Karst has pointed out, "When the Supreme Court and Congress imposed a uniform national principle of racial nondiscrimination on the South, they did not destroy the functions of local communities. Rather, they opened new opportunities for citizen participation in local public life. Localism was not suppressed; it was set free from the stifling effects of a racially exclusive definition of community."[68] There are powerful institutional reasons that federal power in general and congressional power in particular are needed to effectuate meaningful protection of rights of belonging. Those reasons include the fact that Congress represents an extended republic of diverse individuals and is thus unlikely to target legislation at any particular vulnerable group. In addition, structural features of the federal government, including the importance of uniformity of fundamental rights, the effectiveness of centralized enforcement of those rights, and the distance between the federal government and the agents of local oppression, enhance Congress's institutional capacity to protect rights of belonging.

James Madison believed that the size of the federal government and its republican nature would ensure against tyrannical factions taking over that government and imposing oppressive measures against minorities. Modern-day federalists often point out one of the structural protections that Madison advocated, the federalist system of overlapping sovereignties, as a justification for preserving state autonomy from federal intervention. However, contrary to their suggestion, Madison did not think that the system of dual sovereignties alone would be sufficient to protect individual rights. More importantly, at the time of the framing of the Constitution, Madison believed that states, and not the federal government, posed the greatest danger to individual rights and liberties.[69] He believed that Congress had to protect individuals from state governments because Congress represented an extended republic that would be less likely than states to oppress minorities and deny individual rights.[70] As Madison's theory of the extended republic indicates, while Congress may not always provide the most expansive rights, Congress is institutionally less likely than the states to take rights of belonging *away* from its citizens. Because Congress represents the people of the nation as a whole, Congress is uniquely situated to take a leadership role in creating a nationally uniform baseline of rights of belonging.

The passage of time has proven that Madison was correct in his view that Congress would be less likely than states to act to deprive citizens of rights of belonging.[71] However, counterexamples exist where Congress has acted to restrict rights of belonging. The Indian Removal Act of 1830, the Chinese Exclusion Act of 1882, and the restrictions on public benefits for noncitizens in the Personal Responsibility and Work Opportunity Act of 1996 are just a few examples of Congress affirmatively acting to exclude groups from our national community.[72] Moreover, periods in which Congress expanded rights of belonging have frequently been followed by periods in which it contracted rights that it had previously created.[73] For example, the post–Reconstruction Era Congress amended much of the Reconstruction Era legislation, drastically reducing the enforceability of its protections.[74] Similarly, only thirteen years after Congress enacted the Wagner Act, it significantly limited the rights of unionized workers in the Taft Hartley Act of 1947.[75] More recently, in the Personal Responsibility Act of 1996, Congress dismantled large pieces of the federal safety net that it created during the New Deal and the War against Poverty. In addition to these affirmative acts, there are countless instances in which Congress has failed to legislate in the face of an arguably desperate need for rights of belonging.[76] These statutes illustrate the fact that Congress can take rights of belonging away as well as bestow them.

Nevertheless, these counterexamples do not justify court-imposed limitations on congressional power to protect rights of belonging. Throughout history, Congress has only twice actively legislated to prohibit states from protecting rights of belonging—that is, the Fugitive Slave Acts of 1793 and 1850. The glaring exception of the Fugitive Slave Acts is less significant when one considers that Congress enacted those statutes prior to the Civil War and the Reconstruction Amendments, in which Congress for the first time adopted the role of protector of rights of belonging. Since the Fourteenth Amendment, Congress has not legislated to prevent states from bestowing rights of belonging on their citizens. As Madison predicted, because members of Congress represent such an enormously diverse polity, they have been significantly less likely than state legislatures to take away rights of belonging.

The only contemporary measure comparable to the nineteenth-century Fugitive Slave Acts is the Defense of Marriage Act (DOMA) of 1996.[77] In that statute, Congress defined marriage as between one "man" and one "woman" for determining the meaning of any act of Congress, or of any ruling, regulation, or interpretation of administrative bureaus and agencies of the United States,[78] and eliminated from the full faith and credit requirement the recognition of same-sex relationships, entered into under the laws of one state, by other states.[79] DOMA reflects a regressive, exclusionary view of rights of belonging and is thus at first glance comparable to the Fugitive Slave Acts. However, the differences between the measures illustrate the extent to which Congress now defers to the states setting a ceiling on rights of belonging.

DOMA differs from the Fugitive Slave Act in two important respects. First, DOMA's definition of marriage only directly applies to the federal government; DOMA does not prohibit states from implementing their own definitions of marriage. Second, rather than ordering states not to recognize same-sex marriages conducted in other states, DOMA merely gives states the choice not to do so. Like the first provision, this second provision does not order states to deny rights of belonging but simply authorizes them to do so, and thus differs significantly from the Fugitive Slave Act, which took choice away from the states.[80] Crucially, state legislatures that wish to authorize gay marriage within their jurisdiction retain their power to do so even after DOMA. Therefore, while DOMA does affect federal employees, and has symbolic significance as a reflection of congressional intent with regard to rights of belonging of gays and lesbians, it has no practical impact on the power of states to enact laws protecting these rights. In DOMA, Congress deferred to the states to regulate one of the most volatile social issues in the beginning of the twenty-first century, the legality of gay marriage.

That Congress has not used its broadened powers to directly limit states' protection of rights of belonging even in this context may calm concerns that it will do so in the future. Nevertheless, it is clear that the fact that Congress represents an extended republic alone does not make it superior to state legislatures as a protector of rights of belonging. As we have seen, Madison's argument that local constituencies are more homogeneous and susceptible to capture can cut both ways. First, local factions can also be progressive and protective. State legislatures may be more likely than Congress to legislate to *oppress* minority groups in the midst, but they may also be more likely than Congress to legislate to *protect* their interests. Second, and more importantly, prejudice does not only occur locally but is often a national phenomenon. While support for racial segregation divided the country along sectional lines, the same cannot be said with equal force about discrimination and stereotyping on the basis of sex, age, or sexual minority status, or the exclusion of poor people from the economic life of the country—all of which are prevalent in the larger national constituency that Congress serves, as well as in the smaller constituencies that state legislators serve. Assuming that legislators are motivated by the prejudices of their constituents, it follows that Congress is not significantly more likely to enact rights of belonging to protect those rights than are state legislatures.

However, Congress also enjoys other, more important, institutional strengths. First, Congress is better positioned to discern when new rights of belonging are warranted—and when they are no longer required—than are state legislatures. While only local constituents lobby state legislators, Congress represents the interests of people and communities from all around the country. Accordingly, Congress is in the best position to determine whether there is a pattern of stereotyping, discrimination, economic exclusion, or violence against any particular group that is sufficiently pervasive to threaten that group's ability to belong to America. In addition, Congress has more time and resources at its disposal to solicit testimony and to analyze different recommendations about how to respond to the need for a right of belonging. Moreover, from a public choice perspective, the federal legislature is better situated to enact redistributive policies—like statutes that create rights of belonging and thereby disrupt existing hierarchies of power—than are state legislatures.[81]

Second, the centralized nature of the federal government also makes Congress superior to state legislatures as a protector of rights of belonging. Centralized protection of rights of belonging is important for three reasons. First, by their very nature, human rights should be uniform and should not vary from state to state. Second, centralization of rights of belonging is more efficient and thus furthers effective protection of those rights. Third, a nationally shared understanding of rights of belonging enhances our concept of nationhood and strengthens our national polity. Thus, while categorical allocations of functions can be unrealistic and arbitrary, to the extent that it is possible, "national protection of civil rights is a fundamental component of the successful federalism deal."[82]

Because rights of belonging are fundamental, they should be uniform throughout the country. Arguably, "to speak in terms of rights is to speak the language of universality."[83] This fact is well recognized in the movement for international human rights, and leading liberal philosophers have also argued that uniformity of rights is essential to effective government protection of rights. For example, Ronald Dworkin has argued, "the idea of justice connotes consistency in the law, the notion that all citizens should enjoy the same rights."[84] Similarly, John Rawls opined, "citizens of a just society ought to have the same basic rights."[85] Some critics of a universalist approach to rights have argued that such an approach essentializes dominant western ideology.[86] However, whether or not it is possible to identify universal rights, uniformity of rights has a value in and of itself.

Uniformity of rights of belonging is important from both a symbolic and a practical perspective. First, uniformity of rights has the symbolic value of fairness. Rights of belonging that vary from state to state can cause a perception of injustice and undermine the effectiveness of the rule of law.[87] Centralized federal enforcement of those rights is necessary to prevent this from happening. Uniformity of rights of belonging also has the practical value of enabling mobility. When rights of belonging are uniform, people feel free to travel around the country without fear of entering a less protective jurisdiction. Uniformity of rights of belonging thus also furthers the fundamental right to travel.[88]

A second reason why centralized decision-making is more effective to protect rights of belonging is that it is more efficient than decentralized decision-making. In order to effect widespread change at the state level, advocates must lobby fifty different state legislatures. It is considerably more efficient for them to focus solely on lobbying Congress. Efficiency can be especially important for proponents of rights of belonging, who wish to effect change while public opinion, which can be fleeting, is in their favor. For that reason, decentralized decision-making favors the status quo and disfavors the expansion of rights of belonging, and centralized decision-making favors expansion of those rights.[89]

Finally, centralized enforcement of rights of belonging enhances a sense of nationhood and fosters a strong national political community. A common set of laws, including uniform rights of belonging, aids in building a sense of nationhood because uniform laws foster ties between diverse groups of people. Of course, federalism makes it possible for various communities to exist within a larger political community.[90] But a uniform system of basic rights enables people within those communities to feel that they belong to the national polity as well. In this country, looking to the federal government to protect one's individual rights has become part of our constitutional fabric, as well as our national culture. A common set of rights of belonging helps our heterogeneous population build a sense of political community.[91] Once rights of belonging are enacted at the congressional level they create a seamless web of protection across the nation, which reflects and reinforces the national consensus that the group they protect truly belongs to America.

The final structural argument in favor of congressional protection of rights of belonging is the distance between the federal government and the citizens that it protects.[92] This argument may seem counterintuitive since antifederalists often cite accountability of state officials in favor of state autonomy to make decisions. However, accountability can often prevent state officials from effectively protecting rights of belonging. Almost by definition, people whose rights of belonging need protecting are often unpopular with local and state officials.[93] Federal officials can protect those rights because they are distanced from local prejudices, and because they represent larger constituencies they need not be beholden to prejudiced constituents.[94] Therefore, distance has an important role in making Congress particularly well suited to define and protect rights of belonging.

In sum, on the one hand, it is important for our federalist system to preserve state autonomy to give state and municipal legislatures the flexibility that they need to function as pockets of progressive democracy. On the other hand, rights of belonging are most effectively enforced in a centralized, uniform manner, by a legislative body that represents all of the people of the nation. Only Congress can effectively perform this function. When courts rigidly impose limitations on Congress's power to define and protect rights of belonging, they sacrifice Congress's crucial function in this arena. Rather than rigid limitations, a system of federalism that best protects rights of belonging is one that provides a synthesis of the institutional strengths of both the states and the federal governments, what Michael Zuckert has termed "corrective federalism."[95] Congress must retain the power to provide a uniform baseline of rights, and states must retain the flexibility to experiment with more protective measures. This solution is possible because aside from preventing states from violating rights of belonging, congressional power to define and enforce those rights need not interfere with the general police powers of the state.

James Madison articulated a synthesized version of federalism when he advocated in favor of a federal negative to protect individual rights from state infringement. Congress would serve as a "disinterested and dispassionate umpire in disputes between different passions and interests in the State" and curb "the aggressions of interested majorities on the rights of minorities and of individuals."[96] While the federal negative was central to Madison's vision of the federalist system, Madison did not intend that Congress have the power to oversee all state legislation.[97] At the constitutional convention, Madison explained that states would regulate most matters and that Congress could only intervene when necessary to protect rights from infringement.[98] Corrective federalism was also an important component of the vision of the Framers of the Fourteenth Amendment. Like Madison, John Bingham intended to preserve state autonomy in most areas, but only to prohibit states from intruding on rights of belonging.[99] In John Bingham's vision of citizenship rights, states still retained the power to bestow rights on their citizens, but federal citizenship would provide the standard as a baseline of rights that could not be taken away.[100] Bingham wanted the Fourteenth Amendment to prevent the enforcement of federal laws protecting rights of belonging from yielding to state sovereignty.[101]

Justice William Brennan also articulated a synthesized vision of federalism when he argued that the states and the federal government had important roles in defining and protecting rights of belonging.[102]

Writing at a time when the Supreme Court (of which he was still a member) was, in Brennan's eyes, inadequately protecting individual rights, Brennan urged state courts to step forward and interpret state constitutions to provide for more rights than the Court had identified in the U.S. Constitution.[103] Brennan did not see this experimentation as usurping the role of the federal courts in protecting individual rights, nor did he believe it necessary to restrict federal power in the name of state innovation. Instead, Brennan saw the states and the federal government as working together to protect individual rights.

Justice Brennan did not believe that restricting federal power was necessary for states to protect individual rights because he saw federal law as a baseline, and not a ceiling, for individual rights and liberties.[104] As Brennan indicated, our federalism allows for experimentation with dual systems of protections of rights unless there is a danger that federal law will preempt more progressive state and local laws. In the area of court enforcement of individual rights, which was Brennan's concern, state courts do not have to worry about preemption because when state courts interpret state law, the Supreme Court cannot review or overturn their decisions.[105] Non-preemption provisions in federal statutes protecting rights of belonging perform a similar function.

Justice Brennan's vision of federalism provides a good guideline for understanding the role that state autonomy should take in generating and protecting rights of belonging. States and municipalities do have an important rights-generating role that is often overlooked by constitutional scholars. Their autonomy should be preserved in order to facilitate that role.[106] However, that role does not justify restrictions on congressional power to protect rights of belonging because congressional power can coexist with state autonomy and flexibility in this arena. Alternatively, congressional power to generate and protect rights of belonging is essential to the adequate protection of those rights because only Congress can provide an effective, nationally uniform baseline of fundamental rights. A synthesized system of federalism capitalizes on the institutional strengths of the states and the federal government to maximize protection of rights of belonging.

7

Rights of Belonging and Popular Constitutionalism

Contrary to conventional wisdom, Congress took a leading role in protecting rights of belonging in all three of the eras of our history marked by the most significant expansion of those rights. This history challenges the conventional view that courts, and not legislatures, are best suited to protect rights of belonging. However, history alone is not determinative; Congress has not always acted to protect rights of belonging, and history is not necessarily predictive of the future. Indeed, at the beginning of the twenty-first century it may seem odd to some to even ask the question of whether Congress can adequately protect our rights of belonging, given that the principal legislative initiatives regarding those rights that are currently pending are measures to deny the fundamental right of marriage to gays and lesbians.[1] Nevertheless, when Congress does act to protect rights of belonging, it enjoys significant institutional strengths that make it more effective than courts. In this chapter I examine the institutional strengths and weaknesses of courts and Congress as protectors of rights of belonging and make the case that Congress should be allowed to have the leading role as protector of those rights.

Ideally, both courts and legislatures will act to protect rights of belonging, and judicial review will serve simply as a backstop when legislatures fail to carry out this task.[2] When courts and legislatures are in agreement as to the substance of those rights, there is no need to determine which branch should prevail. The problem arises when courts and legislatures disagree as to the substance of those rights or as to how to resolve conflicts between assertions of rights. In *Katzenbach v. Morgan,* the Warren Court deferred to Congress's definition of rights of belonging, as long as that definition did not violate individual rights. In essence, the Court indicated that it would be willing to serve as a protective backstop.[3] By contrast, in *City of Boerne v. Flores,* the Court held that *only* the Court can decide the extent of individual rights under the Fourteenth Amendment.[4] Thus, the *Boerne* Court made it clear that it was not willing to serve as a mere backstop to Congress. Under *Boerne,* the Court will always prevail in a case of conflict over the meaning of the Fourteenth Amendment. *Boerne* thus poses a direct challenge to Congress's power to protect rights of belonging.[5]

Yet there are strong institutional reasons that Congress should have the autonomy to define the meaning of rights of belonging. Congress's institutional advantages over courts as rights protectors include the legitimacy of democratic rule, the flexibility of legislatures for fashioning remedies, the transparency and accountability of congressional debate, the enforceability of legislation, and the involvement of political actors outside of Congress who fight for constitutional change. These advantages suggest that the political process is actually better suited to protecting rights of belonging than is the institution of judicial review.

In *Boerne,* the Court held itself out as the sole branch suited to defining constitutional norms. However, throughout our history the people and the political branches have often asserted the authority to define and develop those norms.[6] Strikingly, political resistance to the constitutional vision of the courts marked two of the historical periods that represent the most significant expansion of rights of belonging by Congress, Reconstruction and the New Deal Eras. Both eras were marked by robust interpretation of the Constitution outside of the courts, or "popular Constitutionalism."[7] A number of scholars recently have challenged the notion that the Court should have a monopoly over constitutional meaning.[8] Contributing to this debate, political scientists such as Keith Whittington, Stephen Griffin, and Louis Fisher point out that the political branches have a major role in creating constitutional law.[9] Another group of legal scholars, including James Gray Pope, William Forbath, Robert Post and Reva Siegel , argue that popular Constitutionalism is not only common, but it is desirable because it expands the possibilities of constitutional development.[10] Indeed, during Reconstruction, the New Deal, and the Second Reconstruction, popular Constitutionalism brought about the expansion of rights of belonging.

However, popular Constitutionalism has generated resistance from some scholars who believe that judicial review is necessary to ensure the constitutional principle and stability necessary for the adequate protection of our individual rights.[11] As Charles Black expressed this view,

"An active judiciary is the most hopeful bulwark for human rights in the United States" because Congress has neither the structure nor the vision to protect those rights.[12] In the same vein, Judith Baer argues that the insulation from political pressures enjoyed by federal judges is a necessary predicate for effective protection of rights.[13] These scholars articulate the conventional wisdom that the political insulation of federal courts makes them the best branch for protecting rights of belonging.

The link between the courts' political insularity and the protection of rights was articulated most eloquently by Justice Robert Jackson in his 1943 opinion in *West Virginia Board of Education v. Barnette,* holding that states could not require Jehovah's Witnesses to pledge allegiance to the flag. Jackson explained, "The very purpose of the Bill of Rights was to withdraw certain subjects from the vicissitudes of political controversy, to place them beyond reach of majorities and to establish them as legal principles to be applied by courts."[14] Here, Jackson equated rights with the courts and maintained that only federal judges, who are shielded from political pressures, can adequately protect individual rights from infringement. Similarly, a few years before, Justice Harlan Stone had argued that the Court should protect "discrete and insular minorities" in his famous footnote four to the Court's *Carolene Products* decision. Because "discrete and insular minorities" are likely to lose repeatedly in the political process, Stone explained that it is appropriate for courts to exercise judicial review to protect their rights.[15]

Following this line of reasoning, Erwin Chemerinsky insists that advocating constitutional interpretation outside of the courts is dangerous because it threatens the rights-protecting role of the federal courts. Chemerinsky claims, "Popular Constitutionalism would mean that courts would be far less available to protect fundamental rights," and that popular Constitutionalism "risks foreclosing judicial protection for litigants who have nowhere to turn but the courts."[16] Of course, minorities could still try to change unjust policies in the political process, but that challenge would "be transferred from an institution largely insulated from political pressure to one that is highly majoritarian. Checks and balances would be lost."[17] Popular Constitutionalism sounds good, admits Chemerinsky, but "tyranny of the majority" does not.[18] He insists that adequate protection of individual rights requires an institution that is insulated from that tyranny—the federal courts.

However, Chemerinsky's image of courts as countermajoritarian protectors of rights is considerably undermined by evidence that courts simply do not often rule against the will of the majority. To the contrary, political scientists who have studied the relationship between Supreme Court opinions and public opinion have found that courts tend to follow prevailing political winds, not resist them.[19] Most famously, in the 1950s, political scientist Robert Dahl found that the Supreme Court essentially tends to track public opinion, not go against it.[20] More recently, political scientist Thomas Marshall concluded that "overall, the evidence suggests that the modern Court has been an essentially majoritarian institution."[21] Both the history explored in this book and the empirical studies conducted by political scientists show that courts simply have not been the champions of individual rights that one might expect, given their political insularity and their stated willingness to serve in a judicial role.[22]

Legal historian Michael Klarman has also analyzed the historical relationship between courts and individual rights and concluded that the view of federal judges as heroic countermajoritarian heroes is no more than a myth.[23] Klarman maintains that in the vast majority of cases where it acts to protect individual rights, the Court has adopted a strong national consensus and imposed it on outliers. In other decisions, "infrequently, the Court resolves a genuinely divisive issue that rends the nation in half; on these occasions, roughly half the country supports the Court's determination."[24] Likewise, legal historian Lucas Powe points out that even the rulings of the Warren Court, champion of minority rights and individual liberties, were in tune with the majority of public opinion far more often than in opposition to that view.[25]

On the other hand, when federal courts do protect minority rights against the will of the majority, insularity becomes their principal weakness. As Madison realized at the time of the founding of our country, because federal judges are insulated from politics, they are not accountable to the people for their actions and their decisions therefore can lack legitimacy in the eyes of the public.[26] When judges make decisions that are very unpopular, they generate political resistance that hampers the enforceability of their decisions. For example, workers resisted antilabor injunctions during the first third of the twentieth century and developed a constitutional ideology in opposition to the courts.

This dynamic also occurs when courts act to protect rights of belonging. For example, resistance by segregationists greatly impeded the efforts of federal courts to enforce the Court's ruling in *Brown* and protect the rights of belonging of African Americans in the south during the

1950s.[27] Critics of the ruling in *Brown* charged the Court with judicial activism and advocated the impeachment of Chief Justice Earl Warren.[28] Resistance to *Brown* was so widespread that the ruling had virtually no impact on southern schools until after Congress adopted a national policy against segregation in the 1964 Civil Rights Act.[29] Public resistance to the Court's ruling in *Brown* and other decisions protecting minorities may have reduced the effectiveness of courts as guardians of rights of belonging because it hampered the enforceability of their decisions.[30]

Perhaps chastened by that pattern of resistance, the Supreme Court subsequently has cited concerns about its own lack of accountability to explain its reluctance to intrude on the political process to protect individual rights in other contexts. In recent years the Court has largely disavowed its role as countermajoritarian protector of rights. Since the mid 1970s, the Court has rejected arguments that it should extend the judicial solicitude that it had shown toward racial minorities and women to other categories of people including the poor, the elderly, and the disabled. In each of those cases, the Court cited its countermajoritarian nature as the principal reason for its refusal to apply heightened scrutiny. The Court opined that the political process, and not the unaccountable federal courts, were better suited to determining the best policies for addressing the needs of the poor, aged, and disabled.[31] Similarly, in the past thirty years, the Court has been reluctant to expand the list of fundamental rights that receive heightened protection from the courts. In its equal protection jurisprudence, the Court has not identified a fundamental right since the early 1970s, when it rejected the claim of a constitutional right to a minimum income and to education, again citing deference to the political process.[32]

In another line of jurisprudence protecting individual rights, many of the Court's recent substantive due process decisions expressly rely on the political process to determine whether or not a right is "fundamental" and thus subject to heightened protection by the Court. In cases evaluating the scope of the "right to privacy," the Court's test for determining whether a right is fundamental is whether there is a tradition and history of treating that right as a fundamental right. The Court canvasses state law and other political sources to determine whether the "history and tradition" requirement is met.[33] There are important exceptions to this trend, in which the Court has identified individual rights by applying the more countermajoritarian "implicit to the concept of ordered liberty" test. There are also some important recent examples of the Court acting to protect individual rights against infringement by the executive branch.[34] However, to a significant degree, even the Court's jurisprudence belies the notion of the federal courts as "countermajoritarian saviors."[35]

Indeed, Robin West has argued that courts should not be expected to take a proactive role in protecting rights because as an institution, courts are conservative. Courts exist to do legal justice, resolve individual cases, and create and follow precedent, which means that courts will always draw on the past and be reluctant to overrule restrictive precedent.[36] In the same vein, other scholars point out that equating constitutional rights with the judicial process is likely to restrict the scope of those rights. Institutional constraints, including the limits of the Court's enforcement powers and the justiciability restraints imposed by Article III, restrict the Court from enforcing constitutional norms to their "conceptual limits."[37] Their argument is supported by the history explored in this book. When courts and Congress have battled over constitutional meaning, Congress often has taken the position that is more protective of rights of belonging.

The Court's position in *Boerne* is thus harmful to rights of belonging for two reasons. First, it restricts rights of belonging to those that the Court has identified. Even though the Court cited deference to the political process as the reason for upholding classifications that discriminate on the basis of age, poverty, and disability, the Court has applied *Boerne* and struck down the attempts of Congress to prohibit discrimination based on those classifications.[38] The Court has relied on *Boerne* to impose explicit limits on congressional power to protect the aged, the disabled, and other people whom the Court has not identified as belonging to a protected class.[39] In this manner, the Court's monopoly on constitutional meaning directly restricts rights of belonging.

Second, Mark Tushnet points out that even when the Court does not impose direct restrictions on the political branches, the Court's monopoly on constitutional meaning has had an indirect effect on political debates over rights of belonging.[40] He points out that the Court's rejection of constitutional rights for the poor in the early 1970s has made it harder politically for advocates to argue that economic rights are constitutional rights.[41] Prior to those rulings, such arguments were at least politically feasible. Toward the end of the New Deal, President Franklin Roosevelt advocated a "Second Bill of Rights" that would have constitutionalized basic economic rights.[42] The continued political salience of economic rights is reflected in the fact that in the late 1960s, many political leaders advocated a legislative right to a minimum income. Even President Richard Nixon supported such an initiative, and Congress came close to adopting legislation that would have established such a right.[43] Yet today, the Court and most constitutional scholars now see constitutional social welfare rights as unfeasible, primarily because of institutional concerns about court enforcement of those rights.[44]

Tushnet claims that without judicial review, politicians and legal advocates might have followed Roosevelt's vision rather than the Court's and developed a more robust understanding of social welfare rights. Therefore, Tushnet maintains that, on balance, judicial review has had a *negative* impact on individual rights.[45] The Court's cramped view of those rights has stifled a more expansive view based on popular Constitutionalism.

Another scholar who criticizes courts as protectors of rights is Stephen Griffin. Griffin insists that liberals should no longer depend on the Supreme Court to enforce the rights against discrimination afforded in the Equal Protection Clause. According to Griffin, in the last twenty years, "If you are a member of a racial minority, the Supreme Court is not your friend."[46] Along with *Boerne,* Griffin cites the Court's restrictive rulings on affirmative action and limiting the scope of federal voting rights legislation to support his point.[47] Griffin points out that in recent years the political branches, and not the courts, are taking the leading role in protecting individual rights. Rather than these developments being passing phenomena, Griffin maintains, "they are rooted in the current institutional structure of the American state and are thus part of the American Constitutional order."[48] Put simply, equal rights have become politically popular so politicians have enacted statutes expanding those rights.

Robin West has also argued that Congress's interpretation of the Constitution is likely to be more progressive than that of the federal courts.[49] West observes that, unlike Courts, Congress's central mission is not to treat like cases alike—it is to alter and transform, not conserve, the past. West points out that the identity of the federal judges may have an impact as well. She argues that Congress may be institutionally more progressive because members of Congress are more diverse in terms of race and gender than are members of the Court.[50] For all of these reasons, West advocates a "pluralist approach to Constitutional meaning" in which the political branches would have the autonomy to adopt a more expansive interpretation of the Equal Protection Clause than that adopted by the Court.[51] In the same vein, Robert Post and Reva Siegel maintain that Congress is better equipped than courts to enact policies with broad social meanings. Courts are limited in character—only Congress can unilaterally construct social meaning.[52]

Many scholars have argued that Congress simply lacks the institutional capacity to protect individual rights. Critics of Congress argue that its political nature makes it ill suited for determining matters of principle such as rights of belonging.[53] Pluralist democratic theory tells us that constituents will primarily be motivated by their own self-interests rather than the constitutionality of any proposed provision.[54] Members of Congress can attempt to reconcile their constituents' desires with their constitutional principles, but that might not always be an easy task. However, it is not clear that judges always act on isolated principle, either. Federal judges are often selected based on political considerations, and there is ample evidence that judges, like politicians, are influenced by their own political views when they interpret constitutional provisions.[55] Moreover, notwithstanding these contrary pressures, members of Congress do sometimes appear to make decisions based on constitutional principle. Indeed, sometimes constituents demand that their representatives do just that. From the abolitionists in the 1840s to the civil rights activists of the 1960s, the most effective mass political movements have been based on articulating constitutional principle.[56] Their representatives in Congress articulated similar principles when they enacted legislation to protect their rights.

Another troubling aspect of the democratic nature of Congress is the influence that money and special interests have on the political process today. Members of Congress must raise large sums of money to run for reelection and keep their jobs, and this creates a powerful incentive to cater to industry lobbyists and other monied interests and disregard constitutional principles that might interfere with those interests. Special-interest lobbies do not have the same influence on federal judges because judges need not raise campaign funds to keep their jobs. This dynamic is particularly problematic for the economically disadvantaged, who simply lack the resources to lobby their political representatives effectively.[57] However, although the influence of money on politics is irrefutable, Congress has periodically made efforts to limit that influence.[58] Ironically, the Court's rulings striking down campaign finance reform measures, treating corporations as people for the purposes of the

First Amendment, and holding the spending of money to be political speech have created the biggest obstacle to congressional efforts to ameliorate the impact of money on the political process.[59] Moreover, though the economically disadvantaged arguably have the strongest argument of any group for courts to protect their interests under the "representation-reinforcement" theory of judicial review, courts have consistently failed to so protect.[60]

Critics of Congress also argue that its political nature makes it unable to maintain constitutional stability, another prerequisite for the adequate protection of rights of belonging.[61] As political winds change, they argue, so do political positions, including positions on the meaning of the Constitution.[62] However, the argument that judicial review creates more constitutional stability than constitutional construction in the political branches is based on questionable empirical evidence.[63] Courts also change their minds and are constantly developing constitutional doctrine in a manner that may result in significant change.[64] Thus, it is simply inaccurate to say that judicial review creates more constitutional stability than constitutional construction.

Even when courts don't change constitutional doctrine, the Court's rulings do not always give rise to constitutional stability. Courts can clarify the law, but clarity is not the same as stability.[65] This is particularly true when the Court addresses issues about which people hold strong beliefs, including the meaning and scope of rights of belonging. The Supreme Court has been remarkably ineffective in resolving constitutional disputes when it acts alone, without the political branches. Indeed, "the Supreme Court is the 'ultimate interpreter' only when its decisions have been accepted as reasonable and persuasive by the people and other governmental units."[66]

There are many historical examples of this phenomenon. The Court's attempt to resolve the question of slavery in the *Dred Scott* decision was a dismal failure. Instead of calming the tension over slavery, *Dred Scott* was widely condemned by opponents of slavery in the territories and added to the tension that erupted into a Civil War only five years later. Similarly, the Court's rulings during the *Lochner* era gave rise not to constitutional stability but to widespread political opposition. Rather than accept the Court's freedom of contract doctrine as established law, progressives and leaders of the labor movement engaged in a power struggle with courts, advocating measures to limit their jurisdiction and adopting a policy of resisting injunctions that they believed to be unconstitutional. Finally, in *Brown v. Board of Education,* the Court articulated a clear constitutional rule—that race-based segregation in public education was unconstitutional, but the Court's ruling alone did not create constitutional stability. Civil rights activists supported the rule of *Brown,* but it was resisted by a large segment of the American population and did not truly become the law of the land until Congress implemented *Brown*'s promise of equality in the 1964 Civil Rights Act.

Critics also underestimate the stability brought about when the political branches interpret the Constitution. As Larry Kramer points out, "over the course of American history, Constitutional understandings determined in politics have been impressively stable."[67] After all, with its system of checks and balances, our political system is designed to make change difficult. It's arguably easier to change the minds of five people on the Court than those of the entire Congress and the president.[68]

Hence, critics exaggerate the shortcomings of Congress as a protector of rights of belonging. More importantly, when Congress does act to protect rights of belonging, it enjoys important institutional advantages over courts. The first advantage that Congress enjoys as a protector of rights of belonging is the fact that its members are democratically elected. While the *countermajoritarian* nature of federal courts is arguably their greatest strength for protecting individual rights, the *majoritarian* nature of Congress is its greatest strength when it acts to do the same. When Congress acts to protect rights of belonging, it acts on behalf of the majority of people in the entire country. The majoritarian nature of Congress gives it more legitimacy when it acts to protect rights of belonging because members of Congress are more accountable to the people than are federal judges.

Arguably, the political process can only effectively address the needs of minorities when they have a chance to participate in that process. That is the primary reason why scholars such as Black, Baer, and Chemerinsky champion courts as protectors of minority rights. However, these scholars discount the fact that minorities can make gains in the political process because in our pluralist system, political clout can be significant even on the margins.[69] For example, African Americans might make up only 10 percent of our population, but in our closely divided country, few candidates win by a margin of more than 10 percent.[70] At important times in our history, this margin enabled African Americans to achieve political goals, even before the civil rights movement when a sizeable number of them were still disenfranchised. For example, Presidents Roosevelt and Truman issued important executive orders to remedy racial discrimination because the northern African American vote was important in presidential elections in the 1940s. This phenomenon led Robert Dahl to conclude that minorities have a considerable influence in American democracy.[71]

Members of majority groups also have important incentives to protect minority rights. Legal scholar Frank Cross points out that with the exception of immutable characteristics, members of majority groups are always subject to the risk that they might someday become a member of a minority group, such as the disabled or the elderly. This gives them a strong reason to be protective of minority interests. Moreover, members of a majority on one issue might become a minority on another issue. Avoiding oppression thus gives majorities a strong incentive to support rights of belonging.[72] Most important, majorities don't always act out of self-interest, and self-interest does not explain many governmental outcomes.[73] Often, arguments based on moral principles are the most persuasive.

Legislatures as institutions also are arguably better suited than courts for remedying constitutional violations because of their fact-finding capabilities and their flexibility in creating policy.[74] The process of constitutional construction by Congress is less constrained than that of the courts. This allows for more creativity in construing constitutional meaning.[75] By contrast, when courts engage in constitutional interpretation, it is a more technical activity, limited by institutional constraints imposed on the Courts by Article III.[76] In addition, Congress has a number of mechanisms to enable it to fashion remedies for constitutional violations. For one thing, Congress has fact-finding capabilities that are superior to those of the federal courts.[77] Congress also has the flexibility to experiment with remedies, a flexibility that courts lack institutionally.[78] Finally, congressional enforcement of rights of belonging is also more efficient than enforcement by federal courts. Enforcement by the courts requires piecemeal litigation and may result in conflicting precedent from district to district.[79]

The democratic nature of the congressional process itself is another advantage of legislatures as protectors of rights of belonging. Critics of popular Constitutionalism argue that it can lead to incoherence and even mob rule.[80] However, there is a significant difference between constitutional interpretation by "the people" and that by Congress, which is the focus of this book. Unlike the dynamics that sometimes occur when "the people themselves" interpret the Constitution, congressional interpretation of the Constitution occurs within an organized institutional framework and within a defined decision-making process. Members of Congress hold hearings, engage in debates, and vote on whether to adopt constitutional positions. Of course, the congressional process does not ensure that the results will be correct, or just, but neither does the judicial process.

The open deliberation of the congressional process is important because when people argue about what is the best policy, they are more likely to reach the best conclusion and create the best policy.[81] Political actors have an incentive to present their arguments openly in order to generate support from the public and from other political actors. Moreover, congressional debate is particularly robust when considering measures protecting rights of belonging because those discussions concern deeply held values. The process advantage enjoyed by legislatures over courts is especially salient in defining the open ended constitutional provisions that protect individual rights. As Frank Cross has pointed out, "judicial interpretation of the Bill of Rights does in fact, and must inevitably, involve a substantial ideological involvement."[82] Because of their fact-finding capabilities and lack of constraint in constitutional debate, Congress may be better suited than courts to making these value judgments.[83] In contrast to the closed atmosphere of judicial decision-making, the relative transparency of the political process adds to its legitimacy and favors public acceptance of decisions made within that process.

The most important strength of the congressional law-making process is its transparency and the resulting accountability. Congressional debates are considerably more transparent than judicial deliberations, enabling more open debates over the controversial issues relating to protection of rights of belonging. Put simply, congressional debates are open to the public, and members of Congress must answer to their constituents when they are up for reelection. It is important not to exaggerate these aspects of the congressional process. First, even though members of Congress are elected, there are important factors that limit their accountability to the public. Because of the advantages of incumbency, most members of Congress simply aren't at risk of losing their jobs due to one unpopular vote. In addition, the political process is not always transparent. Many (perhaps most) important decisions in Congress are made behind closed doors, and compromises of principle are often made away from the watchful eyes of the people. However, the fact remains that "Congressional decisions still turn on whether appropriate justifications can be found for a vote."[84]

When legislation protecting rights of belonging succeeds, Congress's institutional advantages further the enforceability of congressional measures. Resistance to courts often hampers their ability to effect social change. For example, the Court attempted to resolve the issue of slavery in the *Dred Scott* decision, but it only inflamed resistance by northern abolitionists. Similarly, in the decades leading up to the New Deal Era, workers resisted courts' rulings that purportedly protected their "rights to contract." During the 1960s, the courts and the civil rights activists shared the same goals. However, the striking contrast between the public reaction to the ruling in *Brown* and the passage of the 1964 Civil Rights Act illustrates the enforceability of legislation over court decisions. While the Court's ruling in *Brown* encountered widespread resistance, the 1964 act was met with general acceptance and compliance. This contrast indicates that legislative actions bear a special mark of legitimacy, especially when they act to protect rights of belonging.

Then Solicitor General Archibold Cox emphasized the importance of the involvement of all three branches. Speaking of the success of the 1964 act, he argued that wiping out segregation in places of public accommodation was too much of a burden for the Supreme Court alone.[85] Cox explained that the Court alone probably was not able to "withstand the strains of adjudicating society's most fundamental and divisive public issues."[86] He stated:

> In retrospect, it seems clear that the public accommodations sections of the Civil Rights Act of 1964, after the Supreme Court decision upholding their Constitutionality, commanded far wider and deeper acceptance in all parts of the country, because of the participation of all three branches of government, than would have been accorded a Supreme Court ruling sustaining a claim that private establishments were required to desegregate by reason of the Fourteenth Amendment.[87]

In this way, Cox acknowledged the significance of congressional enforcement of rights of belonging. When the majoritarian body such as Congress acts to protect minorities, he explained, its actions bear a mark of special legitimacy.

Even more important, the people participate more actively in the congressional process than they do in the judicial process. This is particularly important when Congress acts to protect rights of belonging. Congressional protection of rights incorporates both the people whom Congress is acting to protect and the people who have made the decision to open our community and make it more inclusive. Congressional protection of rights of belonging furthers the agency of activists who have fought for constitutional change.

While the vision of the federal courts as "antimajoritarian heroes" protecting the rights of minorities is a powerful vision, those minorities can too easily become lost in that vision. Of course, every groundbreaking lawsuit needs a plaintiff, and the plaintiffs in the lawsuits establishing individual rights throughout our history were often heroic actors. However, lawsuits are the domain of lawyers, and individual plaintiffs often play a minor role in the litigation process.[88] By contrast, thousands of political activists engaged openly and vocally in constitutional advocacy in order to obtain the political victories described in this book. Members of the Reconstruction Congress based their broad view of citizenship in large part on the sacrifices of union soldiers and newly freed slaves who had fought on the side of the Union. Many of them saw national citizenship rights for freed slaves as a "social compact" to reward them for their sacrifices. Labor leaders and rank-and-file union members fought for years for the protections afforded them in New Deal Era protective labor legislation. The Second Reconstruction was brought about primarily as a result of the sacrifices of civil rights activists who fought against segregation. All of these activists were not passive actors experiencing the tyranny of the majority. They fought for major constitutional change, and their fight was successful in the political realm.

When the Court asserts a monopoly over constitutional meaning that is likely to be harmful to the cause of rights of belonging for another reason. It creates a disincentive for Congress to act to protect the rights of its citizens because the Court is likely to strike down any legislation that provides more protection than the courts are ready to give. Because they know they are unlikely to succeed, advocates of rights of belonging are likely to decrease their reliance on the political process and increase their reliance on courts as protectors of rights of belonging. Yet even as the current Supreme Court has placed limits on congressional definition of rights of belonging, it has placed even more onerous limitations on individual enforcement of those rights.[89] Most important, this stance threatens to sever the historical link between rights of belonging and the political process. The final chapter of this book explores this link and explains why the very nature of rights of belonging makes them best enforced by legislatures, not courts.

8

Considering Rights of Belonging, Moral Values, and Community

The model of courts as protectors of rights still retains a strong ideological pull for constitutional law scholars, law students, and attorneys. The link between courts and rights is deeply embedded in their consciousness, so much so that many constitutional scholars simply overlook the role that legislatures have in protecting our rights. This theoretical attachment to courts requires a theoretical explanation. Answering the question of where rights of belonging fit within our constitutional system requires delving into the proper relationship between rights of belonging, moral values, and community. In this chapter I explore the possibility that there is something about rights of belonging themselves that links them to federal courts. I conclude that the opposite is the case. Rights of belonging are best enforced in the political process because they express the values of our national community.

Rights of belonging define the contours of our national community and express that community's values, yet federal courts, by and large, are external to that community, making them ill-suited for defining the community and determining its values. Hence, while courts are well-suited for protecting the liberty interests of the individual against infringement by the community, they are less well-suited for protecting equality-based interests, including rights of belonging, that define the community. Legislatures, in contrast, are elected by the community and thus are intended to reflect the values of the community. The legislative process also is likely to result in a more robust vision of equality. Finally, the process of legislative protection of rights of belonging is salutary because it involves an open dialogue about the identity of the community and the values embodied by the community. Identifying and developing values in our society is "an important part of the way we constitute ourselves as part of the people of the United States."[1] Hence, this dialogue has the salutary effect of strengthening civil society, as well as fostering consensus about the extent and meaning of rights of belonging. Most important, when advocates of rights of belonging engage in this dialogue, they are more effective at bringing about social change.

Philosophers have long debated the proper role that rights have in defining and determining the boundaries of a community. Constitutional scholars tend to view individual rights through the prism of liberalism, based on the primacy of individual rights and premised on the neutrality of the state. Liberal theory views rights as protections for individuals against the community.[2] For example, people may have a right to speak without government restrictions or to protection from government interference in their private lives. This liberal model of rights is based on the view that people need to be protected from each other and that government assumes the role of the protector. Because federal courts act outside the community and are not accountable to the community, they are the governmental entity best suited to protect individuals from the community. Moral values play only a negative part in this scenario. They help to define the community from which the individual needs protection. In the name of individual autonomy, courts shield individuals from intrusive moral values that the community wants to impose on them.[3]

Theoretically, judges enforce this model by remaining neutral and avoiding imposing their values through the lens of constitutional interpretation. In his influential "representation reinforcement" theory, John Hart Ely suggests a means for judges to maintain their neutrality while still protecting individual rights. Ely argues that courts should avoid reading substantive values into the constitution and limit themselves to remedying failures of the political process to meet the needs of what the Court deemed "discrete and insular minorities" in *Carolene Products* footnote four.[4] Under this theory, judges establish and enforce rights of belonging for the individuals who are repeat losers in the political process. Many scholars have seized on this point, arguing in favor of courts as protectors of minority rights.[5] However, these scholars fail to fully appreciate Ely's insight that courts are ill-suited to incorporating values into law. When it comes to rights of belonging, the role of courts is both reactive and restricted. Rights of belonging necessarily will be limited because courts will avoid creating new values.

There are several reasons that courts are simply inadequate for a robust enforcement of rights of belonging. First, while rights of belonging are equality-based rights, court enforcement will tend to privilege liberty interests over equality interests because courts tend to favor individual interests over collective interests. For example, during the *Lochner* era, courts privileged the individual liberty of contract over the equality-based right to join a union and bargain collectively. Since the 1970s, the Court has favored individual liberty over group equality when it interpreted the Equal Protection Clause to impose the requirement of discriminatory intent and to disfavor affirmative action measures.[6] Throughout our history, activists have sensed this dynamic and recognized that while liberty is often expressed in individualistic terms that may be enforceable through the courts, equality is most effectively enforced by collective action.

A second reason that courts are not well-suited to protecting rights of belonging is their institutional commitment to neutrality. Formal neutrality may mask deeply seated inequality in our society and make it harder to remedy that inequality.[7] Feminist legal theorists long have recognized the failure of liberal neutrality to meet the needs of those who historically have been disempowered in our society. For example, Catharine MacKinnon argues that the neutral paradigm simply reinforces the unjust status quo. In her "antisubordination" theory of sex equality, MacKinnon maintains that affirmative, value-laden efforts are needed to address the inequity underlying our economic and social systems.[8] Similarly, Robin West maintains that the negative concept of ordered liberty fails to provide the positive rights that women need the most.[9] West points out that the rights that most women lack, such as the right to economic equality and protection from domestic violence, require affirmative action, not noninterference, by the government. Private actors, not government actors, typically impose most constraints on women's lives. Government action, not government inaction, is required to eliminate those constraints.[10] As these scholars recognize, the disempowered, those most likely to benefit from rights of belonging, are not being well served by the neutrality of the state, posited by the liberal view of rights and enforced by the courts.

Another problem with the court enforcement of rights is its emphasis on the individual and its deemphasis on the value of community. As Mary Anne Glendon argues in her critique of the court-based liberal "rights discourse," that debate is too absolutist and too focused on the individual. Liberal rights discourse also tends to downplay the individual's connection to community by undervaluing individual responsibility to the community. Perhaps most important, the adversarial nature of liberal rights discourse tends to heighten social conflict and inhibit dialogue that could lead to consensus about issues that have crucial importance in our society.[11] Glendon maintains, "Saturated with rights, political language can no longer perform the important function of facilitating public discussion of the right ordering of our lives together."[12] Expressing rights as absolute works well as an advocacy tool within the confines of litigation over those rights, but it inhibits dialogue over the fundamental values that underlie rights of belonging.

When debates over those values are confined to the adversarial litigation process, that process stifles the dialogue over rights, values, and community that is necessary to sustain a healthy civic life. Moreover, divorcing rights from the political process has an overwhelming cost. Increasingly, members of our society feel alienated from that process because it does not speak to the values and concerns that people care about.[13] As Michael Sandel points out, the liberal self-image, based on a volunteerist concept of freedom, is at odds with the actual organization of modern socioeconomic life. Even as we experience more freedom as a result of liberal reforms, we suffer from a growing sense of disempowerment and searching for meaning in institutions outside the secular government.[14]

Liberal theory, which values neutrality and autonomy, thus fails to adequately address the value of self-government and community.[15] By contrast, finding a new way to frame issues of rights and values could help to revitalize our civic culture. As an alternative, the theory of rights of belonging views those rights as connecting the individual with one's community. This view reflects the fact that those rights help to shape our communities. Unlike the liberal theory of rights, which is premised on the neutrality of the decision-maker, the theory of rights of belonging accepts the fact that lawmaking is often based on moral values. People have strong values, and many of them want their governments to act on their values. Moreover, many people organize their lives around their value systems by attending church, volunteering for civic organizations, joining unions, and engaging in political activity.[16]

Something special happens when the majority acts to include and protect minorities in their communities. The community has acted to include the excluded and empower the disempowered. It is important not to overstate the altruistic nature of the phenomenon. Arguably, this phenomenon only occurs when the majority is convinced that expanding rights of belonging is in its own best interest.[17] Historically, this has only occurred when minorities participate in mass movements to demand inclusion.[18] Moreover, including some, but not others, may serve to further disempower those with the least power and further marginalize those on the furthest margins.[19] But when people do voluntarily give up power, they often do it because they feel that it is morally imperative to do so. One notable feature of this process, therefore, is the positive role that moral values can have in determining rights of belonging. In today's political discourse, the concept of "moral values" is often voiced in opposition to rights of belonging, such as the rights of gays and lesbians to marry.[20] Notwithstanding the current political climate, however, moral values long have also had a positive role in establishing rights of belonging.

During all three periods marked by the largest expansions of rights of belonging in our country—Reconstruction, the New Deal, and the Second Reconstruction—moral values played an important part in the political processes leading to those expansions. Prior to the Civil War, abolitionists relied on their religious traditions to argue that slavery was morally wrong. During Reconstruction, the members of Congress who authored the Fourteenth Amendment and the civil rights statutes picked up on this theme, arguing that the federal government had a moral obligation to protect the freed slaves and enable them to become equal citizens. Similarly, labor activists in the first third of the last century made moral arguments in favor of the right to unionize, maintaining that working without the right to bargain collectively was tantamount to slavery. Congress's New Deal program was based to a large degree on the philosophy that the government had a moral obligation to care for the most needy in our society. Finally, the civil rights movement in the 1960s, which took the primary role in bringing about the Second Reconstruction, was to a large degree a church-based movement, with Reverend Martin Luther King and his Southern Christian Leadership Conference, the National Council of Churches, and other religious leaders successfully advocating for civil rights legislation. During these periods, members of Congress responded to the value-based arguments of these advocates and incorporated them into the law of the land.

In contrast to the liberal theory of rights, with its emphasis on neutral process, rights of belonging embody a substantive vision of equality, through which the community undertakes the proactive duty of enforcing the equal rights of its members. The substantive view of equality also has its roots in the Reconstruction Era. The Framers of the Fourteenth Amendment intended the Equal Protection Clause to require the state to act affirmatively to protect each individual's exercise of his or her natural human rights.[21] Robin West explains that this obligation "rested on and presupposed a sense of civic responsibility and obligation to others that is foreign to our modern conception of citizenship."[22] Similarly, Akhil Amar notes that the Framers of the Fourteenth Amendment intended it to give Congress broad powers "to affirm that Blacks were equal citizens worthy of respect and dignity" and enforce the ideal of equal citizenship for all those who have historically been denied equality.[23] The ideals of belonging, protection, and equality, central to the Framers of the Fourteenth Amendment, underlie a rich conception of what it means to belong to our society.

Although it carries the danger of exclusion if taken too literally, the concept of citizenship is especially valuable because it evokes a mutual and engaged relationship between the political community and its members, along with a broad vision of equality among those members.[24] During Reconstruction, many supporters of the Fourteenth Amendment believed in a "social contract" theory of citizenship that linked the concept of equality to community. According to their theory, in exchange for one's allegiance to the national government, the national government would provide protection and treat its citizens equally.[25] Judith Baer describes this vision as "a notion that all human beings have a right to equal respect and concern."[26] The Framers of the Fourteenth Amendment held a broad view of the meaning of national citizenship, encompassing the belonging, protection, and equality of those who fell within their jurisdiction.[27] Similarly, unionists and their supporters in the New Deal Congress believed that increased bargaining power would empower workers and enhance their freedom.[28] They advocated a vision of equality that included economic empowerment as a means toward social justice. During the Second Reconstruction, civil rights activists and their congressional supporters linked racial and economic equality in Title VII of the 1964 Civil Rights Act and other legislation establishing economic rights and prohibiting racial discrimination. In all of these eras, members of Congress defined equality broadly.

The message of inclusion in a community carries a value in and of itself. For example, when a state builds a courthouse with an entrance that is only accessible by a long flight of stairs, the lack of access sends a message to wheelchair-bound litigants that they simply do not belong and that they may be prosecuted not just for breaking the law, but for not belonging.[29] Exclusion creates a psychic injury, not just an economic injury or a frustrating inconvenience. When legislatures act to remedy that exclusion, their recognition of this injury in and of itself sends a strong message of inclusion. Reliance on courts to enforce those rights does not require direct engagement in the community but may instead alienate those who feel that unaccountable judges are forcing rights on them. When rights of belonging are defined and enforced through the political process, the process encourages a national dialogue over the meaning of these rights and the values that underlie them.

As David Engle and Frank Munger argue, the connection between statutes protecting rights of belonging and the evolution of social norms is more complicated than commonly assumed—and does not rely exclusively on judicial enforcement of the rights created by those statutes: "rights can become active in day-to-day life even when individuals do not choose to assert them. Rights can transform the sense of self simply by increasing individuals' perceptions of their own worth, or by reminding them of opportunities they could pursue if they could assume reasonable accommodations and nondiscriminatory behavior by employers."[30] Hence, equality and community are linked in a just society. Because people conceive of their identity as defined to some extent by the community in which they take part, "For them, community describes not just what they *have* as fellow citizens but also what they *are*."[31] People often strongly identify with the community in which they live, and it is human nature to want to belong to that community. Rights of belonging matter not only because they facilitate access to the institutions in one's community, but also because they make people feel as if they are members of that community.

Perhaps the most important normative reason that legislative protection of rights of belonging is superior to the use of judicial review to protect those rights is the stifling effect that judicial review can have on deliberation over values and rights in our society. Robert Cover recognized this fact when he described the judicial process as "jurispathic," killing an alternative vision of what constitutional rights and values are about in our society.[32] By contrast, the consideration of rights of belonging in the political process *starts* a conversation about rights and values, and the meaning of community, in our society. We might not always like the result of that conversation, but the fact that it occurs in and of itself has significant value in a democratic society. One of the principal values of popular constitutionalism is the fact that people who engage in it embrace the Constitution and its meaning.[33]

The political process itself is integrally connected to rights of belonging because engaging in the political process amounts to the assertion of belonging. The democratic nature of legislative protection of rights of belonging is an inherent good because it provides a process for people to work together for social change. The act of political engagement can be empowering and lead to an enhanced sense of community. Voting is an act of belonging because it is an act of self-governance.[34] More active political engagement is even more beneficial for the activist. When people work together to change the law, they share a commitment to common values with other people who have the same goals. This commonality creates a community. Hence, political advocacy on behalf of rights of belonging itself not only helps to foster a healthy democracy but also expands one's sense of belonging. Rights of belonging are thus best enforced by the political branches because there is an integral link between rights of belonging and the political process.

Finally, whether or not rights of belonging are inherently valuable, they are essential to democracy. As Sandel notes, belonging is essential to self-government:

> According to republican political theory, . . . sharing in self-rule . . . means deliberating with fellow citizens about the common good and helping to shape the destiny of the political community. But to deliberate well about the common good requires . . . a knowledge of public affairs and also *a sense of belonging,* a concern for the whole, a moral bond with the community whose fate is at stake.[35]

Liberal political theory fails to place a premium on ensuring the prerequisites to effective self-governance and, as a result, "cannot sustain the kind of political community and civic engagement that [democracy] requires."[36] Indeed, in the absence of rights of belonging, the enterprise of self-government would be tainted unavoidably by the systematic privileging of some citizens over others and the consistent overweighting of their voices in the public debate. The enduring inequality that would result from denying rights of belonging to some members of the community would call the integrity of the entire democratic political community into question.[37] Simply put, in practice, rights of belonging are not a luxury.

Unfortunately, at the turn of the twenty-first century, legal reformers seem to underappreciate the value of participation and democracy to defining and expanding our national community. For the past generation, too many legal reformers have focused primarily on the litigation process, favoring test cases over political action, despite the fact that appointments by conservative presidents have made the federal courts increasingly hostile to rights of belonging over recent years.[38] Meanwhile, a decreasing proportion of our voting population participates in elections because many people feel that the issues that concern them the most simply are not addressed within the political process. While the political process is far from perfect, democracy retains its potential for providing an effective forum of debate over the issues that are the most meaningful to our lives. The scope and definition of our national community, and the extent of our right to belonging to that community, are crucial to the American people. Litigation is simply no substitute for collective political action.

Notes

NOTES TO CHAPTER I

1. *United States v. Carolene Products,* 304 U.S. 144 (1938). *See* JOHN HART ELY, DEMOCRACY AND DISTRUST: A THEORY OF JUDICIAL REVIEW (1980).

2. THE FEDERALIST NO. 78, THE FEDERALIST PAPERS 464, 469 (Alexander Hamilton) (Clinton Rossiter, ed., 1961).

3. A recent Lexis search uncovered 506 law review articles written in the past twenty years advocating the proposition that courts should protect minorities against the will of the majority. For just a few of the many prominent scholars supporting this view, *see* KENNETH L. KARST, BELONGING TO AMERICA: EQUAL CITIZENSHIP AND THE CONSTITUTION 9 (1989); CHARLES L. BLACK, JR., A NEW BIRTH OF FREEDOM: HUMAN RIGHTS, NAMED AND UNNAMED 125 (1997); JUDITH A. BAER, EQUALITY UNDER THE CONSTITUTION: RECLAIMING THE FOURTEENTH AMENDMENT 281 (1983); ELY, *supra* note 1, at 7. *See also* JOHN J. DINAN, KEEPING THE PEOPLE'S LIBERTIES: LEGISLATORS, CITIZENS, AND JUDGES AS GUARDIANS OF RIGHTS (1998) (stating that "the nation's leading law faculty are nearly unanimous" in believing the judiciary is best suited to protecting liberties). *But see* Frank B. Cross, *Institutions and Enforcement of the Bill of Rights,* 85 CORNELL L. REV. 1529 (2000) (questioning this assumption).

4. *See* Jane S. Schacter, Romer v. Evans *and Democracy's Domain,* 50 VAND. L. REV. 361, 362 (1997).

5. It is debatable whether courts in fact have played the role of protecting minorities against majority will. *See* Michael J. Klarman, *Rethinking the Civil Rights and Civil Liberties Revolutions,* 82 VA. L. REV. 1, 6 (1996) (questioning the "conventional wisdom" that courts protect minority rights from oppressive majorities). A complete analysis of this debate is beyond the scope of this book, but I attempt a cursory exploration in chapter 7.

6. This is not to suggest that Congress, or any majoritarian body, always acts to protect individual rights. Of course, examples abound of federal legislation that restricts individual rights, and several of those examples are discussed in this book.

7. *Employment Division v. Smith,* 494 U.S. 872 (1990), *superseded by*

statute Religious Freedom Restoration Act of 1993, Pub. L. No. 103-141, 107 Stat. 1488 (1993), *invalidated by City of Boerne v. Flores,* 521 U.S. 507 (1997) (codified at 42 U.S.C. §§ 2000bb to 2000bb-4 (1994)), *as recognized in Cutter v. Wilkinson,* 125 S. Ct. 2113 (2005).

8. *See Sherbert v. Verner,* 374 U.S. 398 (1963).

9. *See* Tony Mauro, *Is the Court Finally Camera-Ready?* LEGAL TIMES, May 14, 1990, at 10.

10. Religious Freedom Restoration Act of 1993; *Employment Division v. Smith.*

11. The bill was agreed to by voice vote in the House of Representatives and passed by a margin of 97 to 3 in the Senate. 139 CONG. REC. H2356, 2363 (1993); 139 CONG. REC. S14461, 14470 (1993).

12. 139 CONG. REC. at S14465 (statement of Sen. Hatfield); *id.* at S14464 (statement of Sen. Coates).

13. *Id.* at S14469 (statement of Sen. Smith).

14. 139 CONG. REC. at H2360.

15. *See* 139 CONG. REC. at S14461 (statement of Sen. Lieberman); *id.* at S14465 (statement of Sen. Hatfield).

16. 139 CONG. REC. at H2357.

17. 139 CONG. REC. at S14461.

18. Marcia Coyle, Marianne Lavelle, & Claudia MacLachlan, *Religion Bill,* NAT'L. J., November 15, 1993, at 12.

19. Remarks on Signing the Religious Freedom Restoration Act of 1993, 29 *Weekly Comp.* Pres. Doc. 2377 (November 16, 1993).

20. *Boerne,* 521 U.S. at 519–520. Like *Smith, Boerne* overruled existing precedent. Prior to *Boerne,* the Court had applied the deferential "rational basis" test to Congress's use of its Section Five power. *See Katzenbach v. Morgan,* 384 U.S. 641, 651 (1966).

21. *Id.* at 529 (*quoting Marbury v. Madison,* 5 U.S. (1 Cranch) 137, 177 (1803)).

22. *Boerne,* 521 U.S. 507.

23. *See Marbury,* 5 U.S. 179–180 ("the framers of the constitution contemplated that instrument as a rule for the government of courts as well as of the legislature"). *See* Keith E. Whittington, *Extrajudicial Constitutional Interpretation: Three Objections and Responses,* 80 N.C. L. REV. 773, 780 (2002) (differentiating between judicial review, the power of courts to review the constitutionality of the acts of other branches, and judicial supremacy, the theory that only the court can authoritatively interpret the constitution); Robert C. Post & Reva B. Siegel, *Legislative Constitutionalism and Section Five Power: Policentric Interpretation of the Family and Medical Leave Act,* 112 YALE L. J. 1943, 2005–2008 (2003) (discussing the differences between judicial and legislative interpretation of the Constitution).

24. *See* Post & Siegel, *supra* note 23, at 2005–2008.

25. Wilfred M. McClay, Commentary: The Worst Decision since "Dred Scott"? Decision Overturning the Religious Freedom Restoration Act, 104 ASAP 52 (1997).

26. Religious Land Use and Institutionalized Persons Act of 2000, Pub. L. No. 106-274, September 22, 2000, 114 Stat. 803, USCA §§ 2000cc et seq. This statute makes compliance a condition of receipt of federal funds.

27. *See Cutter,* 125 S. Ct. 2113.

28. For a few examples of the extensive literature on this subject, *see* Randy Barnett & Don B. Kates, *Under Fire: The New Consensus on the Second Amendment,* 45 EMORY L. J. 1139, 1141 (1996) (individual right); Sanford Levinson, *The Embarrassing Second Amendment,* 99 YALE L. J. 637 (1989) (individual right). *But see* Carl T. Bogus, *The Hidden History of the Second Amendment,* 31 U.C. DAVIS L. REV. 309 (1998) (no individual right); Andrew D. Herz, *Gun Crazy: Constitutional False Consciousness and Dereliction of Constitutional Responsibility,* 75 B.U. L. REV. 57, 58 (1995) (no individual right). For an in-depth discussion of this debate, *see* David Yassky, *The Second Amendment: Structure, History and Constitutional Change,* 99 MICH. L. REV. 588 (2000).

29. *United States v. Miller,* 307 U.S. 174 (1939). Lower courts have tended to rule against Second Amendment claims. *See* Yassky, *supra* note 28, at 589 n.2.

30. *See* Herz, *supra* note 28, at 58; Stephen Halbrook, *Congress Interprets the Second Amendment: Declarations by a Co-Equal Branch on the Individual Right to Keep and Bear Arms,* 32 TENN. L. REV. 597 (1995). Examples of federal statutes enforcing the right to bear arms include Firearms Owners' Protection Act 1(b), Pub. L. No. 99-308, 100 Stat. 449 (1986) (codified as amended at 18 U.S.C. 921 (2000); Requisitioning Property for National Defense Property Requisition Act, Pub. L. No. 77-274, 55 Stat. 742 (1941), *amended by* Second War Powers Act, Pub. L. No. 77-507, 56 Stat. 176 (1942), Requisitioning of Property for National Defense, Pub. L. No. 78-104, 57 Stat. 271 (1943), Requisition of Property for National Defense, Pub. L. No. 78-378, 58 Stat. 624 (1944), Requisition of Property for National Defense, Pub. L. No. 79-102, 59 Stat. 271 (1945); Freedmen's Bureau Act, 14 Stat. 174, 176–177 (1866). Other proposed measures include the proposed Community Protection Initiative, which would have created a federal right of law enforcement officers to carry a concealed firearm nationwide, notwithstanding state law. *See* Orrin G. Hatch, *The Brady Handgun Prevention Act and the Community Protection Initiative: Legislative Responses to the Second Amendment?,* 1998 BYU L. REV. 103 (1998).

31. *See, e.g.,* Ronald H. Beason, *Printz Punts on the Palladium of Rights: It Is Time to Protect the Rights of the Individual to Keep and Bear Arms,* 50 ALA. L. REV. 561, 562 (1999); Brandon P. Denning, *Gun Shy: The Second Amend-*

ment as an "Underenforced Constitutional Norm," 21 HARV. J. L. & PUB. POL'Y 719, 731 (1998).

32. I owe this observation to a conversation with Randy Barnett.

33. *See* Denise C. Morgan & Rebecca E. Zietlow, *The New Parity Debate: Congress and Rights of Belonging,* 73 CINN. L. REV. 1347 (2005).

34. *See, e.g.,* KARST, *supra* note 3, at 2. Karst's work, however, focuses on the Supreme Court's interpretation of constitutional provisions that ensure belonging. By contrast, in this book I discuss the role of Congress in defining and creating rights that serve that function. The difference in emphasis is quite significant. Because federal courts are not politically accountable, when they create rights of belonging, they impose them externally upon a community. Alternatively, when the legislative branch creates rights of belonging, it represents a decision within the community to effectuate a more inclusive vision of that community. *See infra,* chapter 7.

35. *See* Linda S. Bosniak, *Membership, Equality, and the Difference That Alienage Makes,* 69 N.Y.U. L. REV. 1047, 1059 (1994) (pointing out that conventional scholarship about alienage focuses on "inside" and "outside" immigration law).

36. *Compare* KARST, *supra* note 3, at 173 ("nationalism, nourishing both a national identity and the sense of national community") *with* Linda S. Bosniak, *Constitutional Citizenship through the Prism of Alienage,* 63 OHIO ST. L. J. 1285, 1318 (2002) ("the value of belonging also pre-supposes community boundaries—boundaries which ultimately divide insiders from outsiders"). Of course, it is arguable that, whether or not the national community is drawn to include noncitizens, in order to be a community it must exclude *someone.*

37. Here I do not attempt to provide an exhaustive list of "rights of belonging," nor is such an exhaustive list possible. Instead, in each chapter I explore why the featured statutes protect "rights of belonging." In chapters 7 and 8 I delve more deeply into the significance of the term and its relationship to the theoretical underpinning of my argument.

38. The Supreme Court recognized this when it struck down a state statue banning interracial marriage as violating both the Equal Protection and Due Process Clauses of the Fourteenth Amendment. *See Loving v. Virginia,* 388 U.S. 1 (1967).

39. National Labor Relations Act [Wagner Act], ch. 37,49 Stat. 449 (193) (codified as amended at 29 U.S.C. §§ 11–166 (2000).

40. For example, the debate over whether or not the Fourteenth Amendment was intended to incorporate the bill of rights against the states, which occupied scholars and members of the Supreme Court throughout the twentieth century and into the present, focuses exclusively on Section 1 of that amendment and on the Court's interpretation of the rights embodied in that provision. *See* Bryan H.

Wildenthal, *The Lost Compromise: Reassessing the Early Understanding in Court and Congress on Incorporation of the Bill of Rights in the Fourteenth Amendment,* 61 OHIO ST. L. J. 1051, 1055–1061 (2000) (describing the scholarly exchange). Only recently have constitutional scholars begun to analyze the role that congressional enforcement of the Fourteenth Amendment might have in that debate. *See* Rebecca E. Zietlow, *Congressional Enforcement of Citizenship Rights and John Bingham's Theory of Citizenship,* 36 AKRON L. REV. 717 (2003); James W. Fox, *Re-readings and Misreadings: Slaughter-House, Privileges or Immunities, and Section Five Enforcement Power,* 91 KY. L. J. 67 (2002); William J. Rich, *Taking "Privileges or Immunities" Seriously: A Call to Expand the Constitutional Canon,* 87 MINN. L. REV. 153 (2002). A few other scholars have recently focused on reexamining the structural role that the courts and Congress have in protecting individual rights. *See, e.g.,* Stephen M. Griffin, *Judicial Supremacy and Equal Protection in a Democracy of Rights,* 4 U. PA. J. CONST. L. 281 (2002); Post & Siegel, *supra* note 23, at 2005–2008; William D. Araiza, *Court, Congress and Equal Protection: What Brown Teaches Us about the Section 5 Power,* 47 HOW. L. J. 199 (2004).

41. *See* Mark Tushnet, *Non-Judicial Review,* 40 HARV. J. ON LEGIS. 453 (2003) (describing this phenomena). *See also* KEITH E. WHITTINGTON, CONSTITUTIONAL CONSTRUCTION: DIVIDED POWERS AND CONSTITUTIONAL MEANING 1 (1999) (the Constitution is usually regarded as purely a legal document, to be interpreted by courts, "and the exercise of judicial review is regarded as tantamount to constitutionalism itself').

42. *See* ALEXANDER BICKEL, THE LEAST DANGEROUS BRANCH: THE SUPREME COURT AT THE BAR OF POLITICS 24–26 (1962) ("Courts have certain capacities for dealing with matters of principle that legislatures and executives do not possess. Judges have, or should have, the leisure, the training and the insulation to follow the ways of the scholar in pursuing the ends of government."); Abner J. Mikva, *How Well Does Congress Support and Defend the Constitution?* 61 N.C. L. REV. 587, 610 (1983); Owen Fiss, *The Supreme Court 1978 Term—Foreword: The Forms of Justice,* 93 HARV. L. REV. 1, 9–10 (1979) ("Legislatures are . . . not ideologically committed or institutionally suited to search for the meaning of constitutional values, but instead see their primary function in terms of registering the actual, occurrent preferences of the people—what they want and what they believe should be done.").

43. *See* Larry D. Kramer, *Popular Constitutionalism, circa 2004,* 92 CAL. L. REV. 959 (2004).

44. There are many other works exploring the influence of popular constitutionalism on lawmaking. *See, e.g.,* William N. Eskridge, Jr., *Some Effects of Identity-Based Social Movements on Constitutional Law in the Twentieth Century,* 100 MICH. L. REV. 2062 (2002) (discussing in depth the impact of social

movements on the Court's jurisprudence); Post & Siegel, *supra* note 23, at 2005–2008 (detailing the impact of the feminist movement on Congress and the Court in the 1970s); James Gray Pope, *The Thirteenth Amendment versus the Commerce Clause: Labor and the Shaping of American Constitutional Law, 1921–1957,* 102 COLUM. L. REV. 1 (2002) (exploring the relationship between the labor movement and the congressional process (with a slightly different take from mine)).

45. *See* U.S. CONST. Art. VI, § 3; Louis Fisher, *Constitutional Interpretation by Members of Congress,* 63 N.C. L. REV. 707, 718 (1985).

46. WHITTINGTON, *supra* note 41, at 1.

47. *See* Tushnet, *supra* note 41, at 454.

48. For a good summary of the political science literature on judges and public opinion, *see* Cross, *supra* note 3, at 1553–1559. Barry Friedman agrees that courts reflect public opinion, but he argues that they tend to lag behind public opinion about a ten-year interval. *See* Barry Friedman, *Dialogue and Judicial Review,* 91 MICH. L. REV. 577, 677 (1993).

49. A number of cases applied *Boerne* to strike down provisions of civil rights laws that made them individually enforceable against state governments. *See Board of Trustees v. Garrett,* 531 U.S. 356 (2001); *Kimel v. Florida Board of Regents,* 528 U.S. 62 (2000). The Court has upheld some civil rights statutes in other cases, but in those cases the Court has continued to assert its authority as the ultimate interpreter of the Fourteenth Amendment. *See Nevada Department of Human Resources v. Hibbs,* 538 U.S. 721 (2003); *Tennessee v. Lane,* 541 U.S. 509 (2004).

50. *See United States v. Lopez,* 514 U.S. 549 (1995); *United States v. Morrison,* 529 U.S. 598 (2000).

51. *See, e.g.,* James J. Brudney and Ruth Colker, *Dissing Congress,* 100 MICH. L. REV. 80 (2001); AWAKENING FROM THE DREAM: CIVIL RIGHTS UNDER SIEGE AND THE NEW STRUGGLE FOR EQUAL JUSTICE (Denise C. Morgan, Rachel D. Godsil, & Joy Moses, eds., 2005).

52. *See* MARY ANN GLENDON, RIGHTS TALK: THE IMPOVERISHMENT OF POLITICAL DISCOURSE 6 (1991).

NOTES TO CHAPTER 2

1. Mark A. Graber, *Resolving Political Questions into Judicial Decisions: Tocqueville's Thesis Revisited,* 21 CONST. COMMENT. 485, 486 (2004).

2. PAUL FINKELMAN, AN IMPERFECT UNION: SLAVERY, FEDERALISM AND COMITY (1981).

3. The Privileges and Immunities Clause of Article IV had a nondiscrimination component to it and was intended to require equal treatment to some

extent. ROGERS M. SMITH, CIVIC IDEALS: CONFLICTING VISIONS OF CITIZEN-
SHIP IN U.S. HISTORY (1997). However, as described in this chapter, due in large
part to the issue of slavery, the Privilege and Immunities Clause failed to achieve
that potential.

4. *Dred Scott v. Sanford*, 60 U.S. (19 How.) 393 (1856). *See* FINKELMAN,
IMPERFECT UNION, *supra* note 2, at 274.

5. *See* James S. Liebman & Brandon L. Garrett, *Madisonian Equal Protection*, 104 COLUM. L. REV. 837, 839–840 (2004).

6. THE FEDERALIST NOS. 44, 51 (James Madison) (Clinton Rossiter, ed.,
1961). *See* Paul Finkelman, *James Madison and the Bill of Rights: A Reluctant
Paternity*, 1990 SUP. CT. REV. 301, 308 (1991).

7. THE FEDERALIST NO. 10, 77–78 (James Madison) (Clinton Rossiter, ed.,
1961).

8. Jack N. Rakove, *The Madisonian Theory of Rights*, 31 WM. & MARY L.
REV. 245, 252 (1990); Larry D. Kramer, *Madison's Audience*, 112 HARV. L.
REV. 611, 633 (1999).

9. THE FEDERALIST NO. 10 (James Madison), *supra* note 7, at 78, 80; *see
also* Liebman & Garrett, *supra* note 5, at 858.

10. THE FEDERALIST NO. 51, 321, 321–323 (James Madison) (Clinton Rossiter, ed., 1961).

11. This is not to say that Madison intended to transfer authority from
states to the federal government. Rather, he wanted the federal government to
provide a check on the states. *See* Michael P. Zuckert, *Toward a Corrective Federalism: The United States Constitution, Federalism, and Rights, in* FEDERALISM
AND RIGHTS 75 (Ellis Katz & G. Alan Tarr, eds., 1996).

12. JAMES MADISON, VICES OF THE POLITICAL SYSTEM OF THE UNITED
STATES (1787), *reprinted in* THE PAPERS OF JAMES MADISON 9:346 (Robert A.
Rutland et al., eds. 1975) (Editor's Note on Vices Memo); Rakove, *supra* note
8, at 247; Mark R. Killenbeck, *Madison, M'Culloch, and Matters of Judicial
Cognizance: Some Thoughts on the Nature and Scope of Judicial Review*, 55
ARK. L. REV. 901, 914 (2003).

13. MADISON, VICES OF THE POLITICAL SYSTEM, *supra* note 12, at 350, 354.
Madison's distrust of state legislatures was rooted in his negative experience as
a member of the Virginia state assembly. *See* Rakove, *supra* note 8, at 263;
Kramer, *supra* note 8, at 625.

14. *See* Gary Jeffrey Jacobsohn, *Contemporary Constitutional Theory, Federalism, and the Protection of Rights, in* FEDERALISM AND RIGHTS 35 (Ellis
Katz & G. Alan Tarr, eds., 1996). Madison thought that Congress would be disinterested as to terms of local policy, so that the federal negative would likely
further positive public policy. Zuckert, *supra* note 11, at 85.

15. *See* Kramer, *supra* note 8, at 645.

16. Madison, Vices of the Political System, *supra* note 12, at 357.

17. The Federalist No. 10 (James Madison), *supra* note 7, at 82, 84; Liebman & Garrett, *supra* note 5, at 881.

18. Liebman & Garrett, *supra* note 5, at 839–840, citing Letter from James Madison to George Washington (Apr. 16, 1787), *reprinted in* The Papers of James Madison, *supra* note 12, at 9:383–384. *See also* Kramer, *supra* note 8, at 649; Rakove, *supra* note 8, at 253.

19. Liebman & Garrett, *supra* note 5, at 907; Kramer, *supra* note 8, at 634; *See* Charles F. Hobson, *The Negative on States Laws: James Madison, and the Crisis of Republican Government,* 36 Wm. & Mary Q. 215, 226 (1979).

20. Letter from James Madison to George Washington, *reprinted in* The Papers of James Madison, *supra* note 12, at 9:383–384.

21. The Papers of James Madison, *supra* note 12, at 9:347 (Editor's Note on Vices Memo) ("This federal veto was to be the foundation of the new system."); Kramer, *supra* note 8, at 649; Liebman & Garrett, *supra* note 5, at 845.

22. Hobson, *supra* note 19, at 226.

23. While Larry Kramer emphasizes the role that the negative would have had in protecting liberty interests, Liebman and Garrett maintain that Madison was more concerned about protecting equality interests. Kramer, *supra* note 8, at 634; Liebman & Garrett, *supra* note 5, at 849.

24. Rakove, *supra* note 8, at 252, citing Letter from James Madison to George Washington, *reprinted in* The Papers of James Madison, *supra* note 12, at 9:384.

25. The Federalist No. 10 (James Madison), *supra* note 7, at 81.

26. Letter from James Madison to Thomas Jefferson (Oct. 24, 1788), *reprinted in* The Papers of Madison 10:205, 212 (Robert A. Rutland et al., eds. 1975).

27. Zuckert, *supra* note 11, at 96; Kramer, *supra* note 8, at 634.

28. *See* Kramer, *supra* note 8, at 642. The primary concern of the other federalist delegates was protecting the federal government from state interference. *See id.* at 636, 642–643.

29. *See id.* at 650.

30. *See* R. Smith, *supra* note 3, at 117 (pointing out that the delegates were divided between supporters of an extended national republic and those who supported small republics).

31. Kramer, *supra* note 8, at 651; Liebman & Garrett, *supra* note 5, at 913–917.

32. Liebman & Garrett, *supra* note 5, at 917. U.S. Const. Art. I, § 10 ("No state shall . . . pass any Bill of Attainder, ex post facto Law, or Law impairing the obligation of Contracts.").

33. Liebman & Garrett, *supra* note 5, at 930, 932.

34. THE FEDERALIST NO. 78, 465–466 (Alexander Hamilton) (Clinton Rossiter, ed., 1961).

35. LETTER FROM THOMAS JEFFERSON TO MADISON (Mar. 15, 1789), *reprinted in* CREATING THE BILL OF RIGHTS: THE DOCUMENTARY RECORD FROM THE FIRST FEDERAL CONGRESS 218 (Helen E. Veit et al., eds., 1991).

36. DEBATE IN THE HOUSE OF REPRESENTATIVES (June 8, 1789), *reprinted in* CREATING THE BILL OF RIGHTS, *supra* note 35, at 83.

37. In a speech which Madison gave during the constitutional convention, in which he explained that "in a government modified like this of the United States, the great danger lies rather in the abuse of the community than in the legislative body. . . . But this is not found in either the executive or legislative departments of government, but in the body of the people, operating by the majority against the minority." DEBATES IN HOUSE OF REPRESENTATIVES, CREATING THE BILL OF RIGHTS, *supra* note 35, at 81.

38. Liebman & Garrett, *supra* note 5, at 880; Finkelman, *supra* note 6, at 331.

39. Liebman & Garrett, *supra* note 5, at 880, 906, 908.

40. LETTER FROM JAMES MADISON TO THOMAS JEFFERSON, *reprinted in* THE PAPERS OF MADISON, *supra* note 26, 10:205; Liebman & Garrett, *supra* note 5, at 932.

41. LETTER FROM JAMES MADISON TO THOMAS JEFFERSON, *reprinted in* THE PAPERS OF MADISON, *supra* note 26, 10:205; Liebman & Garrett, *supra* note 5, at 926, 932, 934. This prediction came true in 1957, when President Eisenhower sent federal troops to Little Rock, Arkansas, to aid in enforcing the district court's ruling requiring the desegregation of the local schools. *See* MICHAEL J. KLARMAN, FROM JIM CROW TO CIVIL RIGHTS: THE SUPREME COURT AND THE STRUGGLE FOR RACIAL EQUALITY 326 (2004).

42. THE FEDERALIST NO. 51 (James Madison), *supra* note 10; Liebman & Garrett, *supra* note 5, at 937.

43. Liebman & Garrett, *supra* note 5, at 935–936.

44. Alien and Sedition Acts of 1798, ch. 74, § 2, 1 Stat. 596, 596–597 (1798), *amended by* Espionage Offenses, Pub. L. No. 65-150, 40 Stat. 553 (1918). *See* Rakove, *supra* note 8, at 257; Jean Yarbrough, *Federalism and Rights in the American Founding, in* FEDERALISM AND RIGHTS 68–69 (Ellis Katz & G. Alan Tarr, eds., 1996).

45. LARRY D. KRAMER, THE PEOPLE THEMSELVES: POPULAR CONSTITUTIONALISM AND JUDICIAL REVIEW 146 (2004). Kramer argues that Madison changed his mind because he believed that bickering between state and federal governments, and conflicts between the federal departments over the national bank, indicated a need for a "single authoritative interpreter" of the Constitution. *Id.* at 188.

46. *McCulloch v. Maryland*, 17 U.S. (4 Wheat.) 316 (1819). *See* Killenbeck,

supra note 12, at 920. *Id.* at 924 (citing LETTER FROM JAMES MADISON TO SPENCER ROANE (May 6, 1821), *reprinted in* THE WRITINGS OF JAMES MADISON 8:61 (Gaillard Hunt, ed., 1900) ("Legislative precedents are frequently of a character entitled to little respect, and . . . those of Congress . . . sometimes liable to peculiar distrust.")).

47. *See* R. SMITH, *supra* note 3, at 125.

48. U.S. CONST. Art. IV, § 1.

49. *Id.*, § 2.

50. *Id.*, Art. III, § 2, cl. 1.

51. *See* R. SMITH, *supra* note 3, at 125.

52. Arguably, those mechanisms were intended by some of the Framers as a means to deny individual rights, at least to slaves and free blacks. *See* FINKELMAN, AN IMPERFECT UNION, *supra* note 2, at 8–10 (pointing out that slave masters relied on these clauses to protect their rights to own slaves); *id.* at 32 (pointing out that the Full Faith and Credit Clause was a two-edged sword, requiring free states to recognize the institution of slavery).

53. *See* Finkelman, *James Madison and the Bill of Rights, supra* note 6, at 303.

54. CREATING THE BILL OF RIGHTS, *supra* note 35; Liebman & Garrett, *supra* note 5, at 920.

55. Kramer, *supra* note 8, at 670 (citing THE PAPERS OF JAMES MADISON 12:344 (Charles F. Hobson et al., eds., 1979)). *See also* Finkelman, *James Madison and the Bill of Rights, supra* note 6, at 344.

56. CREATING THE BILL OF RIGHTS, *supra* note 35, at 85 (speech to House of Representatives, June 8, 1789).

57. *See* R. SMITH, *supra* note 3, at 134 (arguing that the Bill of Rights, above all, represented the rise of states' rights and the decline in importance of national citizenship).

58. *See* DAVID P. CURRIE, THE CONSTITUTION IN CONGRESS: THE FEDERALIST PERIOD, 1978–1801, 114–115 (1997).

59. Rakove, *supra* note 8, at 247. *See also* William J. Brennan, Jr., *The Bill of Rights and the States: The Revival of State Constitutions as Guardians of Individual Rights,* 61 N.Y.U. L. REV. 535, 551 (1986) (arguing that the Fourteenth Amendment fulfilled Madison's vision of federalism and rights).

60. *See* Liebman & Garrett, *supra* note 5, at 882; Denise C. Morgan & Rebecca E. Zietlow, *The New Parity Debate: Congress and Rights of Belonging,* 73 CINN. L. REV. 1347 (2005).

61. Liebman & Garrett, *supra* note 5, at 964.

62. Fugitive Slave Act of 1793, 1 Stat. 302 (repealed 1864); Fugitive Slave Act of 1850, 9 Stat. 462 (repealed 1864.

63. *See* PAUL FINKELMAN, SLAVERY AND THE FOUNDERS: RACE AND LIBERTY IN THE AGE OF JEFFERSON 3 (1996).

64. *Id.* at 5.

65. *Id.* at 32.

66. *See* FINKELMAN, AN IMPERFECT UNION, *supra* note 2, at 286.

67. Congress acted early on to *abridge* individual rights in the notorious Alien and Sedition Acts of 1798, which among other things made it a crime to "write, print, utter or publish . . . any false, scandalous or malicious writing . . . against the government of the United States, either House of Congress, or the President." Alien and Sedition Acts of 1798, ch. 74, § 2, 1 Stat. 596, 596–597 (1798), *amended by* Espionage Offenses, Pub. L. No. 65-150, 40 Stat. 553 (1918). *See* CURRIE, THE FEDERALIST PERIOD, *supra* note 58, at 260–261.

68. The clause simply required that fugitives should be "delivered up" on the "demand" of the state or the "claim" of the slave owner. Section 1 of the statute went further, making it the duty of the executive authority of the state to have a person charged with a crime arrested upon the presentation of an indictment or an affidavit. Fugitives from Justice—Fugitives from Labour, ch. 7, § 1, 1 Stat. 302 (1793). Section 2 also stated that the laws of the state into which a slave fled were ineffective to set him free.

69. *See* FINKELMAN, SLAVERY AND THE FOUNDERS, *supra* note 63, at 88.

70. *Id.* at 94.

71. *Id.* at 96.

72. The Supreme Court upheld the act in *Prigg v. Pennsylvania,* based on Congress's implied power to enforce the Fugitive Slave Clause and protect the property rights of slave owners. 41 U.S. (16 Pet.) 539 (1842).

73. *See* Paul Finkelman, *States' Rights North and South in Antebellum America, in* AN UNCERTAIN TRADITION: CONSTITUTIONALISM AND THE HISTORY OF THE SOUTH 125 (Kermit L. Hall & James W. Ely, eds., 1989).

74. *See* Paul Finkelman, *Sorting Out* Prigg v. Pennsylvania, 24 RUTGERS L. J. 605, 664 (1993) ("The 1850 Fugitive Slave Act created exclusive federal power to enforce the Fugitive Slave Clause and placed the prestige of the national government behind the rendition of fugitive slaves.").

75. Finkelman, *Sorting Out, supra* note 74, at 623. Such a scenario happened leading up to the case of *Prigg v. Pennsylvania. Id.* at 613. The Supreme Court also upheld the 1850 act, in *Ableman v. Booth,* 62 U.S. 506 (1859).

76. *See* DAVID P. CURRIE, THE CONSTITUTION IN CONGRESS: THE JEFFERSONIANS, 1801–1829, 258–267 (2001).

77. *See, e.g.,* DAVID P. CURRIE, THE CONSTITUTION IN CONGRESS: DEMOCRATS AND WHIGS, 1829–1861, 3 (2005); CURRIE, THE FEDERALIST PERIOD, *supra* note 58, at 168–169 (debate in second Congress over whether Congress could use the spending power to subsidize the codfish industry by giving them a "bounty"); CURRIE, THE FEDERALIST PERIOD, *supra* note 58, at 222 (fourth congressional debate over Washington's proposal to set up a national university and an agricultural board); CURRIE, THE JEFFERSONIANS, *supra* note 76, at

258–267 (describing the debates over internal improvements during Madison's presidency); Graber, *supra* note 1, at 486 (American system proposals raised constitutional issues).

78. In the early years, they submitted numerous petitions urging Congress to end the slave trade and to protect free northern blacks, but all of those petitions died in committee. *See* David P. Currie, *The Constitution in Congress: Substantive Issues in the First Congress, 1789–1791*, 61 U. CHI. L. REV. 775, 792 (1994); CURRIE, THE FEDERALIST PERIOD, *supra* note 58, at 229; CURRIE, THE JEFFERSONIANS, *supra* note 76, at 223, 226, 228; FINKELMAN, IMPERFECT UNION, *supra* note 2, at 88.

79. Northwest Ordinance of 1787, Art. VI.

80. FINKELMAN, SLAVERY AND THE FOUNDERS, *supra* note 63, at 35.

81. The ambiguity is due to the fact that Article VI was added at the last minute, after little debate over its meaning. *See* FINKELMAN, SLAVERY AND THE FOUNDERS, *supra* note 63, at 35.

82. FINKELMAN, IMPERFECT UNION, *supra* note 2, at 84.

83. *See* CURRIE, THE JEFFERSONIANS, *supra* note 76, at 237–238.

84. 24 ANNALS OF CONG. 1225 (1812), cited by CURRIE, THE JEFFERSONIANS, *supra* note 76, at 221.

85. The bill would have authorized Missouri to form a state government that would have prohibited slavery and provided that all children born within the state would be free as of their twenty-fifth birthday. 33 ANNALS OF CONG. 1166, 1170 (1818). *See* CURRIE, THE JEFFERSONIANS, *supra* note 76, at 234.

86. 35 ANNALS OF CONG. 947 (1820).

87. *Id.* at 424, 426–427, 471. *See* CURRIE, THE JEFFERSONIANS, *supra* note 76, at 235.

88. Compromise of 1820 & Missouri Enabling Acts, ch. 22, § 8, 3 Stat. 545 (1820), *amended by* 3 Stat. 645 (1821), 3 Stat. 645 (1821). The statute was struck down by the Court in the *Dred Scott* case after it had been repealed by the Kansas-Nebraska Act, ch. 59, § 32, 10 Stat. 277, 283 (1854) (Nebraska); *id.* at 289 (Kansas) and reenacted in the Freedom in the States and Territories Abolition of Slavery Act, ch. 11, 12 Stat. 432 (1862) (abolishing slavery in all U.S. territories) in accordance with Lincoln's view that the Supreme Court's interpretation of the Constitution no more bound Congress than Congress's interpretation bound the Court. *See* CURRIE, THE JEFFERSONIANS, *supra* note 76, at 232.

89. CURRIE, THE JEFFERSONIANS, *supra* note 76, at 235. Antislavery members of Congress also argued that banning slavery was analogous to the civil liberties conditions that had been imposed on the state of Louisiana as a condition of its admission. *Id.* at 237. Rep. John Holmes of Massachusetts agreed. *See id.* at 238.

90. 35 ANNALS OF CONG. 1199–1200 (statement of Rep. John Sergeant). *See*

also id. at 126 (statement of Sen. Jonathan Roberts), *id.* at 291 (statement of Sen. William Allen Trimble), *cited in* CURRIE, THE JEFFERSONIANS, *supra* note 76, at 239.

91. CURRIE, THE JEFFERSONIANS, *supra* note 76, at 237.

92. 35 ANNALS OF CONG. 984; CURRIE, THE JEFFERSONIANS, *supra* note 76, at 236, 241.

93. 35 ANNALS OF CONG. 319–320. *See* CURRIE, THE JEFFERSONIANS, *supra* note 76, at 239. The Supreme Court ruled that the commerce power did not extend to the regulation of slaves in *Groves v. Slaughter,* 40 U.S. 449 (1841).

94. At the end of the debate over the first compromise, Georgia Rep. Thomas Cobb was chillingly and sadly prophetic when he warned, "He believed that they were kindling a fire which all the waters of the ocean could not extinguish. It could only be extinguished in blood!" 34 ANNALS OF CONG. 1437 (1819). *See* CURRIE, THE JEFFERSONIANS, *supra* note 76, at 249.

95. CURRIE, THE JEFFERSONIANS, *supra* note 76, at 347 (citing 41 ANNALS OF CONG. 1308 (1824)).

96. *See id.* at 348 ("Thus it was the unworthy cause of slavery that led Southerners to embrace an absurdly narrow interpretation of federal authority, in order to ward off an absurdly broad one.").

97. Bill of Abominations, ch. 55, § 2, 4 Stat. 270, 271–272 (1828).

98. 1 S.C. Stat. at 329–331, *reprinted in* STATE DOCUMENTS IN FEDERAL RELATIONS 170–173 (Herman Vandenburg Ames, ed., 1970); CURRIE, DEMOCRATS AND WHIGS, *supra* note 77, at 104; KEITH E. WHITTINGTON, CONSTITUTIONAL CONSTRUCTION: DIVIDED POWERS AND CONSTITUTIONAL MEANING 73, 78 (1999).

99. A COMPILATION OF THE MESSAGES AND PAPERS OF THE PRESIDENTS 2:617 (James D. Richardson, ed., New York Bureau of National Literature 1897); CURRIE, DEMOCRATS AND WHIGS, *supra* note 77, at 110. Jackson also asked Congress to reduce the tariffs, paving the way to a compromise resolution. *Id.* at 110.

100. CONG. DEB., 21st Cong., 1st Sess. 38 (1830); CURRIE, DEMOCRATS AND WHIGS, *supra* note 77, at 93; WHITTINGTON, *supra* note 98, at 82.

101. The Force Bill passed the Senate 32–1 and the House 149–48, a resounding victory. CONG DEB., 22d Cong, 2d Sess. 688, 1903 (1833); CURRIE, DEMOCRATS AND WHIGS, *supra* note 77, at 115; WHITTINGTON, *supra* note 98, at 72–73.

102. THE JOHN C. CALHOUN PAPERS 11:269–270 (Robert L. Meriwether, ed., 1959); CURRIE, DEMOCRATS AND WHIGS, *supra* note 77, at 101.

103. CURRIE, DEMOCRATS AND WHIGS, *supra* note 77, at 101 (citing LETTER FROM JOHN C. CALHOUN TO VIRGIL MAXCY (Sept. 11, 1830), THE JOHN C. CALHOUN PAPERS, *supra* note 102, at 11:226, 229).

104. Judith A. Baer, Equality under the Constitution: Reclaiming the Fourteenth Amendment 58 (1983).

105. *See* Finkelman, Slavery and the Founders, *supra* note 63, at 1–2.

106. Baer, *supra* note 104, at 60.

107. *Id.*

108. *Barron v. Mayor and City Council of Baltimore,* 32 U.S. (7 Pet.) 243 (1833). Baer, *supra* note 104(quoting Alvan Stewart, *A Constitutional Argument on the Subject of Slavery* (1837), *reprinted in* Jacobus tenBroek, Equal under Law 282–283 (1969)).

109. Joel Tiffany, Treatise on the Unconstitutionality of American Slavery, together with the Powers and Duties of the Federal Government in Relation to That Subject (J. Calyer 1849), *cited in* Michael Kent Curtis, No State Shall Abridge: The Fourteenth Amendment and the Bill of Rights 83 (1986).

110. Curtis, *supra* note 109, at 42; Baer, *supra* note 104, at 60.

111. Curtis, *supra* note 109, at 28.

112. Natualization Acts, ch. 3, 1 Stat. 103, 104 (1790); Currie, *Substantive Issues in the First Congress, supra* note 78, at 823–824.

113. *See* Currie, The Federalist Period, *supra* note 58, at 192.

114. *See* Baer, *supra* note 104, at 60.

115. Mo. Const. of 1820, Art. III, § 26, *cited in* Currie, The Jeffersonians, *supra* note 76, at 245.

116. Compromise of 1820 & Missouri Enabling Acts, *supra* note 88, at § 4, 547; Currie, The Jeffersonians, *supra* note 76, at 246.

117. 37 Annals of Cong. 56–72 (1821); *see also id.* at 545–548 (Rep. John Strode Barbour of Virginia); *id.* at 555 (Rep. Alexander Smyth of Virginia); *id.* at 585 (Rep. Stevenson Archer of Maryland); Currie, The Jeffersonians, *supra* note 76, at 246.

118. 37 Annals of Cong. 571; Currie, The Jeffersonians, *supra* note 76, at 247.

119. 37 Annals of Cong. 1134; Currie, The Jeffersonians, *supra* note 76, at 246. To the contrary, Pinckney probably intended the clause to protect the rights of slaveholders. He was a strong proponent of the rights of slaveholders at the constitutional convention. *See* Finkelman, Imperfect Union, *supra* note 2, at 35.

120. 37 Annals of Cong. 51–56 (Sen. Smith); *id.* at 510 (Rep. William Lowndes of South Carolina); Currie, The Jeffersonians, *supra* note 76, at 247.

121. 37 Annals of Cong. 1079–1080; Currie, The Jeffersonians, *supra* note 76, at 248.

122. Currie, The Jeffersonians, *supra* note 76, at 248.

123. Cong. Globe, 30th Cong., 2d Sess. 418 (1849).

124. *See* Finkelman, Imperfect Union, *supra* note 2, at 236.

125. *See* Cong. Globe, 30th Cong., 2d Sess. 418 (statement of Rep. Robert Rhett of South Carolina).

126. *See* Cong. Globe, 31st Cong., 1st Sess. (1850) (statement of Sen. John Davis of Massachusetts).

127. U.S. Const. Art. IV, § 2, cl. 1 ("The Citizens of each State shall be entitled to all Privileges and Immunities of Citizens in the several states."). *See* Cong. Globe, 30th Cong., 2d Sess. 418–419.

128. *See* Cong. Globe, 30th Cong., 2d Sess. 418.

129. *Id.,* 419.

130. *See* Rebecca E. Zietlow, *Congressional Enforcement of Citizenship Rights and John Bingham's Theory of Citizenship,* 36 Akron L. Rev. 717, 723 (2003).

131. *See* Finkelman, Imperfect Union, *supra* note 2, at 223, 234.

132. *Id.*

133. *See, e.g.,* Cong. Globe, 31st Cong., 1st Sess. (statement of Sen. John Davis).

134. *Id.* (statement of Sen. Henry Clay).

135. *See, e.g.,* Cong. Globe, 30th Cong., 2d Sess. 418 (statement of Rep. Charles Hudson); *id.* at 419 (statement of Rep. George Ashmun); Cong. Globe, 31st Cong., 1st Sess. 123 (statement of John Davis); *id.* at 1654 (statement of Sen. Robert Winthrop); Cong. Globe, 39th Cong., 1st Sess. 475 (1866) (statement of Sen. Lyman Trumbull).

136. *See, e.g.,* Cong. Globe, 31st Cong., 1st Sess. 1654 (statement of Sen. Robert Winthrop).

137. Curtis, *supra* note 109, at 45–46.

138. William J. Rich, *Taking "Privileges or Immunities" Seriously: A Call to Expand the Constitutional Canon,* 87 Minn. L. Rev. 153, 170 (2002).

139. Cong. Globe, 31st Cong., 1st Sess., Sen. App. 288.

140. *Id.*

141. Fugitive Slave Act of 1850, 9 Stat. 462 (repealed 1864). Indeed, the 1850 Fugitive Slave Act denied those accused of being slaves even the barest minimum of due process of law. *See* Finkelman, *Sorting Out, supra* note 74, at 622–623.

142. *Dred Scott v. Sanford,* 60 U.S. (19 How.) 393, 399 (1856) (discussed below).

143. *See* Graber, *supra* note 1, at 522. The most important slavery-related decisions, *Prigg* and *Dred Scott,* are discussed in the text. As Graber notes, other decisions include *Kentucky v. Denison,* 65 U.S. 66 (1860) (national government could not compel a state government to extradite persons accused of

helping fugitive slaves). *See also* ROBERT M. COVER, JUSTICE ACCUSED: ANTI-SLAVERY AND THE JUDICIAL PROCESS 159–193 (1975) (describing lower court enforcements of fugitive slave laws).

144. *Groves v. Slaughter,* 40 U.S. (15 Pet.) 449 (1841).

145. *Prigg v. Pennsylvania,* 41 U.S. (16 Pet.) 539, 612 (1842).

146. BAER, *supra* note 104, at 69.

147. U.S. CONST., Art. IV, § 2, cl. 1.

148. *Barron v. Mayor and City Council of Baltimore,* 32 U.S. (7 Pet.) 243 (1833).

149. *Corfield v. Coryell,* 6 F. Cas. 546, 551–552 (C.C.E.D. Pa. 1823) (No. 3,230).

150. David R. Upham, Corfield v. Coryell *and the Privileges and Immunities of American Citizenship,* 83 TEX. L. REV. 1483, 1483 (2005).

151. *Id.* at 1484.

152. *Dred Scott,* 60 U.S. (19 How.) at 399. *See* FINKELMAN, IMPERFECT UNION, *supra* note 2, at 222.

153. FINKELMAN, IMPERFECT UNION, *supra* note 2, at 222.

154. *Id.* at 223.

155. *Scott v. Emerson,* 15 Mo. 576, 586 (1852). *See* FINKELMAN, IMPERFECT UNION, *supra* note 2, at 226.

156. FINKELMAN, IMPERFECT UNION, *supra* note 2, at 251.

157. *Id.* at 276.

158. *Id.* at 403.

159. *Id.* at 404, 407.

160. *Id.* at 315.

161. ROBERT BURT, THE CONSTITUTION IN CONFLICT 193 (1992).

162. CURTIS, *supra* note 109, at 27.

163. KRAMER, *supra* note 45, at 211.

164. *See* FINKELMAN, IMPERFECT UNION, *supra* note 2, at 274.

165. KRAMER, *supra* note 45, at 212.

166. THE COLLECTED WORKS OF ABRAHAM LINCOLN 2:464–467 (Roy P. Basler, ed., 1955), *cited in* FINKELMAN, IMPERFECT UNION, *supra* note 2, at 316.

167. THE COLLECTED WORKS OF ABRAHAM LINCOLN 3:421 (Roy P. Basler, ed., 1955), *cited in* FINKELMAN, IMPERFECT UNION, *supra* note 2, at 318.

168. For example, in a speech during the Lincoln-Douglas senatorial debate in October 1858, Lincoln stated that "we oppose [the *Dred Scott* decision] as a political rule which shall be binding on the members of Congress or the President to favor no measure that does not actually concur with the principles of that decision. [We] propose resisting it as to have it reversed if we can," *quoted in* THE COLLECTED WORKS OF ABRAHAM LINCOLN, *supra* note 167, at 255. In his first inaugural address, he asserted that although a Supreme Court ruling "must be binding in any case upon the parties to a suit as to the object of that

suit[,] . . . [a]t the same time, the candid citizen must confess that if the policy of the Government upon vital questions affecting the whole people is to be irrevocably fixed by decisions of the Supreme Court, the instant they are made in ordinary litigation between parties in personal actions, the people will have ceased to be their own rules, having to that extent practically resigned their Government into the hands of that eminent tribunal." A COMPILATION OF THE MESSAGES AND PAPERS OF THE PRESIDENTS 6:5, 9–10 (James D. Richardson, ed., New York Bureau of National Literature 1897). *See* WHITTINGTON, *supra* note 98, at 13 (discussing Lincoln's position on *Dred Scott* as a means of constitutional construction).

169. KRAMER, *supra* note 45, at 212.

170. CONG. GLOBE, 36th Cong, 1st Sess. 1839 (1860).

171. CONG. GLOBE, 35th Cong., 1st Sess. 402 (1858).

172. CURTIS, *supra* note 109, at 91.

173. KRAMER, *supra* note 45, at 5, 7, 8.

174. *Id.,* at 54; Graber, *supra* note 1. For example, Jefferson maintained that the 1798 Alien and Sedition Acts were unconstitutional despite lower court rulings upholding the acts (CURRIE, THE JEFFERSONIANS, *supra* note 76), and Jackson vetoed a statute establishing a national bank on the grounds that it was unconstitutional notwithstanding the Court's ruling in *McCulloch v. Maryland,* 17 U.S. (4 Wheat.) 316 (1819) (CURRIE, DEMOCRATS AND WHIGS, *supra* note 77, at 62). Lincoln's reaction to the *Dred Scott* decision is discussed above at *supra* note 168.

175. KRAMER, *supra* note 45, at 209.

176. *See* FINKELMAN, IMPERFECT UNION, *supra* note 2, at 263, 274, 316–318.

177. CONG. GLOBE, 34th Cong., 3d Sess., H.p. app. 140 (1857).

178. CONG. GLOBE, 34th Cong., 1st Sess., H.p. app. 124 (1856). Abolitionists often noted the importance of freedom of expression, as an increasing number of slave states enacted statutes like that of Kansas. *See* AKHIL REED AMAR, THE BILL OF RIGHTS: CREATION AND RECONSTRUCTION 234 (1998); MICHAEL KENT CURTIS, FREE SPEECH, "THE PEOPLE'S DARLING PRIVILEGE": STRUGGLES FOR FREEDOM OF EXPRESSION IN AMERICAN HISTORY (2000).

179. Richard L. Aynes, *On Misreading John Bingham and the Fourteenth Amendment,* 103 YALE L. J. 57, 71 (1993).

180. CONG. GLOBE, 35th Cong., 1st Sess. 982. Similarly, Sen. William Pitt Fessenden of Maine expressly disavowed the validity of the *Dred Scott* decision, stating that he did not believe that *Dred Scott* accurately stated the law. *Id.*

181. CONG. GLOBE, 35th Cong., 1st Sess. 985.

182. This belief was also consistent with that held by the antislavery constitutionalists. *See* AMAR, *supra* note 178, at 156–162.

183. CONG. GLOBE, 35th Cong., 2d Sess. 984 (1858).

184. Aynes, *supra* note 179, at 70.

185. *Id.* at 72.

186. CONG. GLOBE, 37th Cong, 2d Sess. 345 (1862). *See* Rich, *supra* note 138, at 171.

187. CONG. GLOBE, 35th Cong., 1st Sess. 985.

188. *Id.*

189. *Id.* at 984.

190. *Id.* at 402. Rep. Clark Betton Cochrane of New York also argued that the exclusion provision of the Oregon constitution violated the Privileges and Immunities Clause. *Id.* at 980.

191.*Id.* at 1964. Significantly, this list did not include the right to vote, which Bingham expressly disavowed as a right of citizenship.

192. *Id.* at 1966–1967.

193. *Id.* at 974–975 (Rep. Henry Laurens Dawes arguing that the provision preventing people of color from entering contracts, owning property, and suing courts violated the Privileges and Immunities Clause); *id.* at 980 (Rep. Clark Betton Cochrane arguing the same). *See also id.* at 1966–1967 (Sen. Henry Wilson); *id.* at 974–975 (Rep. Henry Laurens Dawes).

194. *Id.* at 970 (Rep. John Bullock Clark, relying on the *Dred Scott* decision as authority for his position that blacks are not, and cannot be citizens of the United States).

195. *Id.* at 1965 (Sens. Lyman Trumbull and Stephen Arnold Douglas); *id.* at 974 (Rep. Linus Bacon Comins).

196. *Id.* at 974.

197. *Id.* at 1965.

198. CONG GLOBE, 39th Cong., 1st Sess. 1122–1123, 1156 (1866). They argued that the Privileges and Immunities Clause of Article IV merely protected citizens of each state while temporarily visiting any other state. *Id.* at 1269. *See* CURTIS, *supra* note 109, at 82 ("Republican speakers supported the bill on grounds of a paramount national citizenship and a national body of fundamental privileges and immunities; the Democratic doctrine was more in keeping with the accepted Supreme Court doctrine.").

199. CURTIS, *supra* note 109, at 46.

200. *Id.* at 48.

201. *Id.* at 35.

202. *Id.* at 40.

203. *Id.* at 40, 30.

204. AMAR, *supra* note 178, at 234.

NOTES TO CHAPTER 3

1. *See* Robert J. Kaczorowski, *Revolutionary Constitutionalism in the Era of the Civil War and Reconstruction*, 61 N.Y.U. L. REV. 863, 872 (1986). *See also*

Daniel A. Farber & John E. Muench, *The Ideological Origins of the Fourteenth Amendment,* 1 CONST. COMMENT. 235, 263 (1984).

2. *See* Kaczorowski, *supra* note 1, at 873. *See also* Farber & Muench, *supra* note 1 at 277; Jack M. Balkin & Sanford Levinson, *Understanding the Constitutional Revolution,* 87 VA. L. REV. 1045, 1097 (2001).

3. *See* MICHAEL KENT CURTIS, NO STATE SHALL ABRIDGE: THE FOURTEENTH AMENDMENT AND THE BILL OF RIGHTS 54 (1986); ROGERS SMITH, CIVIC IDEALS: CONFLICTING VISIONS OF CITIZENSHIP IN U.S. HISTORY 286 (1997).

4. JUDITH A BAER, EQUALITY UNDER THE CONSTITUTION: RECLAIMING THE FOURTEENTH AMENDMENT 31 (1983).

5. *See* James W. Fox, *Citizenship, Poverty and Federalism,* 60 U. PITT. L. REV. 421, 512 (1999).

6. In the past the Court has noted that "the Framers of the Fourteenth Amendment were primarily interested in augmenting the power of Congress, rather than the courts." *Katzenbach v. Morgan,* 384 U.S. 641, 648 n.7, citing JACOBUS TENBROEK, THE ANTISLAVERY ORIGINS OF THE FOURTEENTH AMENDMENT (1951) and Laurent B. Frantz, *Congressional Power to Enforce the Fourteenth Amendment against Private Acts,* 73 YALE L. J. 1353, 1356–1357 (1964).

7. *See* Robert C. Post & Reva B. Siegel, *Equal Protection by Law: Federal Anti-Discrimination Legislation after* Morrison *and* Kimel, 110 YALE L. J. 441, 507 (2000).

8. Freedmen's Bureau Act, 14 Stat. 174, 176–177 (1866). Act of March 2, 1867, ch. 153, 14 Stat. 428, Act of March 23, 1867, ch. 6, 15 Stat. 2; Act of July 1867, ch. 30, 15 Stat. 4 (collectively, "Reconstruction Acts"). Civil Rights Act of 1866, ch. 31, 14 Stat. 27 (codified at 42 U.S.C. §§ 1981–1983 (2000)). For an excellent description of the political dynamics of the Reconstruction Era, *see* MICHAEL LES BENEDICT, A COMPROMISE OF PRINCIPLE (1974).

9. BENEDICT, *supra* note 8, at 23.

10. ERIC FONER, RECONSTRUCTION: AMERICA'S UNFINISHED REVOLUTION 67 (1988).

11. FONER, *supra* note 10, at 78.

12. *Id.* at 163.

13. *Id.* at 199, 227.

14. *Id.* at 229–230; BENEDICT, *supra* note 8, at 23.

15. FONER, *supra* note 10, at 227.

16. BENEDICT, *supra* note 8, at 41.

17. *See Schurz Report on Condition of the South,* CONG. GLOBE, 39th Cong., 1st Sess., Senate Exec Doc. No. 2 (1865); CONG. GLOBE, 39th Cong., 1st Sess. 474 (1866) (statement of Sen. Trumbull); *id.* at 603 (statement of Sen. Wilson); *id.* at 1123 (statement of Rep. Cook); *id.* at 1153 (statement of Rep. Thayer); *id.* at 1832 (1866) (statement of Rep. Lawrence).

18. Cong. Globe, 39th Cong., 1st Sess. 474 (1866). See The Reconstruction Amendments' Debates 121 (Alfred Avins, ed.,1964).

19. Civil Rights Act of 1866, ch. 31, § 1, 14 Stat. 27 (codified at 42 U.S.C. §§ 1981–1982 (2000)).

20. Civil Rights Act of 1866, ch. 31, § 2, 14 Stat. 27 (codified at 42 U.S.C. § 1983 (2000)). *Id.*, §§ 4–10, 14 Stat. 27, 29. *See* Robert J. Kaczorowski, *Congress's Power to Enforce Fourteenth Amendment Rights: Lessons from Federal Remedies the Framers Enacted*, 42 Harv. J. Leg. 187, 260–263 (2005).

21. Cong. Globe, 39th Cong., 1st Sess. 474 (1866).

22. *Id.*

23. *Id.* at 475.

24. *Id.* at 504.

25. *Id.* at 1124.

26. *Id.* at 1151.

27. *Id.* at 528.

28. *Id.* at 630.

29. *Id.* at 1159.

30. *Id.* at 1833.

31. *Id.* at 630, 1119.

32. *Id.* at 1263.

33. *Id.* at 1757.

34. *See* Douglas G. Smith, *Citizenship and the Fourteenth Amendment*, 34 San Diego L. Rev. 681, 695 (1997); Earl Maltz, The Fourteenth Amendment and the Law of the Constitution 9 (2003).

35. *See, e.g.,* Cong. Globe, 39th Cong., 1st Sess. 586 (1866) (statement of Rep. Donnelly) ("Shall the old reign of terror revive in the south, when no northern man's life was worth an hour's purchase?"); *id.* at 1263 (1866) (statement of Rep. Broomall).

36. *Id.* at 474, 599 (statements of Sen. Trumbull).

37. *See* Earl Maltz, Civil Rights, The Constitution, and Congress, 1863–1869, 63–64 (1990).

38. Cong. Globe, 39th Cong., 1st Sess. 1292 (1866).

39. Maltz, Fourteenth Amendment, *supra* note 34, at 59.

40. *Id.* at 60–61.

41. *Id.*

42. *Id.* at 62.

43. Cong. Globe, 39th Cong., 1st Sess. 1117 (1866).

44. *Id.* at 1151.

45. *Id.* at 474.

46. *See* Samuel Estreicher, *Federal Power to Regulate Private Discrimination: The Revival of the Enforcement Clauses of the Reconstruction Era Amendments*, 74 Colum. L. Rev. 449, 452 (1974).

47. CONG. GLOBE, 39th Cong., 1st Sess. 474 (1866).

48. *Id.* at 1294. *See* CURTIS, *supra* note 3, at 81.

49. CONG. GLOBE, 39th Cong., 1st Sess. 504 (1866) (statement of Sen. Howard). *See also id.* at 602 (1866) (statement of Sen. Lane); *id.* at 1124, 1151 (1866) (statements of Rep. Thayer). *See also* CURTIS, *supra* note 3, at 79.

50. *See* MALTZ, FOURTEENTH AMENDMENT, *supra* note 34, at 58.

51. CONG. GLOBE, 39th Cong., 1st Sess. 475 (1866).

52. *See, e.g., id.* at 1117 (1866) (statement of Rep. James Wilson); *id.* at 1152 (statement of Rep. Thayer).

53. *Id.* at 474.

54. *Id.* at 1292 (statement of Rep. James Wilson); *id.* at 1836 (statement of Rep. Lawrence).

55. For a detailed comparison of the enforcement provisions of the 1866 Civil Rights Act and the Fugitive Slave Acts, *see* Kaczorowski, *supra* note 20, at 260.

56. CONG. GLOBE, 39th Cong., 1st Sess. 1755 (statement of Rep. Stewart).

57. *Id.* at 605.

58. This interpretation of *Prigg* may be consistent with the intent of the author of the opinion of the Court, Justice Story, who arguably saw *Prigg* primarily as a case about the power of Congress, not the extension of slavery. *See* Paul Finkelman, *Sorting out* Prigg v. Pennsylvania, 24 RUTGERS L. J. 605, 608 (1993).

59. CONG. GLOBE, 39th Cong., 1st Sess. 1776 (1866).

60. *Id.* at 478.

61. *Veto Message of President Andrew Johnson,* March 27, 1866, in CONG. GLOBE, 39th Cong., 1st Sess. 1679 (1866).

62. CONG. GLOBE, 39th Cong., 1st Sess. 505 (1866).

63. *Id.* at 499 (statement of Sen. Cowan). *See also id.* at 476 (statement of Sen. Saulsbury); *id.* at 1776 (statement of Sen. Johnson).

64. *Id.* at 477. *See also id.* at 497 (statement of Sen. Van Winkle); *id.* at 528 (statement of Sen. Davis).

65. *Id.* at 504 (statement of Sen. Johnson); *id.* at 1120 (statement of Rep. Rogers).

66. *Id.* at 475.

67. *Id.* at 1115 (statement of Rep. James Wilson); *id.* at 1152 (statement of Rep. Thayer); *id.* at 528 (statement of Sen. Clark); *id.* at 570 (statement of Sen. Morrill); *id.* at 602 (statement of Sen. Lane). *See also* CURTIS, *supra* note 3, at 91.

68. CONG. GLOBE, 39th Cong., 1st Sess. 1115 (1866).

69. *Id.* at 1263.

70. *Id.* at 1291.

71. *Id. See also* CURTIS, *supra* note 3, at 81.

72. CONG. GLOBE, 39th Cong., 1st Sess. 1267 (1866).

73. *Id.* at 1120 (statement of Rep. Rogers); *id.* at app. 156 (statement of Rep. Delano).

74. The bill originally passed the Senate by a vote of 33 to 12 (Cong. Globe, 39th Cong., 1st Sess. 606–607 (Feb. 2, 1866)) and the House by a vote of 111 to 38 (*id.* at 1367 (March 13, 1866)). The vote to override the veto passed in the Senate by a vote of 33 to 15 (*id.* at 1809 (April 5, 1866)) and the House by a vote of 122 to 41 (*id.* at 1861 (April 7, 1866)). The President's veto had the effect of diminishing differences between Republican factions in the House, as they stood together in opposition to the president. *See* Benedict, *supra* note 8, at 165.

75. Cong. Globe, 39th Cong., 1st Sess. 1861 (1866).

76. *See* Foner, *supra* note 10, at xx; Benedict, *supra* note 8, at 163.

77. *See* Baer, *supra* note 4, at 75.

78. The House approved the amendment on May 14, 1866 (Cong. Globe, 39th Cong., 1st Sess. 2545 (1866)), and the Senate endorsed it on June 13, 1866 (*id.* at 3042). *See* Curtis, *supra* note 3, at 86.

79. *Senate Report No. 112, Proposing a Fourteenth Article of Amendment* (June 8, 1866), Cong. Globe, 39th Cong., 1st Sess. (Joint Committee on Reconstruction). The committee also recommended that the readmission of the southern states depend on their adopting the proposed amendment. Benedict, *supra* note 8, at 169. Within the committee, Bingham was the most insistent on a broad national guarantee of privileges and immunities, consistent with his years of support for such a guarantee. *Id.* at 170.

80. *See* Richard L. Aynes, *On Misreading John Bingham and the Fourteenth Amendment*, 103 Yale L. J. 57, 70–71 (1993).

81. Cong. Globe, 39th Cong., 1st Sess. 429 (1866).

82. *Id.* at 1033.

83. *Id.* at 586.

84. *Id.* at 1835. *See* Curtis, *supra* note 3, at 78.

85. Cong. Globe, 39th Cong., 1st Sess. 1054 (1866).

86. *See* Kaczorowski, *supra* note 20, at 267.

87. *City of Boerne v. Flores*, 521 U.S. 507, 523–524 (1997). Earl Maltz makes the same argument. *See* Maltz, Civil Rights, *supra* note 37, at 55–60.

88. Cong. Globe, 39th Cong., 1st Sess., app. 133 (1866) (statement of Rep. Rogers); *id.* at 1063 (statement of Rep. Hale). Hale explained that his opposition to federal power stemmed from the federalization of slave law in the antebellum era. He claimed that had slavery remained a matter of state law, it would have died a natural death. *Id.* *See also id.* at 1094 (statement of Rep. Hotchkiss) (opposing congressional power).

89. *See* Ruth Colker, *The Supreme Court's Historical Errors in* City of Boerne v. Flores, 43 B. C. L. Rev. 783 (2002).

90. *See* Kaczorowski, *supra* note 20, at 267.

91. CONG. GLOBE, 39th Cong., 1st Sess. 2766 (1866).

92. The amendment passed by a vote of 110 to 37 in the House (*id.* at 1094 (Feb. 28, 1866)) and 33 to 11 in the Senate (*id.* at 3042 (June 13, 1866)).

93. *Id.* at 2768.

94. U.S. CONST., Amend. IV, § 1 ("All persons born or naturalized in the United States, and subject to the jurisdiction thereof, are citizens of the United States and of the State wherein they reside."). The citizenship clause of the Fourteenth Amendment closely resembled that of the 1866 Civil Rights Act. Senator Howard's original draft only referred to persons "born" in the United States. The phrase "or naturalized" was added, without much discussion, pursuant to a last-minute motion by Senator William Fessenden. CONG. GLOBE, 39th Cong., 1st Sess. 3040 (1866).

95. CONG. GLOBE, 39th Cong., 1st Sess. 2890 (1866).

96. *See* Kaczorowski, *supra* note 20, at 263.

97. CONG. GLOBE, 39th Cong., 1st Sess. 3035 (1866).

98. *Id.* at 3037.

99. *See* BENEDICT, *supra* note 8, at 184–188.

100. CONG. GLOBE, 39th Cong., 1st Sess. 1094 (1866).

101. *Id.* at 2459.

102. *See* Douglas Laycock, *Congress and the Ratchet,* 56 MONT. L. REV. 145, 160 (1995).

103. *Dred Scott v. Sanford,* 60 U.S. (19 How.) 393, 404 (1856).

104. *Barron v. Mayor and City Council of Baltimore,* 32 U.S. (7 Pet.) 243 (1833). CONG. GLOBE, 39th Cong., 1st Sess. 1089 (1866) (statement of Rep. Bingham). *See* CURTIS, *supra* note 3, at 129–130. The impact of the Fourteenth Amendment on *Barron* has generated a great deal of academic debate. *See* PAMELA BRANDWEIN, RECONSTRUCTING RECONSTRUCTION: THE SUPREME COURT AND THE PRODUCTION OF HISTORICAL TRUTH 108–110 (1999), and Bryan Wildenthal, *The Lost Compromise: Reassessing the Early Understanding in Court and Congress on Incorporation of the Bill of Rights in the Fourteenth Amendment,* 61 OHIO ST. L. J. 1051, 1070–1074 (2000).

105. *See* FONER, *supra* note 10, at 272. The decisions were *Ex parte Milligan,* 71 U.S. 2 (1866) (voiding the conviction of an Indiana man who had been tried before a military tribunal) and *Cummings v. Missouri,* 71 U.S. 277 (1866) (overturning a requirement in the Missouri constitution that lawyers, ministers, and others swear a loyalty oath). *Id.*

106. *Ex parte McCardle,* 73 U.S. (6 Wall.) 318, 320–321 (1868). For an excellent discussion of this case, *see* William W. Van Alstyne, *A Critical Guide to* Ex parte McCardle, 15 ARIZ. L. REV. 229, 239 (1973).

107. Act of Feb. 5, 1867, ch. 28, § 1, 14 Stat. 385.

108. Repealer Act of 1867, Act of Feb. 5, 1867, ch. 28, § 1, 14 Stat. 385. CONG. GLOBE, 40th Cong., 2d Sess. 2062 (1868).

109. CONG. GLOBE, 40th Cong., 2d Sess. at 2165.

110. *Ex parte McCardle,* 73 U.S. (6 Wall.) at 318, 320–321. *See* Van Alstyne, *supra* note 106, at 248.

111. *McCulloch v. Maryland,* 17 U.S. (4 Wheat.) 316, 421 (1819) ("Let the end be legitimate, let it be within the scope of the constitution, and all means which are appropriate, which are plainly adapted to that end, which are not prohibited, but consist with the letter and spirit of the constitution, are constitutional.").

112. *Prigg v. Pennsylvania,* 41 U.S. (16 Pet.) 539, 615 (1842). *See* AKHIL REED AMAR, THE BILL OF RIGHTS: CREATION AND RECONSTRUCTION 69 (1998). *See also* Finkelman, *supra* note 58, at 614. Congress later enacted the more broadly sweeping Fugitive Slave Act of 1850, upheld by the Court in *Ableman v. Booth,* 21 How. 526 (1859). Congress relied on *Prigg* when enacting the later, more comprehensive, law. AMAR, BILL OF RIGHTS, at 26, 70.

113. *See* Akhil Reed Amar, *Intratextualism,* 112 HARV. L. REV. 747, 825 n.299 (2000); Steven A. Engel, *The* McCulloch *Theory of the Fourteenth Amendment:* City of Boerne v. Flores *and the Original Understanding of Section 5,* 109 YALE L. J. 115, 139 (1999).

114. CONG. GLOBE, 39th Cong., 1st Sess. 1294 (statement of Rep. James Wilson); *id.* at 1153, 1270 (statements of Rep. Lawrence); *id.* at 1833 (statement of Rep. Thayer). *See* Curtis, *supra* note 3, at 82. For a contrary reading, *see* Raoul Berger, *Incorporation of the Bill of Rights of the Fourteenth Amendment: A Nine-Lived Cat,* 42 OHIO ST. L. J. 435, 453–456 (1981).

115. *See* Kaczorowski, *supra* note 1, at 866–867; Farber & Muench, *supra* note 1, at 277. *See also* J. M. Balkin, *The Constitution of Status,* 106 YALE L. J. 2313, 2347 (1997); James W. Fox, Jr., *Re-readings and Misreadings: Slaughterhouse, Privileges or Immunities, and Section Five Enforcement Power,* 91 KY. L. J. 67, 145 (2002). *But see* BRANDWEIN, *supra* note 104, at 57 (arguing that the Republicans did not intend to transform federalism because they did not believe that protecting individual rights would require a broad expansion of federal power). Earl Maltz claims that the Framers of the Fourteenth Amendment wanted its impact on federalism to be limited, maintaining the states' role as primary protector of individual rights. MALTZ, CIVIL RIGHTS, *supra* note 37, at 60. While Maltz is correct that Bingham hoped that states would maintain their authority outside the realm of individual rights, and even that states would protect those rights themselves, the evidence is overwhelming that the Framers wanted Congress to have broad power to step in and protect rights of belonging whenever states failed to do so.

116. CONG. GLOBE, 39th Cong., 1st Sess. 2549 (1866).

117. *See* Kaczorowski, *supra* note 20; William J. Rich, *Taking "Privileges or Immunities" Seriously: A Call to Expand the Constitutional Canon,* 87 MINN. L. REV. 153, 200 (2002).

118. Cong. Globe, 39th Cong., 1st Sess. 1292 (1866).

119. *Id.* at 1294.

120. *Id.* at 1292.

121. *Id.* at 1759.

122. *Id.* at 1033.

123. *Id.*

124. *Id.* at 1090.

125. Kaczorowski, *supra* note 1, at 876.

126. *See* Farber & Muench, *supra* note 1, at 277.

127. For just a few samples of works analyzing the meaning of the Fourteenth Amendment, *see* Curtis, *supra* note 3; Maltz, Fourteenth Amendment, *supra* note 34; Brandwein, *supra* note 104; Baer, *supra* note 4; Harold M. Hyman & William M. Wiecek, Equal Justice under Law: Constitutional Developments, 1835–1875 (1982); William E. Nelson, The Fourteenth Amendment: From Political Principle to Judicial Doctrine (1988); tenBroek, *supra* note 6, and the incorporation debate works, *cited in* note 112, *supra*.

128. *Slaughter-House Cases*, 83 U.S. 36 (1872). *See* Maltz, Fourteenth Amendment, *supra* note 34, at 27.

129. Cong. Globe, 39th Cong., 1st Sess. 1833 (1866).

130. *See* Farber & Muench, *supra* note 1, at 277; Curtis, *supra* note 48, at 64, 76.

131. *See* Aynes, *supra* note 80, at 71.

132. Cong. Globe, 42d Cong., 1st Sess., app. 84 (1871).

133. *See also* D. Smith, *supra* note 34, at 802.

134. Foner, *supra* note 10, at 80.

135. R. Smith, *supra* note 3, at 306.

136. *See, e.g.,* Cong. Globe, 39th Cong., 1st Sess. 630 (1866) (statement of Hubbard). *See* Benedict, *supra* note 8, at 136–137. During the debate over the 1866 act, John Bingham indicated that he agreed with the radicals on this point. Cong. Globe, 39th Cong., 1st Sess. 1291 (1866).

137. This opinion was often expressed by moderate Republicans during the debates over the 1866 act. *See, e.g.,* Cong. Globe, 39th Cong., 1st Sess. 476 (1866) (statement of Sen. Trumbull); *id.* at 504 (statement of Sen. Howard); *id.* at 1117 (statement of Rep. James Wilson). Moderates and conservatives held this view primarily because they believed that a bill providing the right to suffrage would not succeed. *See* Benedict, *supra* note 8, at 152–156.

138. *See* Fox, *supra* note 5, at 503–504; R. Smith, *supra* note 3, at 730; Farber & Muench, *supra* note 1, at 236.

139. *Corfield v. Coryell*, 6 F. Cas. 546 (C.C.E.D. Pa. 1823) (No. 3,230).

140. Cong. Globe, 39th Cong., 1st Sess. 2462, 2765–2766 (1866). In *Corfield*, the court articulated a comprehensive list of the fundamental rights of

"citizens of all free governments," including "protection by the government; the enjoyment of life and liberty, with the right to acquire and possess property of every kind, and to pursue and obtain happiness and safety . . . the right of a citizen of one state to pass through, or to reside in any other state . . . to claim the benefit of writ of habeas corpus . . . (and) to institute and maintain actions of any kind in the courts of the state." *Corfield,* 6 F. Cas. at 551–552.

141. CONG. GLOBE, 39th Cong., 1st Sess. 1757 (1866) (statement of Sen. Trumbull); *id.* at 1117 (statement of Rep. Wilson).

142. *See* MALTZ, FOURTEENTH AMENDMENT, *supra* note 34, at 9–28.

143. CONG. GLOBE, 39th Cong., 1st Sess. 1159 (1866).

144. *Id.* at 2766.

145. *See* Farber & Muench, *supra* note 1, at 251.

146. *See* Rich, *supra* note 117, at 185.

147. FONER, *supra* note 10, at 454.

148. Ku Klux Klan Act of 1871, ch. 22, § 2(3), 17 Stat. 13 (codified in Rev. Stat. of 1874, § 1980, now 42 U.S.C. § 1985(3)). *See also* Enforcement Act of 1870, May 31, 1870, ch. 114, 16 Stat. 140 (codified at 18 U.S.C. § 241 (2005)).

149. *See* CURTIS, *supra* note 3, at 158.

150. *Id.* at 157.

151. Civil Rights Act of 1875, ch. 114, 18 Stat. 335. The Supreme Court struck down the Civil Rights Act of 1875 in the *Civil Rights Cases.*

152. *See* Fox, *supra* note 115, at 137.

153. *See* FONER, *supra* note 10, at 532–533, 555.

154. *Id.* at 556.

155. *See* Xi Wang, *The Making of Federal Enforcement Laws, 1870–1872,* 70 CHI.-KENT L. REV. 1013, 1020 (1995).

156. *Id.* at 1020.

157. Civil Rights Act of 1866 (codified at 42 U.S.C. § 1331).

158. *See* Wildenthal, *supra* note 104; Kevin Christopher Newsom, *Setting Incorporationism Straight: A Reinterpretation of the Slaughter-House Cases,* 109 YALE L. J. 643, 659 (2000).

159. *Slaughter-House Cases,* 83 U.S. 36, 76 (1873).

160. *See* Fox, *supra* note 115, at 148–155.

161. *Id.* at 148.

162. *See* CONG. GLOBE, 43d Cong., 1st Sess. 3452–3454 (1874) (statement of Senator Frelinghuysen); *cited in* Fox, *supra* note 115, at 149.

163. Fox, *supra* note 115, at 155. Moreover, after *Slaughter-House,* the Court issued a series of opinions narrowing its views of the Privileges or Immunities Clause, culminating in a list of federal citizenship rights in the case of *Twining v. New Jersey,* 211 U.S. 78 (1908), a list that many commentators consider paltry and redundant, and may have further dampened congressional in-

terest in developing the privileges and immunities of citizenship. For an excellent discussion of the development of the Court's interpretation of the Privileges or Immunities Clause from *Slaughter-House* to *Twining, see* Bryan H. Wildenthal, *The Road to* Twining: *Reassessing the Disincorporation of the Bill of Rights,* 61 OHIO ST. L. J. 1457 (2000).

164. Civil Rights Act of 1875, 18 Stat. 335.

165. *Civil Rights Cases,* 109 U.S. 3, 11 (1983).

166. *Id.* at 13–14. Years later, in *City of Boerne v. Flores,* the Court cited this language to support its holding that Congress cannot create new substantive constitutional rights but is limited to remedying constitutional violations. However, the opinion in the *Civil Rights Cases* that better reflects the intent of the Framers is not the majority ruling but Justice Harlan's dissent. *See* Rebecca E. Zietlow, *Belonging, Protection and Equality: The Neglected Citizenship Clause and the Limits of Federalism,* 62 U. PITT. L. REV. 281, 326–337 (2000).

167. *Plessy v. Ferguson,* 163 U.S. 537 (1896). *See* KENNETH L. KARST, BELONGING TO AMERICA: EQUAL CITIZENSHIP AND THE CONSTITUTION 58 (1989); ROBERT K. CARR, FEDERAL PROTECTION OF CIVIL RIGHTS: QUEST FOR A SWORD 45 (1947); Julius Chambers, *Protection of Civil Rights: A Constitutional Mandate for the Federal Government,* 87 MICH L. REV. 1599, 1610 (1989).

168. FEDERALISM AND RIGHTS xiii (Ellis Katz & G. Alan Tarr, eds., 1996).

169. BRANDWEIN, *supra* note 104, at 29.

170. *See* Michael Kent Curtis, *John A. Bingham and the Story of American Liberty: The Lost Cause Meets the "Lost Clause,"* 36 AKRON L. REV. 617, 617–621 (2003).

171. *Id. See also* FONER, *supra* note 10.

172. BRANDWEIN, *supra* note 104, at 88.

173. For an excellent description of the incorporation debate, *see* Wildenthal, *supra* note 104, at 1055–1094.

174. *See* BRANDWEIN, *supra* note 104, at 108–109, citing Charles Fairman, *A Reply to Professor Crosskey,* 22 UNIV. CHI. L. REV. 144 (1954).

175. BRANDWEIN, *supra* note 104, at 109, citing William Crosskey, *Charles Fairman, "Legislative History," and the Constitutional Limitations on State Authority,* 22 UNIV. CHI. L. REV. 1 (1954).

176. BRANDWEIN, *supra* note 104, at 107.

177. Charles Fairman, *Does the Fourteenth Amendment Incorporate the Bill of Rights?,* 2 STAN. L. REV. 5, 153–154 (1949).

178. *See, e.g.,* CURTIS, *supra* note 3, at 92–130; Akhil Reed Amar, *The Bill of Rights and the Fourteenth Amendment,* 101 YALE L. J. 1193, 1254–1260, 1269–1272 (1992) (advocating "refined" incorporation); Wildenthal, *supra* note 104. However, the debate continues. *See, e.g.,* Raoul Berger, *Incorporation of the Bill of Rights: Akhil Amar's Wishing Well,* 61 U. CINN. L. REV. 1 (1993).

179. *See* Chambers, *supra* note 167, at 1604–1605.

180. *See* U.S. CONST. Amends. XIII (abolishing slavery and giving Congress the power to "enforce this article by appropriate legislation"); XIV; XV (prohibiting the federal government and states from denying the right to vote on account of race and giving Congress the power to "enforce this article by appropriate legislation"); XIX (prohibiting the denial of the right to vote on account of sex and giving Congress the power to "enforce this article by appropriate legislation"); XXIII (bestowing the right to vote for president on residents of the District of Columbia and giving Congress the power to "enforce this article by appropriate legislation"); XXIV (prohibiting the use of poll taxes as a voting qualification and giving Congress the power to "enforce this article by appropriate legislation"); XXVI (lowering the voting age to eighteen and giving Congress the power to "enforce this article by appropriate legislation").

NOTES TO CHAPTER 4

1. William E. Forbath, *The New Deal Constitution in Exile,* 51 DUKE L. J. 165, 169 (2001).

2. National Labor Relations Act [Wagner Act], ch. 372, 49 Stat. 449 (1935) (codified as amended at 29 U.S.C. §§ 151–166 (2000)); Fair Labor Standards Act, ch. 676, 52 Stat. 1060 (1938) (codified as amended at 29 U.S.C. §§ 201–219 (2000)); Social Security Act, ch. 531, 49 Stat. 620 (1935).

3. Of course, "economic" rights and "human" rights are not necessarily differentiated. Indeed, in many places throughout the world, economic rights such as the rights to housing, health care, and earning a livelihood, are considered to be fundamental human rights. *See* Forbath, *New Deal Constitution, supra* note 1, at 168.

4. *See* William E. Forbath, *Caste, Class and Equal Citizenship,* 98 MICH. L. REV. 1, 4 (1999).

5. Forbath, *New Deal Constitution, supra* note 1, at 196.

6. *NLRB v. Jones,* 332 U.S. 823 (1937).

7. *Iron Molder's Journal* 40 (1904): 750, *cited in* Howell John Harris, *Industrial Democracy and Liberal Capitalism, 1890–1925, in* INDUSTRIAL DEMOCRACY IN AMERICA: THE AMBIGUOUS PROMISE 43, 46 (Nelson Lichtenstein & Howell John Harris, eds., 1993).

8. *See* LIZABETH COHEN, MAKING A NEW DEAL: INDUSTRIAL WORKERS IN CHICAGO, 1919–1939, 6–7 (1990).

9. *Id.* at 257–258.

10. I owe this insight in part to an e-mail from William E. Forbath. E-mail from William E. Forbath, Professor of Law, University of Texas at Austin, to Rebecca Zietlow, Professor of Law, University of Toledo College of Law (July 28, 2005) (on file with author).

11. *See* James Gray Pope, *Labor's Constitution of Freedom*, 106 YALE L. J. 941 (1997).

12. *See* Pope, *Labor's Constitution, supra* note 11, at 943; Forbath, *Caste, Class, supra* note 4, at 4; James Gray Pope, *The Thirteenth Amendment versus the Commerce Clause: Labor and the Shaping of American Constitutional Law*, 102 COLUM. L. REV. 1, 14 (2002).

13. *See* Forbath, *Caste, Class, supra* note 4, at 30.

14. *See* ERIC FONER, FREE SOIL, FREE LABOR, FREE MEN: THE IDEOLOGY OF THE REPUBLICAN PARTY BEFORE THE CIVIL WAR (1995).

15. Lea S. Vandervelde, *The Labor Vision of the Thirteenth Amendment*, 138 U. PA. L. REV. 437, 441–443 (1989).

16. *Id.* at 438, 440, 461. Alexander Tsesis also has recently advocated a broad view of the Thirteenth Amendment's protection of liberty. *See* ALEXANDER TSESIS, THE THIRTEENTH AMENDMENT AND AMERICAN FREEDOM: A LEGAL HISTORY (2004).

17. CONG. GLOBE, 35th Cong., 2d Sess. 985 (1859).

18. The most outspoken opponent of that view was Senator Edgar Cowen, who urged that the Thirteenth Amendment be strictly limited to enslaved blacks. However, Vandervelde argues that Wilson's faction generally carried the day. Vandervelde, *supra* note 15, at 445.

19. Pope, *Labor's Constitution, supra* note 11, at 943, 959; WILLIAM E. FORBATH, LAW AND THE SHAPING OF THE AMERICAN LABOR MOVEMENT 137 (1991).

20. For example, when Andrew Furuseth, leader of the Seaman's Union and AFL principal lobbyist, testified before Congress on behalf of anti-injunction legislation, he decried injunctions enforcing "yellow dog" contracts against union organizers and argued that treating human employment relations as property relations violated the Thirteenth Amendment. FORBATH, *supra* note 19, at 160; Pope, *Thirteenth Amendment, supra* note 12, at 32.

21. Pope, *Labor's Constitution, supra* note 11, at 968.

22. *Id.* at 981.

23. *See id.* at 964.

24. FONER, *supra* note 14, at xxiv.

25. E-mail from Forbath, *supra* note 10.

26. *See* COHEN, *supra* note 8, at 251.

27. *Id.* at 252.

28. Nelson Lichtenstein & Howell John Harris, *Introduction: A Century of Industrial Democracy in America, in* INDUSTRIAL DEMOCRACY IN AMERICA: THE AMBIGUOUS PROMISE 1, 3 (Nelson Lichtenstein & Howell John Harris, eds., 1993); Pope, *Labor's Constitution, supra* note 11, at 994.

29. JOSEPH E. SLATER, PUBLIC WORKERS: GOVERNMENT, EMPLOYEE UNIONS,

THE LAW AND THE STATES, 1900–1962, 48–49 (2004) (citing *Post-Intelligencer,* May 13, 1928).

30. The centrality of citizenship to this ideology became problematic after the war, when employers used the language of industrial democracy and citizenship to divide native and immigrant workers. *See* Joseph A. McCartin, *"An American Feeling": Workers, Managers and the Struggle over Industrial Democracy in the World War I Era, in* INDUSTRIAL DEMOCRACY IN AMERICA: THE AMBIGUOUS PROMISE 67, 79–82 (Nelson Lichtenstein & Howell John Harris, eds., 1993).

31. MELVYN DUBOFSKY, THE STATE AND LABOR IN MODERN AMERICA 13, 19 (1994); FORBATH, *supra* note 19, at 39–40, 50. "Yellow dog" contracts required employees to agree not to join a union as a condition of employment. *See* HARRY A. MILLIS & EMILY CLARK BROWN, FROM THE WAGNER ACT TO TAFT-HARTLEY: A STUDY OF NATIONAL LABOR POLICY AND LABOR RELATIONS 7 (1950).

32. *See e.g., Lochner v. New York,* 198 U.S. 45 (1905); *Adair v. U.S.,* 208 U.S. 161 (1908); *Coppage v. State of Kansas,* 236 U.S. 1 (1915); *Adkins v. Children's Hospital. of the District of Columbia,* 261 U.S. 525 (1923); *In re Jacobs,* 98 N.Y. 98 (1885); *Ritchie v. People of the State of Illinois,* 155 Ill. 98, 40 N.E. 454 (1895). *See also* FORBATH, *supra* note 19, at 39–40, 43–44.

33. DUBOFSKY, *supra* note 31, at 37; MILLIS & BROWN, *supra* note 31, at 10.

34. *See* SLATER, *supra* note 29, at 74.

35. *See generally* FORBATH, *supra* note 19. Forbath has been criticized for overplaying the role that courts had in repressing political action and downplaying labor's involvement in politics during the *Lochner* era. *See* Robin Archer, *Unions, Courts and Parties: Judicial Repression and Labor Politics in Late Nineteenth Century America,* 26 POLITICS & SOCIETY 391, 407 (1998). However, this criticism discounts the work that Forbath has done describing the political battles waged between unions and courts over antilabor injunctions.

36. "Voluntarism" refers to the strategy of labor leaders that unions can best obtain benefits for their members by using weapons of economic pressure such as strikes against individual employers rather than the political process. Federal courts repeatedly issued injunctions prohibiting unions from striking during this era. *See, e.g., Coeur D'Alene Consolidated & Mining Co. v. Miners' Union of Wardner,* 51 F. 260 (C.C.D. Idaho 1892) (union actions to enforce a closed shop and union wage scale were unlawful restraints on the owner's property); *Casey v. Cincinnati Typographical Union, No. 3,* 45 F. 135 (C.C.S.D. Ohio 1891) (same). The Supreme Court often seemed to share the lower courts' antipathy to organized labor. *See, e.g., Loewe v. Lawlor,* 208 U.S. 274 (1908) (union boycotts violate Sherman Anti-trust Act); *Adair,* 208 U.S. 161 (striking down state legislation prohibiting "yellow dog" contracts, whereby employers

required workers to sign a pledge not to join a union as a condition of employment, on the grounds that the statute violated the workers' right to contract). *See* Dubofsky, *supra* note 31, at 24–27. Forbath estimates that courts issued 2,100 antilabor injunctions in the 1920s, enjoining as many as 25 percent of all labor strikes during those years. Forbath, *supra* note 19, at 118.

37. Forbath, *supra* note 19, at 88.

38. *See* Dubofsky, *supra* note 31, at 49.

39. Forbath, *supra* note 19, at 150. During the first two decades of the twentieth century, state legislatures enacted 50 anti-injunction statutes. *Id.* at 147.

40. *See, e.g.,* Melvyn Urofsky, *State Courts and Protective Legislation during the Progressive Era: A Reevaluation,* 72 J. of Am. Hist. 63 (1985); David E. Bernstein, Only One Place of Redress: African Americans, Labor Relations and the Courts from Reconstruction to the New Deal 3 (2001).

41. *See* Aziz Z. Huq, *Peonage and Contractual Liberty,* 101 Colum. L. Rev. 351, 353 (2001).

42. Robert Franklin Hoxie, Trade Unionism in the United States 238 (2d ed., D. Appleton & Co. 1923), *quoted in* Christopher L. Tomlins, The State and the Unions: Labor Relations, Law, and the Organized Labor Movement in America, 1880–1960, 58 (1985).

43. *See* Kenneth M. Casebeer, *Holder of the Pen: An Interview with Leon Keyserling on Drafting the Wagner Act,* 42 U. Miami. L. Rev. 285, 288 (1987). The implicit conflict between individual and collective rights has been a continuous theme in the history of labor and it retains its salience today. *See* Joseph A. McCartin, *Democratizing the Demand for Workers' Rights: Toward a Re-framing of Labor's Argument,* Dissent, Winter 2005, at 61.

44. For an excellent description of their resulting opposition to courts, *see* William G. Ross, A Muted Fury: Populists, Progressives, and Labor Unions Confront the Courts, 1890–1937 (1994).

45. *See* Pope, *Labor's Constitution, supra* note 11, at 967; Forbath, *Caste, Class, supra* note 4, at 54–56.

46. Ross, *supra* note 44, at 1.

47. *Pamphlets in American History,* A Bibliographic Guide to the Microform Collection L69(I) (1969), *cited in* Forbath, *supra* note 19, at 143.

48. Forbath, *supra* note 19, at 127.

49. Ross, *supra* note 44, at 1.

50. *Hammer v. Dagenhart,* 247 U.S. 251 (1918). *See* Ross, *supra* note 44, at 167–170.

51. *See J. W. Bailey v. Drexel Furniture Co.,* 259 U.S. 20 (1922). *See* Ross, *supra* note 44, at 188–189.

52. Ross, *supra* note 44, at 19, 167–170.

53. *Id.* at 156.

54. Clayton Act of 1914, ch. 323, 38 Stat. 730 (codified as amended at 15 U.S.C. §§ 12–27, 29 U.S.C. §§ 52–53 (2005)). This defect was obvious to a number of contemporary observers. *Id.* at 156. *See also* William E. Forbath, *Clayton Act, in* DICTIONARY OF AMERICAN HISTORY (Stanley I. Kutler, ed., 3d ed. 2003).

55. *Duplex Printing Press Co. v. Deering,* 254 U.S. 443 (1921). *See* DUBOFSKY, *supra* note 31, at 101.

56. Federal Anti-Injunction Act [Norris-LaGuardia Act], Pub. L. No. 72-65, ch. 90, 47 Stat. 70 (1932), *amended by* Pub. L. No. 98-620, 98 Stat. 3335 (1984) (codified as 29 U.S.C. §§ 101 et seq.). *See* FORBATH, *supra* note 19, at 162; Pope, *supra* note 12, at 45 (terming the Norris-LaGuardia Act "a triumph for labors' 'freedom constitution'").

57. Federal Anti-Injunction Act (codified as 29 U.S.C. § 101).

58. *See id.* § 102. *See also* Clyde W. Summers, *The Privatization of Personal Freedoms and Enrichment of Democracy: Some Lessons from Labor Law,* 1986 U. ILL. L. REV. 689, 696 (1986); MILLIS & BROWN, *supra* note 31, at 20. During the debate over the Wagner Act, its proponents often cited the promise of freedom embodied in the preamble to Norris-LaGuardia.

59. *Lauf v. E. G. Shinner Co.,* 303 U.S. 323 (1938).

60. ROBERT F. HIMMELBERG, THE GREAT DEPRESSION AND THE NEW DEAL 7 (2001).

61. *Id.* at 9–10.

62. *Id.* at 3.

63. *See* Mark Barenberg, *The Political Economy of the Wagner Act: Power, Symbol, and Workplace Cooperation,* 106 HARV. L. REV. 1381, 1393 (1993).

64. MILLIS & BROWN, *supra* note 31, at 20. Labor's political clout actually peaked after the passage of the Wagner Act, when John Lewis formed the CIO and campaigned on Roosevelt's behalf in 1936. DUBOFSKY, *supra* note 31, at 133; KEVIN J. MCMAHON, RECONSIDERING ROOSEVELT ON RACE: HOW THE PRESIDENCY PAVED THE ROAD TO *BROWN* 56 (2004).

65. IRVING BERNSTEIN, THE NEW DEAL COLLECTIVE BARGAINING POLICY 129 (1950; reissued 1975).

66. Casebeer, *supra* note 43, at 299–300; TOMLINS, *supra* note 42, at 100.

67. National Industrial Recovery Act, June 16, 1933, ch. 90, 48 Stat. 195.

68. MILLIS & BROWN, *supra* note 31, at 19.

69. *Id.* at 21; MCMAHON, *supra* note 64, at 33.

70. JAMES A. GROSS, THE MAKING OF THE NATIONAL LABOR RELATIONS BOARD: A STUDY IN ECONOMICS, POLITICS AND LAW, 1933–1937, 1:14 (1974) ("For workers, however, the meaning of Section 7(a) was plain: President Roosevelt wanted them to join unions."); MILLIS & BROWN, *supra* note 31, at 22.

For example, John Lewis and the UMW organized more than 40,000 workers in the two years after § 7(a) was enacted. McMahon, *supra* note 64, at 35.

71. Millis & Brown, *supra* note 31, at 22.

72. *See* I. Bernstein, New Deal Policy, *supra* note 65, at 57.

73. Gross, *supra* note 70, at 14.

74. *Id.*

75. *Interborough Rapid Transit Co. v. Lavin,* 247 N.Y. 65, 159 N.E. 863 (1928).

76. *See* Casebeer, *supra* note 43, at 326.

77. Much of this "common law" later became the basis for provisions of the Wagner Act. Millis & Brown, *supra* note 31, at 24; Gross, *supra* note 70, at 52; *but see* Gross, *supra* note 70, at 33 (NLB decided policy questions only as a last resort).

78. Gross, *supra* note 70, at 11, 35; I. Bernstein, New Deal Policy, *supra* note 65, at 87.

79. 73 Cong. Rec. 2926, S. 2926, 73rd Cong., 2d Sess. (1934).

80. 78 Cong. Rec. 3443, S. 2926 (1934) (explanatory statement by Sen. Wagner upon introducing the bill). *See* I. Bernstein, New Deal Policy, *supra* note 65, at 62.

81. Robert Wagner, Senator of New York, Speech at the Conference of Code Authorities in Washington, D.C. (March 5, 1934), *in* 78 Cong. Rec. 3678.

82. 78 Cong. Rec. 12027 (statement of Sen. Robert La Follette).

83. I. Bernstein, New Deal Policy, *supra* note 65, at 110; Gross, *supra* note 70, at 131.

84. Testimony of Labor Secretary Frances Perkins, Hearings before the Senate Committee on Education and Labor, 73rd Cong., 2d Sess., on S. 2926 (March 14, 1934).

85. Senate Committee on Education and Labor, *Hearings, National Labor Relations Board,* 74th Cong., 1st Sess. (1935) 890. *See* I. Bernstein, New Deal Policy, *supra* note 65, at 100; Millis & Brown, *supra* note 31, at 27.

86. The mainstream press remained hostile to the bill, even after it was enacted. For example, the *Boston Herald* called it a "closed shop" bill and the *New York Times* pointed out that the bill directly conflicted with the president's automobile settlement from the year before in which he condoned company unions. I. Bernstein, New Deal Policy, *supra* note 65, at 99.

87. Gross, *supra* note 70, at 69; I. Bernstein, New Deal Policy, *supra* note 65, at 123; Casebeer, *supra* note 43, at 304.

88. Gross, *supra* note 70, at 69, 73.

89. I. Bernstein, New Deal Policy, *supra* note 65, at 123.

90. Irving Bernstein, A History of the American Worker (1933–1941): Turbulent Years 217 (1969); R. W. Fleming, *The Significance of the*

Wagner Act, in LABOR AND THE NEW DEAL 123, 131 (Milton Derber & Edwin Young, eds., 1957).

91. I. BERNSTEIN, AMERICAN WORKER, *supra* note 90, at 224–225.

92. *Id.* at 272, 278, 310, 312–313, 310; ROBERT S. MCELVANE, THE GREAT DEPRESSION: AMERICA 1929–1941, 226–227 (1984).

93. GROSS, *supra* note 70, at 122.

94. D. BERNSTEIN, *supra* note 40, at 88.

95. *See* Barenberg, *supra* note 63, at 1396.

96. DUBOFSKY, *supra* note 31, at 130; GROSS, *supra* note 70, at 95 (employer resistance was intense).

97. D. BERNSTEIN, *supra* note 40, at 67.

98. *Id.* at 110.

99. GROSS, *supra* note 70, at 140.

100. MILLIS & BROWN, *supra* note 31, at 27.

101. D. BERNSTEIN, *supra* note 40, at 108.

102. *Id.* at 106; GROSS, *supra* note 70, at 69, 138.

103. Hearings before the Senate Committee on Education and Labor, April 2, 1935 (citing *Coppage* and *Adair*).

104. *Id.*

105. *Id.*

106. *See* Forbath, *New Deal Constitution, supra* note 1, at 198.

107. Robert Wagner, Senator of New York, Speech at the Conference of Code Authorities, *supra* note 81.

108. 79 CONG. REC. 12044 (1934).

109. Casebeer, *supra* note 43, at 329.

110. 79 CONG. REC. 12019 (1934).

111. 78 CONG. REC. 9060–9061 (1935).

112. Speech by Representative William P. Connery, Jr., given on the radio on May 31, 1935, reprinted in 79 CONG. REC. 8536 (1935).

113. 79 CONG. REC. 9700 (1935).

114. *Id.* at 9708.

115. *Id.* at 9714.

116. *See* MILLIS & BROWN, *supra* note 31, at 3; MCMAHON, *supra* note 64, at 55.

117. Pope, *Thirteenth Amendment, supra* note 12, at 14.

118. Senate Report No. 1184, 79 CONG. REC. 2926 (1934).

119. 79 CONG. REC. 2368 (1935).

120. *New York Times Magazine,* May 9, 1937, 23, *cited in* MILLIS & BROWN, *supra* note 31, at 3.

121. Forbath, *Caste, Class, supra* note 4, at 69.

122. 79 CONG. REC. 9691 (1935).

123. 79 CONG. REC. 9061 (1934).

124. 79 Cong. Rec. 9713 (1935).

125. Dubofsky, *supra* note 31, at 129.

126. Millis & Brown, *supra* note 31, at 3.

127. National Labor Relations Board, 74th Cong., 1st Sess., Senate Hearings before Committee on Education and Labor on S. 1958 (March 11–April 2, 1935), *cited in* D. Bernstein, *supra* note 40, at 101.

128. In a subsequent interview, Wagner's chief legislative aide and drafter of the Wagner Act, Leon Keyserling, emphasized this aspect of the act. *See* Casebeer, *supra* note 43, at 296. D. Bernstein, *supra* note 40, at 101.

129. Cohen, *supra* note 8, at 286.

130. Millis & Brown, *supra* note 31, at 30 (citing the National Labor Relations Act, 49 U.S. Stat. 449, statement of findings and policy).

131. *Id.*

132. National Labor Relations Board, 74th Cong., 1st Sess., Senate Hearings before the Committee on Education and Labor on H. 573 (May 2, 1935), at 6, 8, 12–13. *See* D. Bernstein, *supra* note 40, at 114.

133. National Labor Relations Board, 74th Cong., 1st Sess., Senate Hearings before the Committee on Education and Labor on S. 1958 (March 11–April 2, 1935), at 125.

134. *See* D. Bernstein, *supra* note 40, at 104.

135. Pope, *Thirteenth Amendment, supra* note 12, at 14.

136. *Id.* at 5.

137. Dubofsky, *supra* note 31, at 127.

138. National Labor Relations Act, 49 U.S. Stat. 449, statement of findings and policy. *See* Millis & Brown, *supra* note 31, at 30.

139. *See generally* Pope, *Thirteenth Amendment, supra* note 12; Forbath, *New Deal Constitution, supra* note 1.

140. D. Bernstein, *supra* note 40, at 90.

141. Pope, *Thirteenth Amendment, supra* note 12, at 51–53.

142. *Id. See also* James Gray Pope, *How American Workers Lost the Right to Strike, and Other Tales,* 103 Mich. L. Rev. 518 (2004).

143. Forbath, *New Deal Constitution, supra* note 1, at 175.

144. 79 Cong. Rec. 8470 (1935).

145. *Id.*

146. *See* Forbath, *New Deal Constitution, supra* note 1, at 198 n.146.

147. *A.L.A. Schechter Poultry Corporation v. United States,* 295 U.S. 495 (1935). Gross, *supra* note 70, at 140.

148. National Labor Relations Board files, memorandum from Laurence A. Knapp to the NLRB, n.d., p. 1.

149. 79 Cong. Rec. 7648 (May 16, 1935) (statement of Mr. Wagner).

150. 79 Cong. Rec. 7670. *See also id.* at 9687 (statement of Mr. Connery).

151. Clayton Act of 1914, October 15, 1914, ch. 323, 38 Stat. 730 (codified

as amended at 15 U.S.C. §§ 12–27, 29 U.S.C. §§ 52–53 (2005)). 79 CONG. REC. 7668–7669.

152. 79 CONG. REC. 7675 (1935). One hour later, the bill passed the Senate by a vote of 63 to 12. 79 CONG. REC. 7681 (1935).

153. I owe this insight to a conversation with Jim Pope.

154. Forbath, *New Deal Constitution, supra* note 1.

155. 79 CONG. REC. 7648 (1935).

156. *A.L.A. Schechter Poultry Corporation v. United States,* 295 U.S. 495 (1935).

157. D. BERNSTEIN, *supra* note 40, at 131. Prior to *Schechter,* the president's attitude toward the bill had been measured at best. DUBOFSKY, *supra* note 31, at 128; MCMAHON, *supra* note 64, at 52.

158. DUBOFSKY, *supra* note 31, at 128; D. BERNSTEIN, *supra* note 40, at 128.

159. MCMAHON, *supra* note 64, at 48.

160. D. BERNSTEIN, *supra* note 40, at 121; MCMAHON, *supra* note 64, at 52.

161. *See* D. BERNSTEIN, *supra* note 40, at 128.

162. GROSS, *supra* note 70, at 144.

163. D. BERNSTEIN, *supra* note 40, at 121.

164. MILLIS & BROWN, *supra* note 31, at 28.

165. 79 CONG. REC. 9681 (1935).

166. *See, e.g., id.* at 9686 (statement of Mr. Tarver) and 9689 (statement of Mr. Rich).

167. *Id.* at 9701.

168. *See id.* at 9679 (statement of Mr. Cox).

169. *Id.* at 9693.

170. *Id.* at 9692.

171. D. BERNSTEIN, *supra* note 40, at 123.

172. Speech by Rep. William P. Connery, Jr., given on the radio on May 31, 1935, reprinted in 79 CONG. REC. 8536 (1935).

173. 79 CONG. REC. 8816 (1935).

174. *Id.* at 8817.

175. *Id.* at 9680.

176. *Id.* at 9714.

177. *Id.* at 9698, 9714.

178. D. BERNSTEIN, *supra* note 40, at 124.

179. 79 CONG. REC. 9704 (1935).

180. *Id.* at 9709.

181. D. BERNSTEIN, *supra* note 40, at 116–117.

182. *See* GROSS, *supra* note 70, at 145, citing oral history interview with P. Levy.

183. *See* MCMAHON, *supra* note 64, at 50.

184. 79 CONG. REC. 9676–9711, 9715–9731, esp. 9680, 9683, 9727, 9729–9731; MILLIS & BROWN, *supra* note 31, at 28.

185. 79 CONG. REC. 10259, 10300.

186. However, the president's support for the bill was "tepid." *See* GROSS, *supra* note 70, at 147. Even after the act's passage, Roosevelt remained reluctant to support the public policy of collective bargaining. *See* GROSS, *supra* note 70, at 212.

187. Pope, *Thirteenth Amendment, supra* note 12, at 67 n.325.

188. *Id.*

189. D. BERNSTEIN, *supra* note 40, at 116.

190. *See* MILLIS & BROWN, *supra* note 31, at 28.

191. D. BERNSTEIN, *supra* note 40, at 117.

192. *Id.* at 128.

193. *See, e.g., Hammer v. Dagenhart,* 247 U.S. 251 (1918) (striking down a federal statute that prohibited shipping products in interstate commerce that had been manufactured by minors); *A.L.A Schechter Poultry Corporation v. United States,* 295 U.S. 495 (1935) (striking down provisions of the National Industrial Relations Act that authorized the president to regulate hours and wages of workers in the poultry industry). *See* Pope, *Thirteenth Amendment, supra* note 12, at 67.

194. Bituminous Coal Conservation Act, August 30, 1935, ch. 824, 49 Stat. 991. *Carter v. Carter Coal,* 298 U.S. 238 (1936).

195. *See Myers v. Bethlehem Shipbuilding Corp.,* 88 F.2d 154, 156 (2d Cir. 1937); *Foster Bros. Mfg. Co. v. NLRB,* 85 F.2d 984, 986–987 (4th Cir. 1986); *Fruehauf Trailer Co. v. NLRB,* 85 F.2d 391, 392 (6th Cir. 1936); *Pratt v. Stout,* 85 F.2d 172, 177–178 (8th Cir. 1986); *NLRB v. Friedman-Harry Marks Clothing Co.,* 85 F.2d 1, 2 (2d Cir. 1936); *NLRB v. Jones & Laughlin Steel Corp.,* 83 F.2d 998, 998 (5th Cir. 1946); GROSS, *supra* note 70, at 205.

196. GROSS, *supra* note 70, at 149.

197. *Id.* at 211.

198. MCMAHON, *supra* note 64, at 73.

199. GROSS, *supra* note 70, at 209.

200. *See* ROSS, *supra* note 44, at 193, GROSS, *supra* note 69, at 216.

201. GROSS, *supra* note 70, at 223.

202. MCMAHON, *supra* note 64, at 66.

203. Pope, *Thirteenth Amendment, supra* note 12, at 77–78. *See also* MCMAHON, *supra* note 64, at 86.

204. DUBOFSKY, *supra* note 31, at 137.

205. Pope, *Thirteenth Amendment, supra* note 12, at 77.

206. DUBOFSKY, *supra* note 31, at 138–139.

207. *See* Pope, *Thirteenth Amendment, supra* note 12, at 80.

208. *Id.* at 75–76. *See also* MCMAHON, *supra* note 64, at 37. Toward the

end of his presidency, Roosevelt embraced the link between economic and human rights even more firmly, declaring that "Every man has a right to life," and this means a "right to make a comfortable living" in his "Second Bill of Rights." *See* Forbath, *Caste, Class, supra* note 4, at 68.

209. Typescript of speech, "Industrial Democracy," John L. Lewis papers, State Historical Society of Wisconsin, Madison, *cited in* Dubofksy, *supra* note 31, at 139.

210. *The Constitution of the United States Was a Layman's Document, Not a Lawyer's Contract* (Sept. 17, 1937), in FRANKLIN D. ROOSEVELT, THE PUBLIC PAPERS AND ADDRESSES OF FRANKLIN D. ROOSEVELT 359, 6:362–363 (Samuel I. Rosenman, ed., 1941).

211. *Id.* at 366.

212. *The Three Hundred and Forty-Second Press Conference* (Feb. 5, 1937), in FRANKLIN D. ROOSEVELT, THE PUBLIC PAPERS AND ADDRESSES OF FRANKLIN D. ROOSEVELT 6:35, 44 (Samuel I. Rosenman, ed., 1941).

213. GROSS, *supra* note 70, at 225.

214. MCMAHON, *supra* note 64, at 78–79; DUBOFSKY, *supra* note 31, at 147.

215. *West Coast Hotel v. Parrish,* 300 U.S. 379 (1937) (reversing *Adkins v. Children's Hospital,* 261 U.S. 525 (1923)). Whether or not Roberts's switch was a response to Roosevelt's plan, or whether it was really a switch at all, is a matter that has been hotly contested by scholars. *See, e.g.,* Felix Frankfurter, *Mr. Justice Roberts,* 104 U. PA. L. REV. 311, 313 (1955); Michael Ariens, *A Thrice-Told Tale, or Felix the Cat,* 107 HARV. L. REV. 620 (1994); Barry Friedman, *A Reaffirmation: The Authenticity of the Roberts Memorandum,* 142 U. PA. L. REV. 1985 (1994); and Barry Friedman, *Switching Time and Other Thought Experiments: The Hughes Court and Constitutional Transformation,* 142 U. PA. L. REV. 1891, 1983 (1994).

216. *NLRB v. Jones & Laughlin Steel Corp.,* 301 U.S. 1 (1937). The Court continued its deferential approach to the commerce power in two subsequent rulings upholding other landmark New Deal measures—the Fair Labor Standards Act in *United States v. Darby,* 312 U.S. 100 (1941), and the Agricultural Adjustment Act in *Wickard v. Filburn,* 317 U.S. 111 (1942).

217. Pope, *Thirteenth Amendment, supra* note 12, at 97.

218. *New York Times,* April 13, 1937, p. 20 col. 1, *cited by* GROSS, *supra* note 70, at 229.

219. *See* GROSS, *supra* note 70, at 226–227; DUBOFSKY, *supra* note 31, at 145; Pope, *Thirteenth Amendment, supra* note 12, at 96; Drew D. Hansen, *The Sit-Down Strikes and the Switch in Time,* 46 WAYNE L. REV. 49, 50 (2000).

220. DUBOFSKY, *supra* note 31, at 129.; Karl Klare, *Judicial Deradicalization of the Wagner Act and the Origins of Modern Legal Consciousness, 1937–1941,* 62 MINN. L. REV. 265, 290 (1977–1978).

221. Forbath, *Caste, Class, supra* note 4, at 67. *See also* ERIC FONER, THE STORY OF AMERICAN FREEDOM 196 (1998) ("Like the Civil War, the New Deal recast the idea of freedom by linking it to the expanding power of the national state.")

222. HIMMELBERG, *supra* note 60, at 14.

223. *See* BRUCE ACKERMAN, WE THE PEOPLE: TRANSFORMATIONS 2:310–311 (1998). *But see* Michael J. Klarman, *Constitutional Fact/Constitutional Fiction: A Critique of Bruce Ackerman's Theory of Constitutional Moments,* 44 STAN. L. REV. 759, 771 (1992).

224. Klare, *supra* note 220. *See also* Katherine Van Wezel Stone, *The Post-War Paradigm in American Labor Law,* 90 YALE L. J. 1509 (1981).

225. TOMLINS, *supra* note 42, at 327.

226. *See* Klare, *supra* note 220, at 270; TOMLINS, *supra* note 42, at 60.

227. The Taft Hartley Act, 61 Stat. 137 (1947), created a category of unfair union practices, created management rights, enabled workers more easily to choose nonunion employment options, limited union rights to strike and boycott, and offered employers and workers the ability to challenge unions more effectively. The act reestablished the right of federal courts to issue antistrike injunctions, in effect amending the Norris-La Guardia Act, 61 Stat. 137 (1947). DUBOFSKY, *supra* note 31, at 199, 201.

228. *Id. See also* James J. Brudney, Sara Schiavoni, & Deborah J. Meritt, *Judicial Hostility toward Labor Unions? Applying the Social Background Model to a Celebrated Concern,* 60 OHIO ST. L. J. 1675 (1999); Klare, *supra* note 220, at 270; Pope, *American Workers, supra* note 142, at 519.

229. *See Thornhill v. Alabama,* 310 US 88, 101 (1940) (picketing as civil liberty), overturned in *Teamster v. Vogt,* 354 U.S. 284, 289 (1957); *Hague v. CIO,* 307 U.S. 496, 512 (1939) (free speech rights), *cited in* Pope, *Thirteenth Amendment, supra* note 12, at 103–104.

230. *See NLRB v. Mackay Radio & Telegraph Co.,* 304 U.S. 333, 345–346 (1938). Section 13 of the NLRA expressly protects the workers' right to strike.

231. Casebeer, *supra* note 43, at 353.

232. Pope, *American Workers, supra* note 142, at 527.

233. *Consolidated Edison Co. v. NLRB,* 305 U.S. 197 (1938) (remedial power); *NLRB v. Fansteel Metalurgical Corp.,* 306 U.S. 240 (1939) (sit-down strikes).

234. *See* Pope, *American Workers, supra* note 142, at 519.

235. *Id.* at 525.

236. *Report on the American Workforce* 69 (Dept. of Labor 2001), LEO TROY, TRADE UNION MEMBERSHIP, 1897–1962, 1–2 (National Bureau of Economic Research 1965). Union membership reached its peak in the mid 1950s. In 1955, some 16,042,700 workers belonged to unions, representing 31.7 percent of the civilian workforce. *Id.*

237. Casebeer, *supra* note 43, at 321.

238. *See* Forbath, *Caste, Class, supra* note 4, at 23.

239. *See* D. Bernstein, *supra* note 40, at 7.

240. *See, e.g.,* Alex Lichtenstein, *Book Review,* 50 LABOUR [CANADA] 340 (2002); Clarence Taylor, *Book Review,* 21 LAW & HISTORY REV. 431 (2003); James D. Schmidt, *Book Review,* 68 JOURNAL OF SOUTHERN HISTORY 724 (2002). *But see* David T. Beito, *Book Review,* 10 GEO. MASON L. REV. 293 (2001); Michael S. Mayer, *Book Review,* 89 JOURNAL OF AMERICAN HISTORY 255 (2002).

241. Vandervelde, *supra* note 15, at 466.

242. *Id.* at 466.

243. CONG. GLOBE, 39th Cong., 1st Sess. 343 (1866), *cited in* Vandervelde, *supra* note 15, at 481.

244. DUBOFSKY, *supra* note 31, at 187.

245. 79 CONG. REC. 9720 (1935); *See* MARTHA BIONDI, TO STAND AND FIGHT: THE STRUGGLE FOR CIVIL RIGHTS IN POSTWAR NEW YORK CITY 42 (2003) (discussing Marcantonio).

246. *See* D. BERNSTEIN, *supra* note 40, at 124; Forbath, *Caste, Class, supra* note 4, at 76.

247. DUBOFKSY, *supra* note 31, at 131; MCMAHON, *supra* note 64, at 50–52.

248. Agricultural and domestic workers were also excluded from the protections of the Social Security Act, and state-level administration of programs such as Unemployment Insurance and Aid to Families with Dependent Children was also a concession to southern representatives who feared federal interference in the states' treatment of poor blacks. *See* Forbath, *Caste, Class, supra* note 4, at 77.

249. *Id.*

250. COHEN, *supra* note 8, at 337.

251. Forbath, *Caste, Class, supra* note 4, at 83–84.

252. COHEN, *supra* note 8, at 340.

253. *Id.* at 367–368.

254. BIONDI, *supra* note 245, at 17.

255. DUBOFSKY, *supra* note 31, at 187.

256. Forbath, *Caste, Class, supra* note 4, at 81–82.

257. DUBOFKSY, *supra* note 31, at 223.

258. *See, e.g., Smith v. Allwright,* 321 U.S. 649 (1944) (striking down all-white primaries); *Shelley v. Kraemer,* 334 U.S. 1 (1948) (striking down racially restrictive covenants); *Missouri ex rel Gaines v. Canada,* 305 U.S. 337 (1938) (requiring the state of Missouri to provide access to law school for a black plaintiff); *Sweatt v. Painter,* 339 U.S. 629 (1950) (holding that a racially segregated state law school violated the Equal Protection Clause).

NOTES TO CHAPTER 5

1. *See* Michael J. Klarman, *Rethinking the Civil Rights and Civil Liberties Revolutions*, 82 VA. L. REV. 1 (1996).

2. Civil Rights Act of 1964, Pub. L. No. 88-352, July 2, 1964, 78 Stat. 241 (codified at 42 U.S.C. § 2000 et seq. (1994)). *See* Robert C. Post & Reva B. Siegel, *Equal Protection by Law: Federal Anti-Discrimination Legislation after Morrison and* Kimel, 110 YALE L. J. 441, 447 (2000).

3. *Brown v. Board of Education,* 347 U.S. 483 (1954).

4. *See* Klarman, *supra* note 1, at 19 (citing scholars who argue that *Brown* proves that Courts are "counter-majoritarian heroes" who protect minority rights).

5. While Title VII originally only applied to private employers, Congress expanded its coverage in 1972 to state employees.

6. Civil Rights Act of 1964, Title VI, 42 U.S.C. § 2000d (1994).

7. The most effective enforcement mechanisms were Title III, which authorized the attorney general to sue to enforce the provisions of the act; Title VI, which enabled the federal government to end federal funding of programs that discriminated on the basis of race, ethnicity, or religion; and Title VII, which established the federal Equal Employment Opportunity Commission.

8. *See* NICHOLAS LEMANN, THE PROMISED LAND: THE GREAT BLACK MIGRATION AND HOW IT CHANGED AMERICA 111, 137, 182 (1992).

9. JOHN F. KENNEDY, PUBLIC PAPERS, 1963, 469 (1964); CHARLES & BARBARA WHALEN, THE LONGEST DEBATE: A LEGISLATIVE HISTORY OF THE 1964 CIVIL RIGHTS ACT xx (1985).

10. *CQ Weekly Report* 281 (Feb. 7, 1964); *see* THE CIVIL RIGHTS ACT OF 1964: THE PASSAGE OF THE LAW THAT ENDED RACIAL SEGREGATION (Robert D. Loevy, ed., 1997).

11. Civil Rights Act of 1963, Additional Views of Hon. William T. McCulloch, Hon. John V. Lindsay, Hon. William T. Cahill, Hon. Garner E. Shriver, Hon. Clark McGregor, Hon. Charles McC. Mathias, Hon. James E. Bromwell, 88th Cong. § 1, Report 914, Part 2 (1963).

12. MARTHA BIONDI, TO STAND AND FIGHT: THE STRUGGLE FOR CIVIL RIGHTS IN POSTWAR NEW YORK CITY 3 (2003).

13. *Id.* at 17.

14. *Id.* at 18.

15. *See* KEVIN J. MCMAHON, RECONSIDERING ROOSEVELT ON RACE: HOW THE PRESIDENCY PAVED THE ROAD TO *BROWN* 40 (2004); BIONDI, *supra* note 12, at 165.

16. *See, e.g.,* MCMAHON, *supra* note 15, at 127, 180.

17. ROBERT K. CARR, FEDERAL PROTECTION OF CIVIL RIGHTS: QUEST FOR A

SWORD 1 (1947); Risa Goluboff, *The Thirteenth Amendment and the Lost Origins of Civil Rights,* 50 DUKE L. J. 1609, 1688 (2001).

18. Exec. Order No. 8802, 6 Fed. Reg. 3109 (1941). Roosevelt created the commission in response to the threat of civil rights leader A. Philip Randolph to stage a march on Washington demanding an end to race discrimination in employment. Twenty-two years later, Randolph played an important part in organizing the 1963 March on Washington to lobby for what became the 1964 Civil Rights Act. *See* ROBERT D. LOEVY, TO END ALL SEGREGATION: THE POLITICS OF THE PASSAGE OF THE CIVIL RIGHTS ACT OF 1964, 1 (1990). Although symbolically significant, the first FEPC had a staff of only eight members, lacked enforcement powers, and disbanded in 1943. *Id.*

19. *See* MCMAHON, *supra* note 15, at 177.

20. Exec. Order No. 9808, 11 Fed. Reg. 14153 (1946).

21. *See* TO SECURE THESE RIGHTS: THE REPORT OF THE PRESIDENT'S COMMITTEE ON CIVIL RIGHTS (U.S. Government Printing Office 1947).

22. *Id.* at 132.

23. The act provided more authority for the Department of Justice to address race discrimination in voting, assist in school desegregation cases and secure nondiscrimination in federal programs. In addition, the president's bill would create a federal Community Relations Service to assist in mediating racial disputes, extend the U.S. Commission on Civil Rights for four more years, and provide statutory authority for the president's Commission on Equal Opportunity. Whalen, *supra* note 9, at 11, 18. All of these measures were among the recommendations listed in TO SECURE THESE RIGHTS, *supra* note 21.

24. TAYLOR BRANCH, PARTING THE WATERS: AMERICA IN THE KING YEARS 1954–63, 15 (1988).

25. DAVID J. GARROW, BEARING THE CROSS: MARTIN LUTHER KING, JR. AND THE SOUTHERN CHRISTIAN LEADERSHIP CONFERENCE 157 (1986).

26. *Id.* at 155; *see* BURKE MARSHALL, FEDERALISM AND CIVIL RIGHTS ix, 49 (1964); Post & Siegel, *supra* note 2, at 492.

27. *See generally* GARROW, *supra* note 25; BRANCH, *supra* note 24.

28. GARROW, *supra* note 25, at 154; BRANCH, *supra* note 24, at 314, 413 (1988).

29. *United States v. Carolene Products Co.,* 304 U.S. 144 (1938).

30. *Id.*

31. *Korematsu v. United States,* 323 U.S. 214 (1944) (upholding the evacuation and internment of Japanese Americans during World War II).

32. *Smith v. Allwright,* 321 U.S. 649 (1944).

33. *Morgan v. Commonwealth of Virginia,* 328 U.S. 373 (1946).

34. *Shelley v. Kraemer,* 334 U.S. 1 (1948).

35. *Brown v. Board of Education,* 347 U.S. 483 (1954).

36. *See, e.g., Mayor of Baltimore v. Dawson,* 350 U.S. 877 (1955) (beaches);

Gayle v. Browder, 352 U.S. 903 (1956) (buses); *Holmes v. Atlanta,* 350 U.S. 879 (1955) (golf courses); *New Orleans City Park Improvement Ass'n v. Detiege,* 358 U.S. 54 (1958) (parks); *see also* KENNETH L. KARST, BELONGING TO AMERICA: EQUAL CITIZENSHIP AND THE CONSTITUTION 80 (1989).

37. *See* LUCAS A. POWE, THE WARREN COURT AND AMERICAN POLITICS 39 (2000); Klarman, *supra* note 1, at 19.

38. *See* Klarman, *supra* note 1, at 8. In 1954, at least 80 percent of white southerners were opposed to ending school segregation; *see* Lucas A. Powe, *supra* note 37, at 39.

39. GERALD N. ROSENBERG, THE HOLLOW HOPE: CAN COURTS BRING ABOUT SOCIAL CHANGE? 49–50, 70–71 (1991).

40. *Id.* at 79.

41. *Id.* at 91.

42. *Id.* at 43.

43. *Id.* at 79.

44. *See* POWE, *supra* note 37, at 78 (*quoting* USCCR 1969, at 2).

45. *See id.* at 58–59.

46. *Id.* at 89–90.

47. *Id.* at 52.

48. *See Bell v. Maryland,* 378 U.S. 226 (1964) (appendix).

49. *United States v. Stanley,* 109 U.S. 3 (1883).

50. RICHARD C. CORTNER, CIVIL RIGHTS AND PUBLIC ACCOMMODATIONS: THE HEART OF *ATLANTA MOTEL* AND *MCCLUNG* CASES 4–5 (2001).

51. The Court's divided opinion in one of the "sit-in" cases, *Bell v. Maryland,* indicates the extent of the Justices' indecision about the state action problem. *See Bell v. Maryland,* 378 U.S. 226 (1964). For an excellent discussion of the dynamics on the Court with regard to the state action issue while Congress was considering the 1964 Civil Rights Act, *see* POWE, *supra* note 37, at 227–229 (2000).

52. *See* CORTNER, *supra* note 50, at 7.

53. BIONDI, *supra* note 12, at 54.

54. *See* MCMAHON, *supra* note 15, at 99–100.

55. LOEVY, *supra* note 18, at 26.

56. *Id.* at 150–151.

57. WHALEN, *supra* note 9, at xvi.

58. ROSENBERG, *supra* note 39, at 167.

59. Civil Rights Act of 1957, Pub. L. No. 85-315, September 9, 1957, 71 Stat. 634 (codified at 42 U.S.C. § 1995). *See* MARSHALL, *supra* note 26, at 7; LEMANN, *supra* note 8, at 111, 137.

60. *See* LOEVY, *supra* note 18, at 36.

61. *Id.* at 154.

62. GARROW, *supra* note 25, at 244 (1986).

63. *Id.* at 249.

64. WHALEN, *supra* note 9, at xx; POWE, *supra* note 37, at 223–225.

65. *See* BRANCH, *supra* note 24, at 344, 319.

66. *See* LOEVY, *supra* note 18, at 8.

67. MARSHALL, *supra* note 26, at 38, 82.

68. Kennedy's bill did not address employment discrimination. Instead, the president called for passage of federal employment practices legislation that was already pending in Congress. 109 CONG. REC. 11, 159–161 (1963); John G. Stewart, *The Senate and Civil Rights, in* THE CIVIL RIGHTS ACT OF 1964: THE PASSAGE OF THE LAW THAT ENDED RACIAL SEGREGATION 149, 156 (Robert D. Loevy, ed., 1997).

69. WHALEN, *supra* note 9, at 5; Stewart, *supra* note 68, at 260.

70. WHALEN, *supra* note 9, at 9, 166.

71. *Id.* at 199.

72. *Id.* at 4; LOEVY, *supra* note 18, at 26.

73. WHALEN, *supra* note 9, at 84.

74. *Id.* at 11–13.

75. *Id.* at 15.

76. *Id.* at 19.

77. Although President Kennedy did not appear at the march, he met with King and other civil rights leaders immediately following the demonstration to express his support. *See* GARROW, *supra* note 25, at 269–286.

78. GARROW, *supra* note 25, at 291.

79. WHALEN, *supra* note 9, at 34–35.

80. *Id.* at 75.

81. LYNDON B. JOHNSON, PAPERS 1963–64, at 1:12 (1965).

82. He declared, "As far as the writ of Federal law will run, we must abolish not some but all racial discrimination. . . . Let this session of Congress be known as the session which did more for civil rights than the last hundred sessions combined." President Lyndon B. Johnson, State of the Union Address 1964, *in* CQ *Almanac* 862 (1964) (*cited in* LOEVY. *supra* note 18, at iii).

83. WHALEN, *supra* note 9, at 83, 96, 125–126, 173–177. Clarence Mitchell, the NAACP lobbyist, and Dick Russell, the bill's principal opponent in the Senate, agreed on this point. Said Mitchell, "President Johnson made a greater contribution to giving a dignified and hopeful status to Negroes in the United States than any other president, including Lincoln, Roosevelt and Kennedy." Interview of Clarence Mitchell, Jr., (April 30, 1969) *in* Oral History Collection (LBJ Library, tape 2, 30); LOEVY, *supra* note 18, at 333. Russell said that Lyndon Johnson had "more to do with [cloture's] success than any other man." *Chicago Daily News*, June 11, 1964, at 16; WHALEN, *supra* note 9, at 203.

84. WHALEN, *supra* note 9, at 89–90.

85. *Id.* at 90, 98–99.

86. LOEVY, *supra* note 18, at 120; WHALEN, *supra* note 9, at 115.

87. LOEVY, *supra* note 18, at 121.

88. *See* CONG. REC. 110, pt. 2, 2578–2580 (1964) (Rep. St. George); LOEVY, *supra* note 18, at 120; CONG. REC. 110, pt. 2, 2581 (1964) (Rep. May).

89. She said, "At the risk of being called an Aunt Jane, if not an Uncle Tom, let us not add any amendment that would get in the way of our primary objective." CONG. REC. 110, pt. 2, 2581 (1964); LOEVY, *supra* note 18, at 121.

90. LOEVY, *supra* note 18, at 125.

91. *Id.*

92. CONG. REC. 110, pt. 2, 2705–2805 (1964).

93. *See* CORTNER, *supra* note 50, at 14.

94. CONG. REC. 110, 2774.

95. WHALEN, *supra* note 9, at 4.

96. LOEVY, *supra* note 18, at 159.

97. *Id.* at 160.

98. Hubert Humphrey's public support for civil rights dated back to at least 1948. At the Democratic Convention that year, then mayor of Minneapolis Humphrey gave a speech in which he urged the Democratic Convention to accept the cause of civil rights. *See* Henry M. Jackson tribute, CONG. REC.1, 95th Cong., 2d Sess., January 24, 1978, vol. 124, pt. 1, 576 (*cited in* WHALEN, *supra* note 9, at 136). Humphrey's call was successful, and the Democrats adopted the most progressive civil rights platform in history, prompting a faction of segregationists, led by Strom Thurmond, to storm out of the convention center. *Id.*

99. *Id.* at 137.

100. They appointed two "title captains," one Democrat and one Republican, for each title of the bill. The job of a "title captain" was to actively work on the Senate floor when their particular title was being considered. This approach also served the purpose of getting more people actively involved in the passage of the bill. LOEVY, *supra* note 18, at 145–146.

101. WHALEN, *supra* note 9, at 126.

102. *Id.*

103. *Id.* at 82, 84.

104. Stewart, *supra* note 68, at 177.

105. Senate cloture proceedings, June 10, 1964; CONG. REC., June 10, 1964, pt. 10, 13307–13337; WHALEN, *supra* note 9, at 200.

106. *See* Hubert H. Humphrey, *Memorandum on Senate Consideration of the Civil Rights, in* THE CIVIL RIGHTS ACT OF 1964: THE PASSAGE OF THE LAW THAT ENDED RACIAL SEGREGATION 77, 85 (Robert D. Loevy, ed., 1997).

107. On February 18, 1964, Johnson pulled Humphrey aside and told him "the bill can't pass unless you get Ev Dirksen. You and I are going to get Ev." WHALEN, *supra* note 9, at 148.

108. *Id.* at 127.

109. *Id.* at 155.

110. *Id.* at 166.

111. Stewart, *supra* note 68, at 257.

112. *Id.* at 258; WHALEN, *supra* note 9, at 185.

113. *See* WHALEN, *supra* note 9, at 201 (Dirksen brought in the conservative Republican votes by placating states rights' supporters with his non-preemption amendments).

114. *Id.* at 196–197.

115. Senate cloture proceedings, CONG. REC., pt. 10, 13307–13337 (June 10, 1964); WHALEN, *supra* note 9, at 198.

116. WHALEN, *supra* note 9, at 198.

117. *Id.*

118. *Id.* at 227.

119. CORTNER, *supra* note 50, at 24.

120. *New York Herald Tribune,* May 26, 1964, at 1, 4; WHALEN, *supra* note 9, at 187.

121. WHALEN, *supra* note 9, at 107.

122. For a discussion of the evocation of citizenship rights by the Reconstruction Era Congress, *see* Rebecca E. Zietlow, *Belonging, Protection and Equality: The Neglected Citizenship Clause and the Limits of Federalism,* 62 U. PITT. L. REV. 281, 309–316 (2000).

123. *Id.*

124. CONG. GLOBE, 39th Cong., 1st Sess. 868 (1866) (Newell).

125. *Id.* at 1032 (McClurg).

126. *Id.* at 1295 (Wilson).

127. *Id.* at 1182 (Pomeroy).

128. WHALEN, *supra* note 9, at 104–105.

129. Additional Views of Hon. Arch A. Moore, Jr, House Judiciary Report, 88th Cong., 1st Sess., Report No. 914 (1963).

130. LOEVY, *supra* note 18, at 199 (citing Norbert Mills, The Speaking of Hubert Humphrey in Favor of the Civil Rights Act (Ph.D. dissertation, Bowling Green State University, 1974), 55, 79.

131. Stewart, *supra* note 68, at 312.

132. LOEVY, *supra* note 18, at 325.

133. *Id.* at 159.

134. WHALEN, *supra* note 9, at 142.

135. *Id.*

136. African Americans were purposefully excluded from many of the protections provided by New Deal Era legislation because so many of them were domestic and agricultural workers. MCMAHON, *supra* note 15, at 40.

137. Civil Rights Act of 1963, Additional Views of Hon. William T. McCulloch, Hon. John V. Lindsay, Hon. William T. Cahill, Hon. Garner E. Shriver,

Hon. Clark McGregor, Hon. Charles McC. Mathias, Hon. James E. Bromwell, 88th Cong. 1st Sess., Report 914, Part 2 (Dec. 2, 1963).

138. *Civil Rights Cases,* 109 U.S. 3 (1883).

139. LOEVY, *supra* note 18, at 49. *See also* Senate Record, April 8, 1964, at 7212 (letter from the Office of the Deputy Attorney General Nicholas deB. Katzenbach says bill falls within commerce power, citing New Deal cases).

140. *See* Civil Rights Act of 1963, *supra* note 137.

141. *CQ Weekly Report,* Jul. 12, 1963, 1131.

142. In *Shelley v. Kraemer,* 334 U.S. 1 (1948) the Court held that court enforcement of private racially restrictive covenants satisfied the state action requirement of the Fourteenth Amendment.

143. CORTNER, *supra* note 50, at 25.

144. *Id.* at 26.

145. *CQ Weekly Report,* Jul. 12, 1963, 1000; Loevy, *supra* note 10, at 50.

146. *See* "Minority Report upon Proposed Civil Rights Act of 1963," Committee on Judiciary Substitute for H.R. 7152 (citing the *Civil Rights Cases,* stating "It is clearly unconstitutional to bottom any claim of Federal control of state action upon 'custom or usage' involving acts which constitute merely private conduct").

147. WHALEN, *supra* note 9, at 106.

148. *Id.*

149. Senate proceedings, CONG. REC. June 18, 1964, pt. 11, 14275–14281, 14283–14287, 14294–14319, 14326–14336. *See also* "Minority Report upon Proposed Civil Rights Act of 1963, Committee on Judiciary Substitute for H.R. 7152" (Title II violates the Tenth Amendment).

150. LOEVY, *supra* note 18, at 160 (citing Kane dissertation at 49, 110, 130).

151. LESTER MADDOX, SPEAKING OUT: THE AUTOBIOGRAPHY OF LESTER GARFIELD MADDOX 57 (1975) (*cited in* CORTNER, *supra* note 50, at 38). Maddox eventually exploited his opposition to desegregation and successfully ran for governor of Georgia.

152. Strom Thurmond, Radio Statement, In Opposition to Proposed Statute Which Would Make Businessmen Sell and Serve to Negroes (June 6, 1963) (Speeches, Box 19, Thurmond Collection), cited in WHALEN, *supra* note 9, at 164.

153. Senate Apr. 8, 1964, 7205. *See also* Brief on Behalf of the State of New York as *Amicus Curiae* in support of Affirmance, *Heart of Atlanta Motel v. United States,* 379 U.S. 241 (1964) at 1; CORTNER, *supra* note 50, at 93.

154. Post & Siegel, *supra* note 2, at 489.

155. For this reason, William Eskridge and John Ferejohn have described the 1964 Civil Rights Act as a "super statute" that established a new normative framework that had a broad effect on the law. *See* William N. Eskridge, Jr., & John Ferejohn, *Super Statutes,* 50 DUKE L. J. 1215, 1237–1242 (2001).

156. Serena J. Hoy, *Interpreting Equal Protection: Congress, the Court, and the Civil Rights Acts,* 16 J. L.& POL. 381, 401–402 (2000).

157. *Id.* at 391.

158. Post & Siegel, *supra* note 2, at 497. *See also* LOEVY, *supra* note 18, at 326.

159. *See* LOEVY, *supra* note 18, at 40.

160. For example, a February Harris poll showed 68 percent of the American public favoring the bill, and a Harris poll conducted on April 26 revealed public support for the bill at 70 percent, with 63 percent in favor of limiting the debate. WHALEN, *supra* note 9, at 155, 170. Even more important, election returns in the spring primaries showed that supporting civil rights was a winning issue with the northern electorate. *Id.* at 237.

161. CONG. REC. pt. 4, 4741, 4742–4768 (1964); WHALEN, *supra* note 9, at 143.

162. *See* WHALEN, *supra* note 9, at 136, 86.

163. LOEVY, *supra* note 18, at 56.

164. WHALEN, *supra* note 9, at 27, 82.

165. Mitchell was the Washington Chief of the NAACP, who had once worked for Roosevelt's Employment Practices Committee and as a labor secretary for the NAACP. Rauh was a prominent Washington lawyer and vice-chairman of Americans for Democratic Action, a political lobbying organization that traditionally supported liberal causes. *See* LOEVY, *supra* note 18, at 60.

166. *See* Joseph L. Rauh, Jr., *The Role of the Leadership Conference on Civil Rights in the Civil Rights Struggle of 1963–1964, in* THE CIVIL RIGHTS ACT OF 1964: THE PASSAGE OF THE LAW THAT ENDED RACIAL SEGREGATION 49, 62–65 (Robert D. Loevy, ed., 1997).

167. LOEVY, *supra* note 18, at 112.

168. WHALEN, *supra* note 9, at 113 (citing an off-the-record interview with former House member, May 23, 1983).

169. Stewart, *supra* note 68, at 192.

170. *See* Hoy, *supra* note 156, at 394.

171. WHALEN, *supra* note 9, at 165. For example, an important step in the direction of cloture was the decision of Jack Miller, conservative Republican from Iowa, to vote for cloture based on intense church lobbying. *Id.* at 190.

172. *Id.* at 163.

173. Rauh, *supra* note 166, at 67; Humphrey, *supra* note 106, at 89.

174. *See Heart of Atlanta Motel v. United States,* 379 U.S. 241 (1964); *Katzenbach v. McClung,* 379 U.S. 294 (1964).

175. CORTNER, *supra* note 50, at 99.

176. Record, *Heart of Atlanta Motel,* at 56–58; CORTNER, *supra* note 50, at 47.

177. Brief of Appellees, *McClung*, at 29–31; CORTNER, *supra* note 50, at 122.

178. Record, *Heart of Atlanta Motel*, Civil Action No. 9017, at 47–52; CORTNER, *supra* note 50, at 45.

179. CORTNER, *supra* note 50, at 45.

180. *Heart of Atlanta Motel*, at 241.

181. *McClung*, at 294.

182. *Heart of Atlanta Motel*, at 241; *McClung*, at 294. Notably, though Congress had relied on both the commerce power and its power to enforce the Fourteenth Amendment pursuant to Section Five, the Court discussed only the commerce power in its opinions. *See* Post & Siegel, *supra* note 2, at 517.

183. CORTNER, *supra* note 50, at 181.

184. *Id.* As Justice Clark announced the opinion from the bench, Justice Douglas passed a note to Justice Goldberg stating that he was happy they had written separately. Goldberg passed a note back, which said, "Bill: I agree most emphatically. It sounds like hamburgers are more important than human rights. Arthur." *See* CORTNER, *supra* note 50, at 180.

185. Despite the opponents' emphasis on property rights, none of the Court's opinions mentioned those arguments made by opponents of the act, and conference notes suggest that the Justices did not even discuss them in conference over the case. *See* CORTNER, *supra* note 50, at 150.

186. Post & Siegel, *supra* note 2, at 517.

187. TAKING CHARGE: THE JOHNSON WHITE HOUSE TAPES 1963–64, 420–421 (Michael R. Beschloss, ed., 1997); CORTNER, *supra* note 50, at 27.

188. CORTNER, *supra* note 50, at 29, 31.

189. *Wall Street Journal*, July 2, 1964, at 1, 16; CORTNER, *supra* note 50, at 31.

190. President Johnson sent thank you letters to the first three senators who made such speeches. LOEVY, *supra* note 18, at 338.

191. *Time Magazine* 84 (July 7, 1964) 25; CORTNER, *supra* note 50, at 63–64.

192. LOEVY, *supra* note 18, at 331.

193. CORTNER, *supra* note 50, at 182–183.

194. Thanks to Martha Biondi for pointing this out to me.

195. The 1964 act was also more effective than the courts alone in effecting the desegregation of public education. *See* ROSENBERG, *supra* note 39, at 49–50, 70–71; Klarman, *supra* note 1, at 21 ("Only the intervention of the national political branches in the form of the 1964 Civil Rights Act and stringent executive branch enforcement guidelines produced significant amounts of public school desegregation in the late 1960s and early 1970s."). Aggressive executive enforcement was also crucial to the act's success. The federal government poured money into southern schools, and Title VI required nondiscrimination

as a condition of the states' receiving that money. *See* ROSENBERG, *supra* note 39, at 97–99.

196. Stephen M. Griffin, *Judicial Supremacy and Equal Protection in a Democracy of Rights,* 4 U. PA. J. CONST. L. 281, 290 (2002).

197. Robert C. Post, *The Supreme Court 2002 Term. Foreword: Fashioning the Legal Constitution—Culture, Courts and Law,* 117 HARV. L. REV. 4, 23 (2003). *See also* Griffin, *supra* note 196, at 284–285.

198. *See* Eskridge & Ferejohn, *supra* note 155, at 615.

199. Voting Rights Act of 1965, Pub. L. No. 89-110, August 6, 1965, 79 Stat. 437 (codified at 42 U.S.C. §§ 1973 et seq.). GARROW, *supra* note 25, at 161–163; LOEVY, *supra* note 18, at 22. Martin Luther King later took credit for influencing Johnson to support the act. GARROW, supra note 25, at 598.

200. LEMANN, *supra* note 8, at 171.

201. Fair Housing Act, Pub. L. No. 90-284, Title VIII, April 11, 1968, 82 Stat. 81 (codified at 42 U.S.C. § 3616a (1995)) (the act provided federal grants to state or local governments for the purpose of preventing or eliminating discriminatory housing practices).

202. Equal Credit Opportunity Act of 1974, Pub. L. No. 90-321, Title VII as added Pub. L. No. 93-495 Title V, October 28, 1974 88 Stat. 1521 (prohibiting discrimination in lending on the basis of race, religion, sex, and age).

203. Education Amendments of 1972, Title IX, 20 U.S.C. § 1681 (1994) (prohibiting discrimination on the basis of sex in programs or activities receiving federal financial assistance); Pregnancy Discrimination Act, Pub. L. No. 95-555, October 31, 1978, 92 Stat. 2076 (codified at 42 U.S.C. § 2000e-k (1978)). *See also* Women in Apprenticeship and Non-Traditional Occupations Act, Pub. L. No. 102-530, October 27, 1992, 106 Stat. 3465 (codified at 29 U.S.C. §§ 2501–2509) (providing grants to community-based organizations that deliver technical assistance to the preparation of employers to recruit, train, and employ women). *See* Robert C. Post & Reva B. Siegel, *Legislative Constitutionalism and Section Five Power: Policentric Interpretation of the Family and Medical Leave Act,* 112 YALE L. J. 1943 n.158 (2003) (detailing sex equality legislation enacted by Congress in the 1970s). When enacting this legislation, Congress was again responding to the intense political pressure of a popular political movement, Second Wave Feminism, and the women's rights movement. *See id. See also* Reva Siegel, *Text in Context: Gender and the Constitution from a Social Movement Perspective,* 150 U. PA. L. REV. 297 (2001).

204. Rehabilitation Act of 1973, 29 U.S.C. §§ 701–796 (1998) (Supp., May 1999) (prohibiting discrimination against the disabled by recipients of federal funds); Americans with Disabilities Act of 1990, Pub. L. No. 101-336, 104 Stat. 330 (prohibiting discrimination on the basis of disability by state and private employers and requiring state facilities to be accessible to the disabled).

205. Age Discrimination Act of 1975, 42 U.S.C. §§ 6101–6107 (1994) (pro-

hibiting discrimination on the basis of age in programs or activities receiving federal financial assistance).

206. Elementary and Secondary Education Act; Education for All Handicapped Children Act of 1975 (now the Individuals with Disabilities Education Act), 20 U.S.C. § 1400 (1997) (requiring states to provide adequate educational facilities to disabled children to ensure that all disabled children have the availability of a free, appropriate education).

207. For example, in the Economic Opportunity Act of 1964, Congress created ten federal programs to fight poverty, including the Office of Economic Opportunity, Head Start, and Community Action Programs (Pub. L. No. 88-452, August 20, 1964, 78 Stat. 508 (codified as 42 U.S.C. § 2991 et seq.)). *See* LEMANN, *supra* note 8, at 156. Some civil rights leaders, including Martin Luther King, saw economic justice as essential to achieving civil rights. *See* GARROW, *supra* note 25, at 537–540. Forbath, *supra* note 7, at 85–88 (discussing a campaign by some civil rights leaders for economic rights as well as "civil" rights).

208. LEMANN, *supra* note 8, at 191.

209. *See* Post & Siegel, *supra* note 2, at 517.

210. However, Congress often acted first to protect those rights. *See* Post & Siegel, *supra* note 203.

211. Thanks to Owen Fiss for emphasizing this point to me.

212. *NAACP v. Button*, 371 U.S. 415 (1963).

213. *New York Times Co. v. Sullivan*, 376 U.S. 254 (1964).

214. *NAACP v. Alabama ex rel. Patterson*, 357 U.S. 449 (1958).

215. Post & Siegel, *supra* note 2, at 443.

216. *See Katzenbach v. Morgan*, 384 U.S. 641 (1966); *South Carolina v. Katzenbach*, 383 U.S. 301 (1966).

217. *See Jones v. Alfred H. Mayer Co.*, 392 U.S. 409 (1968).

218. 110 CONG. REC. 12,619 (1964).

219. *See* Post & Siegel, *supra* note 2, at 498.

220. *See* MICHAEL KENT CURTIS, NO STATE SHALL ABRIDGE: THE FOURTEENTH AMENDMENT AND THE BILL OF RIGHTS 157 (1986); ROBIN WEST, PROGRESSIVE CONSTITUTIONALISM 34 (1994).

221. Post & Siegel, *supra* note 2, at 480 (pointing out that in *U.S. v. Guest*, 383 U.S. 745 (1966), six members of the Court indicated that they believed the Fourteenth Amendment enforcement power might address private action).

222. Violence against Women Act of 1994, Pub. L. No. 103-322, Title IV, September 13, 1994, 108 Stat. 1902 (codified as 18 U.S.C. §§ 2261–2266 (2000)). *See U.S. v. Morrison*, 529 U.S. 598 (2000).

223. Post & Siegel, *supra* note 2, at 475.

224. Thanks to Bobby Lipkin for pointing this out to me.

225. Hoy, *supra* note 156, at 399.

226. 111 CONG. REC. 1213 (1964) (citing *Simpkins v. Moses Cone Memorial Hospital,* 323 F.2d 957 (4th Cir. 1963)).

227. *Griggs v. Duke Power Co.,* 401 U.S. 424 (1971) (sustaining disparate impact claim under Title VII); *United Steelworkers of America v. Weber,* 443 U.S. 193 (1979) (upholding employer's voluntary adoption of affirmative e action plan).

228. *See* Eskridge & Ferejohn, *supra* note 155, at 623–636.

229. *Id.* at 627–628 (citing Pregnancy Discrimination Act, H.R. 948, 95th Cong., 2d Sess. 1978) (reprinted in 1978 U.S. CODE CONG. & ADMIN. NEWS 4749, at 2).

230. *See* Hoy, *supra* note 156, at 439.

231. *See* Griffin, *supra* note 186, at 287.

232. *Id.*

NOTES TO CHAPTER 6

1. *See* Judith Resnik, *Categorical Federalism: Jurisdiction, Gender and the Globe,* 111 YALE L. J. 619 (2001).

2. *See, e.g.,* Burt Neuborne, *The Myth of Parity,* 90 HARV. L. REV. 1105 (1977); Paul Bator, *The State Courts and Federal Constitutional Litigation,* 22 WM. & MARY L. REV. 605 (1981); Michael E. Solimine & James L. Walker, *Constitutional Litigation in Federal and State Courts: An Empirical Analysis o f Judicial Parity,* 10 HASTINGS CONST. L. Q. 213 (1983); Erwin Chemerinsky, *Parity Reconsidered: Defining a Role for the Federal Judiciary,* 36 UCLA L. REV. 233 (1988); Erwin Chemerinsky, *Ending the Parity Debate,* 71 B.U. L. REV. 593, 594 (1991).

3. For a full discussion of this debate, and the Court's jurisprudence which has occasioned it, *see* Denise C. Morgan & Rebecca E. Zietlow, *The New Parity Debate: Congress and Rights of Belonging,* 73 CINN. L. REV. 1347 (2005).

4. Gary Jeffrey Jacobsohn, *Contemporary Constitutional Theory, Federalism, and the Protection of Rights, in* FEDERALISM AND RIGHTS 29, 33 (Ellis Katz & G. Alan Tarr, eds., 1996) (describing arguments of states' rights federalists). Justice Thomas articulated this view of state sovereignty in his dissent to *U. S. Term Limits, Inc. v. Thornton,* 514 U.S. 779, 847–848 (Thomas, J., dissenting).

5. *See* Marci Hamilton, *Why Federalism Must Be Enforced: A Response to Professor Kramer,* 46 VILL. L. REV. 1069, 1072 (2001).

6. Jacobsohn, *supra* note 4, at 33, 44.

7. *See* Paul Finkelman, *States' Rights North and South in Antebellum America, in* AN UNCERTAIN TRADITION: CONSTITUTIONALISM AND THE HISTORY OF THE SOUTH 125, 135 (Kermit L. Hall & James W. Ely, eds., 1989).

8. *See, e.g.,* the Pennsylvania Personal Liberty Law, "An act to give effect to

the provisions of the constitution of the United States relative to fugitives from labor, for the protection of free people of color, and to prevent kidnapping," ch. L, 1826 Pa. Laws 150 (making it a violation of Pennsylvania law for a slave's "master" to seize and remove a slave from the state); "An Act to Extend the Right of Trial by Jury," act of May 6, 1840, *Laws of New York, 1840,* 174 (guaranteeing a jury trial to all persons seized as fugitive slaves in New York); "An Act More Effectually to Protect the Free Citizens of this State from Being Kidnapped or Reduced to Slavery, act of May 14, 1840, *Laws of New York, 1840,* 319 (authorizing the governor to appoint agents and spend state money to help rescue kidnapped free blacks). For a discussion of these and other laws, *See* Finkelman, *States' Rights, supra* note 7.

9. *See* PAUL FINKELMAN, AN IMPERFECT UNION: SLAVERY, FEDERALISM AND COMITY 147–180 (1981).

10. DAVID CURRIE, THE CONSTITUTION IN CONGRESS: DEMOCRATS AND WHIGS, 1829–1861, 91 (2005). *See generally* FORREST MCDONALD, STATES' RIGHTS AND THE UNION, IMPERIUM IN IMPERIO 1776–1876, ch. 5 (2000).

11. Finkelman, *States' Rights, supra* note 7, at 128.

12. *See* Michael Kent Curtis, *John A. Bingham and the Story of American Liberty: The Lost Cause Meets the Lost "Clause,"* 36 AKRON L. REV. 617 (2003).

13. Michael P. Zuckert, *Toward a Corrective Federalism: The United States Constitution, Federalism, and Rights, in* FEDERALISM AND RIGHTS 75 (Ellis Katz & G. Alan Tarr, eds., 1996).

14. *Brown v. Board of Education,* 347 U.S. 483 (1954). *See* TAYLOR BRANCH, PARTING THE WATERS: AMERICA IN THE KING YEARS 1954–63, 380 (1988); MICHAEL KLARMAN, FROM JIM CROW TO CIVIL RIGHTS: THE SUPREME COURT AND THE STRUGGLE FOR RACIAL EQUALITY 330, 355–356 (2004).

15. *See* Robert F. Kennedy, Foreword to BURKE MARSHALL, FEDERALISM AND CIVIL RIGHTS vii–ix (1964).

16. *See* AKHIL REED AMAR, THE BILL OF RIGHTS: CREATION AND RECONSTRUCTION 304 (1998).

17. *See* Steven Calabresi, *"A Government of Limited and Enumerated Powers": In Defense of* United States v. Lopez, 94 MICH. L. REV. 752, 768–787 (1995); Michael W. McConnell, *Federalism: Evaluating the Founders' Design,* 54 U. CHI. L. REV. 1484, 1503–1504 (1987); John C. Yoo, *Sounds of Sovereignty: Defining Federalism in the 1990s,* 32 IND. L. REV. 27, 28 (1998); Nelson Lund, *Federalism and Civil Liberties,* 45 U. KEN. L. REV. 1045, 1055 (1997); Hamilton, *supra* note 5, at 1072–1074.

18. James Madison, *The Federalist No. 51,* THE FEDERALIST PAPERS 323 (Clinton Rossiter, ed., 1961).

19. *See* McConnell, *supra* note 17, at 1488; Yoo, *supra* note 17, at 41. I refer to these scholars as antifederalists because their work is in the tradition of

those Framers who opposed a strong national government. *See* Kathleen M. Sullivan, *Dueling Sovereignties: U.S. Term Limits, Inc. v. Thornton,* 109 HARV. L. REV. 78, 80 (1995) (referring to "a dramatic antifederalist revival").

20. McConnell, *supra* note 17, at 1503.

21. Yoo, *supra* note 17, at 32, 37; Calabresi, *supra* note 17, at 754; Lund, *supra* note 17, at 1055; Hamilton, *supra* note 17, at 1072. *See also* Lynn A. Baker, *Putting the Safeguards Back into the Political Safeguards of Federalism,* 46 VILL. L. REV. 951, 952, 972 (2001).

22. *See* Resnik, *supra* note 1, at 620.

23. Compare *National League of Cities v. Usery,* 426 U.S. 833 (1976) with *Garcia v. San Antonio Metropolitan Transit Authority,* 469 U.S. 528 (1985).

24. *See* Resnik, *supra* note 1, at 625.

25. *See* Stephen Clark, *Progressive Federalism? A Gay Liberationist Perspective,* 66 ALBANY L. REV. 719 (2003); Lund, *supra* note 17, at 1055. *See also* Richard B. Stewart, *Federalism and Rights,* 19 GA. L. REV. 917, 918 (1985).

26. *See* Clark, *supra* note 25, at 723.

27. *Id.;* Grant S. Nelson & Robert Pushaw, *Rethinking the Commerce Clause: Applying First Principles to Uphold Federal Commercial Regulations but Preserve State Control over Social Issues,* 85 IOWA L. REV. 1, 118 (1999).

28. A. E. Dick Howard, *Does Federalism Secure or Undermine Rights?, in* FEDERALISM AND RIGHTS 17 (Ellis Katz & G. Alan Tarr, eds, 1996).

29. MELVYN DUBOFSKY, THE STATE AND LABOR IN MODERN AMERICA 13–14 (1994).

30. *See* PAUL E. PETERSON, THE PRICE OF FEDERALISM 109 (1995); *Bell v. Maryland,* 378 U.S. 226, 284–285 (1964) (Douglas, J., concurring) (enumerating state and local laws against race discrimination that were enacted prior to the 1964 Civil Rights Act).

31. Employment Non-Discrimination Act of 2001, S. 1284. ENDA was approved by the Senate Health, Education, Labor and Pensions Committee on May 1, 2002, but was never considered by the full Senate. ENDA was reintroduced as Title VII of S. 16, the Equal Rights and Equal Dignity for Americans Act of 2003, on January 7, 2003, and referred to the Senate Committee on Finance on that date.

32. As of spring 2003, fifteen states, the District of Columbia, and 140 municipalities had enacted laws prohibiting discrimination in employment on the basis of sexual orientation. Clark, *supra* note 25, at 720–721.

33. *See* Catherine Powell, *Dialogic Federalism: Constitutional Possibilities for Incorporation of Human Rights Law in the United States,* U. PA. L. REV. 245, 289–290, 277 (2001) (citing SAN FRANCISCO, CAL. ADMINISTRATIVE CODE ch. 12K (2001), *available at* http://www.amlegal.com/sanfranadmin/lptext.dll?f= templates&fn=main-j.htm&2.0).

34. *See, e.g., Kimel v. Florida Board of Regents,* 528 U.S. 62 (2000) (sovereign immunity barred private enforcement of Age Discrimination in Employment Act against state government); *Board of Trustees v. Garrett,* 531 U.S. 356 (2001) (sovereign immunity barred private enforcement of Title I of Americans with Disabilities Act against state government).

35. *See* Lauren K. Robel, *Sovereignty and Democracy: The States' Obligations to Their Citizens under Federal Statutory Law,* 78 IND. L. J. 543, 543 (2003).

36. HB0469, *available at* http://www.legis.state.il.us/legislation/billstatus.asp?DocNum=469.

37. Maine Pub. L. ch. 423 (2003).

38. *Alden v. Maine,* 527 U.S. 706 (1999).

39. *See* Matthew Adler & Seth Kreimer, *The New Etiquette of Federalism: New York, Printz and Yeskey,* 1998 SUP. CT. REV. 71, 78 (1998); Vicki Jackson, *Federalism and the Uses and Limits of Law: Printz and Principle?,* 111 HARV. L. REV. 2180, 2214 (1998); Stewart, *supra* note 25, at 918.

40. *See* Mark C. Gordon, *Differing Paradigms, Similar Flaws: Constructing a New Approach to Federalism in Congress and the Court,* 14 YALE L. & POL'Y REV. 187, 218 (1996). *See also* Nelson & Pushaw, *supra* note 27, at 117.

41. *See* David J. Barron, *The Promise of Cooley's City: Traces of Local Constitutionalism,* 147 U. PA. L. REV. 487, 495 (1999).

42. Clark, *supra* note 25, at 722.

43. Adler & Kreimer, *supra* note 39, at 78; Jackson, *supra* note 39, at 2213–2214; Erwin Chemerinsky, *The Values of Federalism,* 47 FLA. L. REV. 499, 524 (1995); A. E. Dick Howard, *Does Federalism Secure or Undermine Rights?, in* FEDERALISM AND RIGHTS 17 (Ellis Katz & G. Alan Tarr, eds., 1996).

44. *See* Gordon, *supra* note 40, at 220 (cities are closer to the people, serve as better laboratories, and are more flexible than states); Howard, *supra* note 28, at 17.

45. *See* Barron, *supra* note 41, at 549. *See also* Akhil Reed Amar, *The Bill of Rights as a Constitution,* 100 YALE L. J. 1131, 1136–1137 (1991) (advocating the Madisonian insight that "localism and liberty can sometimes work together.")

46. Barron, *supra* note 41, at 561.

47. Adler & Kreimer, *supra* note 39, at 81; Jackson, *supra* note 39, at 2214; Chemerinsky, *supra* note 43, at 524. Stewart, *supra* note 25, at 918.

48. *See* Nelson & Pushaw, *supra* note 27, at 113–114; Keith Aoki, *A Tale of Three Cities: Thoughts on Asian American Electoral and Political Power after 2000,* 8 ASIAN PAC. AM. L. J. 1 (2002).

49. *See* Michael C. Dorf & Charles F. Sabel, *A Constitution of Democratic Experimentalism,* 98 COLUM. L. REV. 267, 318 (1998).

50. Howard, *supra* note 28, at 14.

51. *See* Clark, *supra* note 25, at 727; Barron, *supra* note 41, at 495; Powell, *supra* note 33, at 289–290.

52. Barron, *supra* note 41, at 556.

53. Clark, *supra* note 25, at 749.

54. Steve Clark contests the very notion of fundamental human rights, pointing out that many scholars have recently argued that this notion reflects the imposition of western cultural constructs and accusing supporters of congressional power of making the same mistake. Clark, *supra* note 25, at 753.

55. *Id.* at 746 ("Put starkly, it is the difference between enacting a pro-gay law in San Francisco and enacting one in Congress.").

56. *See* Lund, *supra* note 17, at 1063; Richard Epstein, *Exit Rights under Federalism,* 55 LAW & CONTEMP. PROBS. 147 (1992).

57. *See* BURKE MARSHALL, FEDERALISM AND CIVIL RIGHTS (1964).

58. *See* Laurence Tribe, *Saenz Sans Prophecy: Does the Privileges or Immunities Revival Portend the Future—or Reveal the Structure of the Present?,* 113 HARV. L. REV. 110, 156 (1999) (noting that the federal right to travel enables states to represent centers of democratic choice because people choose their state of residence).

59. Todd E. Pettys, *The Mobility Paradox,* 92 GEO. L. J. 481, 489 (2004).

60. *Id.*

61. *See* KENNETH L. KARST, BELONGING TO AMERICA: EQUAL CITIZENSHIP AND THE CONSTITUTION 68 (1989).

62. *But see* Lund, *supra* note 17, at 1065 (arguing that "even the poorest citizens move").

63. *See* PETERSON, *supra* note 30, at 121–126 (discussing the race-to-the-bottom problem in the welfare context); Gay Gellhorn, *Disability and Welfare Reform: Keep the Supplemental Security Income Program but Reengineer the Disability Determination Process,* 22 FORDHAM URB. L. J. 961, 1001–1103 (1995) ("The result [devolving welfare programs to the states], however, may not be creative experimentation, but more likely 'a race to the bottom.'"); *Devolving Welfare Programs to the States: A Public Choice Perspective,* 109 HARV. L. REV. 1984, 1985 (1996) (discussing the strong possibility that states will engage in "a race to the bottom" in developing block-grant programs).

64. Stewart, *supra* note 25, at 926. *But see* Lund, *supra* note 17, at 1046 ("It would be safe to return the states to their former ascendancy because there is no good reason to fear a 'race to the bottom' in which our important liberties would be lost or badly compromised."); Frank B. Cross, *The Folly of Federalism,* 24 CARDOZO L. REV. 1, 12–18 (2002) (arguing that "the strict race to the bottom theory is largely empirically unsupportable").

65. *See, e.g.,* Title II of the Civil Rights Act of 1964, 42 U.S.C. § 2000a-6; Title VII of the Civil Rights Act of 1964, 42 U.S.C. § 2000e-7; Americans with

Disabilities Act of 1990, Pub. L. No. 101-336, 104 Stat. 330 (codified at 42 U.S.C. § 12201(b)); Age Discrimination in Employment Act, Pub. L. No. 90-202, December 15, 1967, 81 Stat. 602 (codified as amended at 29 U.S.C. §§ 621 et seq.); Fair Housing Act, Pub. L. No. 90-284, Title VIII, April 11, 1968, 82 Stat. 81 (codified as amended at 42 U.S.C. §§ 3601 et seq.; Family Medical Leave Act, of 1993, Pub. L. No. 103-3, February 3, 1993, 107 Stat. 6 (codified at 29 U.S.C. § 2601 et seq.).

66. *See New York Gaslight Club v. Carey*, 447 U.S. 54, 67 (1980); *Alexander v. Gardner-Denver Co.*, 415 U.S. 36, 48–49 (1974) (Title VII); *Treglia v. Town of Manlius*, 313 F.3d 713 (2002) (Americans with Disabilities Act); *Simpson, Alaska State Commission for Human Rights v. Providence Washington Insurance*, 608 F.2d 1171 (1979) (Age Discrimination in Employment Act); *Moody v. Pepsi-Cola Metropolitan Bottling Company, Inc.*, 915 F.2d 201, 210) (1990) (Age Discrimination in Employment Act).

67. For a complete discussion of the preemption issue, *see* Morgan & Zietlow, *supra* note 3, at 1383–1390.

68. KARST, *supra* note 61, at 187.

69. This is not to say that Madison intended to transfer authority from states to the federal government. Rather, he wanted the federal government to provide a check on the states. *See* Zuckert, *supra* note 13, at 78. Later in his life, after the Alien and Sedition Acts of 1798, Madison become more suspicious of the power of the federal legislature and began to believe that Congress also posed a danger to liberty. *See* Jack N. Rakove, *The Madisonian Theory of Rights*, 31 WM. & MARY L. REV. 245, 257 (1990).

70. For a full discussion of Madison's theory of the extended republic and the federal negative, *see* chapter 2, section 1.

71. *See* Larry D. Kramer, *Madison's Audience*, 112 HARV. L. REV. 611, 671 (1999).

72. *See* Indian Removal Act, ch. 148, 4 Stat. 411 (1830). *See* THOMAS R. HIETALA, MANIFEST DESIGN: ANXIOUS AGGRANDIZEMENT IN THE LATE JACKSONIAN AMERICA 136–137 (1985); Chinese Exclusion Act of May 6, 1882, ch. 126, 22 Stat. 58. *See* Gabriel J. Chin, *Regulating Race: Asian Exclusion and the Administrative State*, 37 HARV. C.R.-C.L. REV. 1 (2002); Personal Responsibility and Work Opportunity Reconciliation Act of 1996, Pub. L. No. 104-193, August 22, 1996, 110 Stat. 2105 (codified at 42. U.S.C. §§ 601 et seq.). See chapter 2, where I discuss the Fugitive Slave Acts.

73. *See* DERRICK BELL, SILENT COVENANTS *BROWN V. BOARD* AND THE UNFULLFILLED HOPES FOR RACIAL REFORM 5 (2004) (discussing "the nineteenth century's post-Civil War Reconstruction/Redemption pattern of progress followed by retrogression").

74. ERIC FONER, RECONSTRUCTION: AMERICA'S UNFINISHED REVOLUTION 587 (1988).

75. Taft Hartley Act of 1947, ch. 120, 61 Stat. 136 (codified as amended in scattered sections of 29 U.S.C.).\

76. One obvious example is Congress's failure to enact antilynching legislation. *See* HERBERT SHAPIRO, WHITE VIOLENCE AND BLACK RESPONSE: FROM RECONSTRUCTION TO MONTGOMERY 282–286 (1988).

77. Defense of Marriage Act of 1996, Pub. L. No. 104-199, § 3(a), 110 Stat. 2419 (codified at 1 U.S. C. § 7 (Supp. V 199)).

78. *Id.*

79. *Id.* at § 2(a), 110 Stat. 2419 (codified at 28 U.S.C. § 1738C).

80. Andrew Koppelman argues that states already had the power to deny recognition to gay marriages in other states under the "public policy" exception to choice of law rules. *See* Andrew Koppelman, *Same Sex Marriage, Choice of Law, and Public Policy,* 76 TEX. L. REV. 921, 922 (1998).

81. *See* PETERSON, *supra* note 30, at 16.

82. James F. Blumstein, *Federalism and Civil Rights: Complimentary and Competing Paradigms,* 47 VAND. L. REV. 1251, 1271–1272 (1994).

83. *See* Ellis Katz & G. Alan Tarr, Introduction *in* FEDERALISM AND RIGHTS x (Ellis Katz & G. Alan Tarr, eds., 1996).

84. RONALD DWORKIN, LAW'S EMPIRE 134 (1986).

85. JOHN RAWLS, A THEORY OF JUSTICE 61 (1971).

86. For an excellent discussion of this debate, *see* Tracy Higgins, *Anti-Essentialism, Relativism, and Human Rights,* 19 HARV. WOMEN'S L. J. 89 (1996).

87. *See* Howard, *supra* note 28, at 22–23.

88. *See* Rebecca E. Zietlow, *Belonging, Protection and Equality: The Neglected Citizenship Clause and the Limits of Federalism,* 62 U. PITT. L. REV. 281, 302 (2000).

89. *See* Blumstein, *supra* note 82, at 1259.

90. Howard, *supra* note 28, at 23–24.

91. *Id.* at 23.

92. *See* ROBERT K. CARR, FEDERAL PROTECTION OF CIVIL RIGHTS: QUEST FOR A SWORD 201 (1947).

93. *Id.*

94. *See* Zuckert, *supra* note 13, at 85.

95. *Id.*

96. Rakove, *supra* note 69, at 252, citing Letter from James Madison to George Washington (Apr. 16, 1787), reprinted in JAMES MADISON, THE PAPERS OF JAMES MADISON 9:382, 384 (Robert A. Rutland et al., eds., 1975).

97. THE PAPERS OF JAMES MADISON 9:347 (Editor's Note on Vices Memo) ("This federal veto was to be the foundation of the new system."); Kramer, *supra* note 71, at 649.

98. *See* Zuckert, *supra* note 13, at 86.

99. *Id.* at 87.

100. *See* James W. Fox, Jr., *Re-readings and Misreadings: Slaughter-House, Privileges or Immunities, and Section Five Enforcement Power,* 91 Ky. L. J. 67, 143 (2002), citing Michael P. Zuckert, *Congressional Power under the Fourteenth Amendment: The Original Understanding of Section Five,* 3 Const. Comm. 123, 141 (1986).

101. William J. Rich, *Taking "Privileges or Immunities" Seriously: A Call to Expand the Constitutional Canon,* 87 Minn. L. Rev. 153, 172 (2002).

102. *See* William J. Brennan, Jr., *State Constitutions and the Protection of Individual Rights,* 90 Harv. L. Rev. 489 (1977); William J. Brennan, Jr., *The Bill of Rights and the States: The Revival of State Constitutions as Guardians of Individual Rights,* 61 N.Y.U. L. Rev. 535 (1986).

103. Brennan, *State Constitutions, supra* note 102, at 502; Brennan, *Bill of Rights, supra* note 102, at 551.

104. Brennan, *Bill of Rights, supra* note 102 at 550.

105. Brennan, *State Constitutions, supra* note 102 at 501.

106. *See* Sally F. Goldfarb, *The Supreme Court, the Violence against Women Act, and the Use and Abuse of Federalism,* 71 Fordham L. Rev. 57, 137–146 (2002).

NOTES TO CHAPTER 7

1. *See* Defense of Marriage Act of 1996, Pub. L. No. 104-199, § 3(a), 110 Stat. 2419 (codified at 1 U.S.C. § 7 (Supp. V 199)); Proposed Federal Marriage Amendment.

2. *See* Frank B. Cross, *Institutions and Enforcement of the Bill of Rights,* 85 Cornell L. Rev. 1529, 1576 (2000).

3. *Katzenbach v. Morgan,* 384 U.S. 641 (1966). The Court upheld a Section Five–based voting rights statute that provided a wide-ranging remedy beyond that previously ordered by the federal courts. The Court opined, "It is not for us to review the congressional resolution of these factors. It is enough that we be able to perceive a basis upon which Congress might resolve the conflict as it did." *Id.* at 653. In a footnote, the Court noted that "Section Five grants Congress no power to restrict, abrogate or dilute these guarantees," indicating a willingness to intervene if Congress did so. *Id.* at 651 n.10.

4. *See City of Boerne v. Flores,* 521 U.S. 507, 519 (1997). Many scholars have challenged the Court's ruling in *Boerne. See, e.g.,* Douglas Laycock, *RFRA, Congress and the Ratchet,* 56 Mont. L. Rev. 145 (1995); David Cole, *The Value of Seeing Things Differently:Boerne v. Flores and Congressional Enforcement of the Bill of Rights,* 1997 Sup. Ct. Rev. 31.

5. Thanks to Michael Les Benedict for making this point in a conversation. The Court also denied Congress the autonomy to protect rights of belonging in *United States v. Morrison,* 529 U.S. 598 (2000) by characterizing the Civil

Rights remedy of the Violence against Women Act as a family law measure. *See* Judith Resnik, *Categorical Federalism: Jurisdiction, Gender and the Globe*, 111 YALE L. J. 619, 628 (2001).

6. *See* LARRY D. KRAMER, THE PEOPLE THEMSELVES: POPULAR CONSTITUTIONALISM AND JUDICIAL REVIEW (2004).

7. *See* Larry D. Kramer, *Popular Constitutionalism, circa 2004*, 92 CAL. L. REV. 959 (2004).

8. For an excellent summary of recent works in this era, *see* Kramer, *supra* note 7.

9. *See* STEPHEN M. GRIFFIN, AMERICAN CONSTITUTIONALISM: FROM THEORY TO POLITICS 45 (1996); LOUIS FISHER, CONSTITUTIONAL DIALOGUES 231–275 (1988); KEITH E. WHITTINGTON, CONSTITUTIONAL CONSTRUCTION: DIVIDED POWERS AND CONSTITUTIONAL MEANING 1 (1999).

10. Early works advocating this viewpoint include SANFORD LEVINSON, CONSTITUTIONAL FAITH (1988), and Robert M. Cover, *Nomos and Narrative*, 97 HARV. L. REV. 4 (1983). *See also* James Gray Pope, *Labor's Constitution of Freedom*, 106 YALE L. J. 941, 943 (1997); William E. Forbath, *The New Deal Constitution in Exile*, 51 DUKE L. J. 165 (2001); Reva Siegel, *Text in Context: Gender and the Constitution from a Social Movement Perspective*, 150 U. PA. L. REV. 297, 312–313 (2001); Robert C. Post, *The Supreme Court 2002 Term. Foreword: Fashioning the Legal Constitution—Culture, Courts and Law*, 117 HARV. L. REV. 4 (2003); Robert C. Post & Reva B. Siegel, *Legislative Constitutionalism and Section Five Power: Policentric Interpretation of the Family and Medical Leave Act*, 112 YALE L. J. 1943 (2003).

11. *See, e.g.*, Erwin Chemerinsky, *In Defense of Judicial Review: A Reply to Professor Kramer*, 92 CAL. L. REV. 1013 (2004).

12. CHARLES L. BLACK, JR., A NEW BIRTH OF FREEDOM: HUMAN RIGHTS, NAMED AND UNNAMED 124, 126–127 (1997). However, Black does note that Congress also has the responsibility to affirmatively provide constitutional rights. *Id.* at 137.

13. JUDITH BAER, EQUALITY UNDER THE CONSTITUTION: RECLAIMING THE FOURTEENTH AMENDMENT 281–282 (1983).

14. *West Virginia Board of Education v. Barnette*, 319 U.S. 624 (1943) (holding unconstitutional a state law that required all children in public schools to salute and pledge allegiance to the flag).

15. *United States v. Carolene Products*, 304 U.S. 144 n.4 (1938). *Carolene Products* footnote four has been called "the most celebrated footnote in Constitutional law." Lewis Powell, Carolene Products *Revisited*, 82 COLUM. L. REV. 1087, 1087 (1982).

16. Chemerinsky, *supra* note 11, at 1013–1014.

17. *Id.* at 1016.

18. *Id.* at 1014.

19. *See* Robert Dahl, *Decision-Making in a Democracy: The Supreme Court as a National Policy-Maker,* 6 J. Pub. L. 279, 284 (1957). When it comes to rights of belonging, the fact that the Court changes its view in accordance with evolving and contested social norms often has a positive impact. For example, the Court did exactly that in *Brown,* and in its cases striking down "archaic and overbroad" generalizations about gender roles. *See* Robert C. Post & Reva B. Siegel, *Equal Protection by Law: Federal Anti-Discrimination Legislation after Morrison and Kimel,* 110 Yale L. J. 441, 514 (2000).

20. Dahl, *supra* note 19, at 293–294.

21. Thomas R. Marshall, Public Opinion and the Supreme Court 192 (1989). *See also* Cross, *supra* note 2, at 1555; Barry Friedman, *Dialogue and Judicial Review,* 91 Mich. L. Rev. 577, 677 (1993).

22. *See* Keith E. Whittington, *Extrajudicial Constitutional Interpretation: Three Objections and Responses,* 80 N.C. L. Rev. 773, 831 (2002); Kramer, *supra* note 7, at 997; Cross, *supra* note 2, at 1555.

23. Michael J. Klarman, *Rethinking the Civil Rights and Civil Liberties Revolutions,* 82 Va. L. Rev. 1, 6–7 (1996). *See also* Stephen M. Griffin, *Judicial Supremacy and Equal Protection in a Democracy of Rights,* 4 U. Pa. J. Const. L. 281, 295 (2002) (arguing that the politicization of the judicial selection process means that "the vocabulary of the counter-majoritarian difficulty no longer makes sense").

24. *See* Klarman, *supra* note 23.

25. *See* Lucas A. Powe, The Warren Court and American Politics 501 (2000). Notwithstanding this observation, Powe insists that judicial review is superior to "popular Constitutionalism" in protecting individual rights. *See* Lucas A. Powe, *Are "The People" Missing in Action (and Should Anyone Care?)* (review of Larry Kramer, The People Themselves), 83 Tex. L. Rev. 855, 893 (2005).

26. For a complete discussion of Madison's reservations about courts as protectors of rights, *see* chapter 2.

27. *See* Powe, *Missing in Action, supra* note 25, at 866–870.

28. One example of this criticism was the "Southern Manifesto," a resolution adopted by southern members of Congress. 102 Cong. Rec. 4515–4516 (March, 12 1956) (Southern Manifesto). The principal accusation of the manifesto was the charge that "We regard the decision of the Supreme Court in the school cases as a clear abuse of judicial power. It climaxes a trend in the Federal judiciary undertaking to legislate, in derogation of the authority of Congress, and to encroach upon the reserved rights of the states and the people." *Id.*

29. *See* Gerald N. Rosenberg, The Hollow Hope: Can Courts Bring about Social Change? 49–53 (1991); Klarman, *supra* note 23, at 21.

30. Of course, popular resistance to courts' decisions protecting rights is not a justification for courts to avoid politically unpopular decisions.

31. *See Dandridge v. Williams,* 397 U.S. 471, 486 (1970) (poverty); *Massachusetts Board of Retirement v. Murgia,* 427 U.S. 307, 315 (1976) (age); *Cleburne v. Cleburne Living Center,* 473 U.S. 432, 443 (1985) (disability).

32. *Dandridge v. Williams,* 397 U.S. 471 (1970) (minimum income); *San Antonio v. Rodriguez,* 411 U.S. 1 (1973).

33. *See, e.g., Cruzan v. Director, Missouri Department of Health,* 497 U.S. 261 (1990); *Washington v. Glucksberg,* 521 U.S. 702 (1997) .

34. *See, e.g., Planned Parenthood v. Casey,* 505 U.S. 833 (1992); *Lawrence v. Texas,* 539 U.S. 558 (2003); *Hamdi v. Rumsfeld,* 542 U.S. 507 (2004).

35. See Michael J. Klarman, *Rethinking the Civil Rights and Civil Liberties Revolutions,* 82 VA. L. REV. 1, 10 (1996).

36. ROBIN WEST, PROGRESSIVE CONSTITUTIONALISM 311 (1994).

37. *See* Cole, *supra* note 4, at 60–61.

38. *See* Post & Siegel, *supra* note 19, at 467; Kramer, *supra* note 6, at 219.

39. Even when Congress does legislate to protect people who fall into a protected class that has been identified by the Court, the Court has struck down those attempts as "inappropriate" when they are inconsistent with remedies that the Court would impose. For example, Congress intended the Violence against Women Act (Pub. L. No. 103-322, Title IV, September 13, 1994, 108 Stat. 1902 (codified as 18 U.S.C. §§ 2261–2266 (2000)) to protect women from gender-motivated violence. Despite the fact that the Court has identified gender as a protected class warranting heightened scrutiny, the Court struck down the provision of VAWA creating a federal cause of action for victims of gender-motivated violence in *United States v. Morrison.* The Court simply did not believe that the statute was an appropriate remedy for gender discrimination. By contrast, in *Nevada Department of Human Resources v. Hibbs,* 538 U.S. 721 (2003), the Court upheld the Family Medical Leave Act because the act was consistent with court-imposed remedies for gender-based discrimination. *See* Rebecca E. Zietlow, *Juriscentrism and the Original Meaning of Section Five,* 13 TEMPLE POL. & CIV. RTS L. REV. 485, 511–512 (2004).

40. MARK TUSHNET, TAKING THE CONSTITUTION AWAY FROM THE COURTS 172 (1999).

41. *Id.* at 168.

42. *Id.* at 171.

43. Tellingly, President Lyndon Johnson viewed the economic legislation of his War on Poverty as a key element of his 1964 reelection campaign. *See* ROBERT D. LOEVY, TO END ALL SEGREGATION: THE POLITICS OF THE PASSAGE OF THE CIVIL RIGHTS ACT OF 1964, 8 (1990). For an excellent account of the welfare rights movement and the campaign for a minimum income, *see* MARTHA DAVIS, BRUTAL NEED: LAWYERS AND THE WELFARE RIGHTS MOVEMENT (1993).

44. Tushnet, *supra* note 40, at 169.

45. *Id.*

46. Griffin, *supra* note 23, at 282.

47. *Id.* at 303–305.

48. *Id.*

49. West, *supra* note 36, at 311.

50. *Id.* at 298.

51. *Id.* at 69.

52. *See* Post & Siegel, *supra* note 19, at 514–515, 519.

53. *See, e.g.,* Abner J. Mikva, *How Well Does Congress Support and Defend the Constitution?*, 61 N.C. L. REV. 587, 610 (1983); Owen Fiss, *The Supreme Court 1978 Term. Foreword: The Forms of Justice,* 93 HARV. L. REV. 1, 9–10 (1979).

54. *See* Cole, *supra* note 4, at 62.

55. *See* Cross, *supra* note 2, at 1543.

56. *See* Kramer, *supra* note 7, at 1000. *See also* JOHN W. KINGDON, CONGRESSMEN'S VOTING DECISIONS 47 (3d ed. 1989).

57. *See* KENNETH L. KARST, BELONGING TO AMERICA: EQUAL CITIZENSHIP AND THE CONSTITUTION 135 (1989).

58. *See, e.g.,* Federal Election Campaign Act of 1971, Pub L. 92-225, February 7, 1972, 86 Stat. 3, 2 U.S.C. § 431; Bipartisan Campaign Reform Act of 2002, Pub. L. No. 107-155, March 27, 2002, 116 Stat. 81, 2 U.S.C. § 441 et seq.

59. *See Buckley v. Valeo,* 424 U.S. 1 (1976). Of course, many members of Congress may appreciate the Court's intervention in this realm since it allows them to "pass the buck" while the Court preserves the status quo. Indeed, in the most recent election finance reform bill, Congress included a "fast track" provision enabling swift judicial review of the measure. *See McConnell v. Federal Election Commission,* 540 U.S. 93 (2003).

60. *See* Rebecca E. Zietlow, *Exploring a Substantive Approach to Equal Justice under Law,* 28 N.M. L. REV. 411 (1998).

61. *See, e.g.,* Larry Alexander & Frederick Schauer, *On Extrajudicial Constitutional Interpretation,* 110 HARV. L. REV. 1359, 1371 (1997).

62. *See* Larry Alexander & Frederick Shauer, *Defending Judicial Supremacy: A Reply,* 17 CONST. COMM. 455, 464 (2000).

63. *See* Kramer, *supra* note 7, at 987.

64. *See* Tushnet, *supra* note 40, at 180 ("It is not as if the Constitution does not get amended. It does—when the Supreme Court reinterprets the Constitution to satisfy contemporary political desires."). A significant example of the Court's overruling itself is *Employment Division v. Smith,* 494 U.S. 872 (1990), which inspired RFRA and eventually brought about the Court's ruling in *Boerne,* overruled twenty-seven years of precedent and drastically altered the meaning of the Free Exercise Clause. Similarly, the Court's ruling in *Boerne* overruled thirty years of precedent by replacing the "rational basis" test with the "congruence and proportionality" test as applied to Congress's Section Five power.

65. Whittington, *supra* note 22, at 790.

66. Louis Fisher, *Constitutional Interpretation by Members of Congress*, 63 N.C. L. REV. 707, 716–717 (1985).

67. Kramer, *supra* note 7, at 987.

68. *Id.* at 988. Tushnet, *supra* note 40, at 52

69. *See* Whittington, *supra* note 22, at 835.

70. Tushnet, *supra* note 40, at 159.

71. Cross, *supra* note 2, at 165, citing ROBERT DAHL, A PREFACE TO DEMO-CRATIC THEORY 146 (1956).

72. Cross, *supra* note 2, at 1563–1564.

73. *Id.* at 1567–1568.

74. *See* Cole, *supra* note 4, at 62.

75. Whittington, *supra* note 9, at 5; Cross, *supra* note 2, at 1549.

76. For example, federal courts are limited to hearing "cases and controversies" between actual parties who have standing to bring suit in Article III courts.

77. *See* Fisher, *supra* note 66, at 747; WHITTINGTON, *supra* note 9, at 822.

78. The Court often cites the lack of flexibility as a reason for deferring to the political process. *See, e.g., Cleburne v. Cleburne Living Center,* 473 U.S. 432, 443 (1985); *see also* William D. Araiza, *Court, Congress and Equal Protection: What* Brown *Teaches Us about the Section 5 Power,* 47 HOW. L. J. 199, 226–227 (2004).

79. Senator Hubert Humphrey cited his frustration with the piecemeal enforcement of *Brown* as a motivating factor for Title VI of the 1964 Civil Rights Act, which prohibits race discrimination by recipients of federal funds and provides a mechanism for executive enforcement of its provisions. 111 CONG. REC. 1213 (1964).

80. *See, e.g.,* Powe, *supra* note 25, at 857.

81. *See* Griffin, *supra* note 23, at 300.

82. Cross, *supra* note 2, at 1544–1545.

83. *Id.*

84. Kramer, *supra* note 7, at 1001.

85. ARCHIBOLD COX, THE WARREN COURT: CONSTITUTIONAL DECISIONS AS AN INSTRUMENT OF REFORM 40 (1968).

86. *Id.*

87. Cox, *supra* note 85, at 139. RICHARD C. CORTNER, CIVIL RIGHTS AND PUBLIC ACCOMMODATIONS: THE *HEART OF ATLANTA MOTEL* AND *McCLUNG* CASES 192 (2001).

88. *See* Herb Eastman, *Speaking Truth to Power: The Language of Civil Rights Litigators,* 104 YALE L. J. 763 (1995); Pope, *supra* note 10, at 1012.

89. *See* Denise C. Morgan & Rebecca E. Zietlow, *The New Parity Debate: Congress and Rights of Belonging,* 73 CINN. L. REV. 1347 (2005).

NOTES TO CHAPTER 8

1. MARK TUSHNET, TAKING THE CONSTITUTION AWAY FROM THE COURTS 174 (1999). *See* LARRY D. KRAMER, THE PEOPLE THEMSELVES: POPULAR CONSTITUTIONALISM AND JUDICIAL REVIEW 8 (2004).

2. *See* RONALD DWORKIN, LAW'S EMPIRE 134 (1986); JOHN RAWLS, A THEORY OF JUSTICE 61 (1971).

3. *See* MARY ANN GLENDON, RIGHTS TALK: THE IMPOVERISHMENT OF POLITICAL DISCOURSE 14 (1991).

4. *See* JOHN HART ELY, DEMOCRACY AND DISTRUST: A THEORY OF JUDICIAL REVIEW (1980).

5. *See, e.g.,* KENNETH L. KARST, BELONGING TO AMERICA: EQUAL CITIZENSHIP AND THE CONSTITUTION 9 (1989); CHARLES L. BLACK, JR., A NEW BIRTH OF FREEDOM: HUMAN RIGHTS, NAMED AND UNNAMED 125 (1997); JUDITH A. BAER, EQUALITY UNDER THE CONSTITUTION: RECLAIMING THE FOURTEENTH AMENDMENT 281 (1983); ELY, *supra* note 4, at 7. *See also* JOHN J. DINAN, KEEPING THE PEOPLE'S LIBERTIES: LEGISLATORS, CITIZENS, AND JUDGES AS GUARDIANS OF RIGHTS x (1998) (stating that "the nation's leading law faculty are nearly unanimous" in believing the judiciary is best suited to protecting liberties). *But see* Frank B. Cross, *Institutions and Enforcement of the Bill of Rights,* 85 CORNELL L. REV. 1529 (2000) (questioning this assumption).

6. *See Washington v. Davis,* 426 U.S. 229 (1976) (discriminatory intent); *Richmond v. J. A. Croson Co.,* 488 U.S. 469 (1989) (affirmative action); *Adarand Constructors v. Pena,* 515 U.S. 200 (1995). *But see Grutter v. Bollinger,* 539 U.S. 306 (2003). For a classic discussion of group versus individual rights, *see* Owen M. Fiss, *Groups and the Equal Protection Clause,* 5 PHIL. & PUB. AFF. 107 (1976).

7. *See* Charles R. Lawrence, *The Id, the Ego and Equal Protection: Reckoning with Unconscious Racism,* 39 STAN. L. REV. 317 (1987).

8. CATHARINE MACKINNON, TOWARD A FEMINIST THEORY OF THE STATE 165 (1989).

9. ROBIN WEST, PROGRESSIVE CONSTITUTIONALISM 109 (1994).

10. *Id.* at 115. *See also* Rebecca E. Zietlow, *Exploring a Substantive Approach to Equal Justice under Law,* 28 NEW MEXICO L. REV. 411, 429–433 (1998).

11. GLENDON, *supra* note 3, at 14.

12. *Id.* at xi.

13. *Id.* at x; MICHAEL SANDEL, DEMOCRACY'S DISCONTENT (1996).

14. SANDEL, *supra* note 13, at 202.

15. SANDEL, *supra* note 13, at 4.

16. *See* GEORGE LAKOFF, MORAL POLITICS: HOW LIBERALS AND CONSERVATIVES THINK 384–385 (2002).

17. *See* Derrick Bell, Brown v. Board of Education *and the Interest-Convergence Dilemma,* 93 HARV. L. REV. 518, 524–525 (1980).

18. KARST, *supra* note 5, at 5.

19. *Id.* at 2.

20. For example, during the 2004 presidential election, opponents of gay marriage often based their opposition on "moral values."

21. WEST, *supra* note 9, at 38.

22. *Id.*

23. *See* Akhil Reed Amar, *The Supreme Court, 1999 Term. Foreword: The Document and the Doctrine,* 114 HARV. L. REV. 26, 105–108 (2000).

24. Linda S. Bosniak, *Constitutional Citizenship through the Prism of Alienage,* 63 OHIO ST. L. J. 1285, 1288 (2002).

25. *See* Douglas G. Smith, *Citizenship and the Fourteenth Amendment,* 34 SAN DIEGO L. REV. 681, 695 (1997). My theory of rights of belonging has its roots in the Reconstruction era because that period provides an important source of moral insight and a vision of a just society. *See* WEST, *supra* note 9, at 18, 26.

26. BAER, *supra* note 5, at 32.

27. I have made this argument at length elsewhere. *See* Rebecca E. Zietlow, *Civil Rights and Bingham's Theory of Citizenship,* 36 AKRON L. REV. 717 (2003); *Belonging, Protection and Equality: The Neglected Citizenship Clause and the Limits of Federalism,* 62 U. PITT. L. REV. 281 (2000). Similarly, Judith Baer argues that the Framers of the Fourteenth Amendment based their idea of equality not "in terms of similarity or difference, but on equality in terms of entitlement or endowment, a notion that all human beings have a right to equal respect and concern." BAER, *supra* note 5, at 32.

28. Kenneth M. Casebeer, *Holder of the Pen: An Interview with Leon Keyserling on Drafting the Wagner Act,* 42 U. MIAMI L. REV. 285, 320 (1987).

29. The facts described are taken from *Tennessee v. Lane,* 541 U.S. 509 (2004).

30. DAVID M. ENGEL & FRANK W. MUNGER, RIGHTS OF INCLUSION: LAW AND IDENTITY IN THE LIFE STORIES OF AMERICANS WITH DISABILITIES 11 (2003).

31. *See* MICHAEL SANDEL, LIBERALISM AND THE LIMITS OF JUSTICE 173, 150 (1998).

32. *See* Robert M. Cover, *Nomos and Narrative,* 97 HARV. L. REV. 4 (1983).

33. TUSHNET, *supra* note 1, at 174.

34. KARST, *supra* note 5, at 134.

35. SANDEL, *supra* note 13, at 5 (emphasis added).

36. *Id.* at 24.

37. *Id.* at 330–333.

38. *See* GLENDON, *supra* note 3, at 6.

Bibliography

STATUTES

Age Discrimination in Employment Act, Pub. L. No. 90-202, December 15, 1967, 81 Stat. 602 (codified as amended at 24 U.S.C. §§ 621 et seq.)

Alien and Sedition Acts of 1798, ch. 74, § 2, 1 Stat. 596, 596–597 (1798), *amended by* Espionage Offenses, Pub. L. No. 65-150, 40 Stat. 553 (1918)

Americans with Disabilities Act of 1990, Pub. L. No. 101-336, 104 Stat. 330 (codified at 42 U.S.C. § 12201(b))

Bill of Abominations, ch. 55, § 2, 4 Stat. 270, 271–272 (1828)

Bipartisan Campaign Reform Act of 2002, Pub. L. No. 107-155, March 27, 2002, 116 Stat. 81, 2 U.S.C. § 441 et seq.

Bituminous Coal Conservation Act, August 30, 1935, ch. 824, 49 Stat. 991

Chinese Exclusion Act of May 6, 1882, ch. 126, 22 Stat. 58

Civil Rights Act of 1866, ch. 31, 14 Stat. 27 (codified at 42 U.S.C. §§ 1981–1983 (2000))

Civil Rights Act of 1875, ch. 114, 18 Stat. 335

Civil Rights Act of 1957, Pub. L. No. 85-315, September 9, 1957, 71 Stat. 634 (codified at 42 U.S.C. § 1995)

Civil Rights Act of 1964, Pub. L. No. 88-352, July 2, 1964, 78 Stat. 241 (codified at 42 U.S.C. § 2000 et seq. (1994))

Civil Rights Act of 1991, Pub. L. No. 102-166, November 21, 1991, 105 Stat. 1071 (codified at 42 U.S.C. § 2000-2)

Clayton Act of 1914, October 15, 1914, ch. 323, 38 Stat. 730 (codified as amended at 15 U.S.C. §§ 12–27, 29 U.S.C. §§ 52–53 (2005))

Compromise of 1820 & Missouri Enabling Acts, ch. 22, § 8, 3 Stat. 545 (1820), *amended by* 3 Stat. 645 (1821), 3 Stat. 645 (1821)

Defense of Marriage Act of 1996, Pub. L. No. 104-199, § 3(a), 110 Stat. 2419, 2419 (codified at 1 U.S. C. § 7 (Supp. V 199))

Economic Opportunity Act of 1964, Pub. L. No. 88-452, August 20, 1964, 78 Stat. 508 (codified at 42 U.S.C. §§ 2991 et seq.)

Education Amendments of 1972, Title IX, 20 U.S.C. § 1681 (1994)

Elementary and Secondary Education Act; Education for All Handicapped Children Act of 1975 (now the Individuals with Disabilities Education Act), 20 U.S.C. § 1400 (1997)

Enforcement Act of 1870, May 31, 1870, ch. 114, 16 Stat. 140 (codified at 18 U.S.C. § 241 (2005))

Equal Credit Opportunity Act of 1974, Pub. L. No. 90-321, Title VII as added Pub. L. No. 93-495 Title V, October 28, 1974 88 Stat. 1521

Fair Housing Act, Pub. L. No. 90-284, Title VIII, April 11, 1968, 82 Stat. 81 (codified at 42 U.S.C. §§ 3601 et seq. (1995))

Fair Labor Standards Act, ch. 676, 52 Stat. 1060 (1938) (codified as amended at 29 U.S.C. §§ 201–219 (2000)); Social Security Act, ch. 531, 49 Stat. 620 (1935)

Family Medical Leave Act of 1993, Pub. L. No. 103-3, February 3, 1993, 107 Stat. 6 (codified at 29 U.S.C. §§ 2601 et seq. (1998)

Federal Anti-Injunction Act [Norris-LaGuardia Act], Pub. L. No. 72-65, ch. 90, 47 Stat. 70 (1932), *amended by* Pub. L. No. 98-620, 98 Stat. 3335 (1984) (codified as 29 U.S.C. §§ 101 et seq.)

Federal Election Campaign Act of 1971, Pub L. 92-225, February 7, 1972, 86 Stat. 3, 2 U.S.C. § 431

Firearms Owners' Protection Act 1(b), Pub. L. No. 99-308, 100 Stat. 449 (1986) (codified as amended at 18 U.S.C. 921 (2000))

Freedmen's Bureau Act, 14 Stat. 174, 176–177 (1866)

Freedom in the States and Territories Abolition of Slavery Act, ch. 11, 12 Stat. 432 (1862)

Fugitive Slave Act of 1793, ch. 7, 1 Stat. 302 (repealed 1864)

Fugitive Slave Act of 1850, ch. 60, 9 Stat. 462 (repealed 1864)

Indian Removal Act, ch. 148, 4 Stat. 411 (1830)

Kansas-Nebraska Act, ch. 59, § 32, 10 Stat. 277, 283 (1854)

Ku Klux Klan Act of 1871, ch. 22, § 2(3), 17 Stat. 13 (codified in Rev. Stat. of 1874, § 1980, now 42 U.S.C. § 1985(3))

National Industrial Recovery Act, June 16, 1933, ch. 90, 48 Stat. 195

National Labor Relations Act [Wagner Act], ch. 372, 49 Stat. 449 (1935) (codified as amended at 29 U.S.C. §§ 151–166 (2000))

Naturalization Acts, ch. 3, 1 Stat. 103, 104 (1790)

Norris-La Guardia Act. *See* Federal Anti-Injunction Act

Northwest Ordinance of 1787, Art. VI

Personal Responsibility and Work Opportunity Act of 1996, Pub. L. No. 104-193, August 22, 1996, 110 Stat. 2105 (1996) (codified at 42 U.S.C. §§ 601 et seq. (2005))

Pregnancy Discrimination Act, Pub. L. No. 95-555, October 31, 1978, 92 Stat. 2076 (codified at 42 U.S.C. § 2000e-(k) (1978))

"Reconstruction Acts," Act of March 2, 1867, ch. 153, 14 Stat. 428; Act of March 23, 187, ch. 6, 15 Stat. 2; Act of July 1867, ch. 30, 15 Stat. 4

Rehabilitation Act of 1973, 29 U.S.C. §§ 701–796 (1998) (Supp., May 1999)

Religious Freedom Restoration Act [RFRA] of 1993, Pub. L. No. 103-141, 107 Stat. 1488 (1993)

Religious Land Use and Institutionalized Persons Act [RLUIPA] of 2000, Pub. L. No. 106-274, Sept. 22, 2000, 114 Stat. 803, USCA §§ 2000cc et seq.

Repealer Act of 1867, Act of Feb. 5, 1867, ch. 28, § 1, 14 Stat. 385

Requisitioning Property for National Defense Property Requisition Act, Pub. L. No. 77-274, 55 Stat. 742 (1941), *amended by* Second War Powers Act, Pub. L. No. 77-507, 56 Stat. 176 (1942), Requisitioning of Property for National Defense, Pub. L. No. 78-104, 57 Stat. 271 (1943), Requisition of Property for National Defense, Pub. L. No. 78-378, 58 Stat. 624 (1944), Requisition of Property for National Defense, Pub. L. No. 79-102, 59 Stat. 271 (1945)

Social Security Act, ch. 531, 49 Stat. 620 (1935)

Taft-Hartley Act, ch. 120, 61 Stat. 136 (1947) (codified as amended in scattered sections of 29 U.S.C.)

Violence against Women Act, Pub. L. No. 103-322, Title IV, September 13, 1994, 108 Stat. 1902 (codified as 18 U.S.C. §§ 2261–2266 (2000))

Voting Rights Act of 1965, Pub. L. No. 89-110, August 6, 1965, 79 Stat. 437 (codified at 42 U.S.C. §§ 1973 et seq. (2005))

Wagner Act. *See* National Labor Relations Act

Women in Apprenticeship and Non-Traditional Occupations Act, Pub. L. No. 102-530, October 27, 1992, 106 Stat. 3465 (codified at 29 U.S.C. §§ 2501–2509 (2005))

CASES

Ableman v. Booth, 21 How. 526 (1859)

Adair v. U.S., 208 U.S. 161 (1908)

Adarand Constructors v. Pena, 515 U.S. 200 (1995)

Adkins v. Children's Hospital of the District of Columbia, 261 U.S. 525 (1923)

A.L.A. Schechter Poultry Corporation v. United States, 295 U.S. 495 (1935)

Alden v. Maine, 527 U.S. 706 (1999)

Alexander v. Gardner-Denver Co., 415 U.S. 36 (1974)

Barron v. Mayor and City Council of Baltimore, 32 U.S. (7 Pet.) 243 (1833)

Bell v. Maryland, 378 U.S. 226 (1964)

Board of Trustees v. Garrett, 531 U.S. 356 (2001)

Brown v. Board of Education, 347 U.S. 483 (1954)

Buckley v. Valeo, 424 U.S. 1 (1976)

Carolene Products, United States v., 304 U.S. 144 (1938)

Carter v. Carter Coal, 298 U.S. 238 (1936)

Casey v. Cincinnati Typographical Union, No. 3, 45 F. 135 (C.C.S.D. Ohio 1891)

City of Boerne v. Flores, 521 U.S. 507 (1997); 117 S. Ct. 2157 (????)
Civil Rights Cases, 109 U.S. 3 (1983)
Cleburne v. Cleburne Living Center, 473 U.S. 432 (1985)
Coeur D'Alene Consolidated & Mining Co. v. Miners' Union of Wardner, 51 F. 260 (C.C.D. Idaho 1892)
Consolidated Edison Co. v. NLRB, 305 U.S. 197 (1938)
Coppage v. State of Kansas, 236 U.S. 1 (1915)
Corfield v. Coryell, 6 F. Cas. 546 (C.C.E.D. Pa. 1823) (No. 3,230)
Cruzan v. Director, Missouri Department of Health, 497 U.S. 261 (1990)
Cummings v. Missouri, 71 U.S. 277 (1866)
Cutter v. Wilkinson, 125 S. Ct. 2113 (2005)
Dandridge v. Williams, 397 U.S. 471 (1970)
Darby, United States v., 312 U.S. 100 (1941)
Dred Scott v. Sanford, 60 U.S. (19 How.) 393 (1856)
Duplex Printing Press Co. v. Deering, 254 U.S. 443 (1921)
Employment Division v. Smith, 494 U.S. 872 (1990)
Ex parte McCardle, 73 U.S. (6 Wall.) 318 (1868)
Ex parte Milligan, 71 U.S. 2 (1866)
Foster Bros. Mfg. Co. v. NLRB, 85 F.2d 984 (4th Cir. 1986)
Fruehauf Trailer Co. v. NLRB, 85 F.2d 391 (6th Cir. 1936)
Garcia v. San Antonio Metropolitan Transit Authority, 469 U.S. 528 (1985)
Gayle v. Browder, 352 U.S. 903 (1956)
Griggs v. Duke Power Co., 401 U.S. 424 (1971)
Groves v. Slaughter, 40 U.S. (15 Pet.) 449 (1841)
Grutter v. Bollinger, 539 U.S. 306 (2003)
Guest, United States v., 383 U.S. 745 (1966)
Hague v. CIO, 307 U.S. 496 (1939)
Hamdi v. Rumsfeld, 542 U.S. 507 (2004)
Hammer v. Dagenhart, 247 U.S. 251 (1918)
Heart of Atlanta Motel v. United States, 379 U.S. 241 (1964)
Holmes v. Atlanta, 350 U.S., 879 (1955)
In re Jacobs, 98 N.Y. 98 (1885)
Interborough Rapid Transit Co. v. Lavin, 247 N.Y. 65, 159 N.E. 863 (1928)
Jones v. Alfred H. Mayer Co., 392 U.S. 409 (1968)
J. W. Bailey v. Drexel Furniture Co., 259 U.S. 20 (1922)
Katzenbach v. McClung, 379 U.S. 294 (1964)
Katzenbach v. Morgan, 384 U.S. 641 (1966)
Kentucky v. Denison, 65 U.S. 66 (1860)
Kimel v. Florida Board of Regents, 528 U.S. 62 (2000)
Korematsu v. United States, 323 U.S. 214 (1944)
Lauf v. E. G. Shinner Co., 303 U.S. 323 (1938)
Lawrence v. Texas, 539 U.S. 558 (2003)

Lochner v. New York, 198 U.S. 45 (1905)

Loewe v. Lawlor, 208 U.S. 274 (1908)

Lopez, United States v., 514 U.S. 549 (1995)

Loving v. Virginia, 388 U.S. 1 (1967)

Marbury v. Madison, 5 U.S. (1 Cranch) 137 (1803)

Massachusetts Board of Retirement v. Murgia, 427 U.S. 307 (1976)

Mayor of Baltimore v. Dawson, 350 U.S. 877 (1955)

McConnell v. Federal Election Commission, 540 U.S. 93 (2003)

McCulloch v. Maryland, 17 U.S. (4 Wheat.) 316 (1819)

Miller, United States v., 307 U.S. 174 (1939)

Missouri ex rel. Gaines v. Canada, 305 U.S. 337 (1938)

Moody v. Pepsi-Cola Metropolitan Bottling Company, Inc., 915 F.2d 201 (1990)

Morgan v. Commonwealth of Virginia, 328 U.S. 373 (1946)

Morrison, United States v., 529 U.S. 598 (2000)

Myers v. Bethlehem Shipbuilding Corp., 88 F.2d 154 (2d Cir. 1937)

NAACP v. Alabama ex rel. Patterson, 357 U.S. 449 (1958)

NAACP v. Button, 371 U.S. 415 (1963)

National League of Cities v. Usery, 426 U.S. 833 (1976)

Nevada Department of Human Resources v. Hibbs, 538 U.S. 721 (2003)

New Orleans City Park Improvement Ass'n v. Detiege, 358 U.S. 54 (1958)

New York Gaslight Club v. Carey, 447 U.S. 54 (1980)

New York Times Co. v. Sullivan, 376 U.S. 254 (1964)

NLRB [National Labor Relations Board] v. Fansteel Metalurgical Corp., 306 U.S. 240 (1939)

NLRB v. Friedman-Harry Marks Clothing Co., 85 F.2d 1 (2d Cir. 1936)

NLRB v. Jones, 332 U.S. 823 (1937)

NLRB v. Jones & Laughlin Steel Corp., 83 F.2d 998 (5th Cir. 1946)

NLRB v. Mackay Radio & Telegraph Co., 304 U.S. 333 (1938)

Planned Parenthood v. Casey, 505 U.S. 833 (1992)

Plessy v. Ferguson, 163 U.S. 537 (1896)

Pratt v. Stout, 85 F.2d 172 (8th Cir. 1986)

Prigg v. Pennsylvania, 41 U.S. (16 Pet.) 539 (1842)

Richmond v. J. A. Croson Co., 488 U.S. 469 (1989)

Ritchie v. People of the State of Illinois, 155 Ill. 98, 40 N.E. 454 (1895)

Saenz v. Roe, 526 U.S. 489 (1999)

San Antonio v. Rodriguez, 411 U.S. 1 (1973)

Scott v. Emerson, 15 Mo. 576 (1852)

Shelley v. Kraemer, 334 U.S. 1 (1948)

Sherbert v. Verner, 374 U.S. 398 (1963)

Simpkins v. Moses Cone Memorial Hospital, 323 F.2d 957 (4th Cir. 1963)

Simpson, Alaska State Commission for Human Rights v. Providence Washington Insurance, 608 F.2d 1171 (1979)

Slaughter-House Cases, 83 U.S. 36 (1872)

Smith v. Allwright, 321 U.S. 649 (1944)

South Carolina v. Katzenbach, 383 U.S. 301 (1966)

Stanley, United States v., 109 U.S. 3 (1883)

Sweatt v. Painter, 339 U.S. 629 (1950)

Teamster v. Vogt, 354 U.S. 284 (1957)

Tennessee v. Lane, 541 U.S. 509 (2004)

Thornhill v. Alabama, 310 US 88 (1940)

Treglia v. Town of Manlius, 313 F.3d 713 (2002)

Twining v. New Jersey, 211 U.S. 78 (1908)

United Steelworkers of America v. Weber, 443 U.S. 193 (1979)

U.S. Term Limits v. Thornton, 514 U.S. 779, 847–848 (Thomas, J., dissenting)

Washington v. Davis, 426 U.S. 229 (1976)

Washington v. Glucksberg, 521 U.S. 702 (1997)

West Coast Hotel v. Parrish, 300 U.S. 379 (1937)

West Virginia Board of Education v. Barnette, 319 U.S. 624 (1943)

Wickard v. Filburn, 317 U.S. 111 (1942)

BOOKS AND ARTICLES

BRUCE ACKERMAN, WE THE PEOPLE: TRANSFORMATIONS (1998)

Matthew Adler & Seth Kreimer, *The New Etiquette of Federalism: New York, Printz and Yeskey,* 1998 SUP. CT. REV. 71 (1998)

Larry Alexander & Frederick Shauer, *Defending Judicial Supremacy: A Reply,* 17 CONST. COMM. 455 (2000)

Larry Alexander & Frederick Schauer, *On Extrajudicial Constitutional Interpretation,* 110 HARV. L. REV. 1359 (1997)

AKHIL REED AMAR, THE BILL OF RIGHTS: CREATION AND RECONSTRUCTION (1998)

Akhil Reed Amar, *The Bill of Rights and the Fourteenth Amendment,* 101 YALE L. J. 1193 (1992)

Akhil Reed Amar, *The Bill of Rights as a Constitution,* 100 YALE L. J. 1131 (1991)

Akhil Reed Amar, *Intratextualism,* 112 HARV. L. REV. 747 (2000)

Akhil Reed Amar, *The Supreme Court, 1999 Term. Foreword: The Document and the Doctrine,* 114 HARV. L. REV. 26 (2000)

Keith Aoki, *A Tale of Three Cities: Thoughts on Asian American Electoral and Political Power after 2000,* 8 ASIAN PAC. AM. L. J. 1 (2002)

William D. Araiza, *Court, Congress and Equal Protection: What Brown Teaches Us about the Section 5 Power,* 47 HOW. L. J. 199 (2004)

Robin Archer, *Unions, Courts and Parties: Judicial Repression and Labor Politics in Late Nineteenth Century America,* 26 POLITICS & SOCIETY 391 (1998)

Michael Ariens, *A Thrice-Told Tale, or Felix the Cat*, 107 HARV. L. REV. 620 (1994)

AWAKENING FROM THE DREAM: CIVIL RIGHTS UNDER SIEGE AND THE NEW STRUGGLE FOR EQUAL JUSTICE (Denise C. Morgan, Rachel D. Godsil, & Joy Moses, eds., 2005)

Richard L. Aynes, *On Misreading John Bingham and the Fourteenth Amendment*, 103 YALE L. J. 57 (1993)

JUDITH A. BAER, EQUALITY UNDER THE CONSTITUTION: RECLAIMING THE FOURTEENTH AMENDMENT (1983)

Lynn A. Baker, *Putting the Safeguards Back into the Political Safeguards of Federalism*, 46 VILL. L. REV. 951 (2001)

J. M. Balkin, *The Constitution of Status*, 106 YALE L. J. 2313 (1997)

J. M. Balkin & Sanford Levinson, *Understanding the Constitutional Revolution*, 87 VA. L. REV. 1045 (2001)

Mark Barenberg, *The Political Economy of the Wagner Act: Power, Symbol, and Workplace Cooperation*, 106 HARV. L. REV. 1381 (1993)

Randy Barnett & Don B. Kates, *Under Fire: The New Consensus on the Second Amendment*, 45 EMORY L. J. 1139 (1996)

David J. Barron, *The Promise of Cooley's City: Traces of Local Constitutionalism*, 147 U. PA. L. REV. 487 (1999)

Paul Bator, *The State Courts and Federal Constitutional Litigation*, 22 WM. & MARY L. REV. 605 (1981)

Ronald H. Beason, *Printz Punts on the Palladium of Rights: It Is Time to Protect the Rights of the Individual to Keep and Bear Arms*, 50 ALA. L. REV. 561 (1999)

David T. Beito, *Book Review*, 10 GEO. MASON L. REV. 293 (2001)

Derrick Bell, Brown v. Board of Education *and the Interest-Convergence Dilemma*, 93 HARV. L. REV. 518 (1980)

DERRICK BELL, SILENT COVENANTS: *BROWN V. BOARD* AND THE UNFULLFILLED HOPES FOR RACIAL REFORM (2004)

MICHAEL LES BENEDICT, A COMPROMISE OF PRINCIPLE (1974)

Raoul Berger, *Incorporation of the Bill of Rights: Akhil Amar's Wishing Well*, 61 U. CINN. L. REV. 1 (1993)

Raoul Berger, *Incorporation of the Bill of Rights of the Fourteenth Amendment: A Nine-Lived Cat*, 42 OHIO ST. L. J. 435 (1981)

DAVID E. BERNSTEIN, ONLY ONE PLACE OF REDRESS: AFRICAN AMERICANS, LABOR RELATIONS AND THE COURTS FROM RECONSTRUCTION TO THE NEW DEAL (2001)

IRVING BERNSTEIN, A HISTORY OF THE AMERICAN WORKER (1933–1941): TURBULENT YEARS (1969)

IRVING BERNSTEIN, THE NEW DEAL COLLECTIVE BARGAINING POLICY (1950; reissued 1975)

Alexander Bickel, The Least Dangerous Branch: The Supreme Court at the Bar of Politics (1962)

Martha Biondi, To Stand and Fight: The Struggle for Civil Rights in Postwar New York City (2003)

Charles L. Black, Jr., A New Birth of Freedom: Human Rights, Named and Unnamed (1997)

James F. Blumstein, *Federalism and Civil Rights: Complimentary and Competing Paradigms,* 47 Vand. L. Rev. 1251 (1994)

Carl T. Bogus, *The Hidden History of the Second Amendment,* 31 U.C. Davis L. Rev. 309 (1998)

Linda S. Bosniak, *Constitutional Citizenship through the Prism of Alienage,* 63 Ohio St. L. J. 1285 (2002)

Linda S. Bosniak, *Membership, Equality, and the Difference That Alienage Makes,* 69 N.Y.U. L. Rev. 1047 (1994)

Taylor Branch, Parting the Waters: America in the King Years 1954–63 (1988)

Pamela Brandwein, Reconstructing Reconstruction: The Supreme Court and the Production of Historical Truth (1999)

William J. Brennan, Jr., *The Bill of Rights and the States: The Revival of State Constitutions as Guardians of Individual Rights,* 61 N.Y.U. L. Rev. 535 (1986)

William J. Brennan, Jr., *State Constitutions and the Protection of Individual Rights,* 90 Harv. L. Rev. 489 (1977)

James J. Brudney & Ruth Colker, *Dissing Congress,* 100 Mich. L. Rev. 80 (2001)

James J. Brudney, Sara Schiavoni, & Deborah J. Meritt, *Judicial Hostility toward Labor Unions? Applying the Social Background Model to a Celebrated Concern,* 60 Ohio St. L. J. 1675 (1999)

Robert Burt, The Constitution in Conflict (1992)

Steven Calabresi, *"A Government of Limited and Enumerated Powers": In Defense of* United States v. Lopez, 94 Mich. L. Rev. 752 (1995)

The John C. Calhoun Papers (Robert L. Meriwether, ed., 1959)

Robert K. Carr, Federal Protection of Civil Rights: Quest for a Sword (1947)

Kenneth M. Casebeer, *Holder of the Pen: An Interview with Leon Keyserling on Drafting the Wagner Act,* 42 U. Miami L. Rev. 285 (1987)

Julius Chambers, *Protection of Civil Rights: A Constitutional Mandate for the Federal Government,* 87 Mich L. Rev. 1599 (1989)

Erwin Chemerinsky, *Ending the Parity Debate,* 71 B.U. L. Rev. 593 (1991)

Erwin Chemerinsky, *In Defense of Judicial Review: A Reply to Professor Kramer,* 92 Cal. L. Rev. 1013 (2004)

Erwin Chemerinsky, *Parity Reconsidered: Defining a Role for the Federal Judiciary,* 36 UCLA L. Rev. 233 (1988)

Erwin Chemerinsky, *The Values of Federalism,* 47 Fla. L. Rev. 499 (1995)

Gabriel J. Chin, *Regulating Race: Asian Exclusion and the Administrative State,* 37 Harv. C.R.-C.L. Rev. 1 (2002)

The Civil Rights Act of 1964: The Passage of the Law That Ended Racial Segregation (Robert D. Loevy, ed., 1997)

Stephen Clark, *Progressive Federalism? A Gay Liberationist Perspective,* 66 Albany L. Rev. 719 (2003)

Lizabeth Cohen, Making a New Deal: Industrial Workers in Chicago, 1919–1939 (1990)

David Cole, *The Value of Seeing Things Differently:* Boerne v. Flores *and Congressional Enforcement of the Bill of Rights,* 1997 Sup. Ct. Rev. 31

Ruth Colker, *The Supreme Court's Historical Errors in* City of Boerne v. Flores, 43 B. C. L. Rev. 783 (2002)

The Collected Works of Abraham Lincoln (Roy P. Basler, ed., 1955)

A Compilation of the Messages and Papers of the Presidents (James D. Richardson, ed., New York Bureau of National Literature 1897)

Richard C. Cortner, Civil Rights and Public Accommodations: The Heart of Atlanta Motel and McClung Cases (2001)

Robert M. Cover, Justice Accused: Antislavery and the Judicial Process (1975)

Robert M. Cover, *Nomos and Narrative,* 97 Harv. L. Rev. 4 (1983)

Archibold Cox, The Warren Court: Constitutional Decisions as an Instrument of Reform (1968)

Marcia Coyle, Marianne Lavelle, & Claudia MacLachlan, *Religion Bill,* Nat'l. J., November 15, 1993, at 12

Creating the Bill of Rights: The Documentary Record from the First Federal Congress (Helen E. Veit et al., eds., 1991)

Frank B. Cross, *The Folly of Federalism,* 24 Cardozo L. Rev. 1 (2002)

Frank B. Cross, *Institutions and Enforcement of the Bill of Rights,* 85 Cornell L. Rev. 1529 (2000)

William Crosskey, *Charles Fairman, "Legislative History," and the Constitutional Limitations on State Authority,* 22 Univ. Chi. L. Rev. 1 (1954)

David P. Currie, The Constitution in Congress: Democrats and Whigs, 1829–1861 (2005)

David P. Currie, The Constitution in Congress: The Federalist Period, 1978–1801 (1997)

David P. Currie, The Constitution in Congress: The Jeffersonians, 1801–1829 (2001)

David P. Currie, *The Constitution in Congress: Substantive Issues in the First Congress, 1789–1791,* 61 U. Chi. L. Rev. 775 (1994)

Michael Kent Curtis, Free Speech, "the People's Darling Privilege": Struggles for Freedom of Expression in American History (2000)

Michael Kent Curtis, *John A. Bingham and the Story of American Liberty: The Lost Cause Meets the "Lost Clause,"* 36 AKRON L. REV. 617 (2003)

MICHAEL KENT CURTIS, NO STATE SHALL ABRIDGE: THE FOURTEENTH AMENDMENT AND THE BILL OF RIGHTS (1986)

Robert Dahl, *Decision-Making in a Democracy: The Supreme Court as a National Policy-Maker,* 6 J. PUB. L. 279, 284 (1957)

MARTHA DAVIS, BRUTAL NEED: LAWYERS AND THE WELFARE RIGHTS MOVEMENT (1993)

Brandon P. Denning, *Gun Shy: The Second Amendment as an "Underenforced Constitutional Norm,"* 21 HARV. J. L. & PUB. POL'Y 719 (1998)

Devolving Welfare Programs to the States: A Public Choice Perspective, 109 HARV. L. REV. 1984 (1996)

DICTIONARY OF AMERICAN HISTORY (Stanley I. Kutler, ed., 3d ed. 2003)

JOHN J. DINAN, KEEPING THE PEOPLE'S LIBERTIES: LEGISLATORS, CITIZENS, AND JUDGES AS GUARDIANS OF RIGHTS (1998)

Michael C. Dorf & Charles F. Sabel, *A Constitution of Democratic Experimentalism,* 98 COLUM. L. REV. 267 (1998)

MELVYN DUBOFSKY, THE STATE AND LABOR IN MODERN AMERICA (1994)

RONALD DWORKIN, LAW'S EMPIRE (1986)

Herb Eastman, *Speaking Truth to Power: The Language of Civil Rights Litigators,* 104 YALE L. J. 763 (1995)

JOHN HART ELY, DEMOCRACY AND DISTRUST: A THEORY OF JUDICIAL REVIEW (1980)

DAVID M. ENGEL & FRANK W. MUNGER, RIGHTS OF INCLUSION: LAW AND IDENTITY IN THE LIFE STORIES OF AMERICANS WITH DISABILITIES (2003)

Steven A. Engel, *The McCulloch Theory of the Fourteenth Amendment:* City of Boerne v. Flores *and the Original Understanding of Section 5,* 109 YALE L. J. 115 (1999)

Richard Epstein, *Exit Rights under Federalism,* 55 LAW & CONTEMP. PROBS. 147 (1992)

William N. Eskridge, Jr., *Some Effects of Identity-Based Social Movements on Constitutional Law in the Twentieth Century,* 100 MICH. L. REV. 2062 (2002)

William N. Eskridge, Jr., & John Ferejohn, *Super Statutes,* 50 DUKE L. J. 1215 (2001)

Samuel Estreicher, *Federal Power to Regulate Private Discrimination: The Revival of the Enforcement Clauses of the Reconstruction Era Amendments,* 74 COLUM. L. REV. 449 (1974)

Charles Fairman, *Does the Fourteenth Amendment Incorporate the Bill of Rights?,* 2 STAN. L. REV. 5 (1949)

Charles Fairman, *A Reply to Professor Crosskey,* 22 UNIV. CHI. L. REV. 144 (1954)

Daniel A. Farber & John E. Muench, *The Ideological Origins of the Fourteenth Amendment,* 1 CONST. COMMENT. 235 (1984)

FEDERALISM AND RIGHTS (Ellis Katz & G. Alan Tarr, eds., 1996)

THE FEDERALIST PAPERS (Clinton Rossiter, ed., 1961)

PAUL FINKELMAN, AN IMPERFECT UNION: SLAVERY, FEDERALISM AND COMITY (1981)

Paul Finkelman, *James Madison and the Bill of Rights: A Reluctant Paternity,* 1990 SUP. CT. REV. 301 (1991)

PAUL FINKELMAN, SLAVERY AND THE FOUNDERS: RACE AND LIBERTY IN THE AGE OF JEFFERSON (1996)

Paul Finkelman, *Sorting Out* Prigg v. Pennsylvania, 24 RUTGERS L. J. 605 (1993)

LOUIS FISHER, CONSTITUTIONAL DIALOGUES (1988)

Louis Fisher, *Constitutional Interpretation by Members of Congress,* 63 N.C. L. REV. 707 (1985)

Owen M. Fiss, *Groups and the Equal Protection Clause,* 5 PHIL. & PUB. AFF. 107 (1976)

Owen M. Fiss, *The Supreme Court 1978 Term?Foreword: The Forms of Justice,* 93 HARV. L. REV. 1 (1979)

R. W. Fleming, *The Significance of the Wagner Act, in* LABOR AND THE NEW DEAL 123 (Milton Derber & Edwin Young, eds., 1957)

ERIC FONER, FREE SOIL, FREE LABOR, FREE MEN: THE IDEOLOGY OF THE REPUBLICAN PARTY BEFORE THE CIVIL WAR (1995)

ERIC FONER, RECONSTRUCTION: AMERICA'S UNFINISHED REVOLUTION (1988)

ERIC FONER, THE STORY OF AMERICAN FREEDOM (1998)

William E. Forbath, *Caste, Class and Equal Citizenship,* 98 MICH. L. REV. 1 (1999)

WILLIAM E. FORBATH, LAW AND THE SHAPING OF THE AMERICAN LABOR MOVEMENT (1991)

William E. Forbath, *The New Deal Constitution in Exile,* 51 DUKE L. J. 165 (2001)

James W. Fox, *Citizenship, Poverty and Federalism,* 60 U. PITT. L. REV. 421 (1999)

James W. Fox, *Re-readings and Misreadings: Slaughter-House, Privileges or Immunities, and Section Five Enforcement Power,* 91 KY. L. J. 67 (2002)

Felix Frankfurter, *Mr. Justice Roberts,* 104 U. PA. L. REV. 311 (1955)

Laurent B. Frantz, *Congressional Power to Enforce the Fourteenth Amendment against Private Acts,* 73 YALE L. J. 1353 (1964)

Barry Friedman, *Dialogue and Judicial Review,* 91 MICH. L. REV. 577 (1993)

Barry Friedman, *A Reaffirmation: The Authenticity of the Roberts Memorandum,* 142 U. PA. L. REV. 1985 (1994)

Barry Friedman, *Switching Time and Other Thought Experiments: The Hughes Court and Constitutional Transformation,* 142 U. PA. L. REV. 1891 (1994)

DAVID J. GARROW, BEARING THE CROSS: MARTIN LUTHER KING, JR. AND THE SOUTHERN CHRISTIAN LEADERSHIP CONFERENCE (1986)

Gay Gellhorn, *Disability and Welfare Reform: Keep the Supplemental Security Income Program but Reengineer the Disability Determination Process,* 22 FORDHAM URB. L. J. 961 (1995)

MARY ANN GLENDON, RIGHTS TALK: THE IMPOVERISHMENT OF POLITICAL DISCOURSE (1991)

Sally F. Goldfarb, *The Supreme Court, the Violence against Women Act, and the Use and Abuse of Federalism,* 71 FORDHAM L. REV. 57 (2002).

Risa Goluboff, *The Thirteenth Amendment and the Lost Origins of Civil Rights,* 50 DUKE L. J. 1609 (2001)

Mark C. Gordon, *Differing Paradigms, Similar Flaws: Constructing a New Approach to Federalism in Congress and the Court,* 14 YALE L. & POL'Y REV. 187 (1996)

Mark A. Graber, *Resolving Political Questions into Judicial Decisions: Tocqueville's Thesis Revisited,* 21 CONST. COMMENT. 485 (2004)

STEPHEN M. GRIFFIN, AMERICAN CONSTITUTIONALISM: FROM THEORY TO POLITICS (1996)

Stephen M. Griffin, *Judicial Supremacy and Equal Protection in a Democracy of Rights,* 4 U. PA. J. CONST. L. 281 (2002)

JAMES A. GROSS, THE MAKING OF THE NATIONAL LABOR RELATIONS BOARD: A STUDY IN ECONOMICS, POLITICS AND LAW, 1933–1937 (1974)

Stephen Halbrook, *Congress Interprets the Second Amendment: Declarations by a Co-Equal Branch on the Individual Right to Keep and Bear Arms,* 32 TENN. L. REV. 597 (1995)

Marci Hamilton, *Why Federalism Must Be Enforced: A Response to Professor Kramer,* 46 VILL. L. REV. 1069 (2001)

Drew D. Hansen, *The Sit-Down Strikes and the Switch in Time,* 46 WAYNE L. REV. 49 (2000)

Orrin G. Hatch, *The Brady Handgun Prevention Act and the Community Protection Initiative: Legislative Responses to the Second Amendment?,* 1998 BYU L. REV. 103 (1998)

Andrew D. Herz, *Gun Crazy: Constitutional False Consciousness and Dereliction of Constitutional Responsibility,* 75 B.U. L. REV. 57 (1995)

THOMAS R. HIETALA, MANIFEST DESIGN: ANXIOUS AGGRANDIZEMENT IN THE LATE JACKSONIAN AMERICA (1985)

Tracy Higgins, *Anti-Essentialism, Relativism, and Human Rights,* 19 HARV. WOMEN'S L. J. 89 (1996)

ROBERT F. HIMMELBERG, THE GREAT DEPRESSION AND THE NEW DEAL (2001)

Charles F. Hobson, *The Negative on States Laws: James Madison, and the Crisis of Republican Government*, 36 WM. & MARY Q. 215 (1979)

Serena J. Hoy, *Interpreting Equal Protection: Congress, the Court, and the Civil Rights Acts*, 16 J. L.& POL. 381 (2000)

Aziz Z. Huq, *Peonage and Contractual Liberty*, 101 COLUM. L. REV. 351 (2001)

HAROLD M. HYMAN & WILLIAM M. WIECEK, EQUAL JUSTICE UNDER LAW: CONSTITUTIONAL DEVELOPMENTS, 1835–1875 (1982)

INDUSTRIAL DEMOCRACY IN AMERICA: THE AMBIGUOUS PROMISE (Nelson Lichtenstein & Howell John Harris, eds., 1993)

Vicki Jackson, *Federalism and the Uses and Limits of Law: Printz and Principle?*, 111 HARV. L. REV. 2180 (1998)

LYNDON B. JOHNSON, PAPERS 1963–64 (1965)

Robert J. Kaczorowski, *Congress's Power to Enforce Fourteenth Amendment Rights: Lessons from Federal Remedies the Framers Enacted*, 42 HARV. J. LEG. 187 (2005)

Robert J. Kaczorowski, *Revolutionary Constitutionalism in the Era of the Civil War and Reconstruction*, 61 N.Y.U. L. REV. 863 (1986)

KENNETH L. KARST, BELONGING TO AMERICA: EQUAL CITIZENSHIP AND THE CONSTITUTION (1989)

JOHN F. KENNEDY, PUBLIC PAPERS, 1963 (1964)

Mark R. Killenbeck, *Madison, M'Culloch, and Matters of Judicial Cognizance: Some Thoughts on the Nature and Scope of Judicial Review*, 55 ARK. L. REV. 901 (2003)

JOHN W. KINGDON, CONGRESSMEN'S VOTING DECISIONS (3d ed. 1989)

Karl Klare, *Judicial Deradicalization of the Wagner Act and the Origins of Modern Legal Consciousness, 1937–1941*, 62 MINN. L. REV. 265 (1977–1978)

Michael J. Klarman, *Constitutional Fact/Constitutional Fiction: A Critique of Bruce Ackerman's Theory of Constitutional Moments*, 44 STAN. L. REV. 759 (1992)

MICHAEL J. KLARMAN, FROM JIM CROW TO CIVIL RIGHTS: THE SUPREME COURT AND THE STRUGGLE FOR RACIAL EQUALITY (2004)

Michael J. Klarman, *Rethinking the Civil Rights and Civil Liberties Revolutions*, 82 VA. L. REV. 1 (1996)

Andrew Koppelman, *Same Sex Marriage, Choice of Law, and Public Policy*, 76 TEX. L. REV. 921 (1998)

Larry D. Kramer, *Madison's Audience*, 112 HARV. L. REV. 611 (1999)

LARRY D. KRAMER, THE PEOPLE THEMSELVES: POPULAR CONSTITUTIONALISM AND JUDICIAL REVIEW (2004)

Larry D. Kramer, *Popular Constitutionalism, circa 2004*, 92 CAL. L. REV. 959 (2004)

George Lakoff, Moral Politics: How Liberals and Conservatives Think (2002)

Charles R. Lawrence, *The Id, the Ego and Equal Protection: Reckoning with Unconscious Racism,* 39 Stan. L. Rev. 317 (1987)

Douglas Laycock, *RFRA, Congress and the Ratchet,* 56 Mont. L. Rev. 145 (1995)

Nicholas Lemann, The Promised Land: The Great Black Migration and How It Changed America (1992)

Sanford Levinson, Constitutional Faith (1988)

Sanford Levinson, *The Embarrassing Second Amendment,* 99 Yale L. J. 637 (1989)

Alex Lichtenstein, *Book Review,* 50 Labour [Canada] 340 (2002)

James S. Liebman & Brandon L. Garrett, *Madisonian Equal Protection,* 104 Colum. L. Rev. 837 (2004)

Robert D. Loevy, To End All Segregation: The Politics of the Passage of the Civil Rights Act of 1964 (1990)

Nelson Lund, *Federalism and Civil Liberties,* 45 U. Ken. L. Rev. 1045 (1997)

Catharine MacKinnon, Toward a Feminist Theory of the State (1989)

James Madison, The Papers of James Madison (vols. 9 and 10, Robert A. Rutland et al., eds., 1975; vol. 12, Charles F. Hobson et al., eds., 1979)

James Madison, The Writings of James Madison (vol. 8, Gaillard Hunt, ed., 1900)

Earl Maltz, Civil Rights, The Constitution, and Congress, 1863–1869 (1990)

Earl Maltz, The Fourteenth Amendment and the Law of the Constitution (2003)

Burke Marshall, Federalism and Civil Rights (1964)

Thomas R. Marshall, Public Opinion and the Supreme Court (1989)

Tony Mauro, *Is the Court Finally Camera-Ready?* Legal Times, May 14, 1990, at 10

Michael S. Mayer, *Book Review,* 89 Journal of American History 255 (2002)

Joseph A. McCartin, *Democratizing the Demand for Workers' Rights: Toward a Re-framing of Labor's Argument,* Dissent, Winter 2005, at 61

Wilfred M. McClay, Commentary: The Worst Decision since "Dred Scott"? Decision Overturning the Religious Freedom Restoration Act, 104 ASAP 52 (1997)

Michael W. McConnell, *Federalism: Evaluating the Founders' Design,* 54 U. Chi. L. Rev. 1484 (1987)

Forrest McDonald, States' Rights and the Union, Imperium in Imperio 1776–1876 (2000)

Robert S. McElvane, The Great Depression: America 1929–1941 (1984)

Kevin J. McMahon, Reconsidering Roosevelt on Race: How the Presidency Paved the Road to *Brown* (2004)

Abner J. Mikva, *How Well Does Congress Support and Defend the Constitution?* 61 N.C. L. Rev. 587 (1983)

Harry A. Millis & Emily Clark Brown, From the Wagner Act to Taft-Hartley: A Study of National Labor Policy and Labor Relations (1950)

Denise C. Morgan & Rebecca E. Zietlow, *The New Parity Debate: Congress and Rights of Belonging*, 73 Cinn. L. Rev. 1347 (2005)

Grant S. Nelson & Robert Pushaw, *Rethinking the Commerce Clause: Applying First Principles to Uphold Federal Commercial Regulations but Preserve State Control over Social Issues*, 85 Iowa L. Rev. 1 (1999)

William E. Nelson, The Fourteenth Amendment: From Political Principle to Judicial Doctrine (1988)

Burt Neuborne, *The Myth of Parity*, 90 Harv. L. Rev. 1105 (1977)

Kevin Christopher Newsom, *Setting Incorporationism Straight: A Reinterpretation of the Slaughter-House Cases*, 109 Yale L. J. 643 (2000)

Paul E. Peterson, The Price of Federalism (1995)

Todd E. Pettys, *The Mobility Paradox*, 92 Geo. L. J. 481 (2004)

James Gray Pope, *How American Workers Lost the Right to Strike, and Other Tales*, 103 Mich. L. Rev. 518 (2004)

James Gray Pope, *Labor's Constitution of Freedom*, 106 Yale L. J. 941 (1997)

James Gray Pope, *The Thirteenth Amendment versus the Commerce Clause: Labor and the Shaping of American Constitutional Law, 1921–1957*, 102 Colum. L. Rev. 1 (2002)

Robert C. Post, *The Supreme Court 2002 Term. Foreword: Fashioning the Legal Constitution? Culture, Courts and Law*, 117 Harv. L. Rev. 4 (2003)

Robert C. Post & Reva B. Siegel, *Equal Protection by Law: Federal Anti-Discrimination Legislation after* Morrison *and* Kimel, 110 Yale L. J. 441 (2000)

Robert C. Post & Reva B. Siegel, *Legislative Constitutionalism and Section Five Power: Policentric Interpretation of the Family and Medical Leave Act*, 112 Yale L. J. 1943 (2003)

Lucas.A. Powe, *Are "The People" Missing in Action (and Should Anyone Care?)* (review of Larry Kramer, The People Themselves), 83 Tex. L. Rev. 855 (2005)

Lucas A. Powe, The Warren Court and American Politics (2000)

Catherine Powell, *Dialogic Federalism: Constitutional Possibilities for Incorporation of Human Rights Law in the United States*, U. Pa. L. Rev. 245 (2001)

Lewis Powell, Carolene Products *Revisited*, 82 Colum. L. Rev. 1087 (1982)

Jack N. Rakove, *The Madisonian Theory of Rights*, 31 Wm. & Mary L. Rev. 245 (1990)

John Rawls, A Theory of Justice (1971)

THE RECONSTRUCTION AMENDMENTS' DEBATES (Alfred Avins, ed., 1967)

Judith Resnik, *Categorical Federalism: Jurisdiction, Gender and the Globe,* 111 YALE L. J. 619 (2001)

William J. Rich, *Taking "Privileges or Immunities" Seriously: A Call to Expand the Constitutional Canon,* 87 MINN. L. REV. 153 (2002)

Lauren K. Robel, *Sovereignty and Democracy: The States' Obligations to Their Citizens under Federal Statutory Law,* 78 IND. L. J. 543 (2003)

FRANKLIN D. ROOSEVELT, THE PUBLIC PAPERS AND ADDRESSES OF FRANKLIN D. ROOSEVELT (Samuel I. Rosenman, ed., 1941)

GERALD N. ROSENBERG, THE HOLLOW HOPE: CAN COURTS BRING ABOUT SOCIAL CHANGE? (1991)

WILLIAM G. ROSS, A MUTED FURY: POPULISTS, PROGRESSIVES, AND LABOR UNIONS CONFRONT THE COURTS, 1890–1937 (1994)

MICHAEL SANDEL, DEMOCRACY'S DISCONTENT (1996)

MICHAEL SANDEL, LIBERALISM AND THE LIMITS OF JUSTICE (1998)

Jane S. Schacter, Romer v. Evans *and Democracy's Domain,* 50 VAND. L. REV. 361 (1997)

James D. Schmidt, *Book Review,* 68 JOURNAL OF SOUTHERN HISTORY 724 (2002)

HERBERT SHAPIRO, WHITE VIOLENCE AND BLACK RESPONSE: FROM RECONSTRUCTION TO MONTGOMERY (1988)

Reva Siegel, *Text in Context: Gender and the Constitution from a Social Movement Perspective,* 150 U. PA. L. REV. 297 (2001)

JOSEPH E. SLATER, PUBLIC WORKERS: GOVERNMENT, EMPLOYEE UNIONS, THE LAW AND THE STATES, 1900–1962 (2004)

Douglas G. Smith, *Citizenship and the Fourteenth Amendment,* 34 SAN DIEGO L. REV. 681 (1997)

ROGERS M. SMITH, CIVIC IDEALS: CONFLICTING VISIONS OF CITIZENSHIP IN U.S. HISTORY (1997)

Michael Solimine & James L. Walker, *Constitutional Litigation in Federal and State Courts: An Empirical Analysis o f Judicial Parity,* 10 HASTINGS CONST. L. Q. 213 (1983)

STATE DOCUMENTS IN FEDERAL RELATIONS (Herman Vandenburg Ames, ed. 1970)

STATUTORY HISTORY OF THE UNITED STATES: CIVIL RIGHTS (Bernard Schwartz, ed., 1970)

Richard B. Stewart, *Federalism and Rights,* 19 GA. L. REV. 917 (1985)

Kathleen M. Sullivan, *Dueling Sovereignties:* U.S. Term Limits, Inc. v. Thornton, 109 HARV. L. REV. 78 (1995)

Clyde W. Summers, *The Privatization of Personal Freedoms and Enrichment of Democracy: Some Lessons from Labor Law,* 1986 U. ILL. L. REV. 689 (1986)

Taking Charge: The Johnson White House Tapes 1963–64 (Michael R. Beschloss, ed., 1997)

Clarence Taylor, *Book Review,* 21 Law & History Rev. 431 (2003)

Jacobus tenBroek, The Antislavery Origins of the Fourteenth Amendment (1951)

Jacobus tenBroek, Equal under Law (1969)

Christopher L. Tomlins, The State and the Unions: Labor Relations, Law, and the Organized Labor Movement in America, 1880–1960 (1985)

To Secure These Rights: The Report of the President's Committee on Civil Rights (U.S. Government Printing Office 1947)

Laurence Tribe, *Saenz Sans Prophecy: Does the Privileges or Immunities Revival Portend the Future?or Reveal the Structure of the Present?,* 113 Harv. L. Rev. 110 (1999)

Leo Troy, Trade Union Membership, 1897–1962 (National Bureau of Economic Research 1965)

Alexander Tsesis, The Thirteenth Amendment and American Freedom: A Legal History (2004)

Mark Tushnet, *Non-Judicial Review,* 40 Harv. J. on Legis. 453 (2003)

Mark Tushnet, Taking the Constitution Away from the Courts (1999)

An Uncertain Tradition: Constitutionalism and the History of the South 125 (Kermit L. Hall & James W. Ely, eds., 1989)

David R. Upham, Corfield v. Coryell *and the Privileges and Immunities of American Citizenship,* 83 Tex. L. Rev. 1483 (2005)

Melvyn Urofsky, *State Courts and Protective Legislation during the Progressive Era: A Reevaluation,* 72 J. of Am. Hist. 63 (1985)

William W. Van Alstyne, *A Critical Guide to* Ex parte McCardle, 15 Ariz. L. Rev. 229 (1973)

Lea S. Vandervelde, *The Labor Vision of the Thirteenth Amendment,* 138 U. Pa. L. Rev. 437 (1989)

Katherine Van Wezel Stone, *The Post-War Paradigm in American Labor Law,* 90 Yale L. J. 1509 (1981)

Xi Wang, *The Making of Federal Enforcement Laws, 1870–1872,* 70 Chi.-Kent L. Rev. 1013 (1995)

Robin West, Progressive Constitutionalism (1994)

Charles & Barbara Whalen, The Longest Debate: A Legislative History of the 1964 Civil Rights Act (1985)

Keith E. Whittington, Constitutional Construction: Divided Powers and Constitutional Meaning (1999)

Keith E. Whittington, *Extrajudicial Constitutional Interpretation: Three Objections and Responses,* 80 N.C. L. Rev. 773 (2002)

Bryan H. Wildenthal, *The Lost Compromise: Reassessing the Early Understanding in Court and Congress on Incorporation of the Bill of Rights in the Fourteenth Amendment*, 61 OHIO ST. L. J. 1051 (2000)

Bryan H. Wildenthal, *The Road to* Twining: *Reassessing the Disincorporation of the Bill of Rights*, 61 OHIO ST. L. J. 1457 (2000)

David Yassky, *The Second Amendment: Structure, History and Constitutional Change*, 99 MICH. L. REV. 588 (2000)

John C. Yoo, *Sounds of Sovereignty: Defining Federalism in the 1990s*, 32 IND. L. REV. 27 (1998)

Rebecca E. Zietlow, *Belonging, Protection and Equality: The Neglected Citizenship Clause and the Limits of Federalism*, 62 U. PITT. L. REV. 281 (2000)

Rebecca E. Zietlow, *Congressional Enforcement of Citizenship Rights and John Bingham's Theory of Citizenship*, 36 AKRON L. REV. 717 (2003)

Rebecca E. Zietlow, *Exploring a Substantive Approach to Equal Justice under Law*, 28 N.M. L. REV. 411 (1998)

Rebecca E. Zietlow, *Juriscentrism and the Original Meaning of Section Five*, 13 TEMPLE POL. & CIV. RTS L. REV. 485 (2004)

Michael P. Zuckert, *Congressional Power under the Fourteenth Amendment: The Original Understanding of Section Five*, 3 CONST. COMM. 123 (1986)

Index

A. L. A. Schechter Poultry Corp. v. United States, 81, 83–87
abolitionists, 34, 93
accountability: of Congress, 11, 154, 156–57; federalism and, 134–35; states and, 129, 142; Supreme Court lack of, 85, 149
Ackerman, Bruce, 91
activists, 2, 158
adversarial litigation process, 163
affirmative action, 126, 151, 162
African Americans: migration to North, 136; in military, 42; New Deal and, 94–96, 113; northern, civil rights movement and, 99; voting margins and, 154–55. See also *Brown v. Board of Education;* Civil Rights Act of 1964; civil rights movement
agricultural workers, 94
Aiken, William, 40
Alden v. Maine, 133
Alien and Sedition Acts of 1798, 17
Amar, Akhil, 165
Amendments to the Constitution: First, 2–5, 7, 65, 70, 124, 152–53; Second, 2, 5–6; Fifth, 26, 49, 50; Tenth, 23, 46, 125. See also Fifteenth Amendment; Fourteenth Amendment; Thirteenth Amendment
American Anti-Slavery Society, 25
American Federation of Labor (AFL), 66, 69–71, 94
American system, 22
antifederalists, 19, 131, 142
anti-injunction legislation, 68–71
antipoverty legislation, 124
antislavery constitutionalists, 25–26, 33–34, 38
Article III, 150, 155

Ashmun, George, 28, 29
Auto-Lite strike (1934), 74

Baer, Judith, 30, 38, 147, 165
Barron v. Mayor and City Council of Baltimore, 26, 30, 33, 35, 37, 53, 61
belonging, rights of. See rights of belonging
Benedict, Michael Les, 40
Bernstein, David, 93, 95, 96
Bernstein, Irving, 87
Bill of Rights, 12, 45; federal citizenship and, 49; federal negative and, 16–17; Fourteenth Amendment and, 61–62; ideological interpretation of, 156; Madison's view, 18–19; privileges and immunities of citizenship, 56; slavery and, 25–26, 30; state responsibility to enforce, 55
Bingham, John, 48, 62, 111, 143; criticism of *Dred Scott,* 33; national citizenship, view of, 34–36; original draft of Fourteenth Amendment, 26, 43, 49–50, 52; speech introducing Fourteenth Amendment, 55–56; workers' rights and, 65, 66
Biondi, Martha, 95–96
Birmingham demonstrations, 104
Bituminous Coal Act (1935), 88
Black, Charles, 146–47
Black Codes, 40–42
"Black Monday," 83
Blanton, Thomas, 84
Blue Eagle, 73
Boerne. See City of Boerne v. Flores
bottom-up reforms, 135
Bradley, Bill, 3
Brandwein, Pamela, 61, 62
Brennan, William, 143–44

Brooks, Jack, 4

Broomall, John, 43, 47

Brown, Clarence, 118

Brown v. Board of Education, 1, 6, 7, 97, 126; protection of discrete and insular minorities, 100–101; public reaction to, 101–2, 121–22, 130, 157; resistance to, 148–49, 154

Buchanan, James, 31, 47

Burrill, James, 26–27

business leaders: compliance with Civil Rights Act of 1964, 122; influence of, 152–53; opposition to Wagner Act, 74–75; support for Roosevelt, 71, 73

Butler, Andrew, 29

Byrd, Robert, 110

Calhoun, John, 22, 23–25, 55, 130

campaign finance reform measures, 152–53

Carolene Products. See *United States v. Carolene Products*

Carpenter, Rep., 78

CBS news, 105

Celler, Emmanuel, 105, 108, 118

checks and balances, 14, 147, 154

Chemerinsky, Erwin, 147

child labor, 70

Chinese Exclusion Act of 1882, 138

Citizens' Councils of America, 122

citizenship, 13, 60; as baseline of rights, 143–44; Citizenship Clause of Fourteenth Amendment, 44, 51–53; community and, 164; congressional power to define, 45, 91; equal, 6–7; free blacks and, 21–22, 26–29, 31–34, 42–43; in home state, 18, 35; national vs. state, 30–31, 34–36; privileges and immunities of, 56–57; slavery and, 19–37; substantive component, 48–49

Citizenship Clause (Fourteenth Amendment), 44, 51–53

citizenship gap, 112

City of Boerne v. Flores, 4–5, 10, 50, 52, 127, 146; as harmful to rights of belonging, 150–51

civil rights, 57; lobbying for, 118–19; post-1964, 123–24; Section Five power and, 114–15, 117, 121, 124–26

Civil Rights Act of 1866, 39–42; congres-

sional power and, 44–47, 55; declared unconstitutional, 51–52; *Dred Scott* and, 47–48; exclusion of Native Americans from, 43–44

Civil Rights Act of 1875, 59, 97, 102–3; struck down by Supreme Court, 60, 114

Civil Rights Act of 1957, 103–4

Civil Rights Act of 1964, 7, 8, 149; amendments proposed, 117, 119; citizenship language used, 111–12; cloture, 109–10; commerce power and, 100, 114, 120; constitutionality of, 113–15, 119–21; federalism-based critique, 115–17, 120; filibusters, 103–5, 108–10, 117; Kennedy and, 106–7; as paradigm for congressional action, 123–24; property rights and, 115–16, 120; public response to, 105–6, 109, 121–23; Reconstruction language used in debate, 98, 111–13; state action doctrine and, 114–15; success of, 117–18, 122; symbolic impact of, 98; Title II, 97, 109, 110, 122; Title VI, 126; Title VII, 97–98, 107–10, 113, 122, 126, 165

Civil Rights Cases, 60–61, 102–3, 114–15, 117, 125–26

civil rights movement, 97, 100–101; demonstrations, 103–4, 106; expansion into South, 100, 103–4; Fourteenth Amendment and, 100–101; influence of labor movement on, 95–96; in north, 99, 103; public opinion and, 104–5. *See also* Civil Rights Act of 1964

Civil Rights Restoration Act of 1991, 126

Civil Rights Section (Justice Department), 99

Civil War, 38, 112, 130

Clark, Sen., 42, 116

Clark, Steve, 135

Clark, Tom C., 121

Clay, Henry, 22, 24, 27

Clayton Act (1914), 70–71, 81

Clinton, Bill, 4

cloture, 109–10

coal miners, 66, 88

Coates, Dan, 3

collective bargaining. See right to organize

Comins, Linus, 36

commerce, 100, 114; as argument for right to organize, 79–81, 84–86.

See also commerce clause; commerce power

commerce clause, 20, 79, 113–15

commerce power, 29, 70, 113–15; civil rights legislation and, 100, 120, 124–25; Court deference to, 114, 120, 124–25; right to organize and, 79–81, 84–86

common law, 68, 70, 72, 80, 92

community: Court deemphasis on, 162–63; message of inclusion, 163–66; political, 134–35, 141–42; values of, Congress and, 160–61; of workers, 64–65

Confederate Congress, 22

Confederate states, 38

Congress: accountability of, 11, 154, 156–57; anti-Court sentiment, 59–60, 70–71, 80–83, 85–86, 89; anti-injunction legislation, 68–71; as best suited to protect rights, 1–2, 11, 145; constitutional meaning and, 8–9, 151–56; as danger to liberty, 17–18; deference toward Court, 124–27; disincentives to act, 158; efficiency of, 129; elections, 32, 74; free exercise of religion and, 2–5; incumbency, 156; institutional advantages of, 146, 154, 157; legitimacy of, 157; as majoritarian body, 1, 154–55, 157; monied interests and, 152–53; open deliberation process, 156–57, 160–61; participation of people and, 157–58; political objectives, 9–10; power of derived from people, 17; pre-Civil War failure to protect individual rights, 19–20; role in protection of rights, 1–2, 5, 7, 37, 113, 123; *Schecter* ruling and, 83–84; Second Amendment and, 2, 5–6; segregationists in, 103; slaveholders, protection of, 20–22; values of community and, 160–61. *See also* enforcement powers of Congress

Congressional Globe, 48

Congress of Industrial Organizations (CIO), 94, 95–96

congruence and proportionality test, 4

Connery, William, 77, 85, 94

Connor, Bull, 104

Constitution: Article I, Section 10, 16, 19; authority of the people to interpret, 90; commerce clause, 20, 79, 113–15;

Diversity Clause (Article III), 18; Due Process Clause, 25, 26, 45, 50; Fugitive Slave Clause, 20–21; Full Faith and Credit Clause, 18; limits on congressional power, 12, 51, 55; pre-Civil War, 12; slavery and, 25; structural measures for protecting liberty, 14; Supremacy Clause, 16; Three-Fifths Clause, 20; transition and, 86; Virginia ratifying convention, 30–31. *See also* Amendments to the Constitution; Fifteenth Amendment; Fourteenth Amendment; Privileges and Immunities Clause (Article IV); Thirteenth Amendment

constitutional construction, 9, 153–55

constitutional convention, 15–17, 143

constitutionalism. *See* popular constitutionalism

constitutional meaning, 2–4, 7–8; Civil Rights Act of 1964 and, 113–14; Congressional interpretation of, 8–9, 151–56; constitutional stability, 153–54; pluralist approach to, 151–52, 154; Supreme Court monopoly on, 150

constitutional stability, 153–54

constitution of freedom, 71

contractual liberty view, 64, 68–69, 75, 153–54, 157, 162

Convention on the Elimination of All Forms of Discrimination against Women (CEDAW), 133

Cook, Burton, 42

Cooper, John Sherman, 114

Corfield v. Coryell, 30–31, 57

corrective federalism, 143

Court-packing plan, 86, 89, 90

courts: accountability, lack of, 148–49; affirmative action, limits on, 151, 162; anti-labor position, 85–86; congressional power limited by, 4, 10–11, 32, 60–61, 70, 132, 150; congressional suspicion of, 59–60; conservative constitutional doctrines, 69–70, 75–76, 146, 150; contractual liberty view, 68–70, 75, 153–54, 157, 162; enforceability limited, 148–50; failure to protect rights, 5–6, 50, 69, 80–82; ideological involvement of judges, 156; as ill-suited to protect rights, 1–2, 11, 145, 156, 161; injunctions against labor, 68–71;

courts (*continued*)
  insulation of, 1, 11, 16–17, 147–49;
  limitations of, 148–50, 161–62; minorities, role in protection of, 7, 100–101,
  154–56; neutral paradigm, 161–63; as
  obstacle to social reform, 63–64; resistance to, 146, 148–49, 153–54, 157;
  transparency, lack of, 156. *See also* judicial review; Supreme Court
Cover, Robert, 166
Cowen, Ecker, 94
Cox, Archibald, 157
Cross, Frank, 155, 156
Crosskey, William, 61–62
cultural relativism, 135
Curtis, Michael Kent, 58

Dahl, Robert, 148, 155
Debs, Eugene, 67
Declaration of Independence, 25, 56, 99
Defense of Marriage Act (DOMA),
  139–40
democracy: decreasing voter turnout, 168;
  industrial, 67, 73, 78; judicial interference in, 1–2; right to organize linked to,
  67, 77–78
Democratic Study Group, 119
Democrats, 36
departmentalism, 34
Dirksen, Everett, 109–10, 112, 117
discrete and insular minorities, 1, 7,
  100–101, 147, 161
discriminatory intent, 162
disempowered, inclusion of, 163–66
disparate impact litigation, 126
DOMA. *See* Defense of Marriage Act
Donnelly, Ignatius, 49
Douglas, Steven, 33, 36, 121
Dred Scott v. Sanford, 13, 29–36, 153,
  157; 1866 Civil Rights Act and, 47–48
due process, 120, 149
Due Process Clause, 25, 26, 45, 49, 50
Dworkin, Ronald, 141

Eastland, James, 105, 108
economic equality, 73
economic rights, 150–51
economy, effect of race discrimination on,
  113–14, 124
Education Amendments of 1972, 123

Eisenhower, Dwight, 111
Ellender, Allen, 122, 125
Ely, John Hart, 161
Emancipation Proclamation, 98–99, 101
Emery, James, 75
Employee Non-Discrimination Act, 132
Employment Division v. Smith, 2–3
Enforcement Act of 1870, 58
Enforcement Act of 1871, 58, 59
enforcement powers of Congress, 157;
  1866 Civil Rights Act and, 44–47;
  Article IV power to admit states, 23;
  commerce power, 29, 64, 70, 113–15,
  120, 124–25; constitutional limits on,
  13, 51, 55; Court limitations on, 4,
  10–11, 32, 60–61, 70, 132, 150; federalism and expansion of, 54–55; federal
  negative and, 13–19; Fifteenth Amendment, 59, 124; Fourteenth Amendment,
  49–51, 52–54, 102–3, 114; Fugitive
  Slave Clause and, 21, 29–30; internal
  improvements, 20, 21–24; naturalization
  and, 26, 45; as necessary for baseline of
  rights of belonging, 128, 129, 140–42;
  restricted to state action, 114; right to
  define citizenship, 45, 91; Section Five
  enforcement power, 4, 54, 102–3,
  114–15, 117, 121, 124–26; Thirteenth
  Amendment, 39, 44–47, 79, 124. *See
  also* Congress
Engle, David, 166
entitlements, 6, 38
equal citizenship, 6–7
Equal Credit Opportunity Act of 1974,
  123
equality, 162; protection from majority
  rule, 1–2; of rights, 58; substantive view
  of, 164–65
Equal Protection Clause (Fourteenth
  Amendment), 6, 56, 101, 151–52, 162,
  165
Establishment Clause, 5
executive orders, 99, 155
extended republic, 14–15, 19, 129,
  137–38, 140

factions, 13–15, 19, 134, 138
Fair Employment Practices Commission
  (FEPC), 94, 99
Fair Housing Act, 123

Fairman, Charles, 61–62
fairness, 141
Federal Anti-Injunction Act (1932), 71
federal government: court limitations on, 132; distance from people, 142; protective role of, 66, 161; rights-generating function of, 35
federalism, 14, 129–31; accountability and, 134–35; Civil Rights Act of 1964 and, 115–17, 120; decentralization, 133–34; expansion of, 116–17; expansion of congressional power and, 54–55; non-preemption provision, 144; political community and, 134–35; restrictions on, 136–37; values of, 133–37. *see also* states' rights federalism
Federalist No. 10, 13
Federalist No. 51, 14
federal negative, 13–19, 143
feminist movement, 108
Fessenden, William, 33, 36, 111
Fifteenth Amendment, 59, 100, 123, 124
Fifth Amendment, 26, 49, 50
filibusters, 103–5, 108–10, 117, 123
Finkelman, Paul, 20
First Amendment, 65, 70, 124, 152–53; Free Exercise Clause, 2–5, 7
Fisher, Louis, 146
Flint, Michigan, strike, 89, 90
Foner, Eric, 40, 59
Forbath, William, 63, 68, 80–81, 146
Fourteenth Amendment, 7, 19, 48–49, 146; antislavery constitutionalists and, 25–26; Bill of Rights and, 61–62; Bingham on, 55–56; Citizenship Clause, 44, 51–53; Civil Rights Act of 1964 and, 99, 112–13, 121; civil rights movement and, 100–101; debate over ratification, 36; freedom from involuntary servitude, 65–66; mandates federal role in protection of rights, 130; Necessary and Proper Clause (Article I), 54; original draft, 26, 43, 49–50, 52; rejection of states' rights federalism, 130; revised version, 50–51; Section Five enforcement power, 4, 54, 102–3, 114–15, 121, 124–26; Section One, 26, 43, 52–53, 57; Sections Two through Four, 52; as self-enforcing, 52–53
Fourth World Conference on Women, 133

Fox, James, 60
Framers of the Constitution, 1, 30–31; federal negative and, 13–19, 143. *See also* Hamilton, Alexander; Jefferson, Thomas; Madison, James
Framers of the Fourteenth Amendment, 25–26, 50–57, 125, 143, 165
free blacks, citizenship and, 21–22, 26–29, 31–34, 42–43
Freedmen's Bureau Act, 39
freedom, labor's constitution of, 71
freedom, language of, right to organize and, 66, 77, 79–80
freedom of association, 71
freedom of expression, 65, 77
Freedom Riders, 100
Free Exercise Clause (First Amendment), 2–5, 7
free labor ideology, 65–68
Freund, Paul, 114–15
Friendly, Fred, 105
Fugitive Slave Act of 1793, 20–21, 45–46, 139
Fugitive Slave Act of 1850, 20–21, 29–30, 37, 46, 139
Fugitive Slave Clause, 20–21, 29–30
fugitive slave laws, northern opposition to, 129–30, 132
Full Faith and Credit Clause, 18, 139

Garrison, William Lloyd, 25, 79
gays and lesbians, marriage and, 134, 139–40, 145
Glendon, Mary Anne, 162–63
Goldberg, Arthur J., 121
Goldwater, Barry, 115
Gompers, Samuel, 66, 69–70
Goodlatte, Bob, 3
Great Depression, 66, 71–72
Great Society program, 124
Green, Edith, 107
Griffin, Stephen, 146, 151
Griffiths, Martha, 107, 108
Groves v. Slaughter, 29
gun control legislation, 5

Hale, Robert, 50
Halleck, Charles, 85, 118
Hamilton, Alexander, 1, 16–17
Hatfield, Mark, 3

Heart of Atlanta Motel v. United States,
   120–21, 124
heightened scrutiny, 100, 149
Henderson, Sen., 51
Higby, William, 50
history and tradition requirement, 149
Hoar, Samuel, 28–29
Hobson, Charles, 15
Hollis, Louis W., 121–22
Hollister, Rep., 84
Hotchkiss, Rep., 52
House Judiciary Committee, 105
House Labor Committee, 84, 87
House Rules Committee, 103, 105, 107
Howard, Jacob, 42, 50–51, 57
Hoxie, Robert F., 69
H.R. 7152. *see* Civil Rights Act of 1964
Hubbard, John, 42–43
Hudson, Charles, 28, 29
Humphrey, Hubert, 109–10, 112, 119,
   126
Hyde, Henry, 3–4

Illinois, 31, 36, 133
implicit to the concept of ordered liberty
   test, 149
inclusion, message of, 163–66
Indian Removal Act of 1830, 138
individual rights: Congress, role in protecting, 1–2, 5, 7, 37, 113, 123; congressional failure to protect, pre–Civil War,
   19–20; decentralized conception of, 135;
   judicial review and, 16–17, 151; lack of
   power to enforce, 12, 20–21, 158–59;
   protected by federal system, 131; of
   slaveholders, 20–22, 29; slavery and,
   19–37; states as danger to, 14–19, 37,
   135–36; structural measures for protecting, 13–14. *See also* citizenship; rights of
   belonging
industrial democracy, 67, 73, 78
injunctions, 68–71, 81
insularity of courts, 1, 11, 16–17, 147–49
interest groups, 134, 152–53
interposition, 28, 101, 102
interstate commerce. *See* commerce
Iron Molder's Journal, 64

Jackson, Andrew, 24, 34, 55
Jackson, Robert, 147

Javitz, Jacob, 118
Jefferson, Thomas, 16, 34
Jim Crow system, 61
Johnson, Andrew, 39, 46, 53, 55
Johnson, Lyndon, 98–99, 106–7, 111,
   118–20, 124
Johnson, Sen., 46
Joint Committee on Reconstruction, 26,
   36, 41, 48–49, 111–12
judges. *See* courts
judicial review, 1, 145–47; heightened
   scrutiny, 100, 149; individual rights and,
   16–17, 151; rational basis scrutiny, 2;
   representation reinforcement theory,
   1–2, 153, 161; right to organize and,
   76; strict scrutiny, 2; values, effect of on,
   166–67. *See also* courts; Supreme Court
jurisdictional provision of 1867, 53
justice, 141
Justice Department, 98, 99, 104

Kansas territory, 34–35
Karst, Kenneth, 6, 137
Katzenbach, Nicholas, 104
Katzenbach v. McClung, 120
Katzenbach v. Morgan, 145
Keating, Kenneth, 115
Kennedy, John F., 104, 106–7, 118
Kennedy, Robert, 104, 114–15
Keyserling, Ken, 77, 92, 93
Kilpatrick, James J., 102
King, Martin Luther, 104, 106, 119, 124,
   164
Klare, Karl, 91
Klarman, Michael, 148
Korematsu v. United States, 100
Kramer, Larry, 9, 154
Kuchel, Tom, 109
Ku Klux Klan, 58, 59

labor: enhanced political clout, 71–72;
   investigative hearings, 88–89; race rela-
   tions and, 93–94; slaves and, 65–66;
   successes, 63–64, 70; Thirteenth
   Amendment and, 93–94. *See also* New
   Deal; right to organize; Wagner Act
Labor Department, 73
La Follette, Robert, 88–89
Lawrence, William, 42, 49–50, 56
lawsuits, 158, 163

Leadership Conference on Civil Rights, 109, 118–19
legislative veto. *See* federal negative
legitimacy, 157
Levy, Philip, 87
Lewis, John, 90
liberalism: community, deemphasis on, 162–63; failures of, 167–68; limitations of, 161–64, 167–68
liberty, 7; collective, 67, 69; contractual, 64, 68–70, 75, 153–54, 157, 162; individual, 13–14, 67, 69
Lincoln, Abraham, 34, 36, 130; First Inaugural Address, 33; linked with 1964 Civil Rights Act, 98–99; opposition to *Dred Scott*, 33, 86
Lindsay, John, 99, 118
lobbyists, 118–19, 152–53
localism, 134, 137
Lochner era, 68–69, 93, 153
Locke, John, 43
Loevy, Robert, 117–18
Louisiana, 22
Louisiana Territory, 31

MacKinnon, Catharine, 162
Maddox, Lester, 115–16, 122
Madison, James, 8, 12, 37, 90, 139; Bill of Rights, view of, 18–19; Congress, suspicion of, 17–18; extended republic theory of, 14–15, 19, 129, 137–38, 140; federal negative and, 13–19, 143; letter to George Washington, 15–16; on protection of individual liberty, 131; Vices Memo, 14
Maine, 36, 133
majority rule, 1–2, 78, 154–55, 157
Mansfield, Mike, 108–9
Marbury v. Madison, 4, 32
Marcantonio, Vito, 77, 94
March on Washington (1963), 106
marriage legislation, 134, 139–40, 145
Marshall, Burke, 104, 105–6, 120
Marshall, John, 18
Marshall, Thomas, 148
Marshall, Thurgood, 101
Massachusetts, 29, 36
McCardle, William, 53
McCulloch, William (Bill), 99, 105–6, 108, 112, 118

McCulloch v. Maryland, 18, 54
Miller, Samuel F., 60
minimum wage law, 90
minorities: discrete and insular, 1, 7, 100–101, 147, 161; influence of, 153–55
Mississippi, 22
Missouri, 23; state Constitution, 26–27
Missouri Compromise, 12, 20, 23, 26–27, 32
Missouri Supreme Court, 31
Mitchell, Clarence, 118, 119
monied interests, influence of, 152–53
Montgomery bus boycott, 100, 103–4
Moore, Archie, 112
moral values: Congress and, 156, 160–61; courts and, 161–62; effect on judicial review, 166–67; neutrality and, 161–63; political process and, 163–64
Morgan, Denise, 6
Morgan v. Commonwealth of Virginia, 100
Moritz, Rep., 86
Motley, Constance Baker, 122
Mudd, Roger, 105
Munger, Frank, 166
Murphy, Frank, 89
Muskie, Edmund, 125, 127

NAACP v. Alabama ex rel Patterson, 124
NAACP v. Button, 124
National Association for the Advancement of Colored People (NAACP), 94, 96
National Association of Manufacturers, 74, 75, 81
national community. *See* community
National Council of Churches, 119, 164
National Industrial Recovery Act (NIRA), 72–73, 82–83, 86–87; Section 7(a), 73–75
National Labor Board (NLB), 72–73
National Labor Relations Act. *See* Wagner Act
National Labor Relations Board (NLRB), 79, 81, 88
Native Americans, 43–44, 138
naturalization, 26, 45
natural law, 25–26, 57, 60
negative, federal. *See* federal negative
neutral paradigm, 161–63

New Deal, 164; 1934 congressional elections and, 74; constitutionality of, 83; First, 72; race discrimination and, 94–96, 113; Second, 91; social citizenship and, 64–65. *See also* National Industrial Recovery Act (NIRA); right to organize; unions; Wagner Act

New Deal Congress, 63–64, 165; mistrust of courts, 80–83, 85–86; mistrust of labor, 82

New Deal Era, 7–8, 9, 158; strikes, 79–80, 86, 89–90

New York Times Co. v. Sullivan, 124

NIRA. *See* National Industrial Recovery Act

Nixon, Richard, 151

NLRB v. Jones and Laughlin Steel Corp., 90–91

Norris, George, 81, 89

Norris-LaGuardia Act, 71, 81

Northern Territories, 23

Northwest Ordinance, 22

Norton, Rep., 86

nullification crisis of 1832, 12, 20, 24–25, 55, 101, 130

Oregon, 35–36

Pennsylvania Personal Liberty Act, 29–30

people: authority of, 17, 142; participation in congressional process, 157–58; rule by, 155–56

Perkins, Frances, 73

Personal Responsibility and Work Opportunity Act of 1996, 138

Pettys, Todd, 136

Pinckney, Charles, 27

Plessy v. Ferguson, 61

pluralism, 151–52, 154

political community, 134–35, 141–42

political process: open deliberation, 156–57, 160–61; participation of people in, 157–58; rights of belonging and, 11, 160, 167; role of moral values in, 163–64; Supreme Court deference to, 150

political rights, 40, 57. *See also* Voting Rights Act of 1965

poor, constitutional rights of, 150–51

Pope, James Gray, 65, 66, 80, 82, 89, 92, 146

popular constitutionalism, 9, 25–26, 34; criticism of, 146–47, 155–56; right to organize and, 70, 75, 85–86

positive rights, 11, 162

Post, Robert, 121, 125, 146, 152

Powe, Lucas, 148

powers of Congress. *See* enforcement powers of Congress

preemption, 144

Pregnancy Discrimination Act of 1978, 123, 126

president, executive orders, 99, 155

presidential elections: 1856, 47; 1860, 32–33, 36

presidential Reconstruction, 40

presidential veto, 42, 48, 53, 55

Prigg v. Pennsylvania, 29, 34, 37, 45–46, 54

primaries, race-based, 100

privacy, right to, 149

Privileges and Immunities Clause (Article IV), 20, 25, 27–28, 30, 56; citizenship in home state and, 18, 35; *Dred Scott* and, 29; Fourteenth Amendment and, 49–50; as self-executing, 45–46

Progressives, 68, 70

property rights, 68; Civil Rights Act of 1964 and, 115–16, 120; of slaveowners, 20–22, 29

Public Resolution 44, 73–74

race based classifications, 100

race discrimination: executive order, 99; fair employment practices and, 116; negative effect on economy, 113–14, 124; New Deal and, 94–96, 113; private, 102–3; segregation, support for, 60–61, 116

race relations, labor movement and, 93–96

Radical Republicans, 40, 52, 57, 59

rational basis scrutiny, 2

Rauh, Joseph, Jr., 118, 119

Rawls, John, 141

Reconstruction Act, 39

Reconstruction Amendments, 37, 38, 54, 80. *See also* Fifteenth Amendment; Fourteenth Amendment; Thirteenth Amendment

Reconstruction Congress (Thirty-Ninth Congress), 38–42, 111–12, 157

Reconstruction Era, 7–8, 9, 164; antislavery constitutionalists, 25–26, 33–34, 38; linked with 1964 Civil Rights Act, 98, 111–13; scholarship on, 61–62
Rehnquist Court, 10, 127
relativism, 135
religion, free exercise of, 2–5
Religious Freedom Restoration Act (RFRA), 3–5
Religious Land Use and Institutionalized Persons Act (RLUIPA), 5
Repealer Act, 53–54
representation reinforcement theory, 1–2, 153, 161
republicanism, 6, 23, 66
Republicans, 37–39; 1858 congressional action and, 32; 1860 presidential election and, 32–33, 36; challenge to *Dred Scott* decision, 32–33; Radical, 40, 52, 57, 59
Reuther, Walter, 118
Rich, Robert, 85
Richmond News Leader, 102
rights: equality of, 58; limitations on individual enforcement of, 158–59; to privacy, 149; of travel, 57, 134–36, 141; uniform, 54–55, 57–58, 129, 135, 141–42. *See also* citizenship; individual rights; rights of belonging; right to organize
rights of belonging, 6–8, 11, 38; Congress as necessary to baseline of, 128, 129, 140–42; congressional power to protect, 8–11, 113, 116; congressional restrictions on, 138–39; connection of individual with community, 163; as essential to self-government, 167–68; freedom from racial discrimination as, 98; limitation of courts to enforce, 161–62; political process and, 11, 160, 167; post-1964 civil rights legislation, 123–24; pre-Civil War context, 12–13; protected by state legislatures, 132–33; right to organize and, 64–65, 93; states' denial of, 135–36; substantive vision of equality, 164–65; unlimited power of state legislatures to define, 128. *See also* individual rights
right to bear arms, 2, 5–6
right to organize, 64–65; democracy linked

to, 67, 77–78; Fourteenth Amendment and, 65–66; as human right, 76, 79–80; interstate commerce argument, 79–81, 84–86; language of freedom used, 66, 77, 79–80; pre-New Deal efforts, 65–71; race issues and, 93–95; slavery language used by supporters, 64–66, 76–77, 89, 93; social citizenship and, 63–65, 76–77, 93, 95–96; Thirteenth Amendment and, 55–56, 79–80
riots, urban, 124
Rogers, Sen., 50
Rolleston, Moreton, 120
Roosevelt, Franklin D.: attacks on Courts, 69; Court-packing plan, 86, 89, 90; dependence on business leaders, 71, 73; executive order, 99, 155; reelection campaign, 89–90; Second Bill of Rights, 150–51; Wagner Act and, 83, 89–90
Ross, Malcolm, 88
Roy, James P., 40
Russell, Richard (Dick), 108, 110, 112, 115
Rustin, Bayard, 106

Sabath, Adolf, 86
Sandel, Michael, 163, 167
Saulsbury, William, 46, 47
Scalia, Antonin, 3
scholarship: on federal negative, 15–16; on New Deal Era, 63; on popular constitutionalism, 146–47, 155–56; on Reconstruction Era, 61–62
Schumer, Charles, 3, 4, 5
Scott, Dred, 31–32
Seaman's Acts, 27–29
Second Amendment, 2, 5–6
Second Bill of Rights, 150–51
Second New Deal, 91
Second Reconstruction, 7, 8, 9, 158, 164, 165. *See also* Civil Rights Act of 1964
Section 7(a) (National Industrial Recovery Act), 73–75
Section Five enforcement power, 4, 54, 102–3, 114–15, 117, 121, 124–26
self-government, 129, 167–68
self-representation, 71
Senate: filibusters, 103–5, 108–10, 117, 123. *See also* Congress
Senate Commerce Committee, 115

Senate Judiciary Committee, 41, 90, 103, 105, 108–9, 115
Senate Labor Committee, 78–79
separation of powers, 14, 90, 110, 115
Shellaburger, Samuel, 55
Shelley v. Kraemer, 100, 114
Siegel, Riva, 121, 125, 146
Sixteenth Street Baptist Church, 106
Slaughter-House Cases, 56, 60
slavery, 12; admission of new states and, 22–23, 26–27, 35–36; antislavery constitutionalists, 25–26, 33–34, 38; Bill of Rights and, 25–26, 30; citizenship and, 19–37; criminalization of antislavery speech, 34–35; fugitive slaves, 20–22; language of used to promote right to organize, 64–66, 76–77, 89, 93; Missouri Compromise, 12, 20, 23, 26–27, 32; northern opposition to, 25–26, 32–33, 129–30, 132; nullification crisis of 1832, 20, 24–25, 55, 101, 130; *Prigg v. Pennsylvania,* 29, 34, 37, 45–46, 54; Seaman's Acts and, 27–29. *See also Dred Scott v. Sanford;* free blacks, citizenship and; *fugitive slave acts;* Privileges and Immunities Clause (Article IV)
slaves, labor status of, 65–66
Smith, Howard, 84–85, 105, 107
Smith, William, 27
Smith v. Allwright, 100
social citizenship, 63–65, 76–77, 93, 95–96
social compact, 43, 158, 165
South Carolina, Seaman's Acts and, 27–29. *See also* nullification crisis of 1832
Southern Christian Leadership Conference, 164
Southern Conference on Human Welfare, 95
sovereign immunity, 10, 133
sovereignty: overlapping, 138; of states, 10, 38, 129
state action requirement, 102–3, 114–15, 125–27
state constitutions, 102
state laws, congressional review of, 15–16
state legislatures, 128; examples of protection by, 132–33; labor legislation, 67–68; limitations of, 129, 140
states: accountability and, 129, 142; admission to Union, 22–23, 26–27, 35–36; autonomy of, 128, 131–32, 137, 142–43; comity between, 28–29, 31; as danger to individual rights and liberties, 14–19, 37, 135–36; enforcement of rights of belonging, 132–33; existence prior to federal government, 129; failure to protect citizens, 58–59; federal negative and, 13–19, 143; as laboratories of experimentation, 128–29, 133–34, 136, 144; limitations on powers of, 18–19, 30; mobility between, 134, 135, 136; neutrality of, 161–62; police power, 135; pro-segregation legislation, 101–2; rights-generating functions of, 132; sovereignty of, 10, 38, 129; structural features of government, 128–29
states' rights federalism, 128–31; antifederalist view, 19, 131, 142
statutory president, 122
Steiwer, Frederick, 82–83
Stevens, Thaddeus, 40, 52
stock market crash (1929), 71
Stone, Harlan, 1, 100, 147
Story, Joseph, 30
strict scrutiny, 2
strikes, 92; Auto-Lite, 1934, 74; Wagner Act and, 79–80, 86, 89–90
Strong, James, 27
substantive due process, 149
Sumner, Charles, 40, 59
Supremacy Clause, 16
Supreme Court: 1964 Civil Rights Act and, 120–21; accountability, lack of, 85, 149; antilabor position, 80–82; *Civil Rights Cases,* 60–61, 102–3, 114–15, 117; common law tradition, 68, 70, 72, 80, 92; congressional power, limits on, 4, 10–11, 32, 60–61, 70, 132, 150; congressional suspicion of, 52–53; as conservative, 151; constitutional meaning, and monopoly on, 150; constitutional stability and, 153–54; deference to Congress, 114, 120, 124–25, 145–46, 150; federal power, limits on, 132; Fourteenth Amendment decisions, 60–61;

inadequate protection of individual rights, 144; injunctions, 68–71, 81; *Lochner* era, 68–69, 93, 153; political process and, 10, 149–50; pro–civil rights stance, 100; pro-labor decisions, 90–91; public influence on, 147–48; resistance to, 153–54; *Slaughter-House Cases*, 56, 60; slavery decisions, 13, 29–36, 39, 45–48; viewed as pro-slavery, 52–53. See also *Brown v. Board of Education;* courts; judicial review

Taft Hartley Act of 1947, 92, 138
Tallmadge, James, 23
Talmadge, Herman, 122
Taney, Roger B., 31–32
Taylor, John, 23
Tenth Amendment, 23, 46, 125
Thayer, Martin, 42, 44
Thirteenth Amendment, 39–40; congressional enforcement powers, 39, 44–47, 79, 124; labor linked with, 93–94; right to organize and, 55–66, 79–80; rule by injunction and, 69–70
Thomas, Jesse, 23
Three-Fifths Clause, 20
Thurmond, Strom, 116
Tiffany, Joel, 26
Title IX (Education Amendments of 1972), 123
Title VII (Civil Rights Act of 1964), 97–98, 107–10, 113, 122, 126, 165
Tomlins, Christopher, 91–92
To Secure These Rights, 99
travel, right to, 57, 134–36
Treatise on the Unconstitutionality of American Slavery (Tiffany), 26
Truax, Charles, 77, 78, 86
Truman, Harry, 99, 155
Trumbull, Lyman, 40–42, 44–45, 47, 55, 57
Tuck, William, 115
Tushnet, Mark, 8, 9, 150–51
Tydings, Millard, 81
Tydings Amendment, 81

uniform rights, 54–55, 57–58, 129, 135, 141–42
Union Army, 35

unions, 7, 67, 71; as community, 64–65; race discrimination by, 93, 96. *See also* right to organize
United Automotive Workers (UAW), 89, 90, 96
United States v. Carolene Products, 1, 100, 147, 161
United States v. Miller, 5
United States v. Morrison, 126, 127

values. *See* moral values
Vesey, Denmark, 27–28
veto, presidential, 42, 48, 53, 55
Vices Memo (Madison), 14
Violence against Women Act, 126
voter turnout, 168
voting rights, 57, 151; Fifteenth Amendment and, 59, 100, 123, 124
Voting Rights Act of 1965, 123, 124, 136

Wagner, Robert, 72–73, 75–77, 87–88, 91; Senate Labor Committee hearing and, 78–79
Wagner Act, 7, 138; business opposition to, 74–75; constitutionality of, 75–76, 82–86; *Dred Scott* compared to, 86, 87; as enhancement of democracy, 78–79; failures of, 91–92; favorable climate for, 71–72; impact of, 92–93; opponents of, 81, 84–85; preamble, 79–80; race issues and, 94; *Schechter* decision and, 81, 83–87; strikes and, 79–80, 86, 89–90; vote on, 87
Wallace, George, 121
Walsh, Sen., 77, 81
Warren, Earl, 149
Warren Court, 1, 121, 145–46, 148; as historical anomaly, 10–11, 127
Washington, Bulrod, 30–31
Webster, Daniel, 24
West, Robin, 150, 151–52, 162, 165
West Coast Hotel V. Parrish, 90
West Virginia Board of Education v. Barnett, 147
Wheeler, Burton, 89
Whittington, Keith, 9, 146
Wilkins, Royces, 121
Williamson, Passmore, 34
Wilson, Henry, 36, 65–66, 93–94

Wilson, James, 30–31, 43, 44, 47, 53, 55
Windom, William, 42, 58
Withrow, Rep., 78
women, 90, 126, 133, 162; Civil Rights Act of 1964 and, 98, 107–8
women's rights movement, 123
Wood, Ruben, 77, 85–86

Worker's Rights Amendment, 80
working-class republicanism, 66
World War II, 99

Yates, Sen., 52
yellow dog contracts, 67, 68

Zuckert, Michael, 143

About the Author

Rebecca E. Zietlow is Charles W. Fornoff Professor of Law and Values at the University of Toledo College of Law, where she teaches constitutional law. Prior to entering academia, she worked as a legal services lawyer on the south side of Chicago.

KF 4764 .Z54 2006
Zietlow, Rebecca E.
Enforcing equality

NOV 2 0 2006